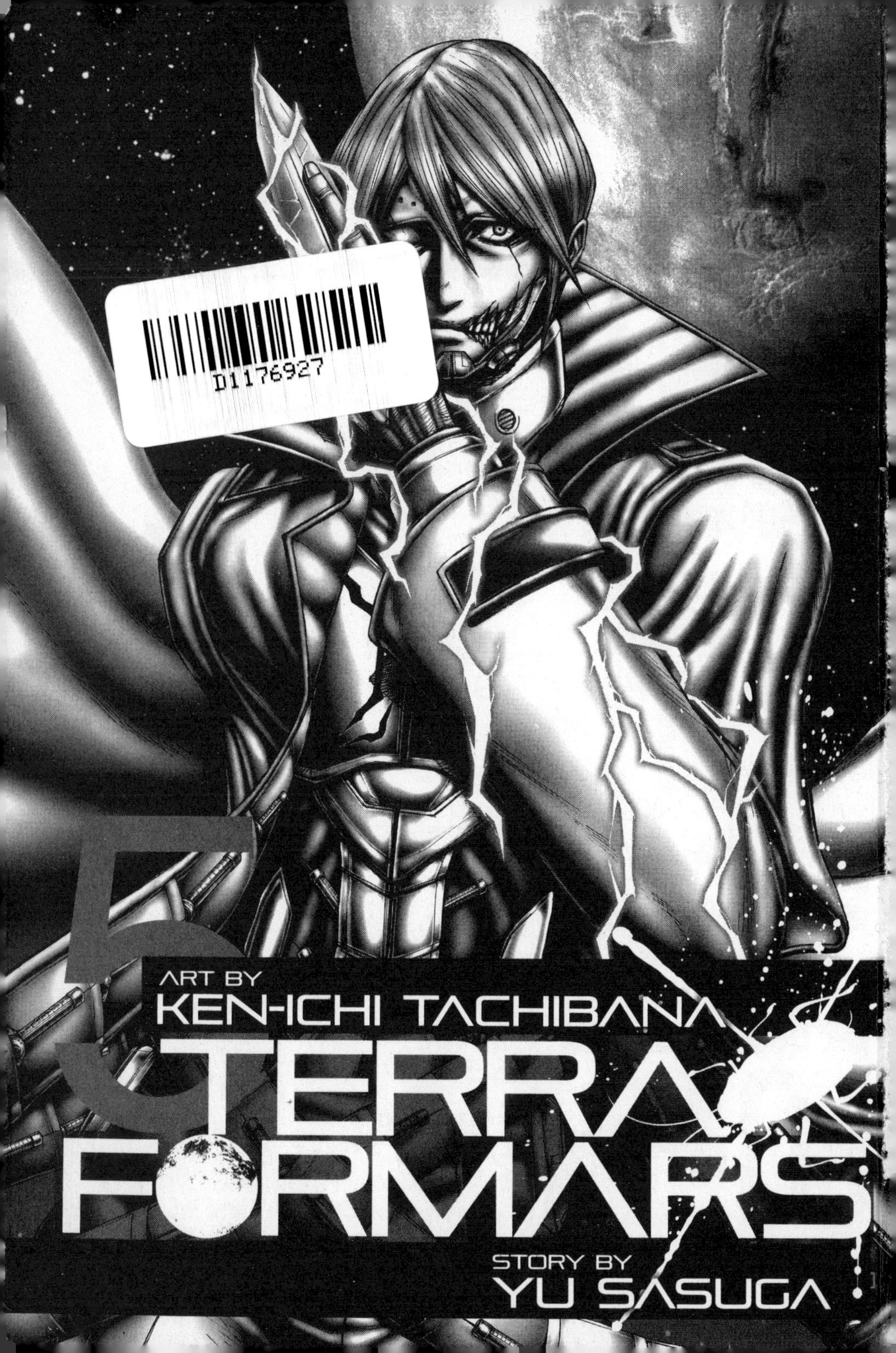
5
ART BY
KEN-ICHI TACHIBANA
TERRA
FORMARS
STORY BY
YU SASUGA

TERRA FORMARS 5

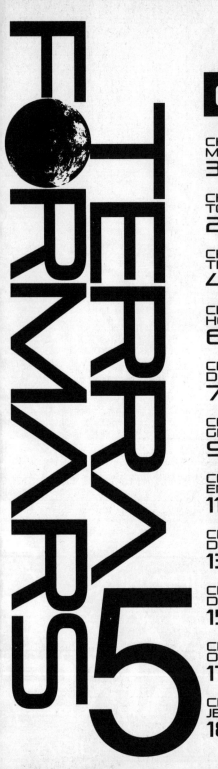

CONTENTS

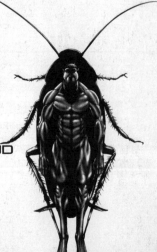

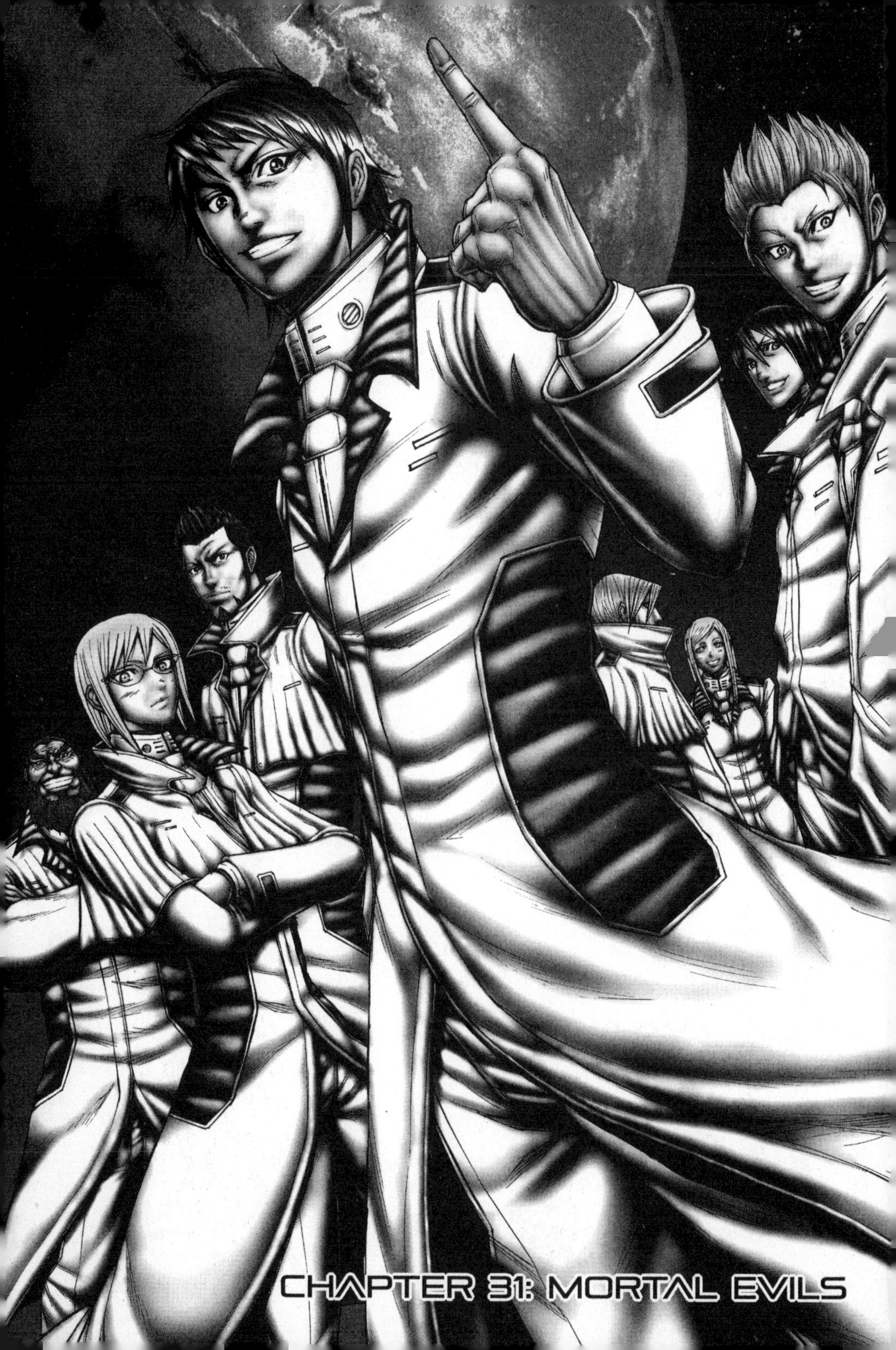
CHAPTER 31: MORTAL EVILS

TERRA FORMARS

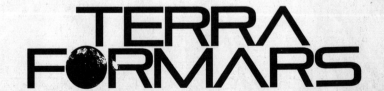

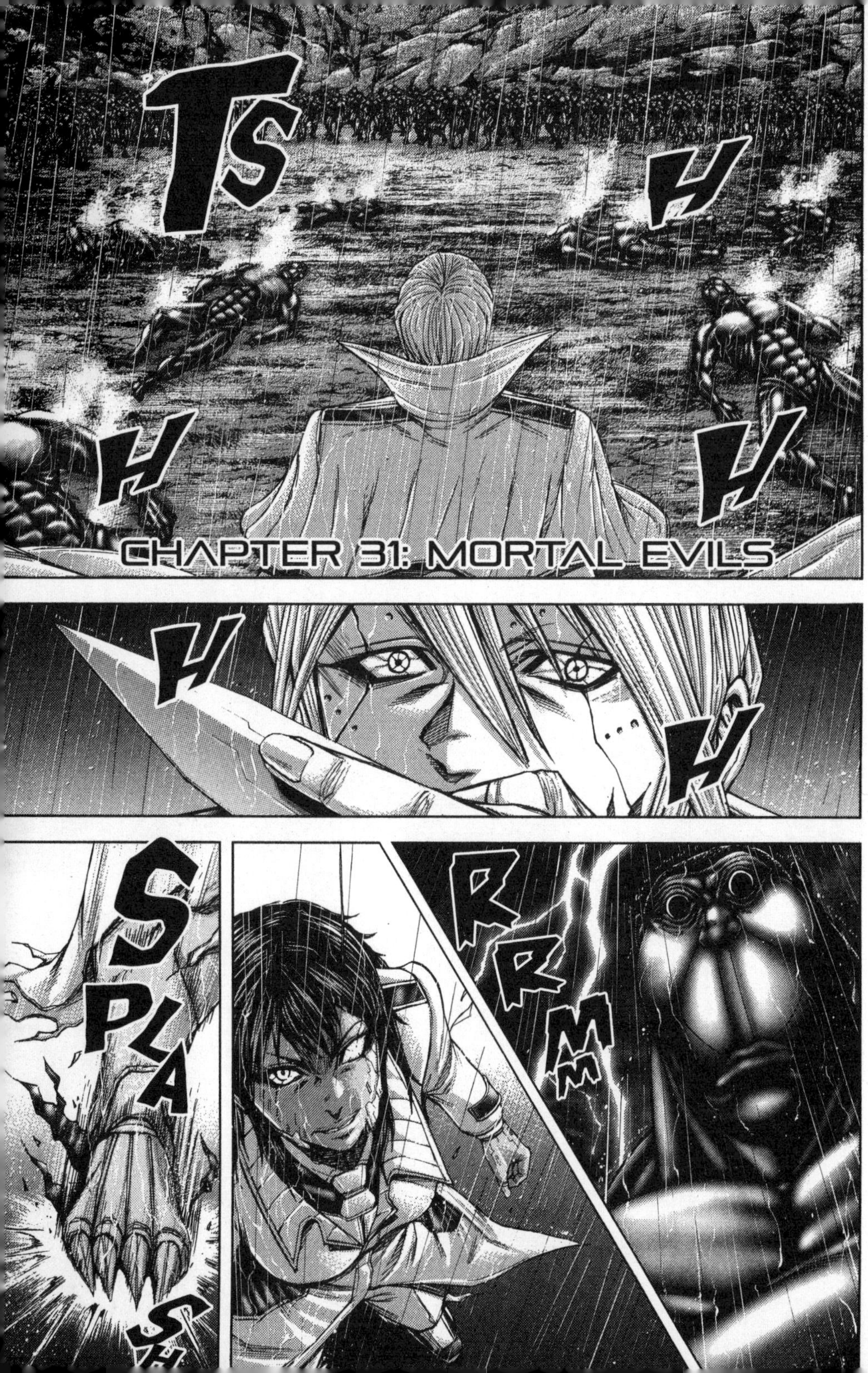
TS
H
H
H
CHAPTER 31: MORTAL EVILS
H
H
RRMM
SPLASH

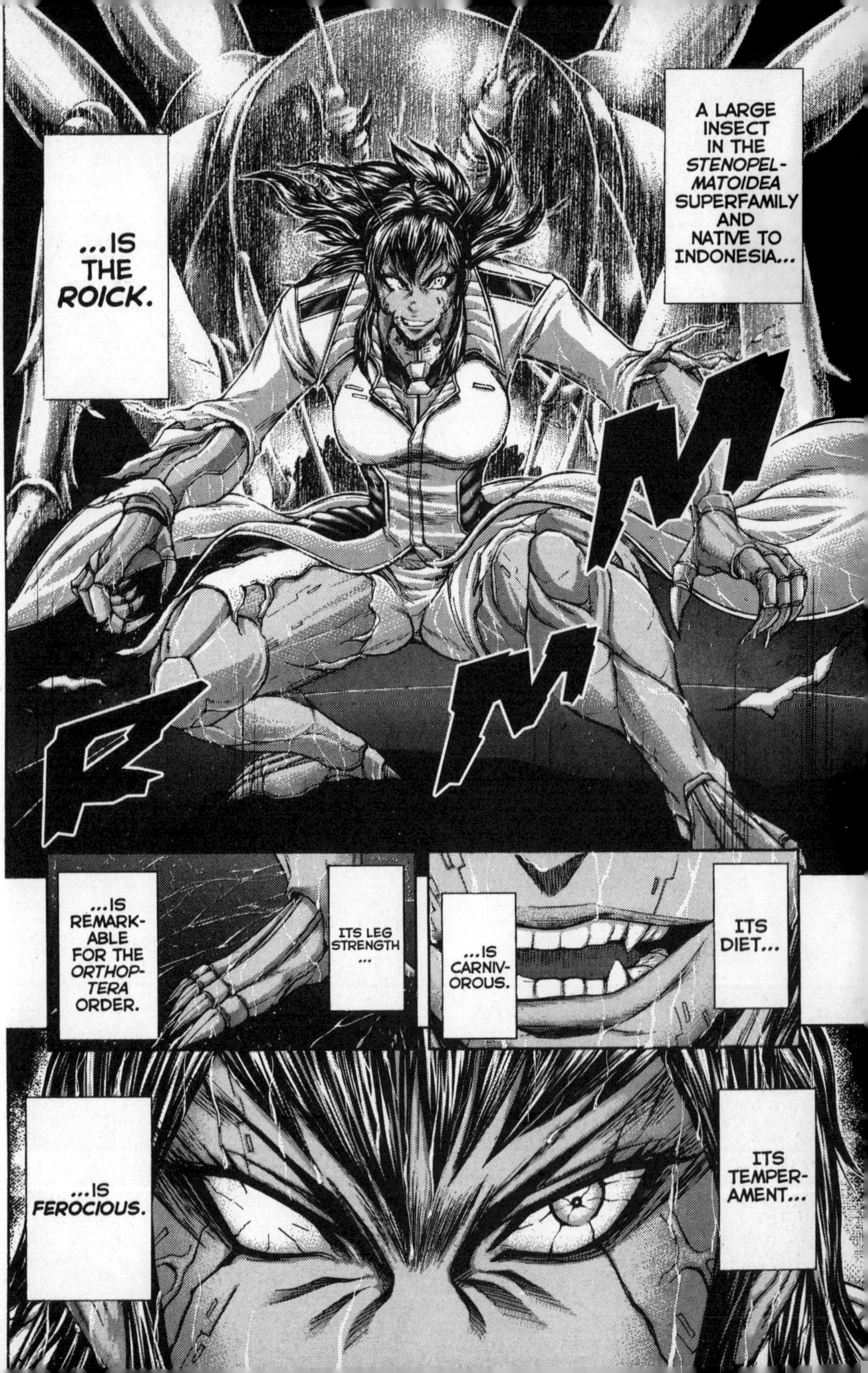
A LARGE INSECT IN THE STENOPELMATOIDEA SUPERFAMILY AND NATIVE TO INDONESIA...
...IS THE ROICK.
RMM
ITS DIET...
...IS CARNIVOROUS.
ITS LEG STRENGTH...
...IS REMARKABLE FOR THE ORTHOPTERA ORDER.
ITS TEMPERAMENT...
...IS FEROCIOUS.

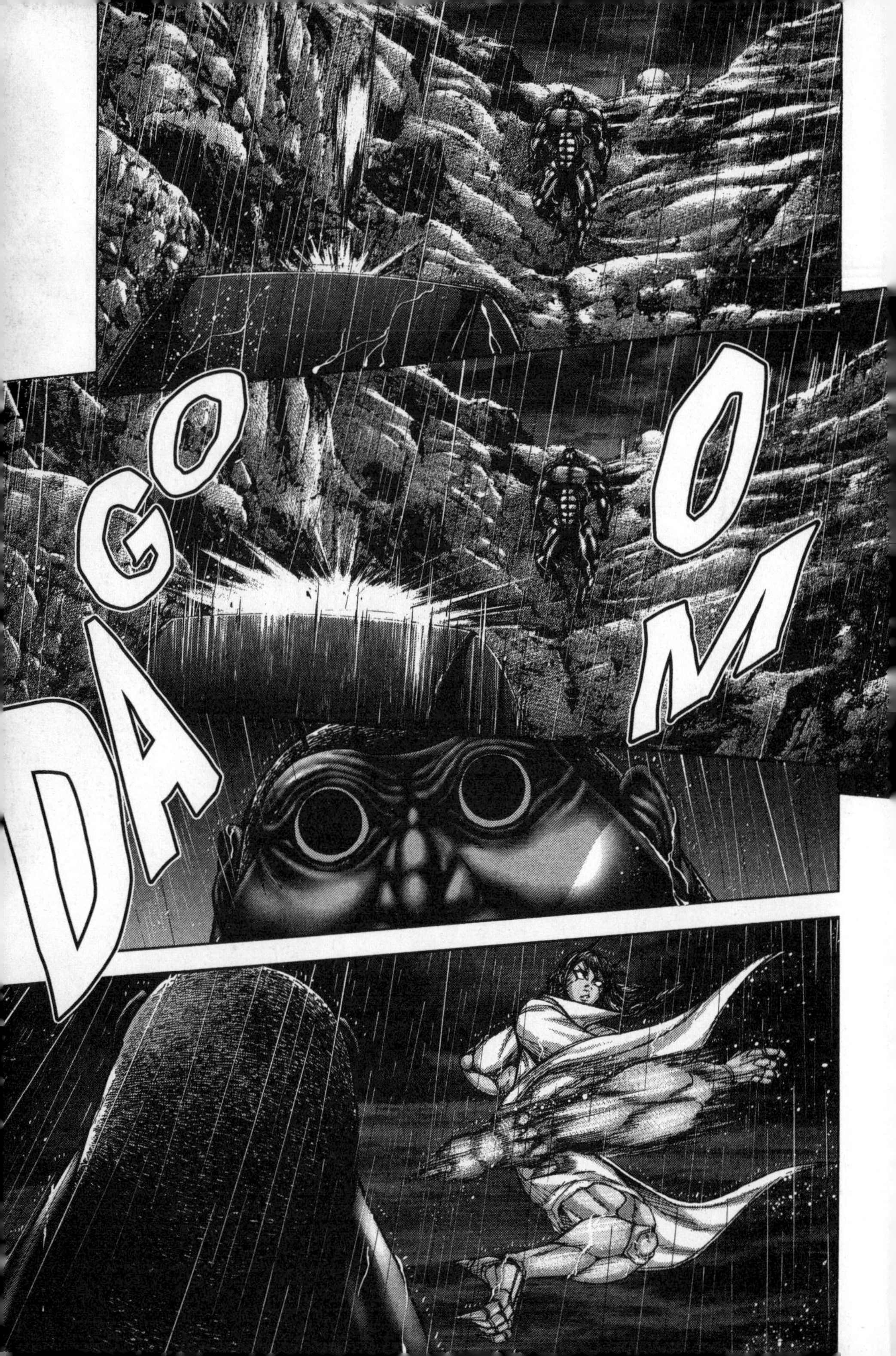
DAGOOM

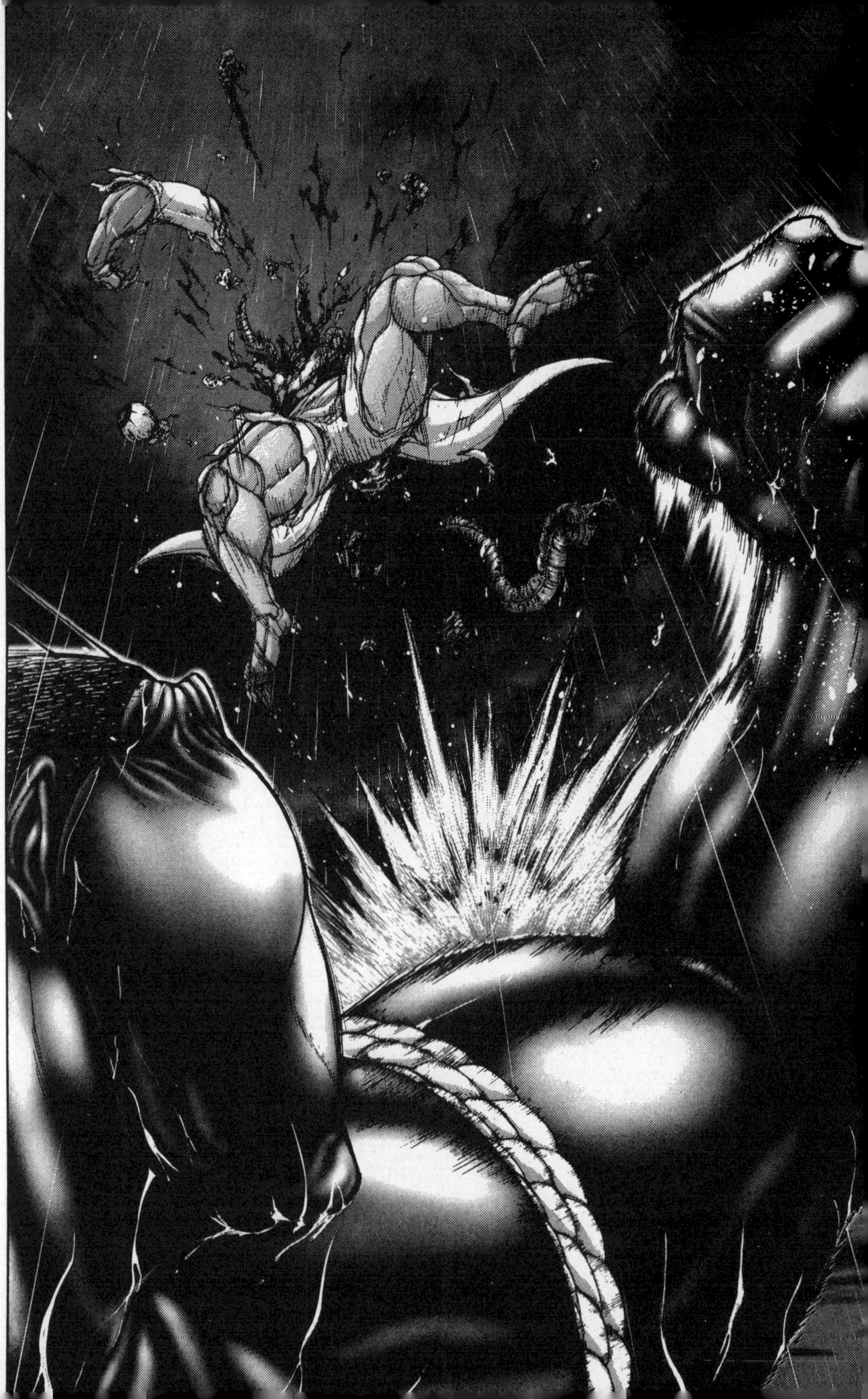

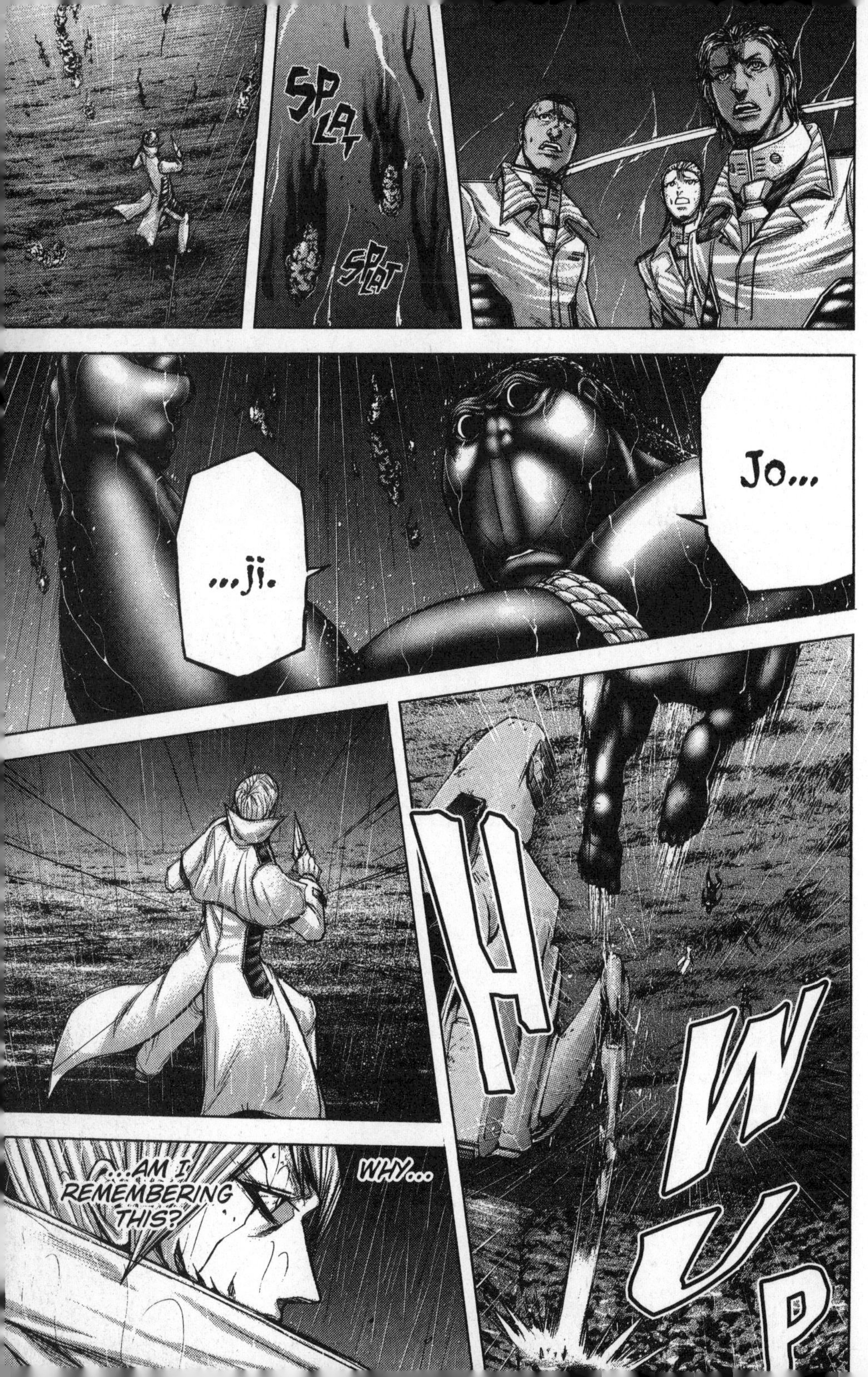
SPLAT
SPLAT
JO...
...ji.
WHUP
WHY...
...AM I REMEMBERING THIS?

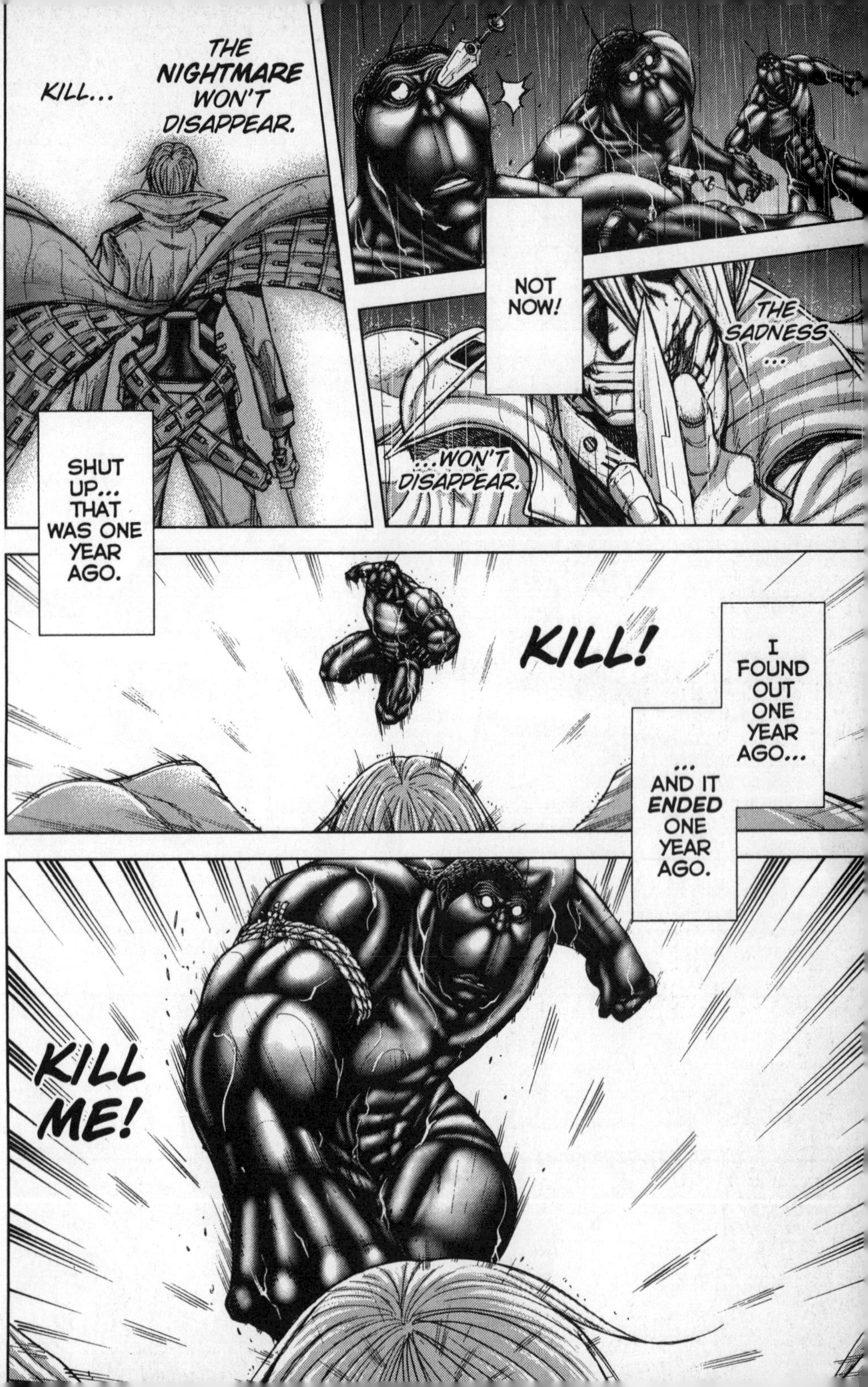
THE SADNESS...
NOT NOW!
...WON'T DISAPPEAR.
THE NIGHTMARE WON'T DISAPPEAR.
KILL...
SHUT UP... THAT WAS ONE YEAR AGO.
I FOUND OUT ONE YEAR AGO...
...AND IT ENDED ONE YEAR AGO.
KILL!
KILL ME!

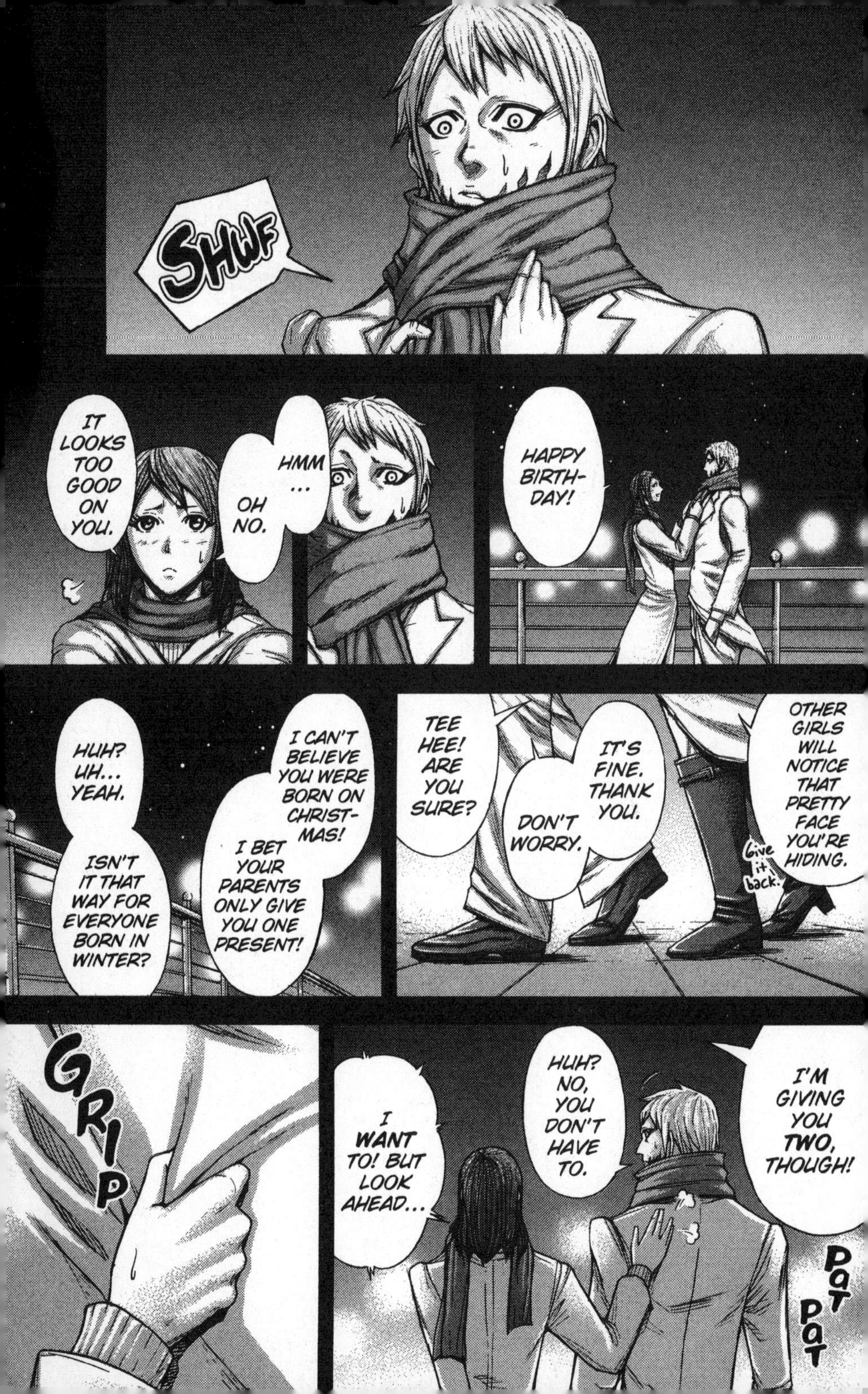
SHWF
HAPPY BIRTHDAY!
HMM...
OH NO.
IT LOOKS TOO GOOD ON YOU.
OTHER GIRLS WILL NOTICE THAT PRETTY FACE YOU'RE HIDING.
Give it back.
IT'S FINE. THANK YOU.
DON'T WORRY.
TEE HEE! ARE YOU SURE?
I CAN'T BELIEVE YOU WERE BORN ON CHRISTMAS!
HUH? UH... YEAH.
I BET YOUR PARENTS ONLY GIVE YOU ONE PRESENT!
ISN'T IT THAT WAY FOR EVERYONE BORN IN WINTER?
I'M GIVING YOU TWO, THOUGH!
HUH? NO, YOU DON'T HAVE TO.
I WANT TO! BUT LOOK AHEAD...
PAT PAT
GRIP

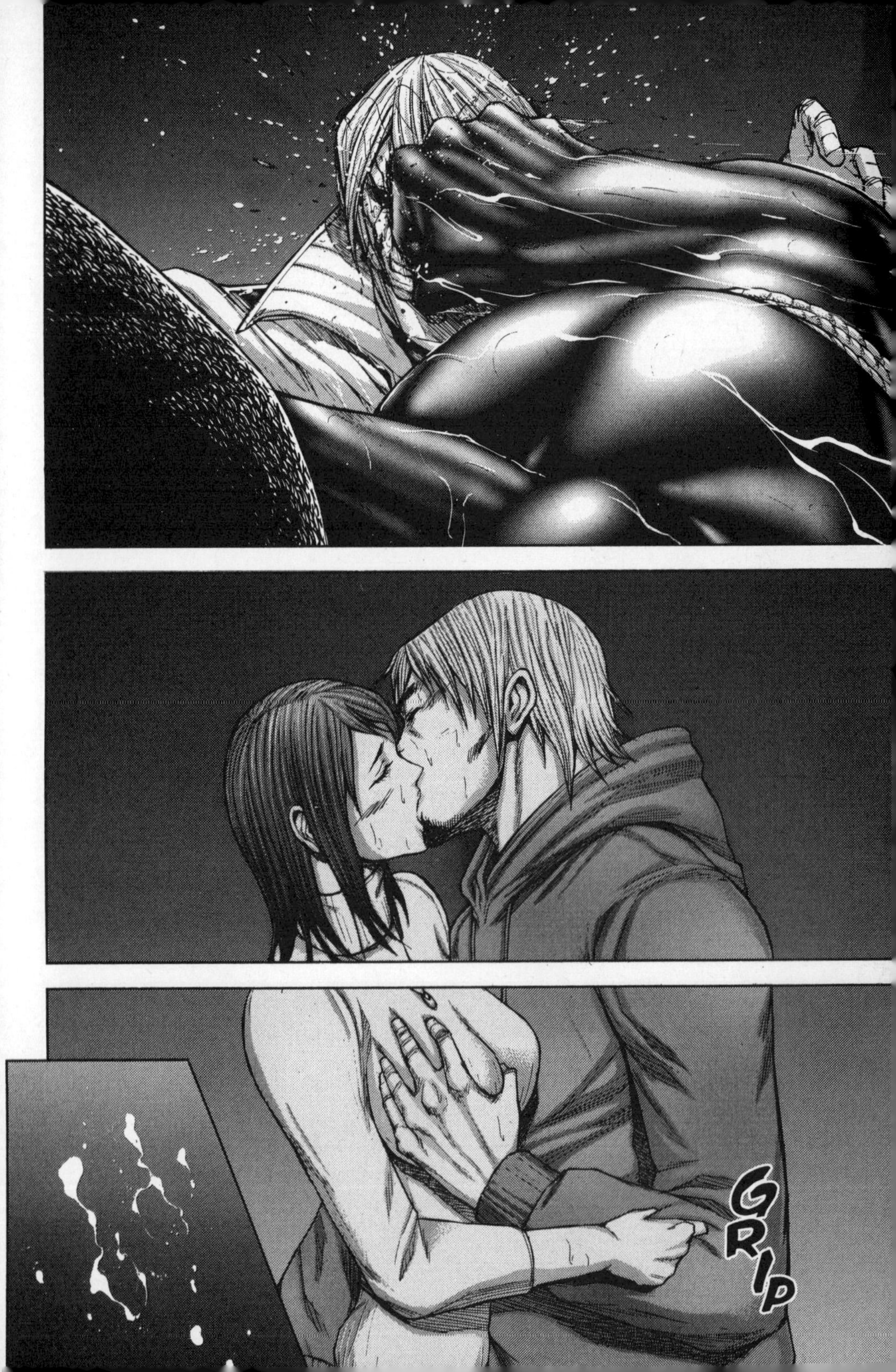
GRIP

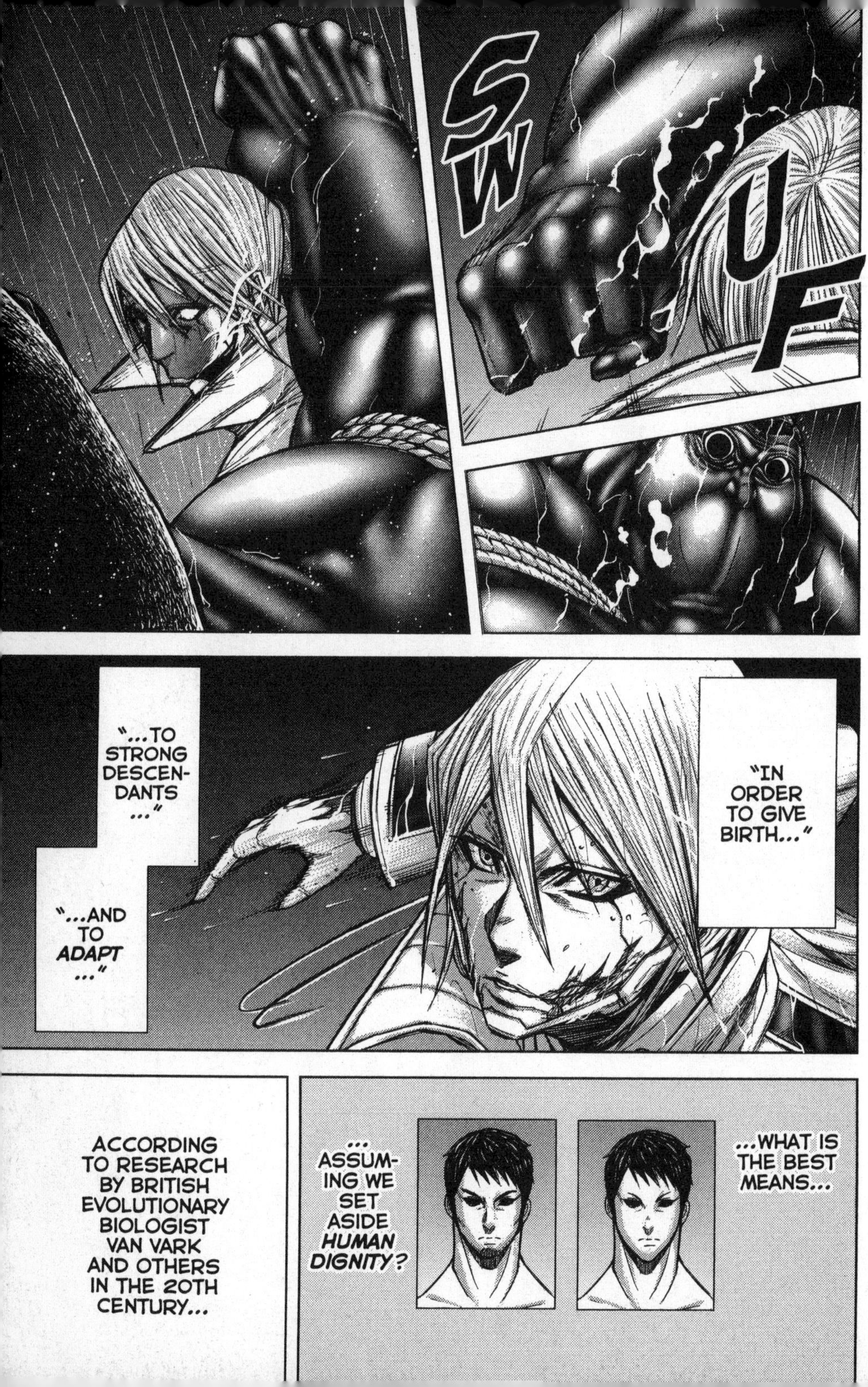
SWUF
"IN ORDER TO GIVE BIRTH..."
"...TO STRONG DESCENDANTS..."
"...AND TO ADAPT..."
...WHAT IS THE BEST MEANS...
...ASSUMING WE SET ASIDE HUMAN DIGNITY?
ACCORDING TO RESEARCH BY BRITISH EVOLUTIONARY BIOLOGIST VAN VARK AND OTHERS IN THE 20TH CENTURY...

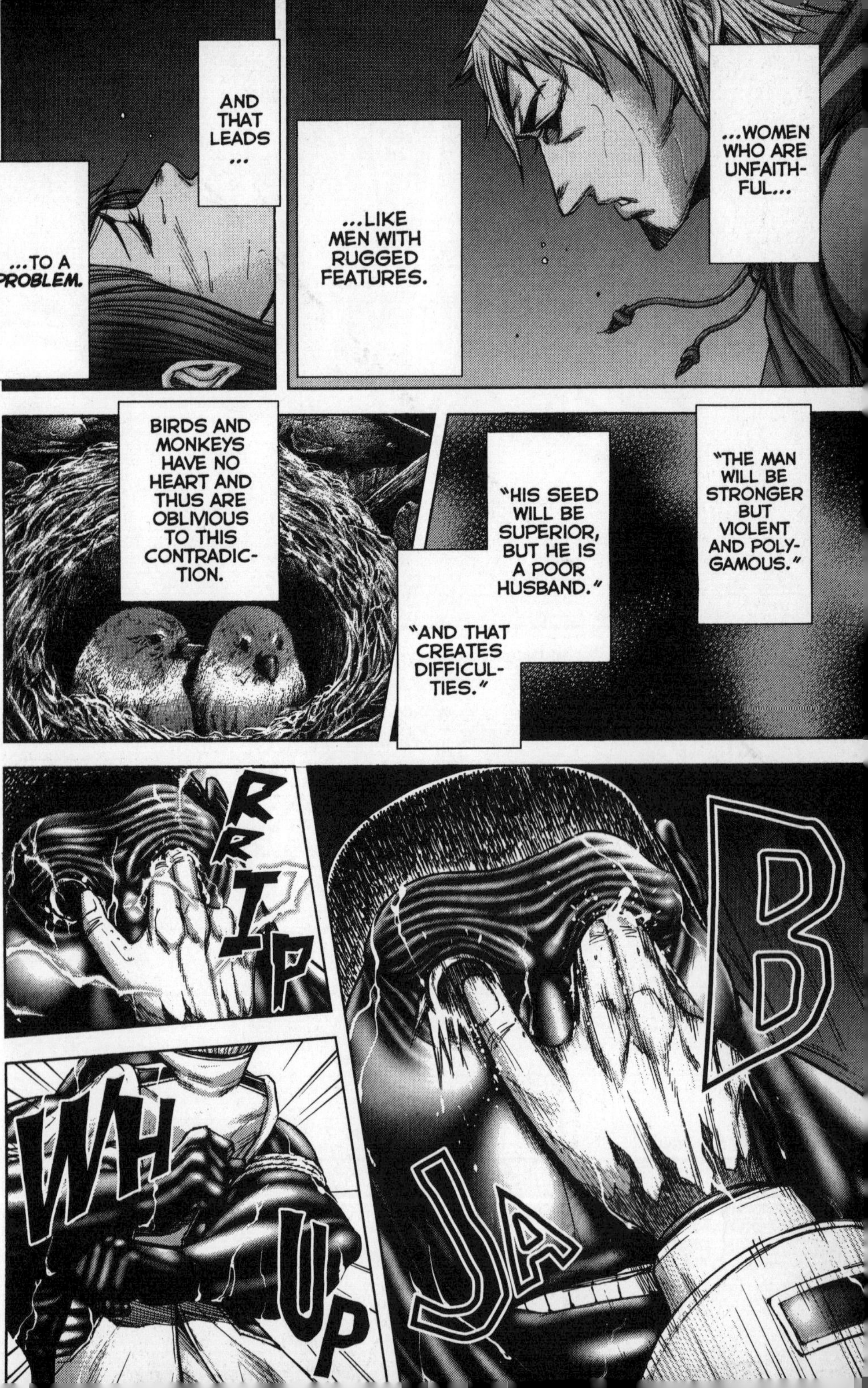
...WOMEN WHO ARE UNFAITHFUL...
...LIKE MEN WITH RUGGED FEATURES.
AND THAT LEADS ...
...TO A PROBLEM.
"THE MAN WILL BE STRONGER BUT VIOLENT AND POLYGAMOUS."
"HIS SEED WILL BE SUPERIOR, BUT HE IS A POOR HUSBAND."
"AND THAT CREATES DIFFICULTIES."
BIRDS AND MONKEYS HAVE NO HEART AND THUS ARE OBLIVIOUS TO THIS CONTRADICTION.
BJA
RRIP
WHUP

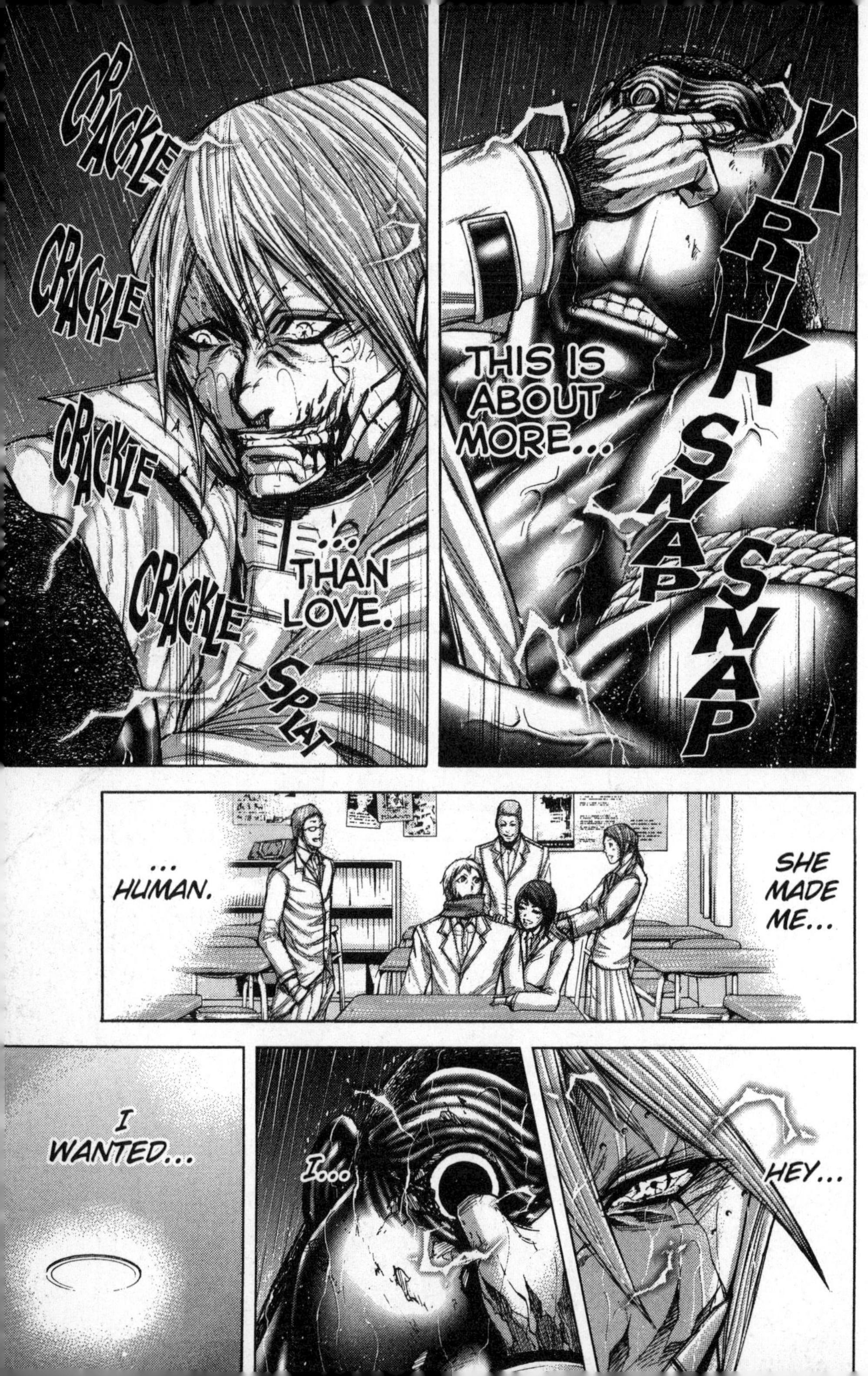
KRIK
THIS IS ABOUT MORE...
SNAP
SNAP
CRACKLE
CRACKLE
CRACKLE
CRACKLE
...THAN LOVE.
SPLAT
SHE MADE ME...
...HUMAN.
HEY...
I...
I WANTED...

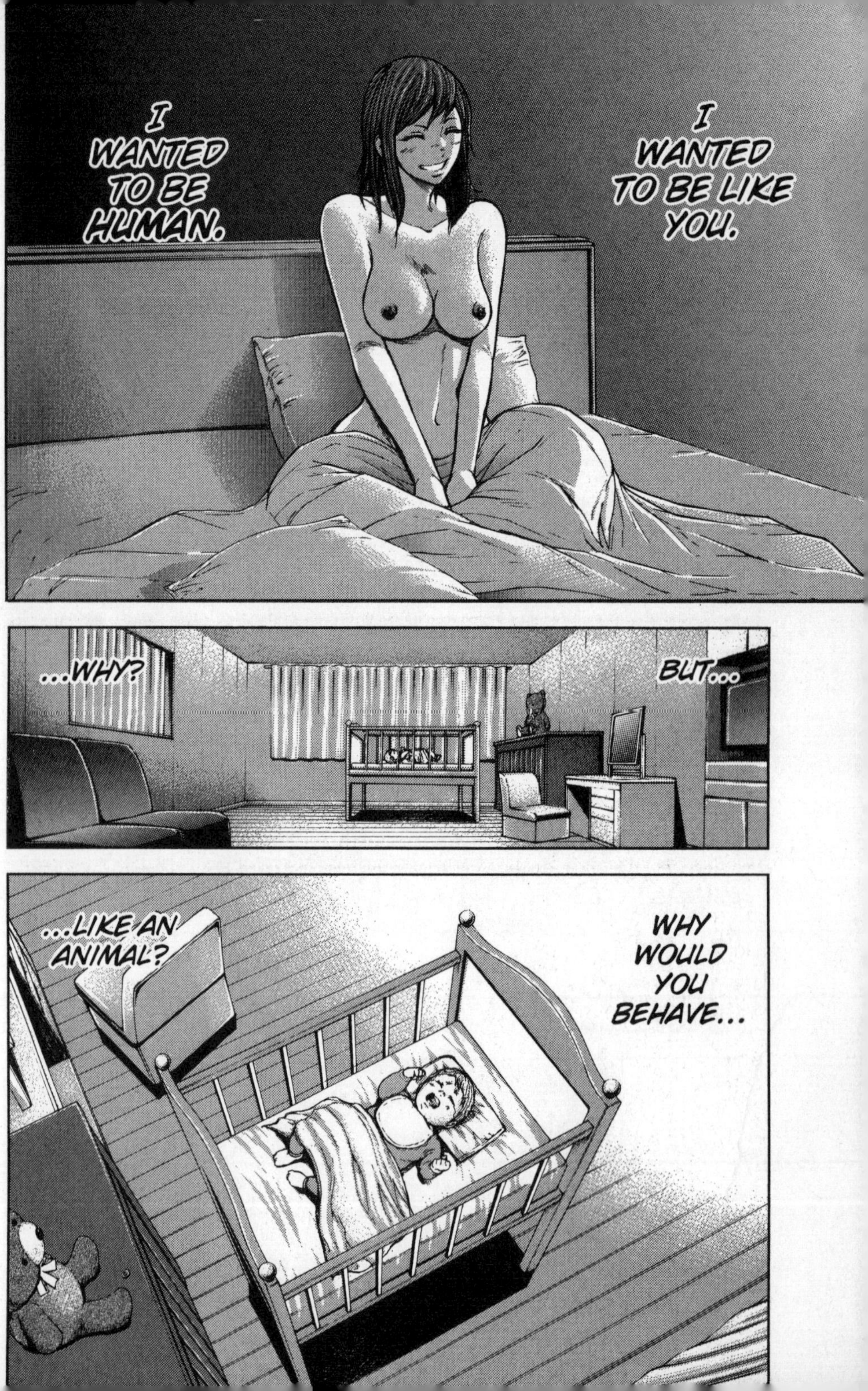
I WANTED TO BE LIKE YOU.
I WANTED TO BE HUMAN.
BUT...
...WHY?
WHY WOULD YOU BEHAVE...
...LIKE AN ANIMAL?

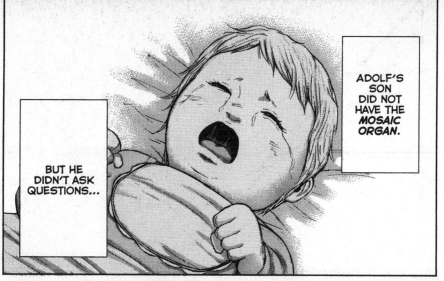

ADOLF'S SON DID NOT HAVE THE *MOSAIC ORGAN*.
BUT HE DIDN'T ASK QUESTIONS...
...BECAUSE HE WAS AFRAID.
LIKE AN ABUSED CHILD WHO FEARS LOSING HIS FAMILY...
...ADOLF FEARED LOSING ANYTHING ELSE.
SHUMP
WAS THAT ADOLF'S WEAK-NESS?
OR WAS IT A *HUMAN* WEAK-NESS?
WHUD
SHE GAVE THAT TO ME...
WHUD

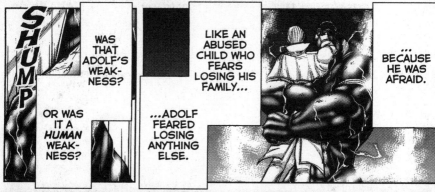

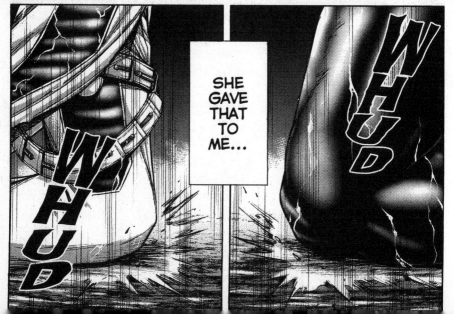

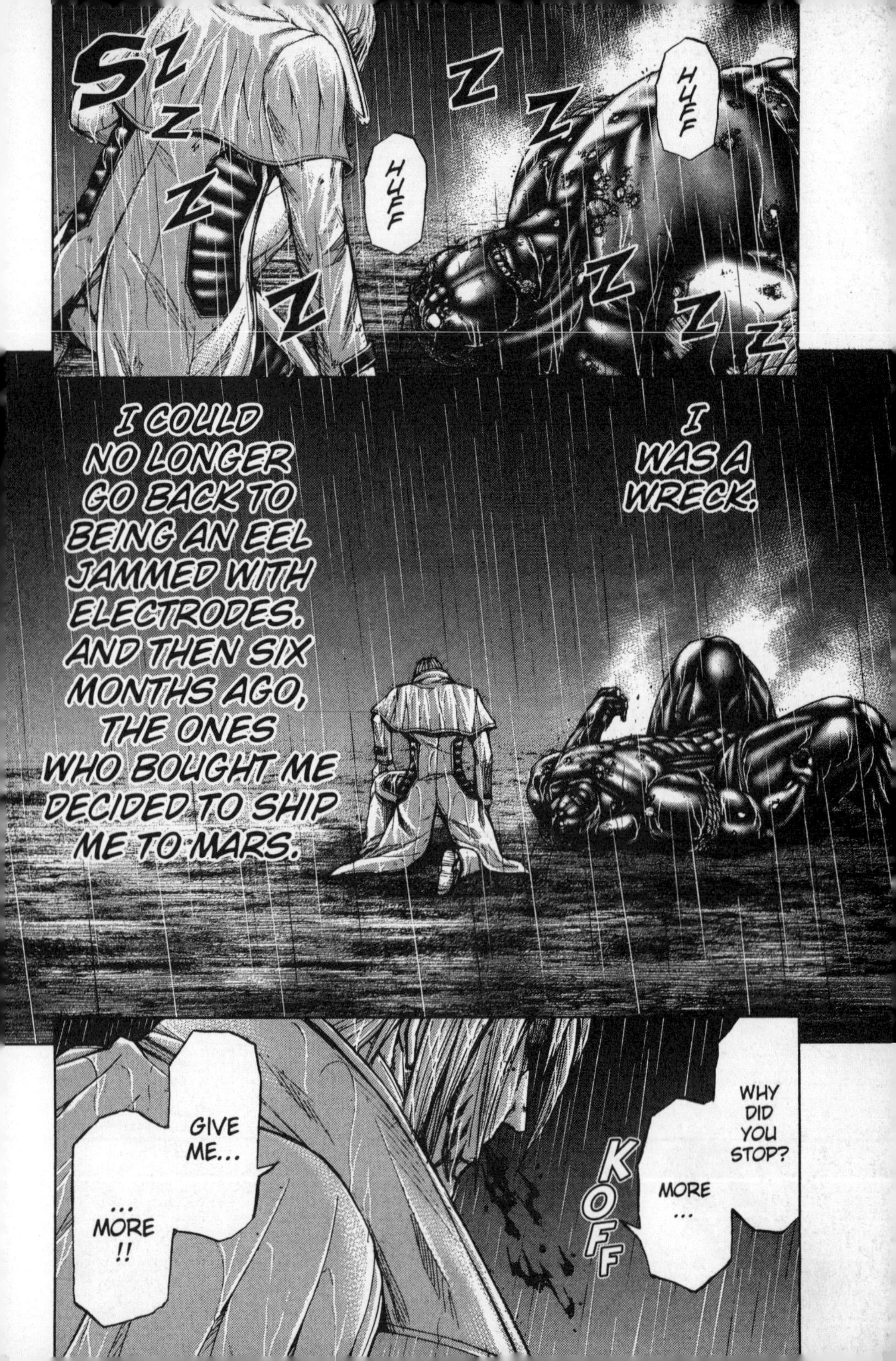
HUFF
HUFF
SIZZZZ
ZZZZZ
I WAS A WRECK.
I COULD NO LONGER GO BACK TO BEING AN EEL JAMMED WITH ELECTRODES. AND THEN SIX MONTHS AGO, THE ONES WHO BOUGHT ME DECIDED TO SHIP ME TO MARS.
WHY DID YOU STOP?
MORE ...
KOFF
GIVE ME...
... MORE !!

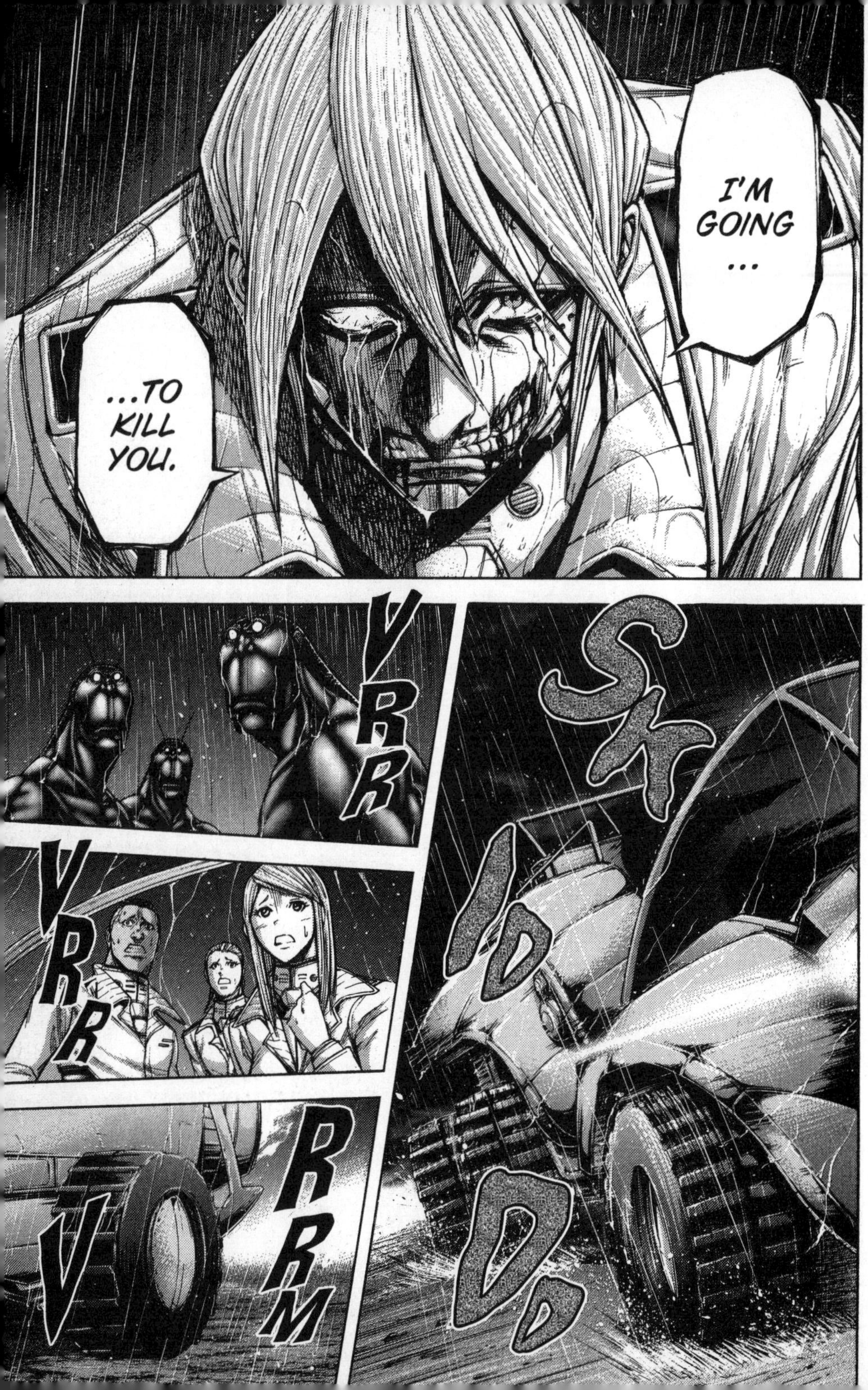
I'M GOING...
...TO KILL YOU.
SKIDDD
VRR
VRR
VRRM

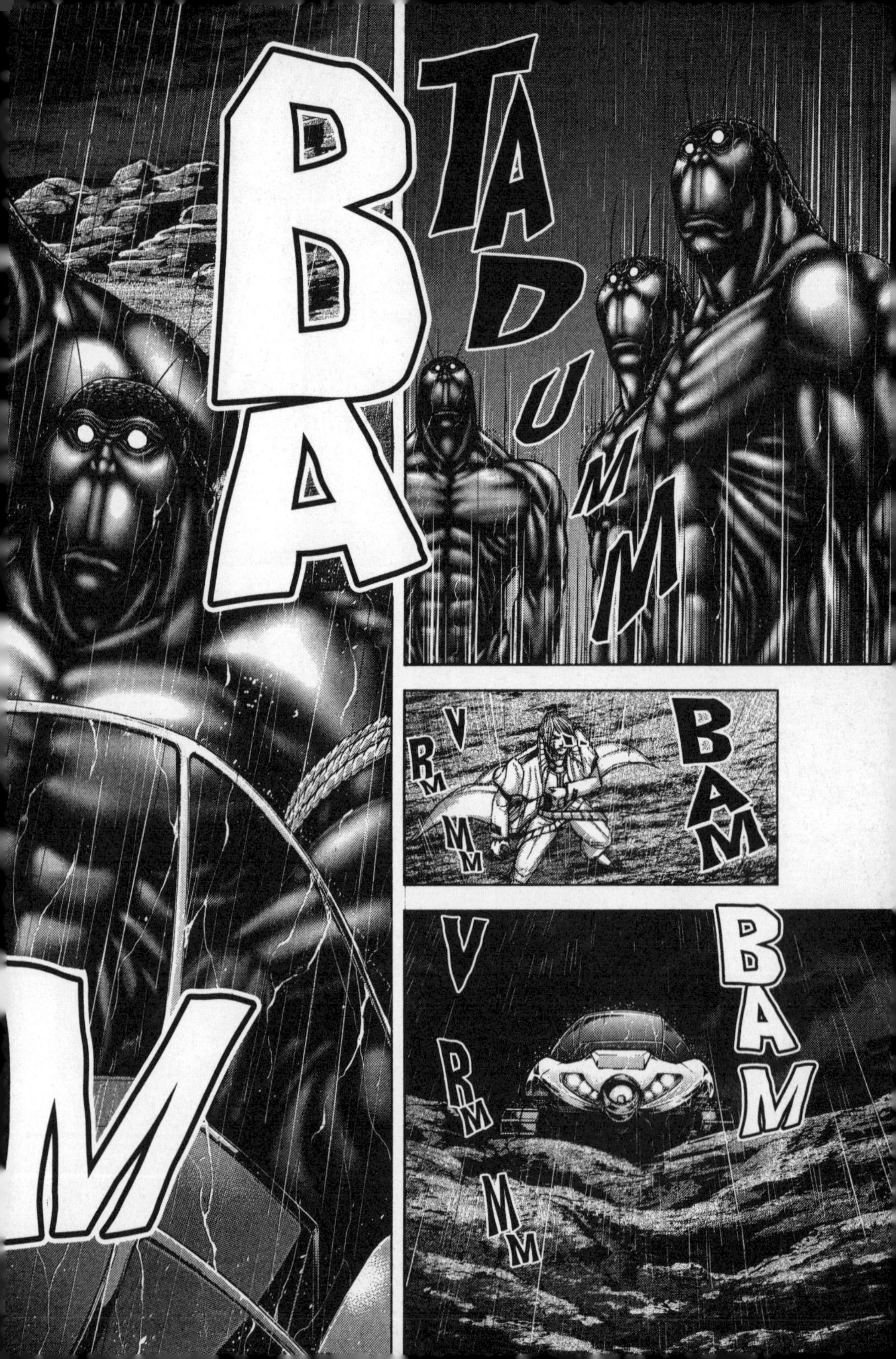
TADUMM
VRMMM
BAM
VRMMM
BAM
BAM

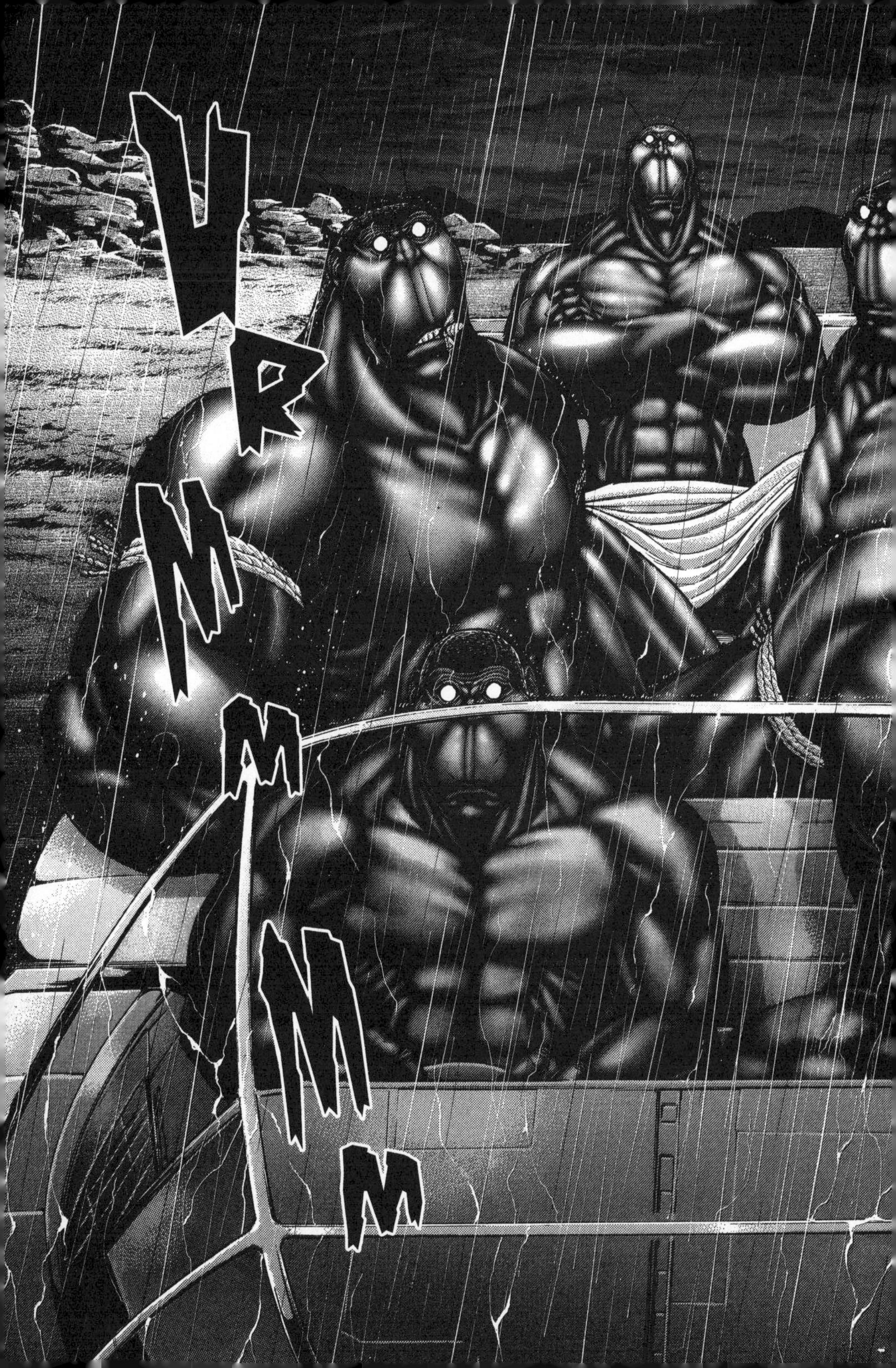
VRMMMM

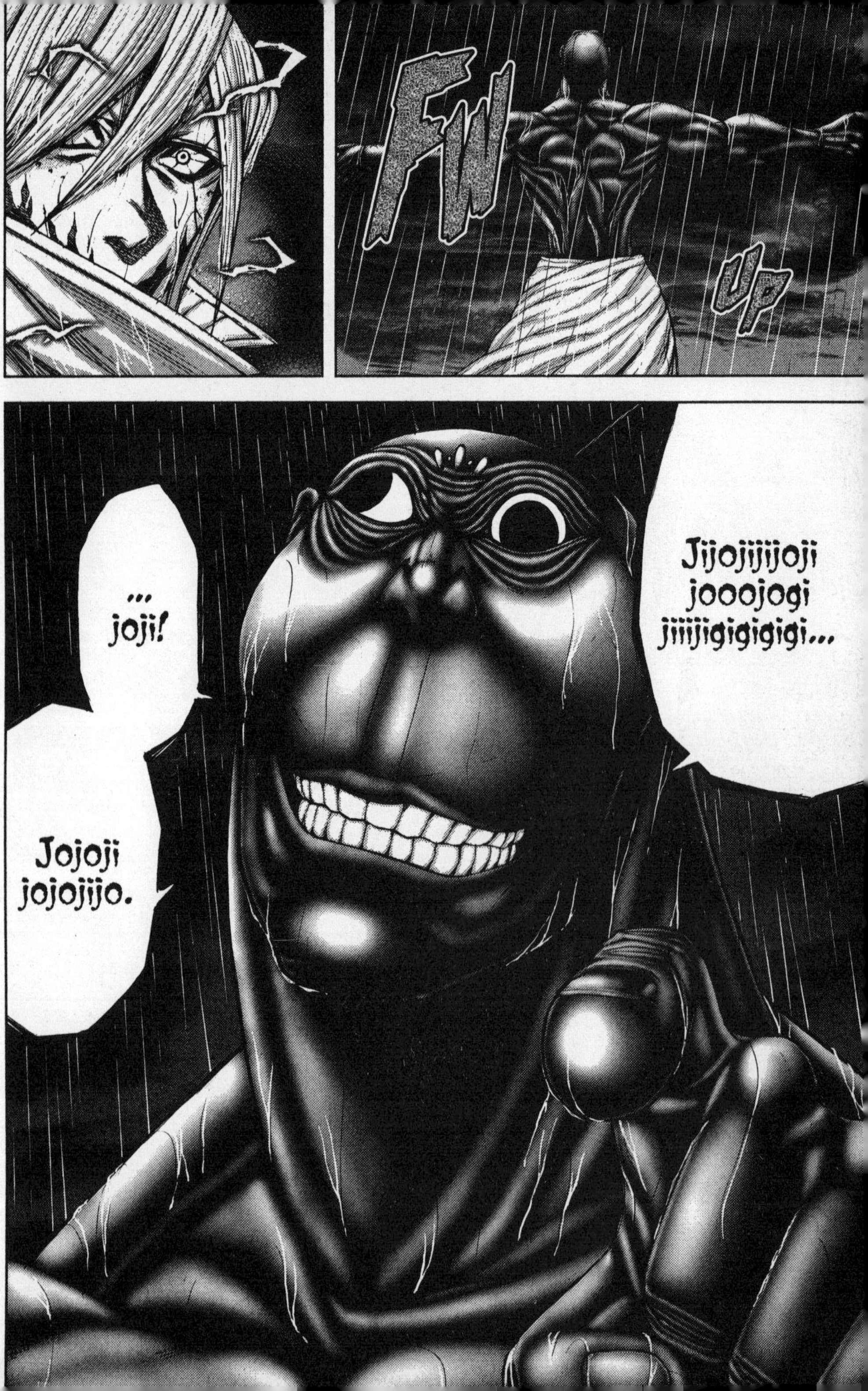
FW
UP
Jijojijijoji jooojogi jiiijigigigigi...
... joji!
Jojoji jojojijo.

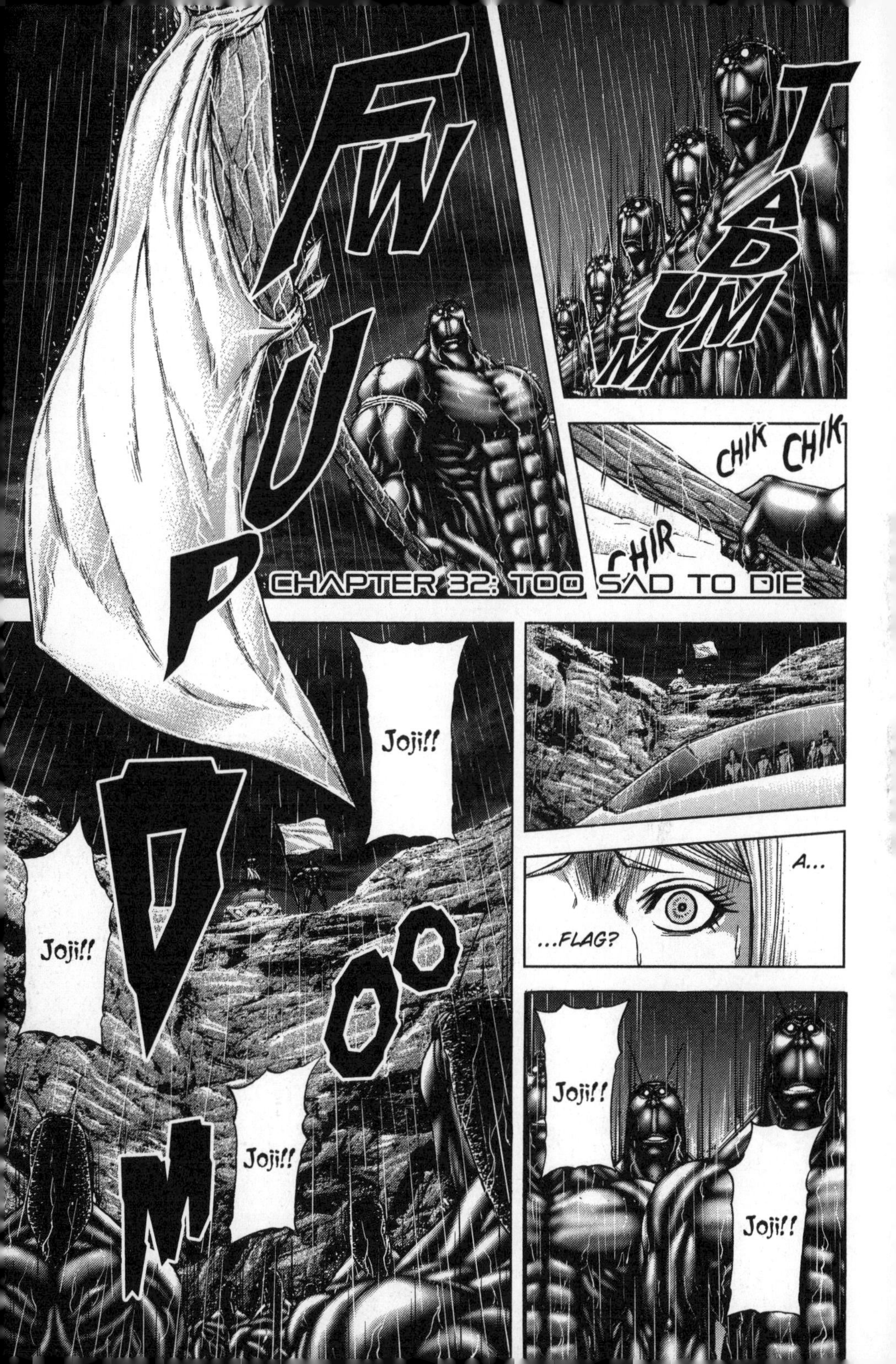
TADUMM
CHIK CHIK
CHIR
CHAPTER 32: TOO SAD TO DIE
FWUP
A...
...FLAG?
Joji!!
Joji!!
Joji!!
DOOOM
Joji!!
Joji!!

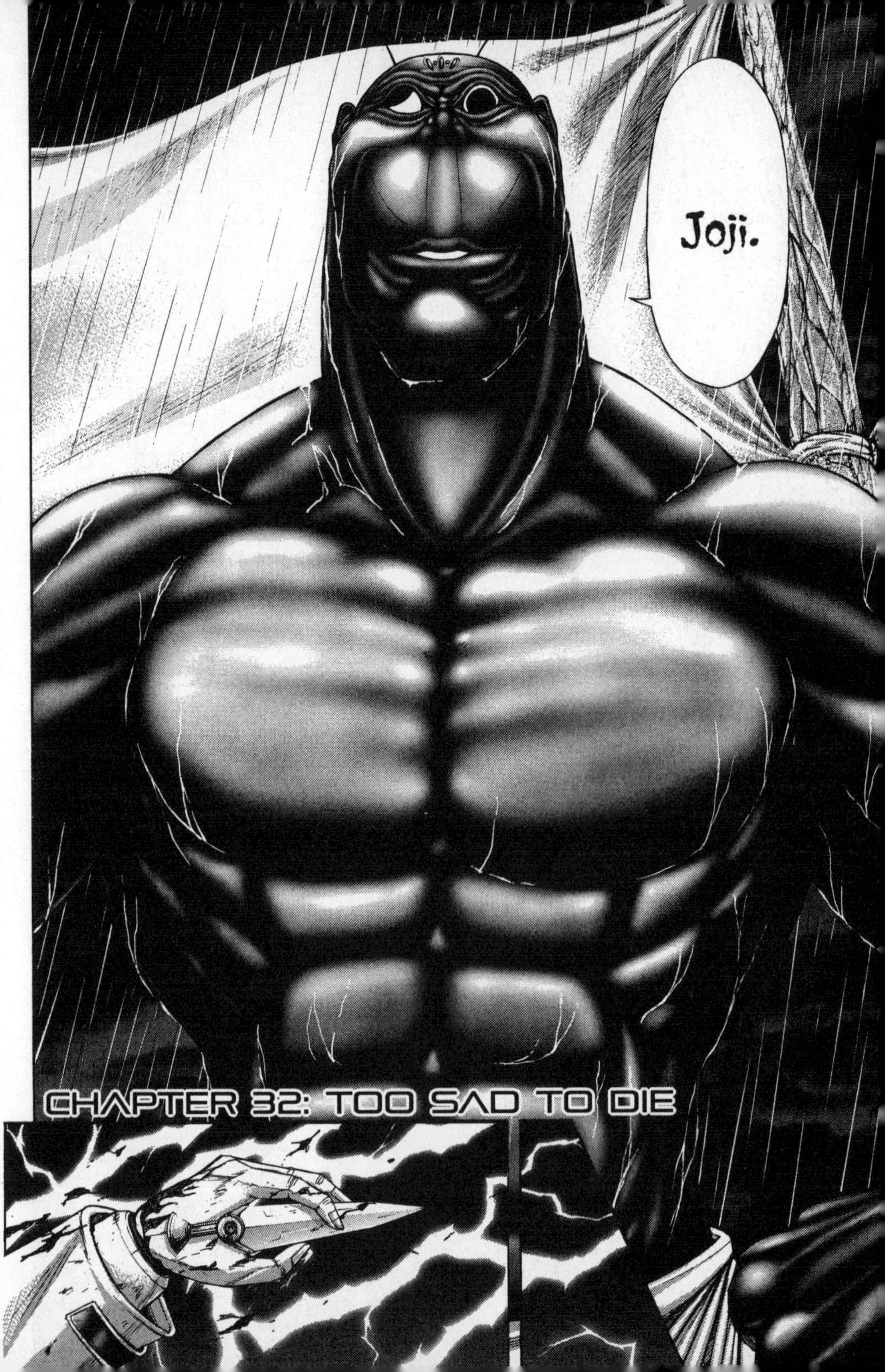
Joji.
CHAPTER 32: TOO SAD TO DIE

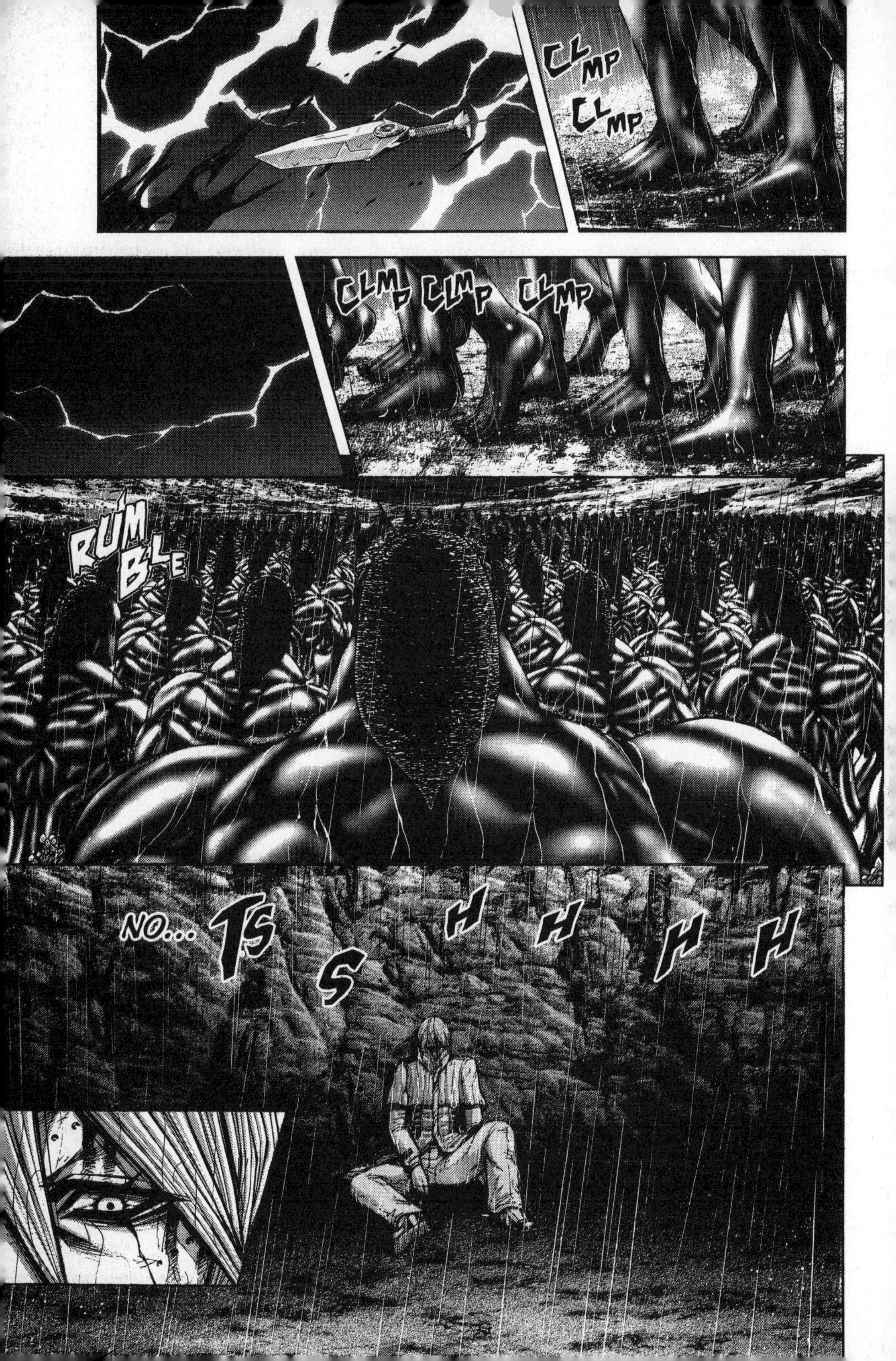
CLMP
CLMP
CLMP CLMP CLMP
RUMBLE
NO...
TSSHHHH

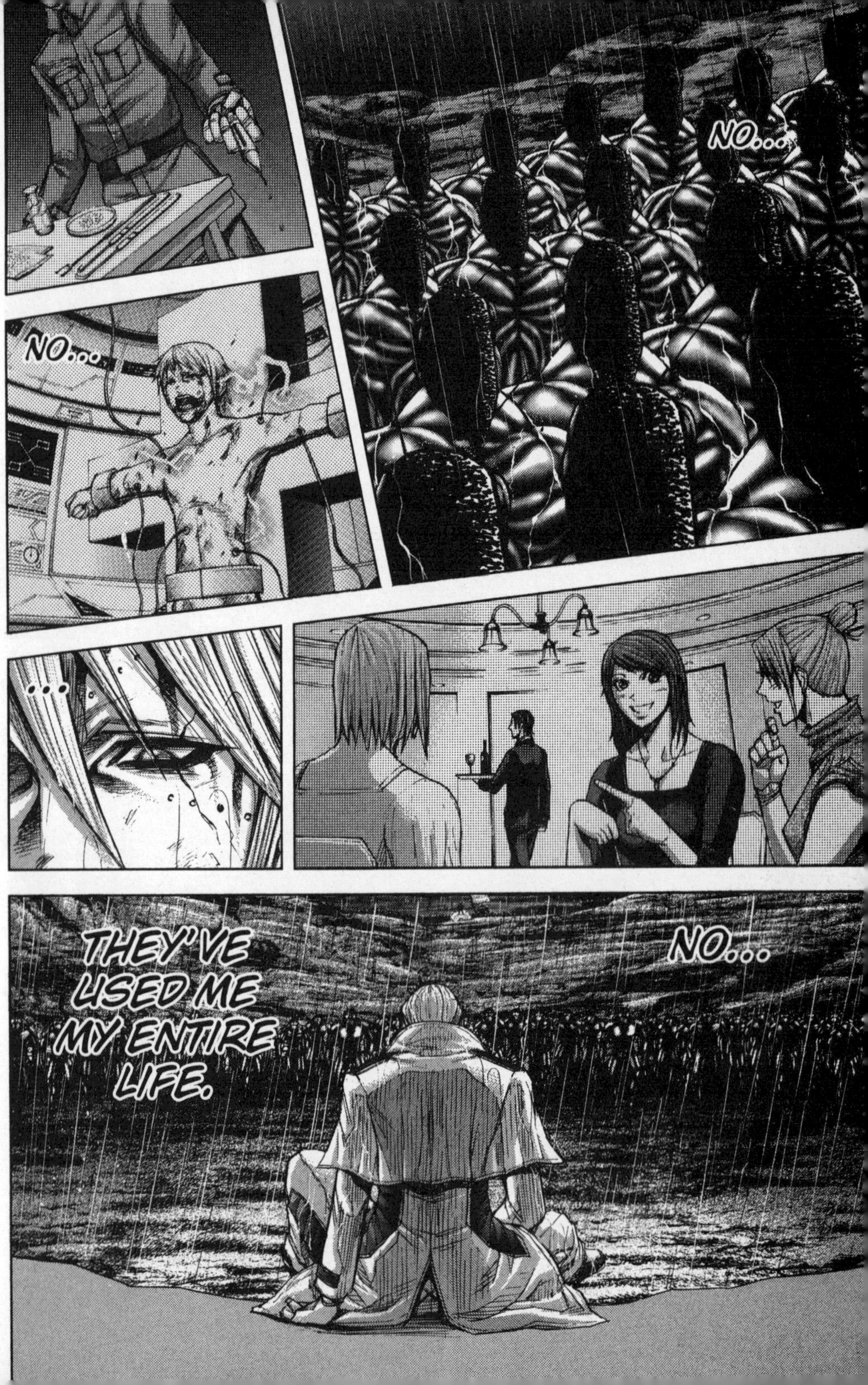
NO...
NO...
...
NO...
THEY'VE USED ME MY ENTIRE LIFE.

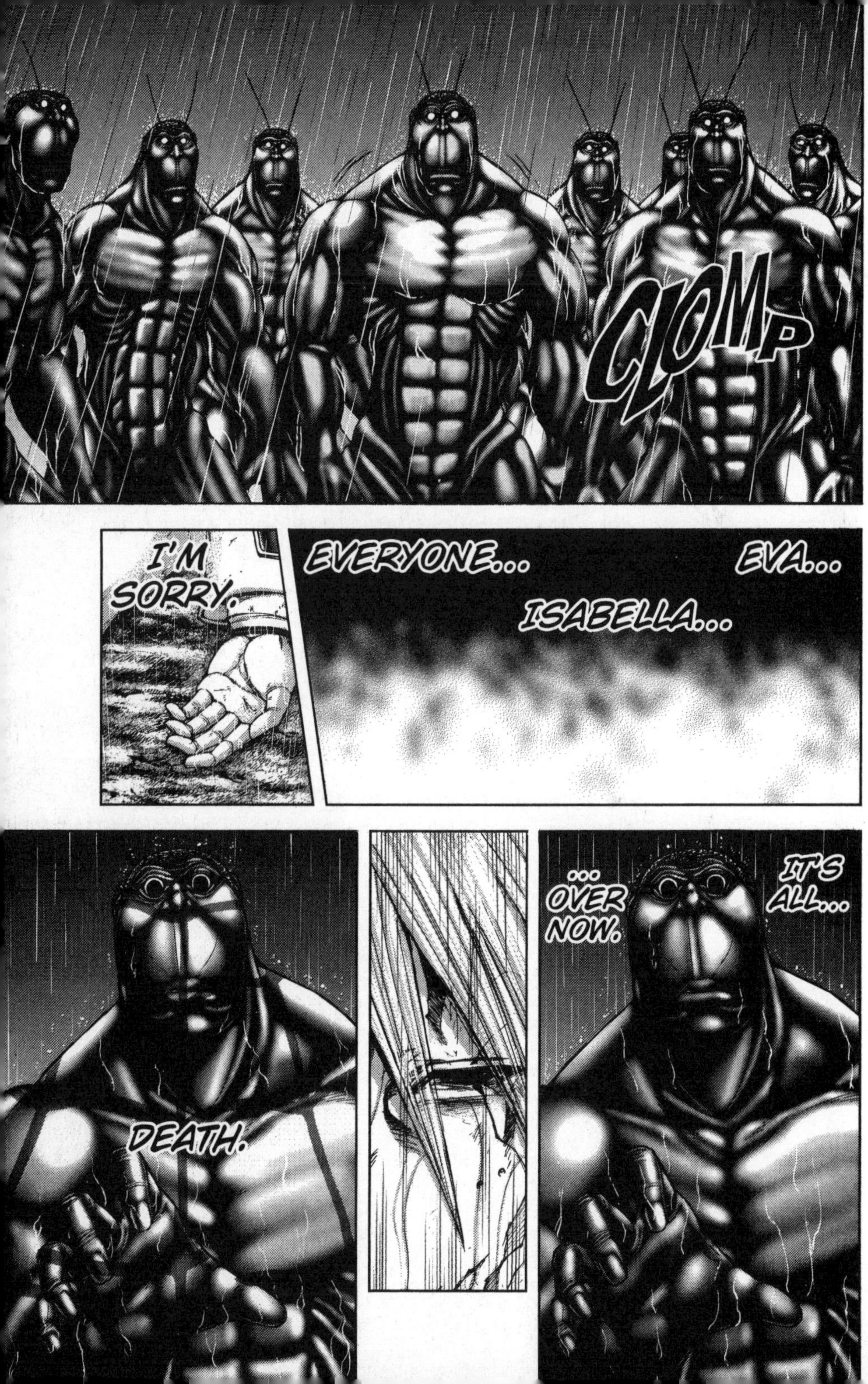
CLOMP
EVA...
EVERYONE...
ISABELLA...
I'M SORRY.
IT'S ALL...
...OVER NOW.
DEATH.

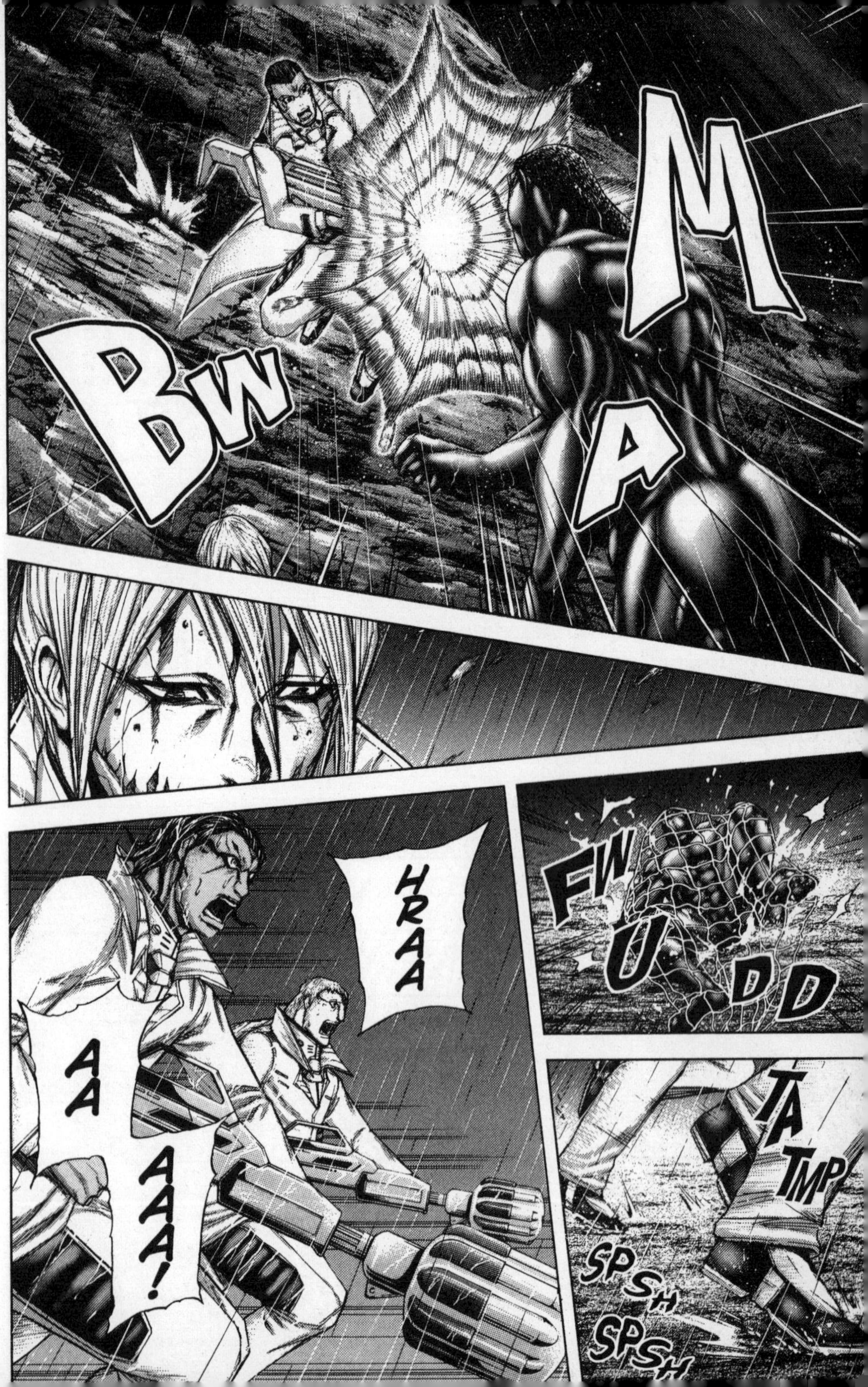
M
A
BW
FW
U
DD
TA
TMP
SPSH
SPSH
HRAAA
AA
AAA
A!

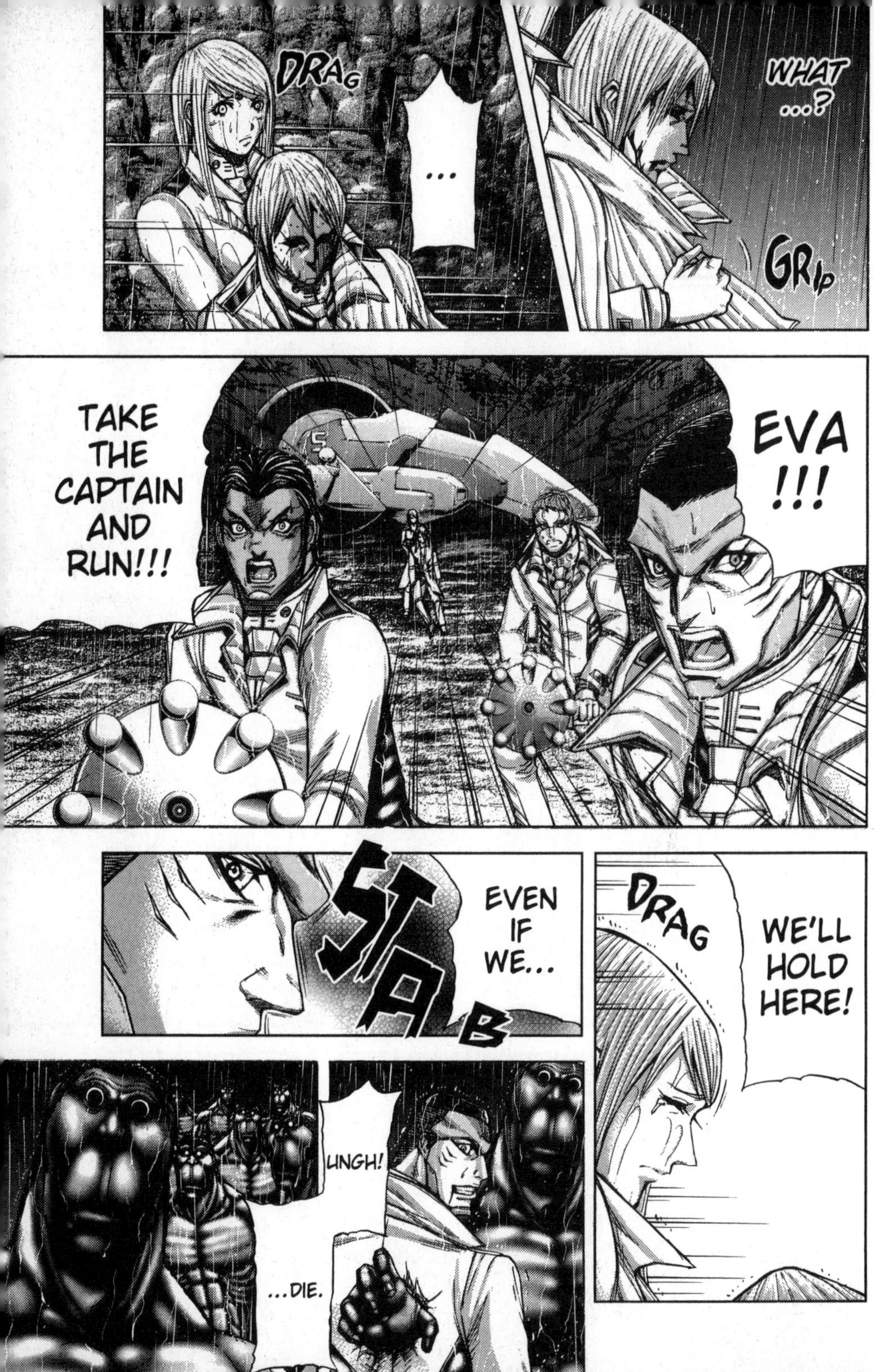
WHAT ...?
GRIP
DRAG
...
EVA !!!
TAKE THE CAPTAIN AND RUN!!!
DRAG
WE'LL HOLD HERE!
STAB
EVEN IF WE...
UNGH!
...DIE.

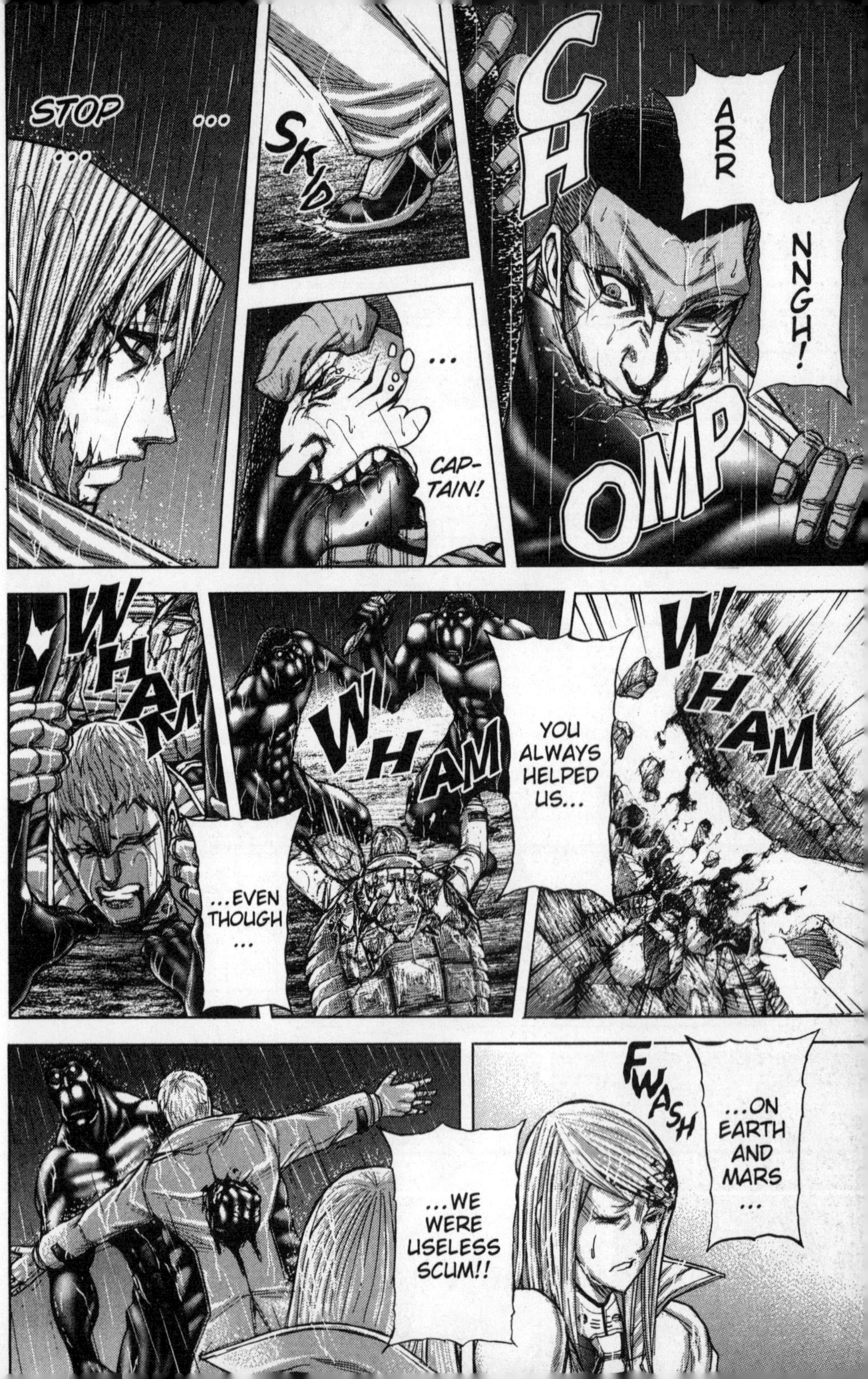
CH
ARR NNGH!
OMP
SKID
...
CAP-TAIN!
STOP ... ...
WHAM
YOU ALWAYS HELPED US...
WHAM
...EVEN THOUGH ...
WHAM
FWASH
...ON EARTH AND MARS ...
...WE WERE USELESS SCUM!!

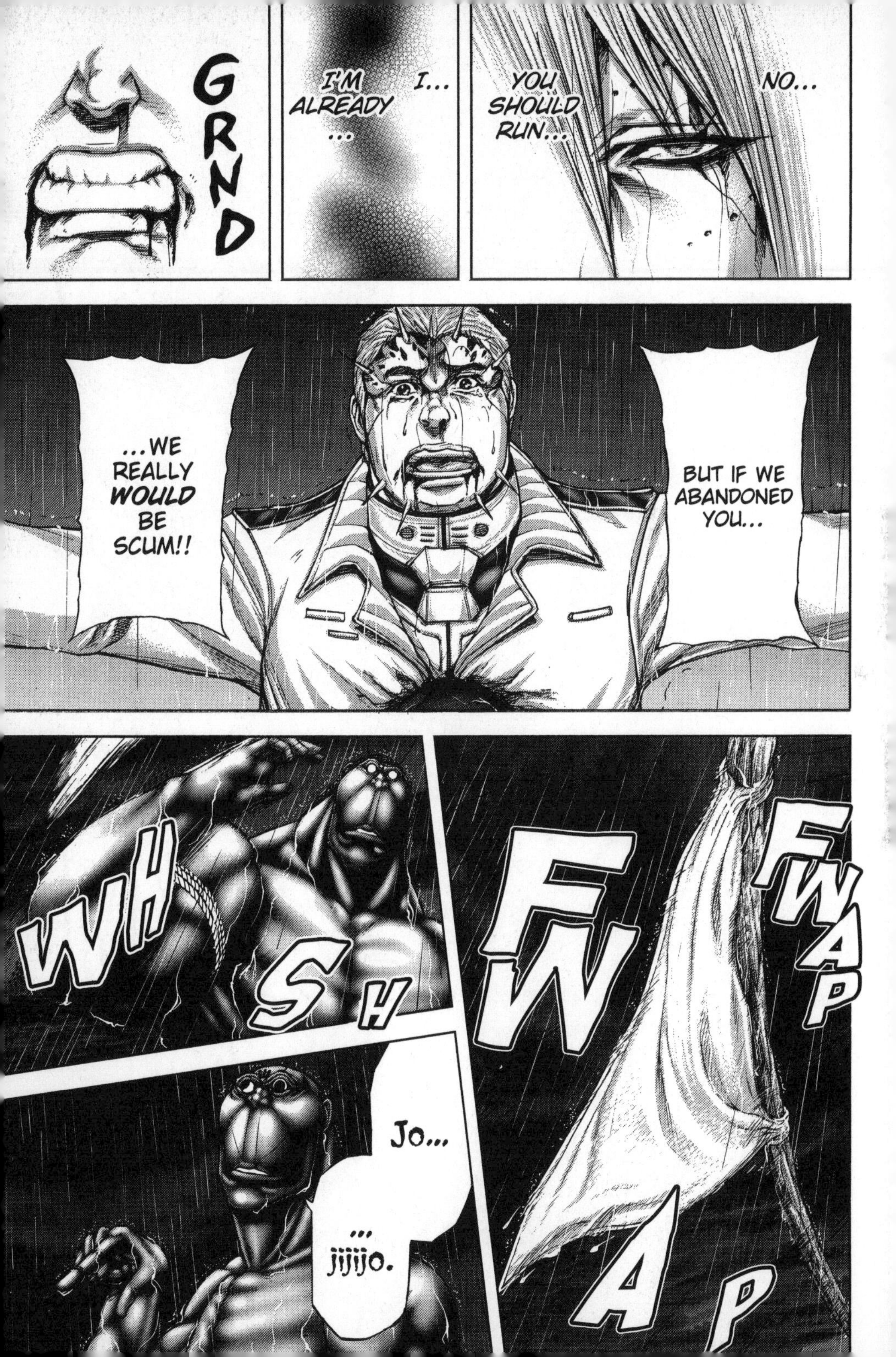
NO...
YOU SHOULD RUN...
I...
I'M ALREADY ...
GRND
BUT IF WE ABANDONED YOU...
...WE REALLY **WOULD** BE SCUM!!
FWAP
FWAP
WHSH
Jo...
...jijijo.

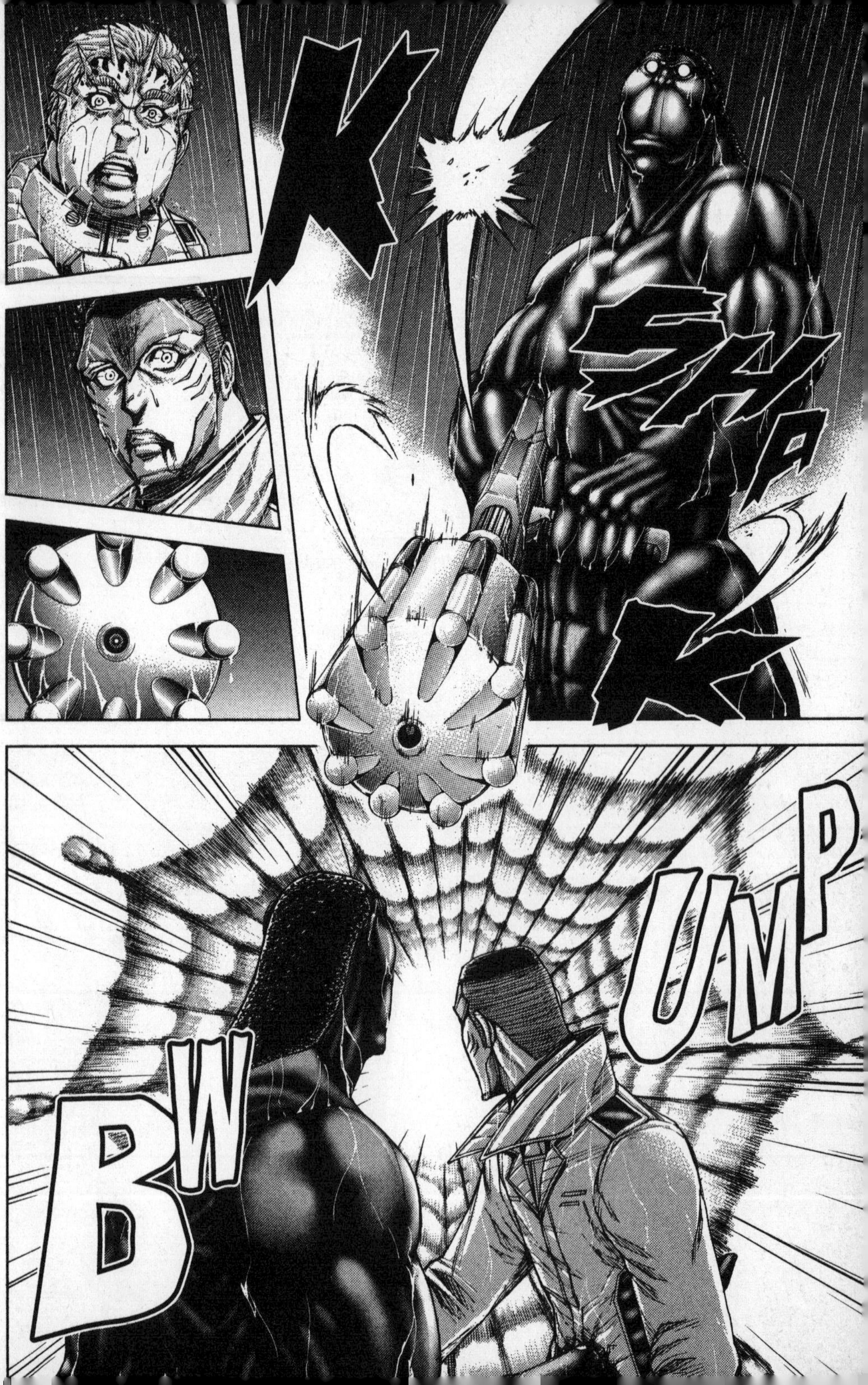
SHAK
K
BWUMP

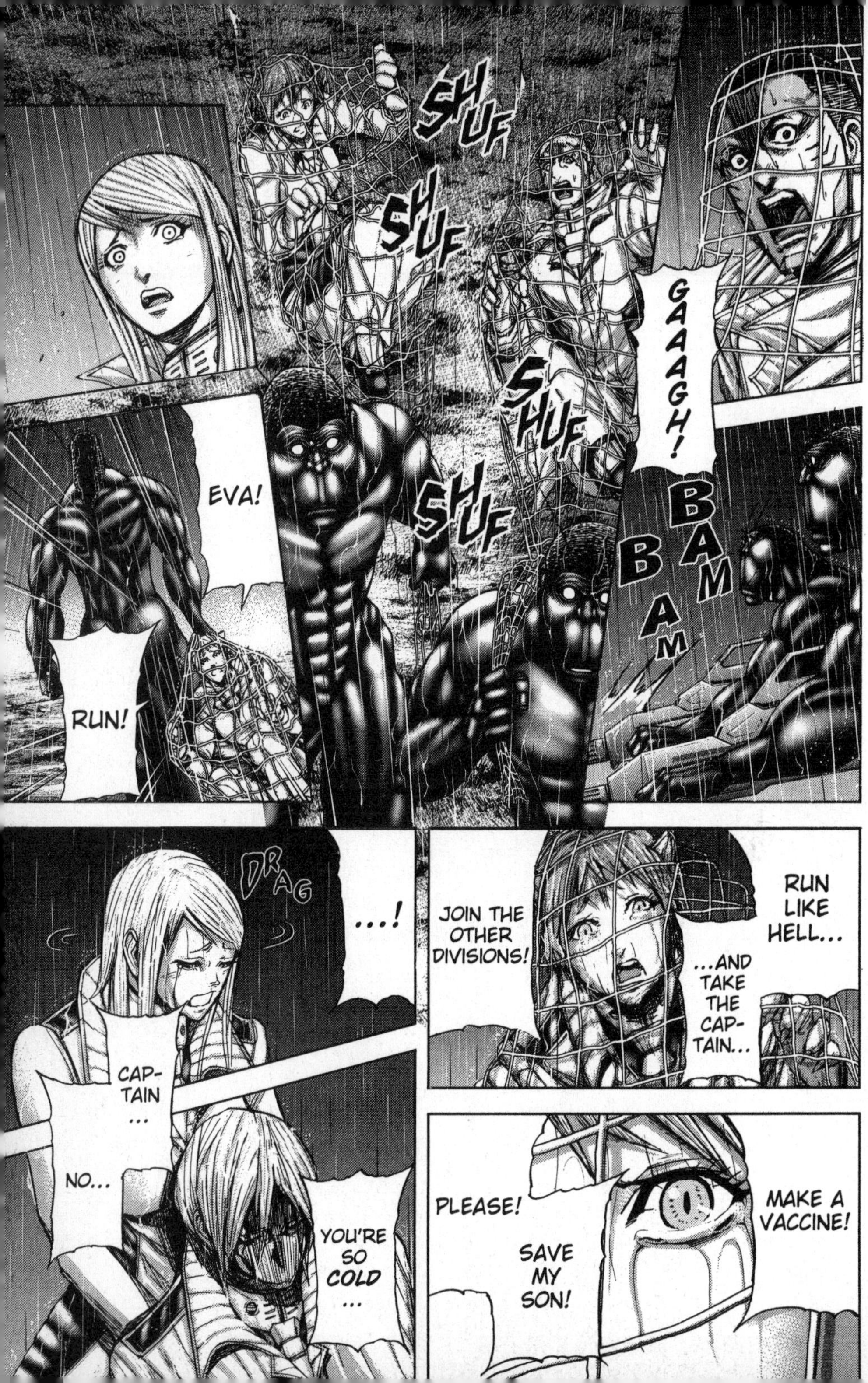
GAAAGH!
SHUF
SHUF
SHUF
SHUF
BAM
BAM
EVA!
RUN!
RUN LIKE HELL...
...AND TAKE THE CAP-TAIN...
JOIN THE OTHER DIVISIONS!
MAKE A VACCINE!
PLEASE!
SAVE MY SON!
DRAG
...!
CAP-TAIN ...
NO...
YOU'RE SO COLD ...

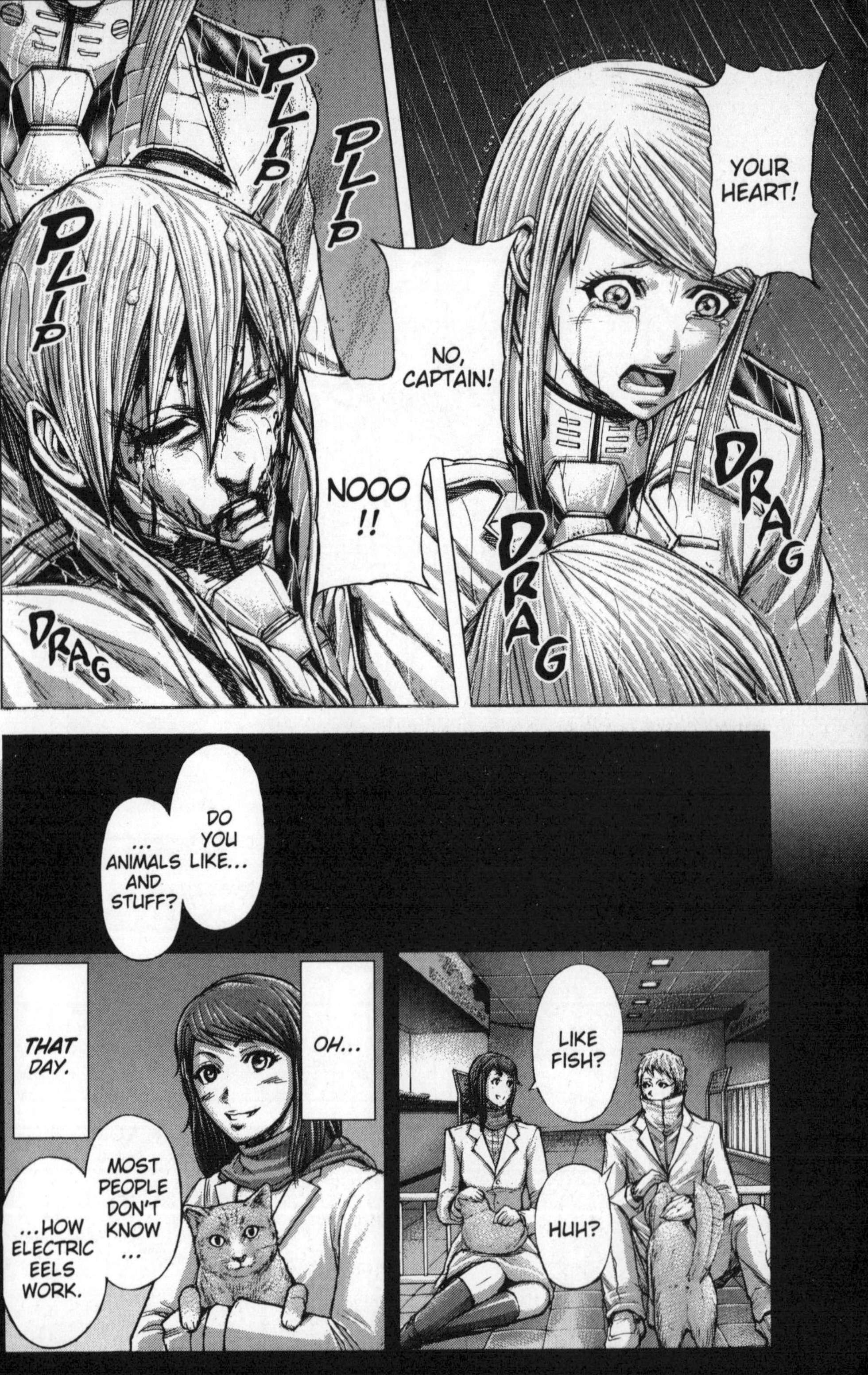
YOUR HEART!
NO, CAPTAIN!
NOOO !!
DRAG DRAG
DRAG
PLIP PLIP PLIP
DRAG
DO YOU LIKE...
...ANIMALS AND STUFF?
LIKE FISH?
HUH?
OH...
THAT DAY.
MOST PEOPLE DON'T KNOW ...
...HOW ELECTRIC EELS WORK.

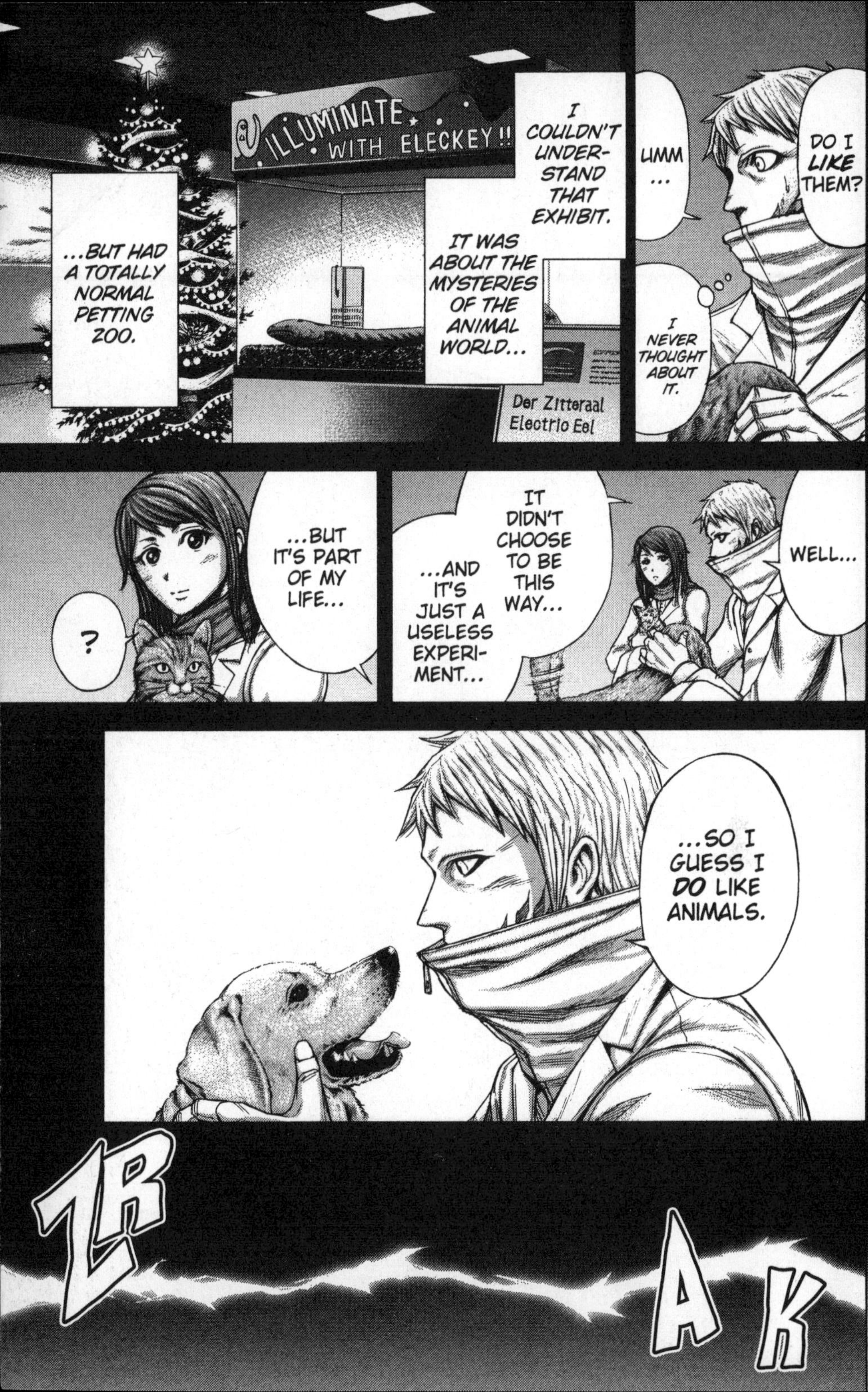
DO I **LIKE** THEM?
UMM...
I NEVER THOUGHT ABOUT IT.
I COULDN'T UNDERSTAND THAT EXHIBIT.
ILLUMINATE WITH ELECKEY!!
IT WAS ABOUT THE MYSTERIES OF THE ANIMAL WORLD...
Der Zitteraal
Electric Eel
...BUT HAD A TOTALLY NORMAL PETTING ZOO.
WELL...
IT DIDN'T CHOOSE TO BE THIS WAY...
...AND IT'S JUST A USELESS EXPERIMENT...
...BUT IT'S PART OF MY LIFE...
?
...SO I GUESS I **DO** LIKE ANIMALS.
ZR A K

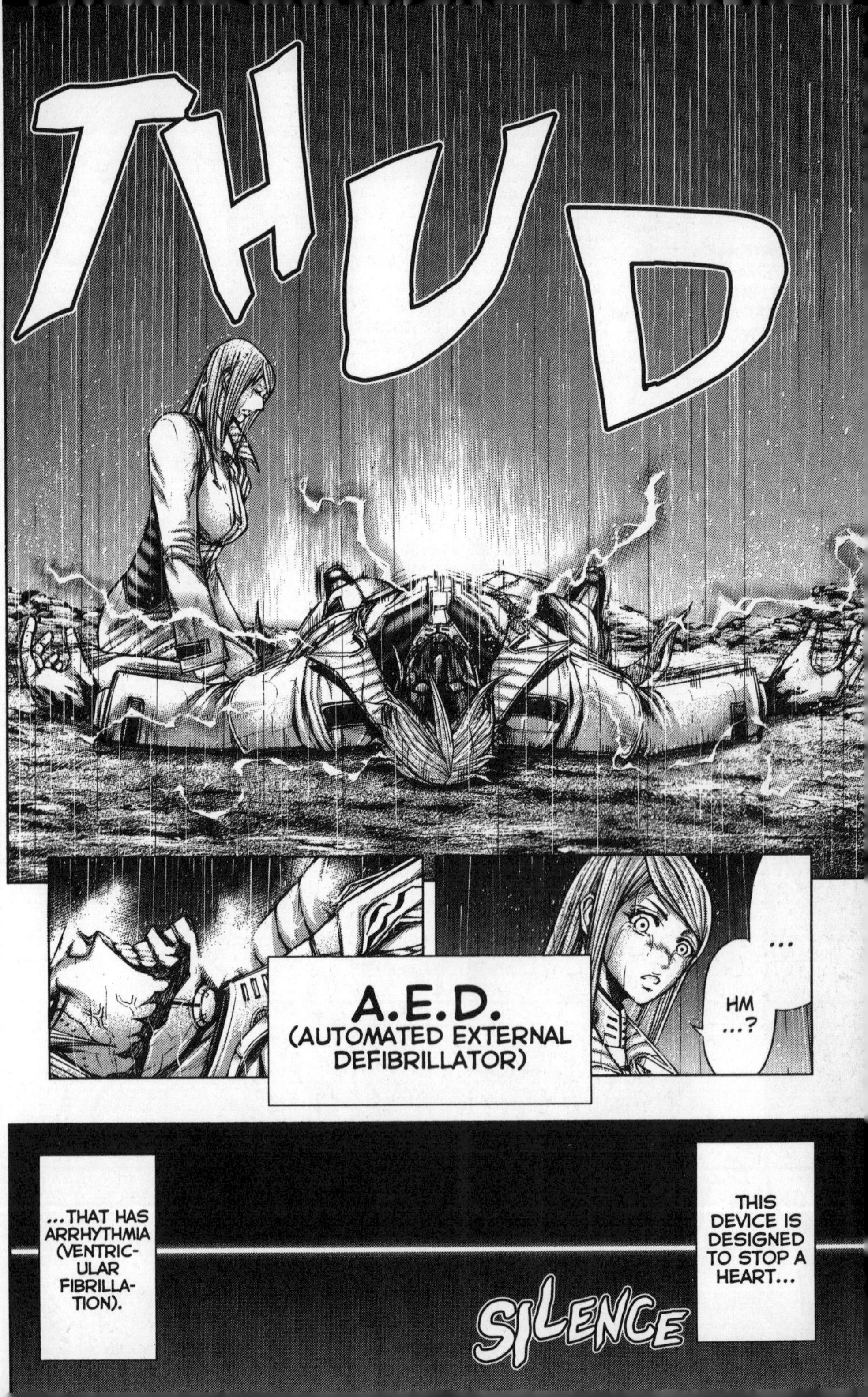
THUD
...
HM ...?
A.E.D. (AUTOMATED EXTERNAL DEFIBRILLATOR)
THIS DEVICE IS DESIGNED TO STOP A HEART...
SILENCE
...THAT HAS ARRHYTHMIA (VENTRICULAR FIBRILLATION).

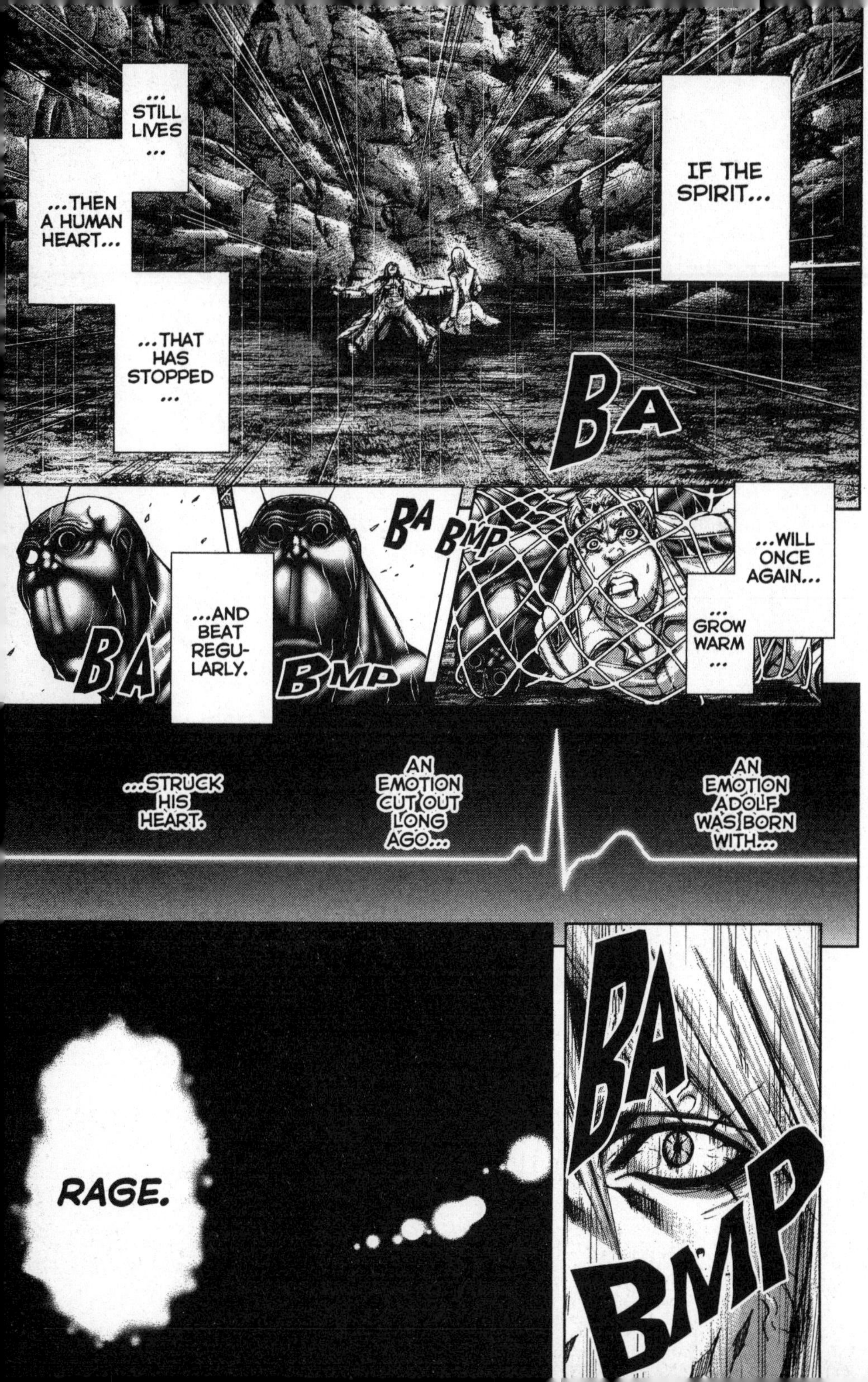
IF THE SPIRIT...
...STILL LIVES...
...THEN A HUMAN HEART...
...THAT HAS STOPPED...
BA
...WILL ONCE AGAIN...
...GROW WARM...
BA BMP
...AND BEAT REGU-LARLY.
BMP
BA
AN EMOTION ADOLF WAS BORN WITH...
AN EMOTION CUT OUT LONG AGO...
...STRUCK HIS HEART.
BA BMP
RAGE.

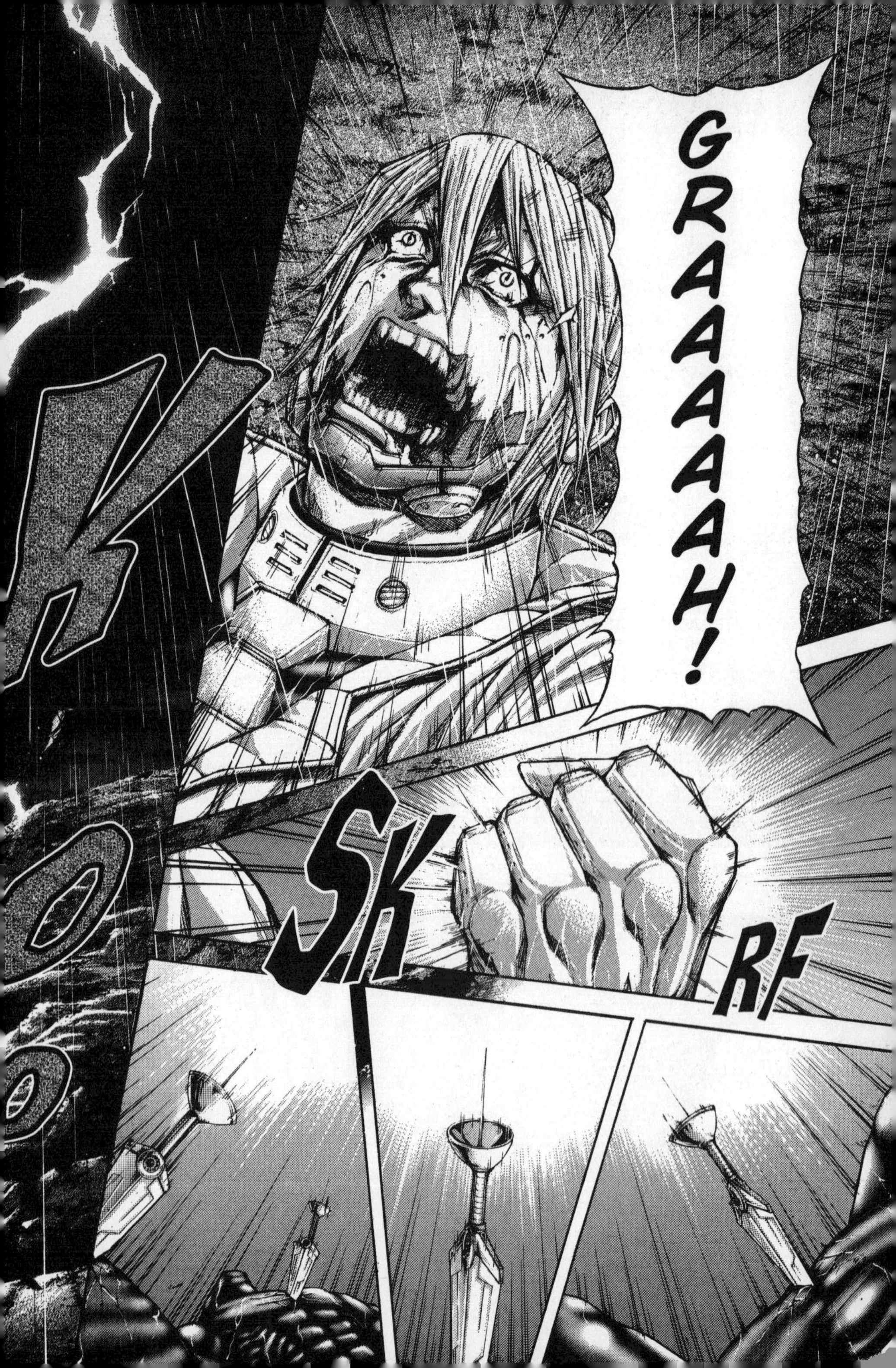
GRAAAAAH!
SK
RF

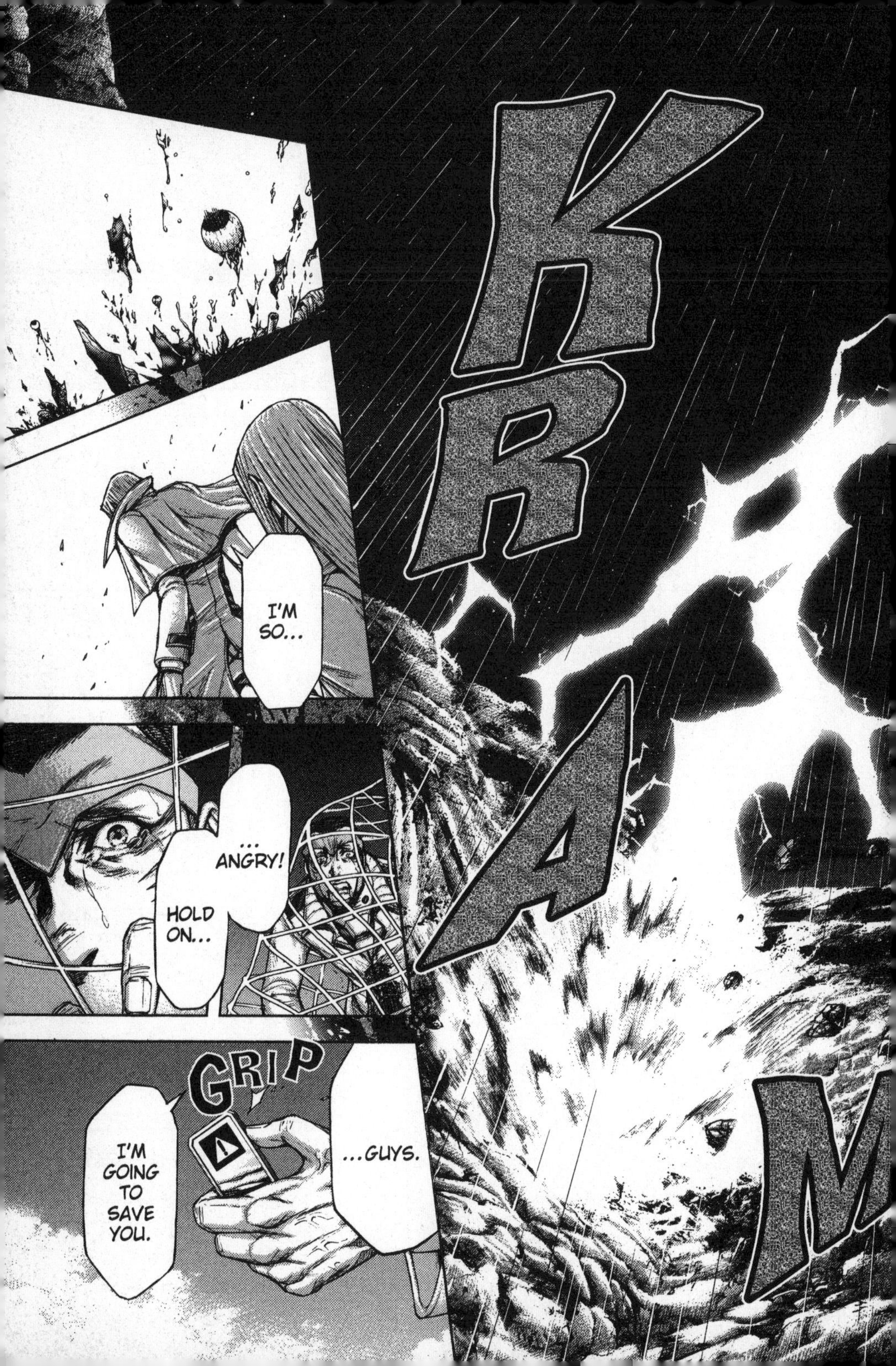
KRAAM
I'M SO...
...ANGRY!
HOLD ON...
...GUYS.
GRIP
I'M GOING TO SAVE YOU.

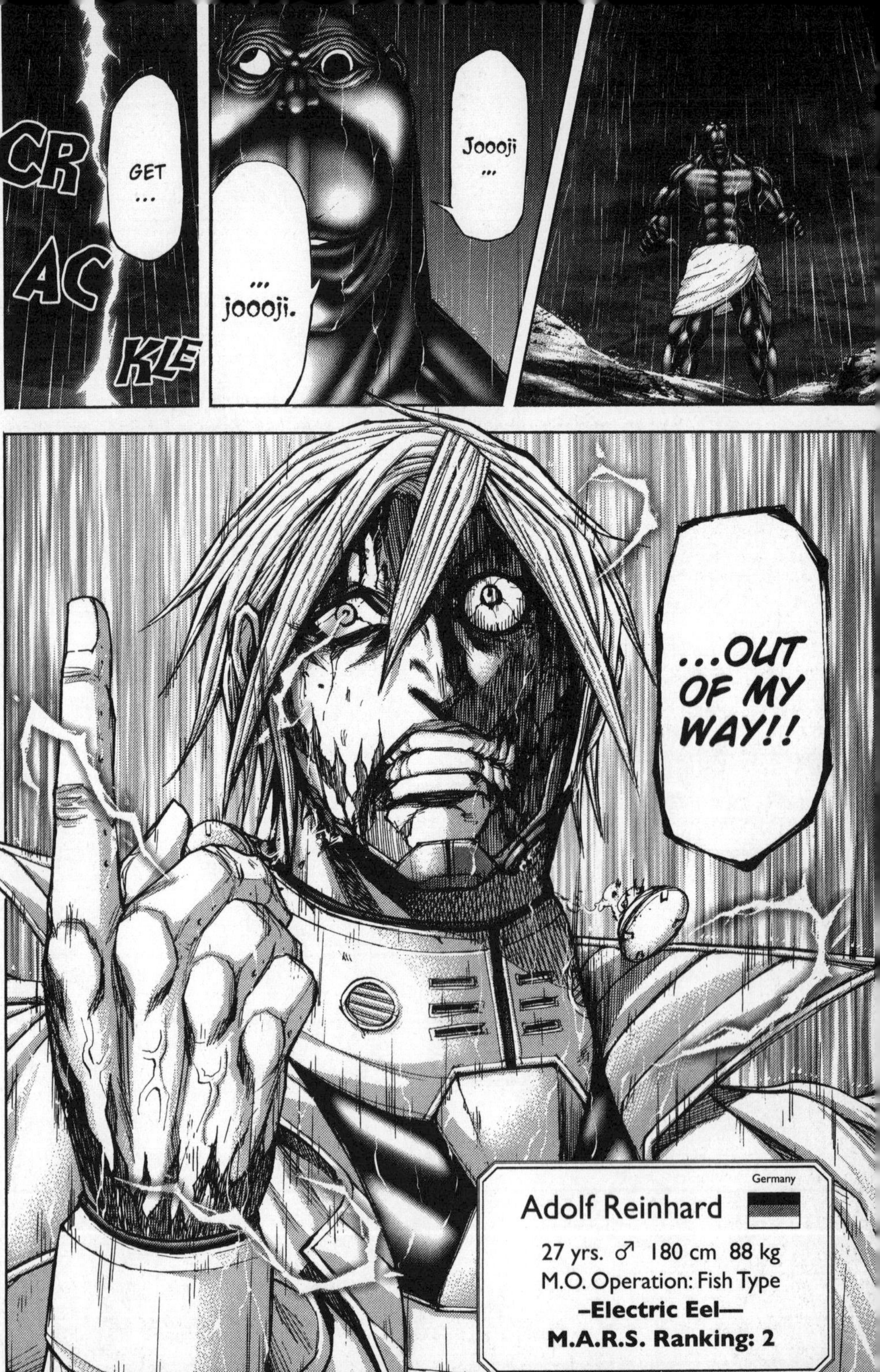
Joooji ...
... joooji.
GET ...
CRACKLE
...OUT OF MY WAY!!
Germany
Adolf Reinhard
27 yrs. ♂ 180 cm 88 kg
M.O. Operation: Fish Type
–Electric Eel—
M.A.R.S. Ranking: 2

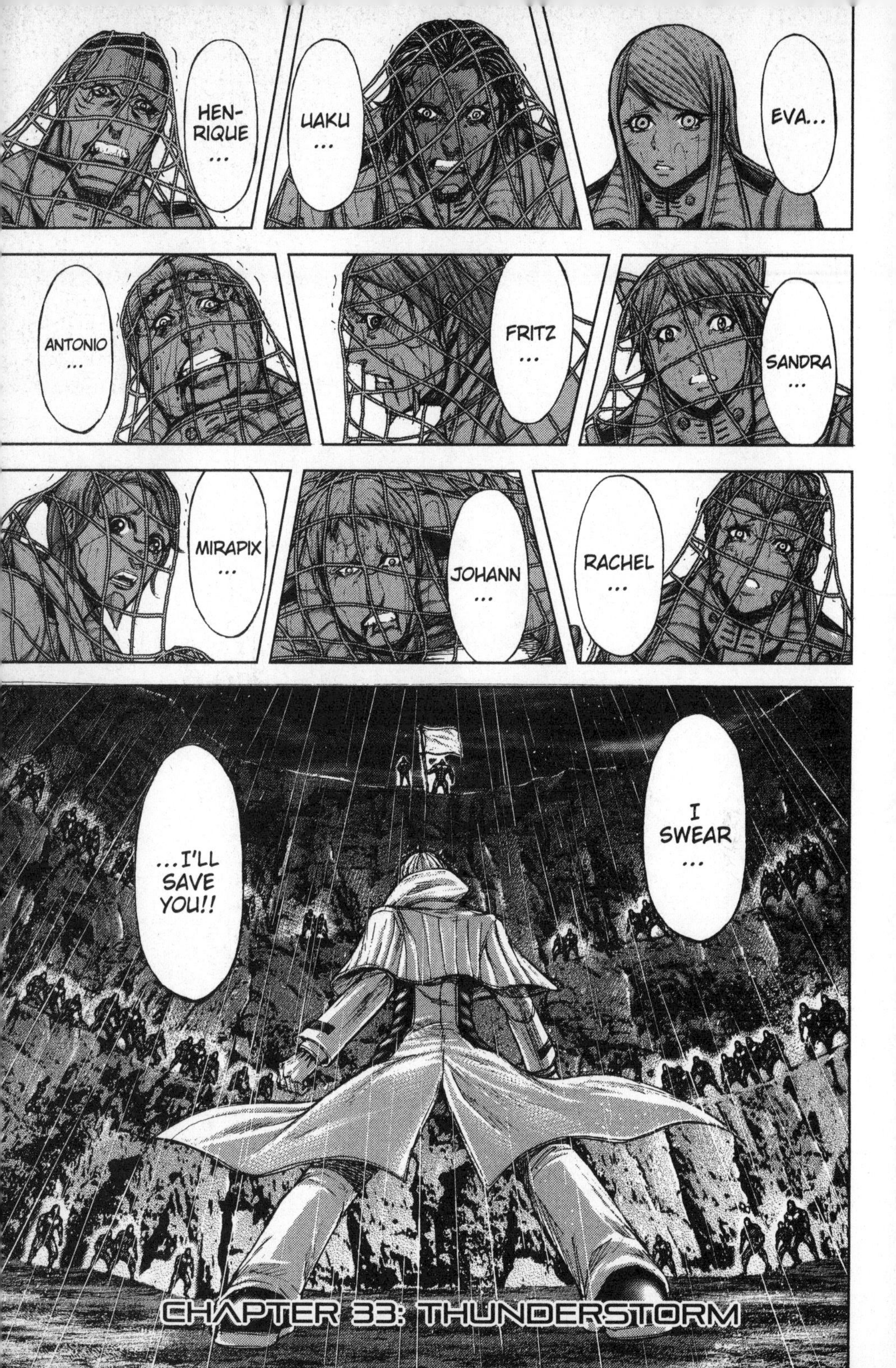
EVA...
UAKU ...
HEN-RIQUE ...
SANDRA ...
FRITZ ...
ANTONIO ...
RACHEL ...
JOHANN ...
MIRAPIX ...
I SWEAR ...
...I'LL SAVE YOU!!
CHAPTER 33: THUNDERSTORM

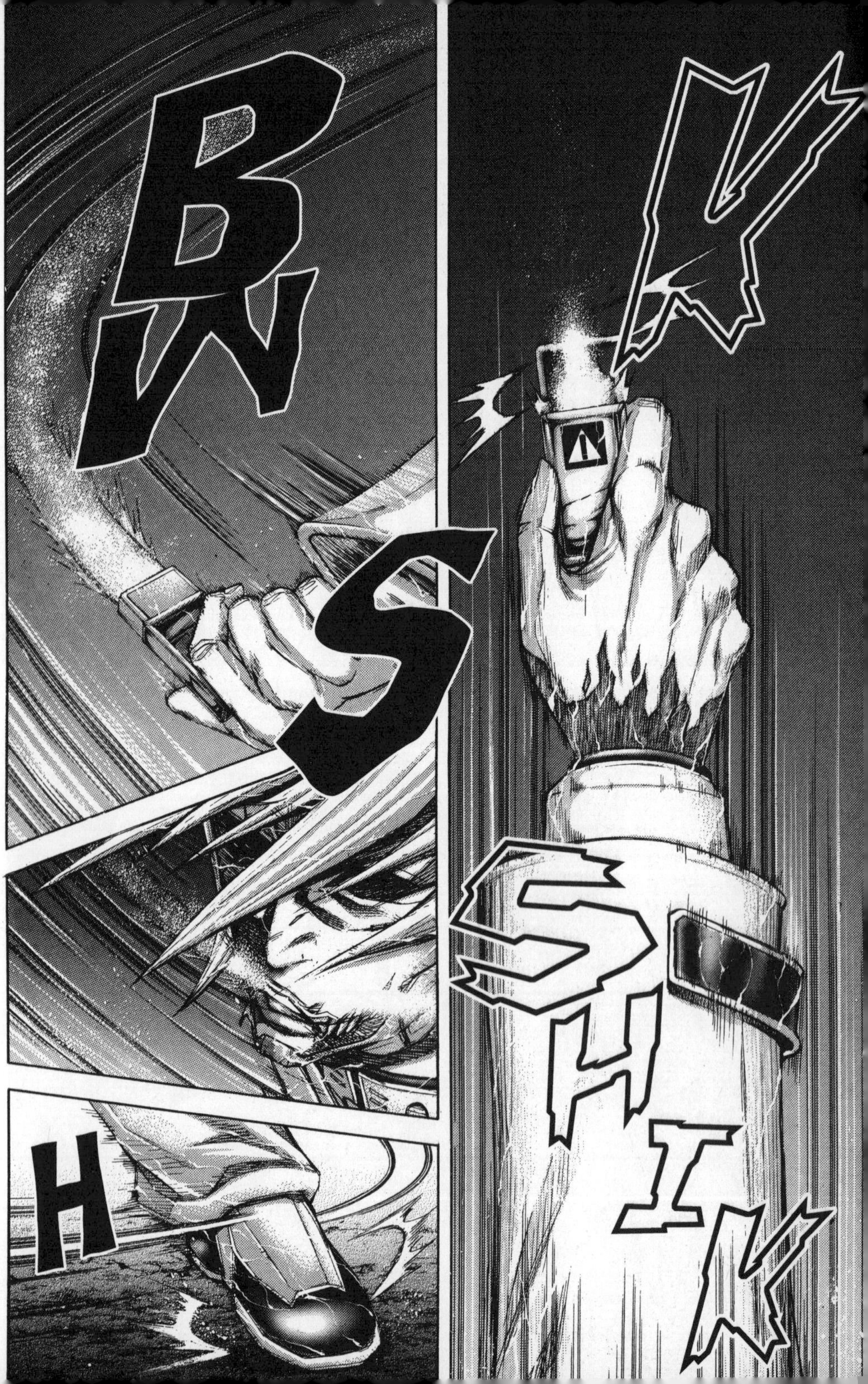
K
SHIK
B
S
H

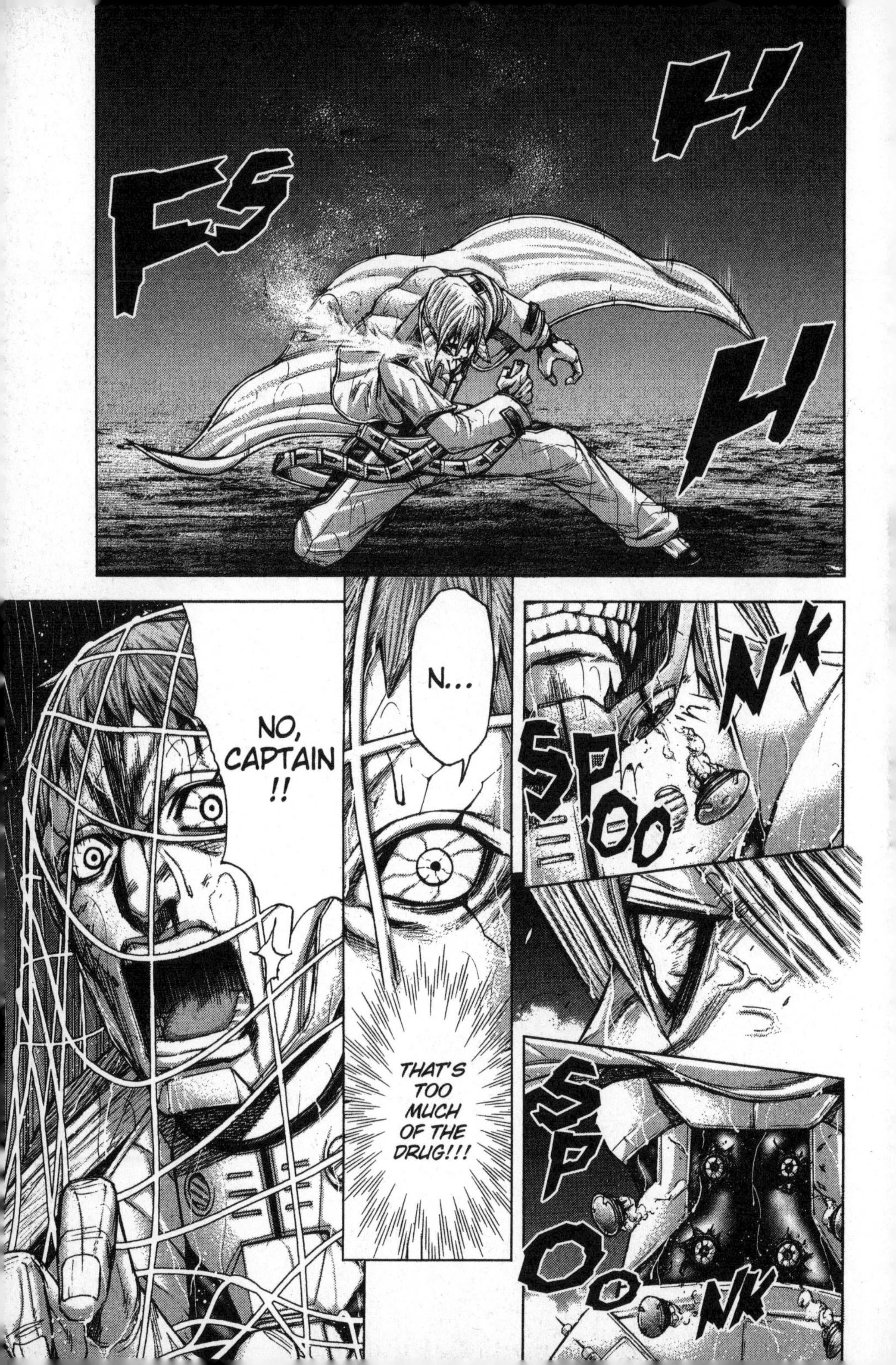
FS
H
H
SPOO
NK
SPOOO
NK
N...
THAT'S TOO MUCH OF THE DRUG!!!
NO, CAPTAIN !!

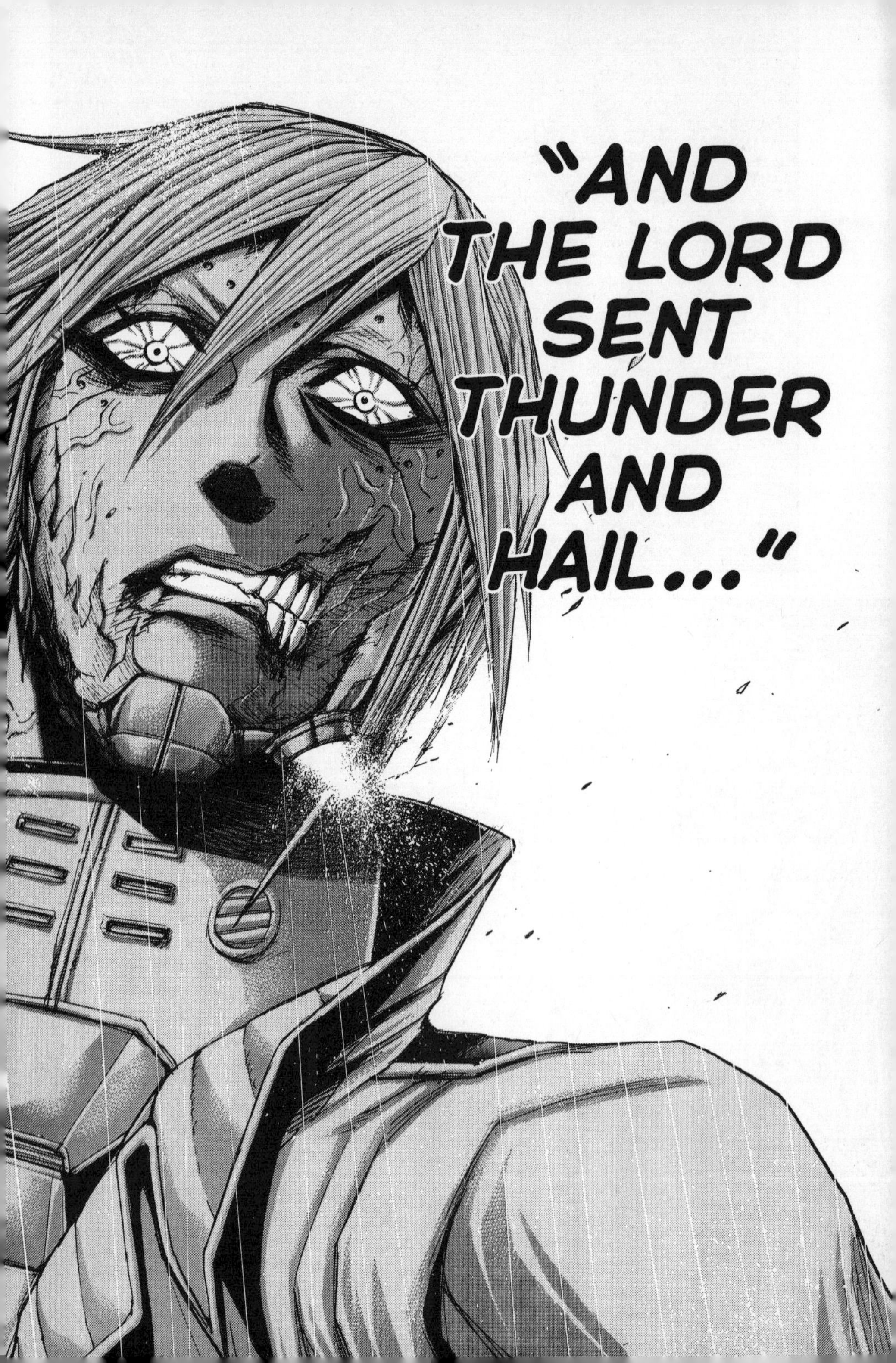
"AND THE LORD SENT THUNDER AND HAIL..."

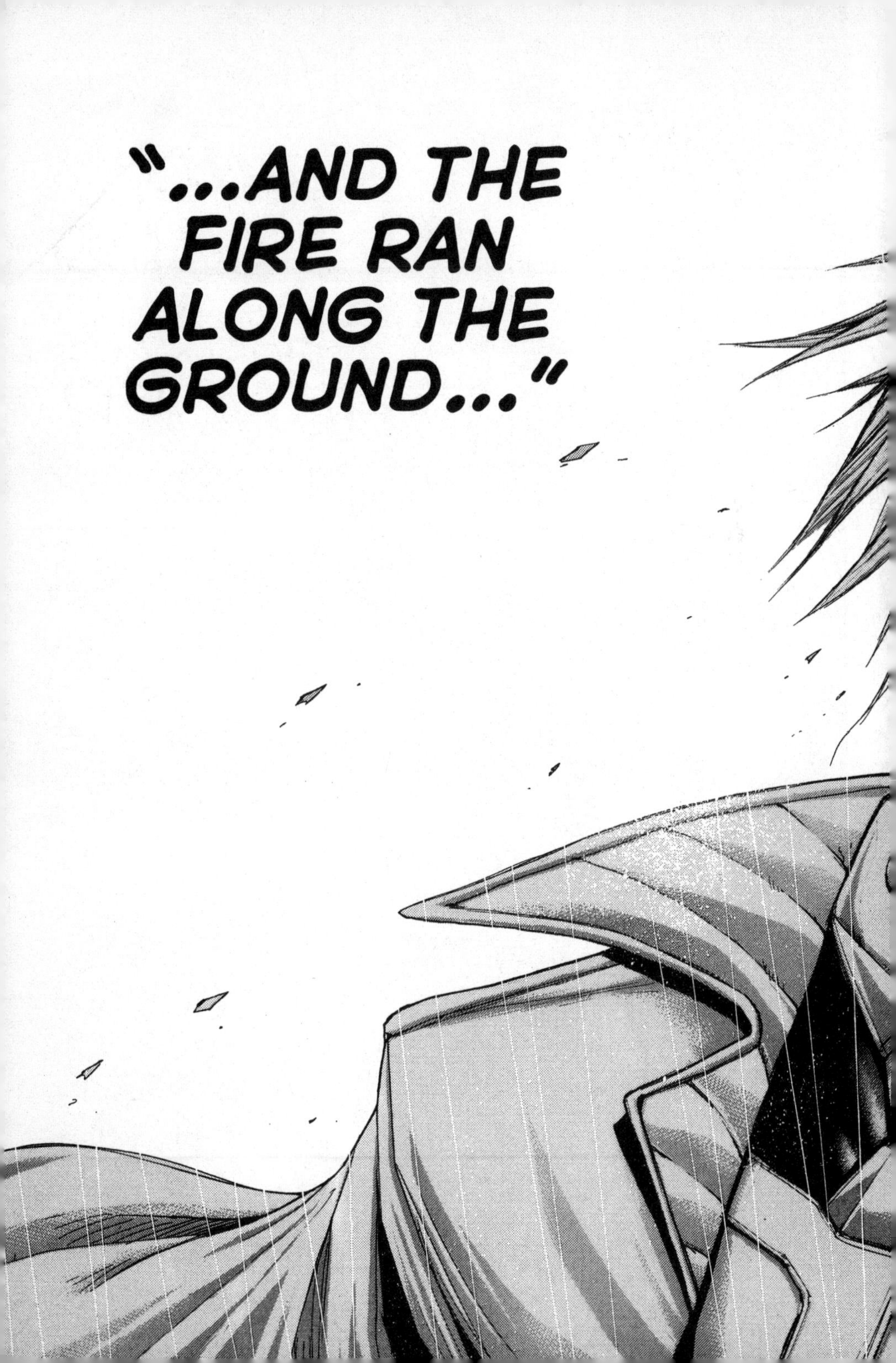
"...AND THE FIRE RAN ALONG THE GROUND..."

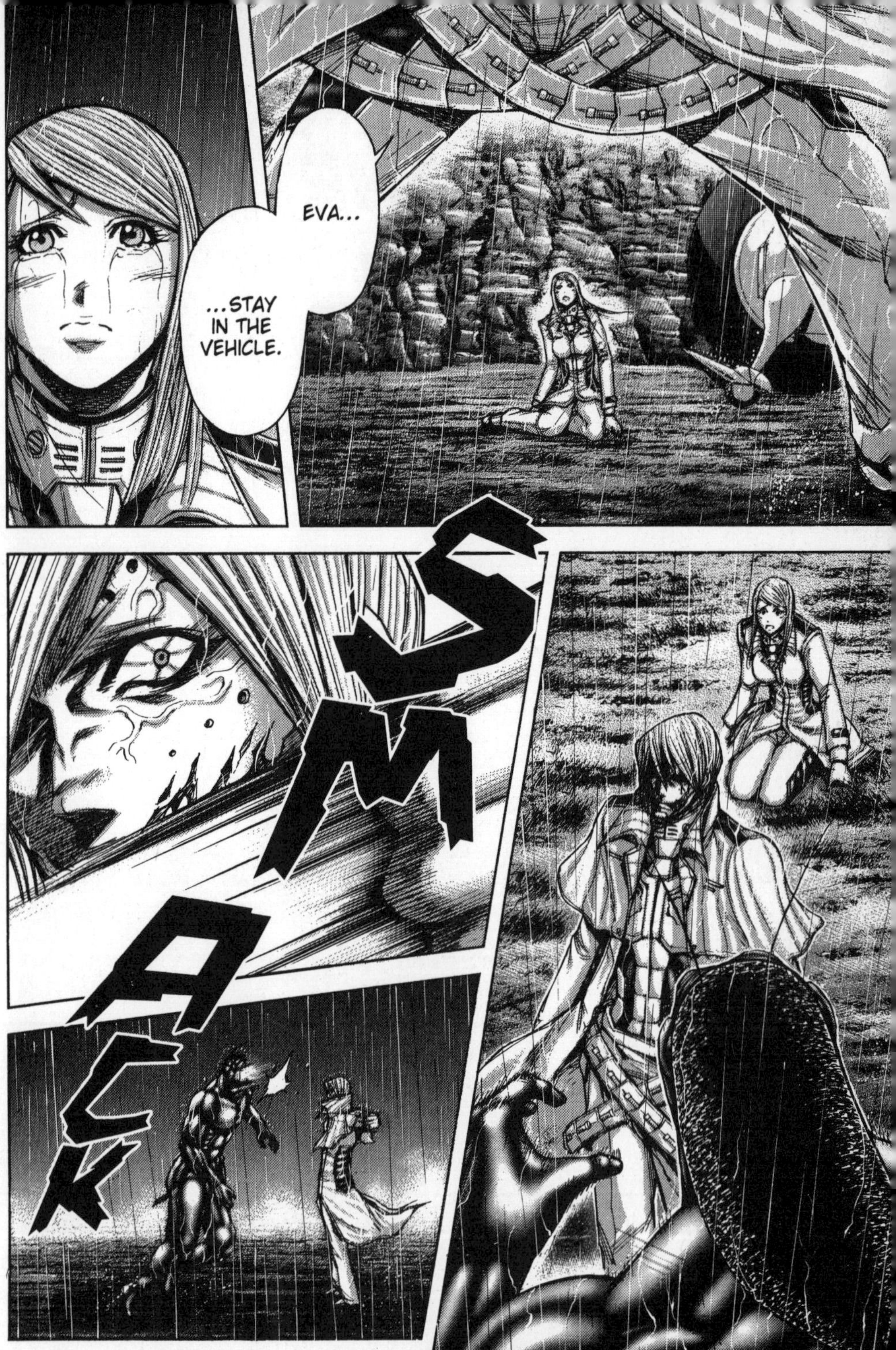
EVA...
...STAY IN THE VEHICLE.
SMACK

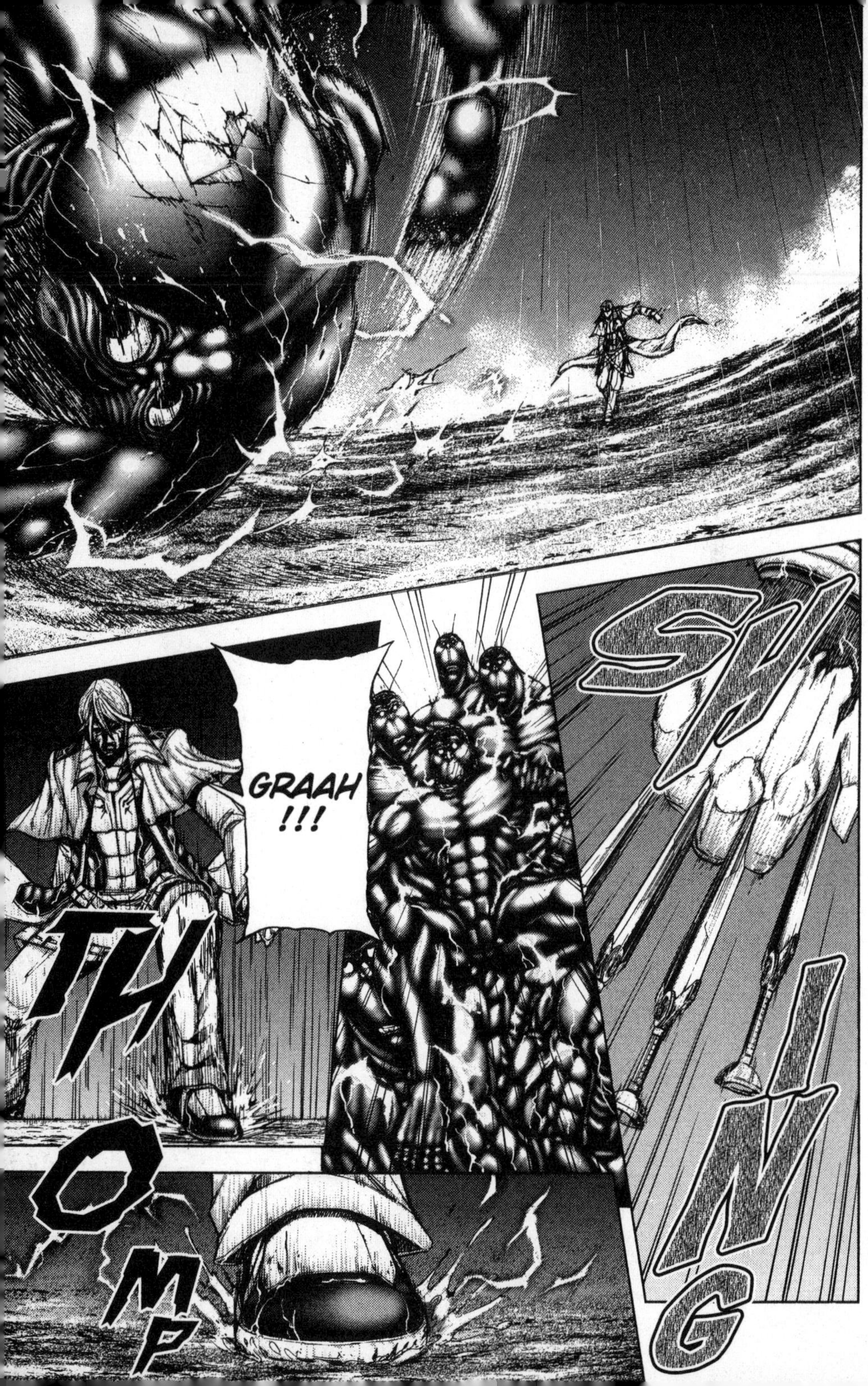
SHING
GRAAH!!!
THOMP

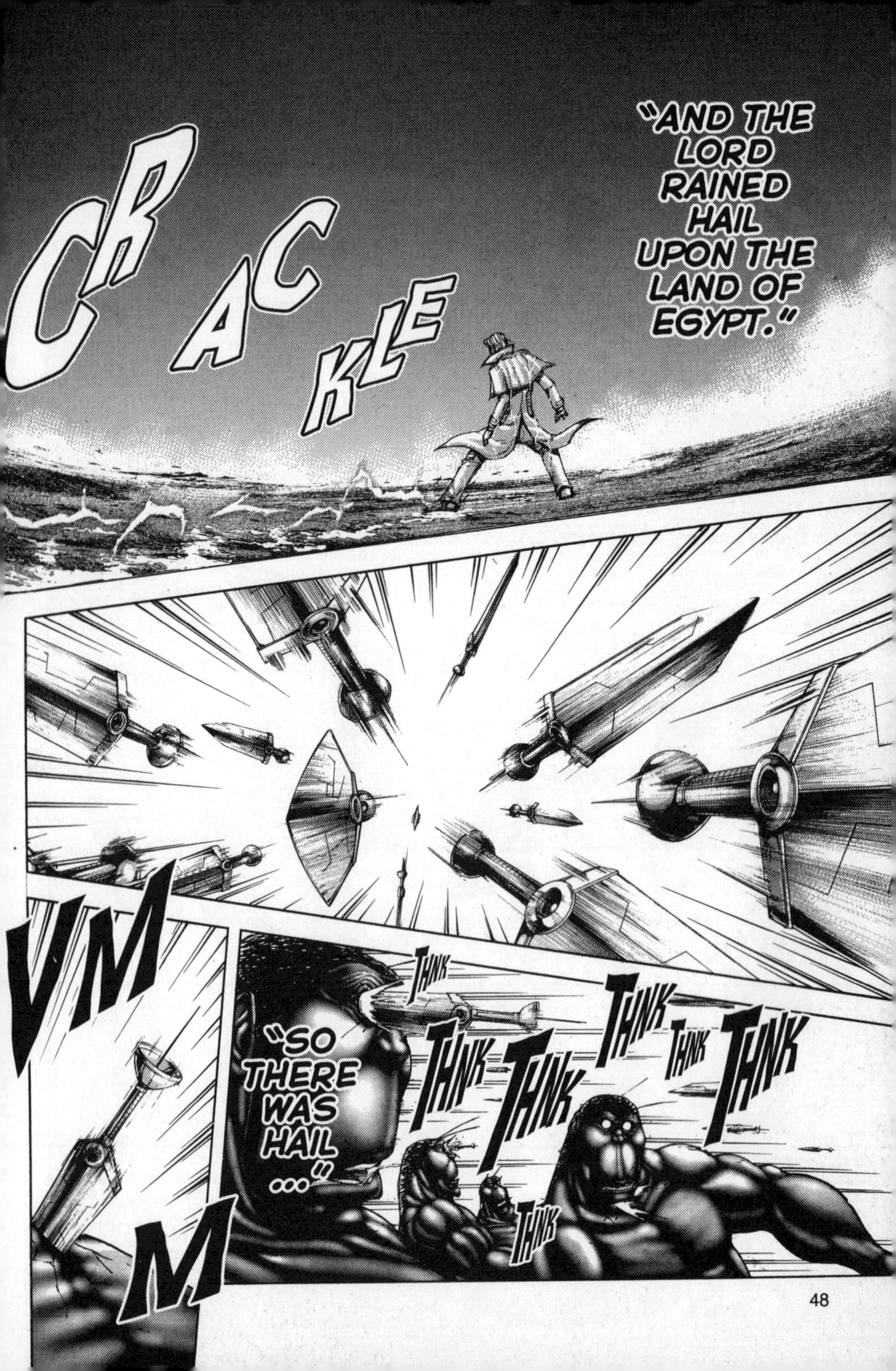
"AND THE LORD RAINED HAIL UPON THE LAND OF EGYPT."
CRACKLE
THNK
THNK THNK THNK THNK THNK
"SO THERE WAS HAIL..."
THNK
VMMM

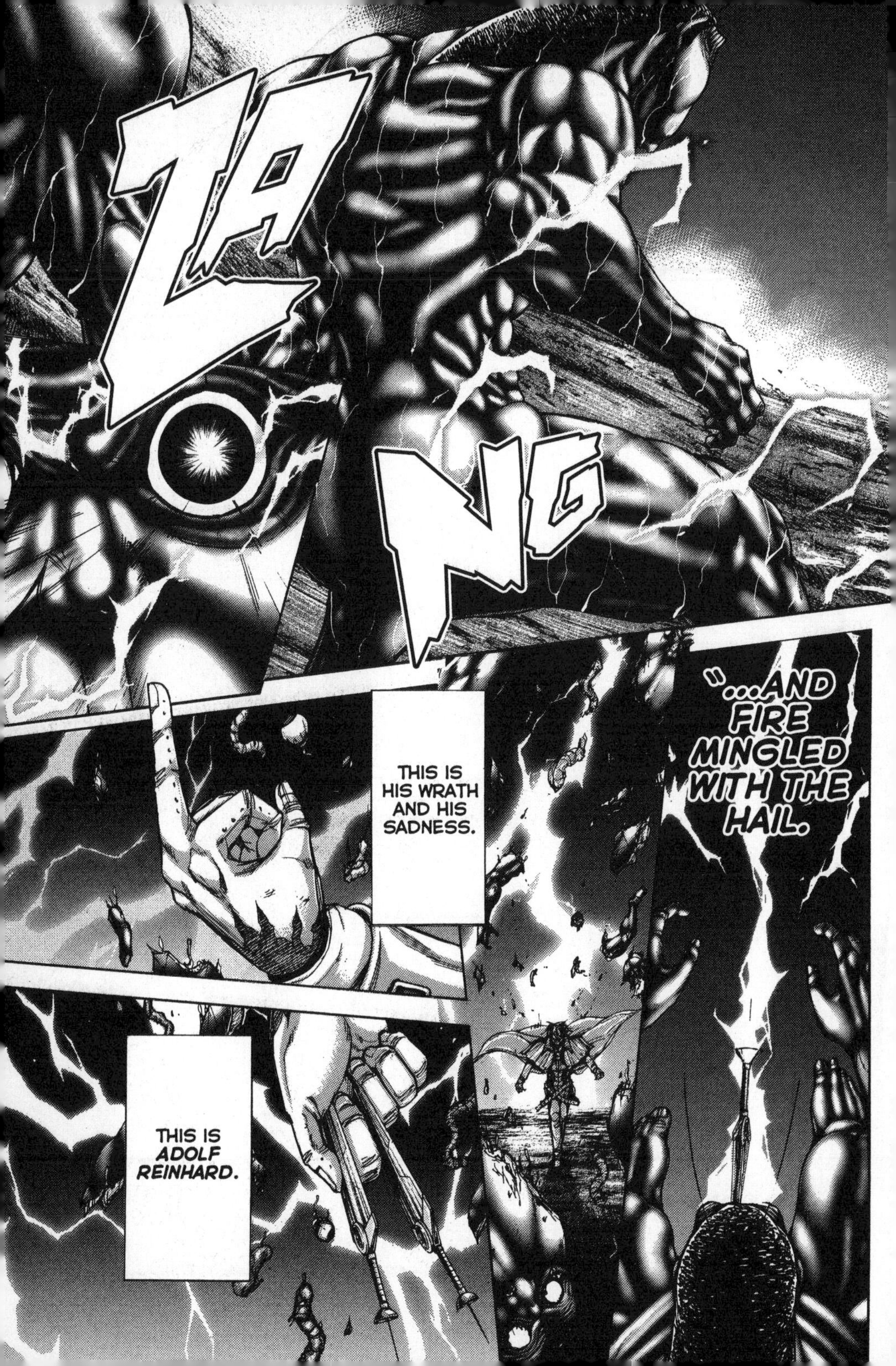
ZANG
"...AND FIRE MINGLED WITH THE HAIL.
THIS IS HIS WRATH AND HIS SADNESS.
THIS IS ADOLF REINHARD.

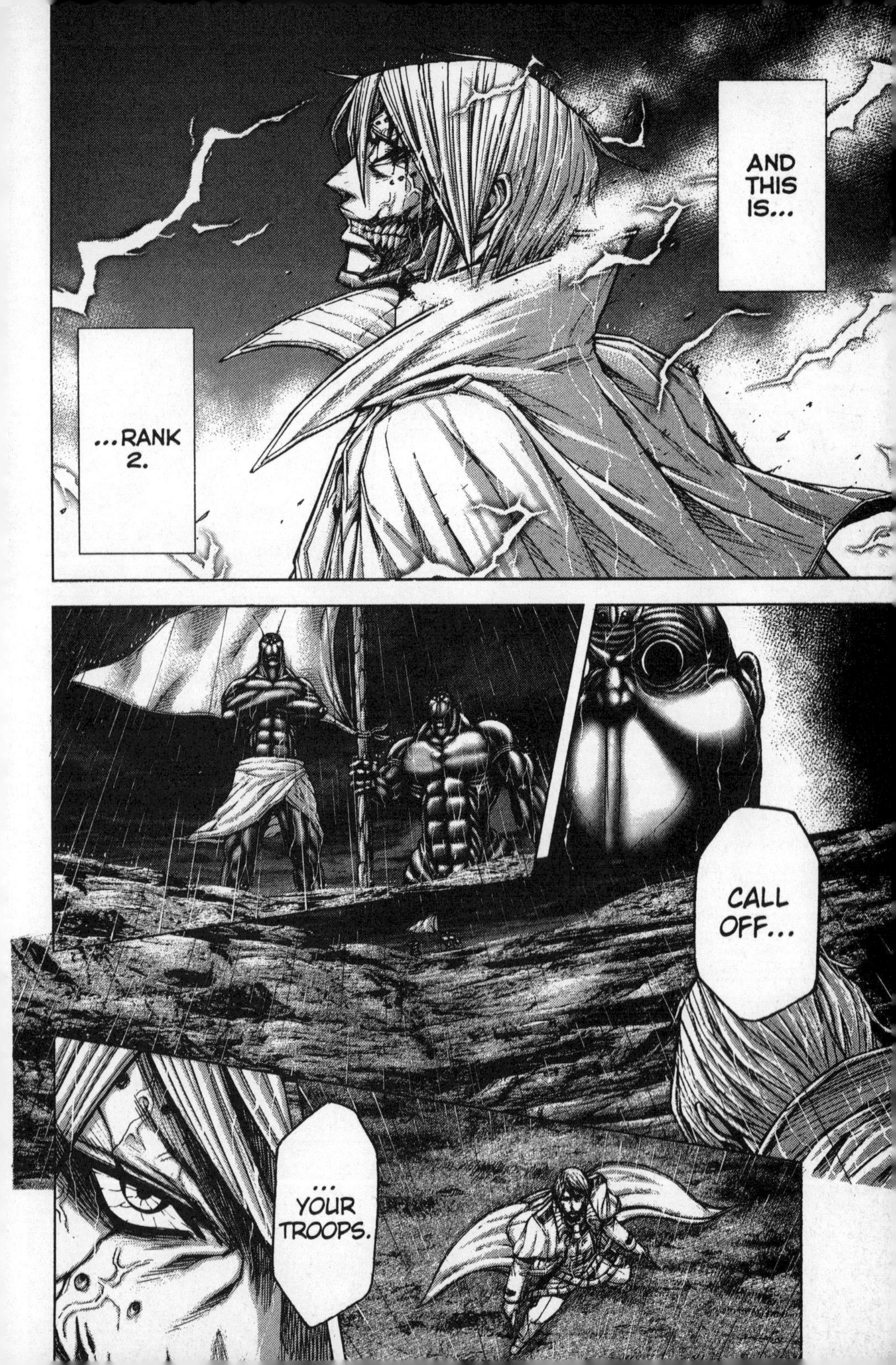
AND THIS IS...
...RANK 2.
CALL OFF...
...YOUR TROOPS.

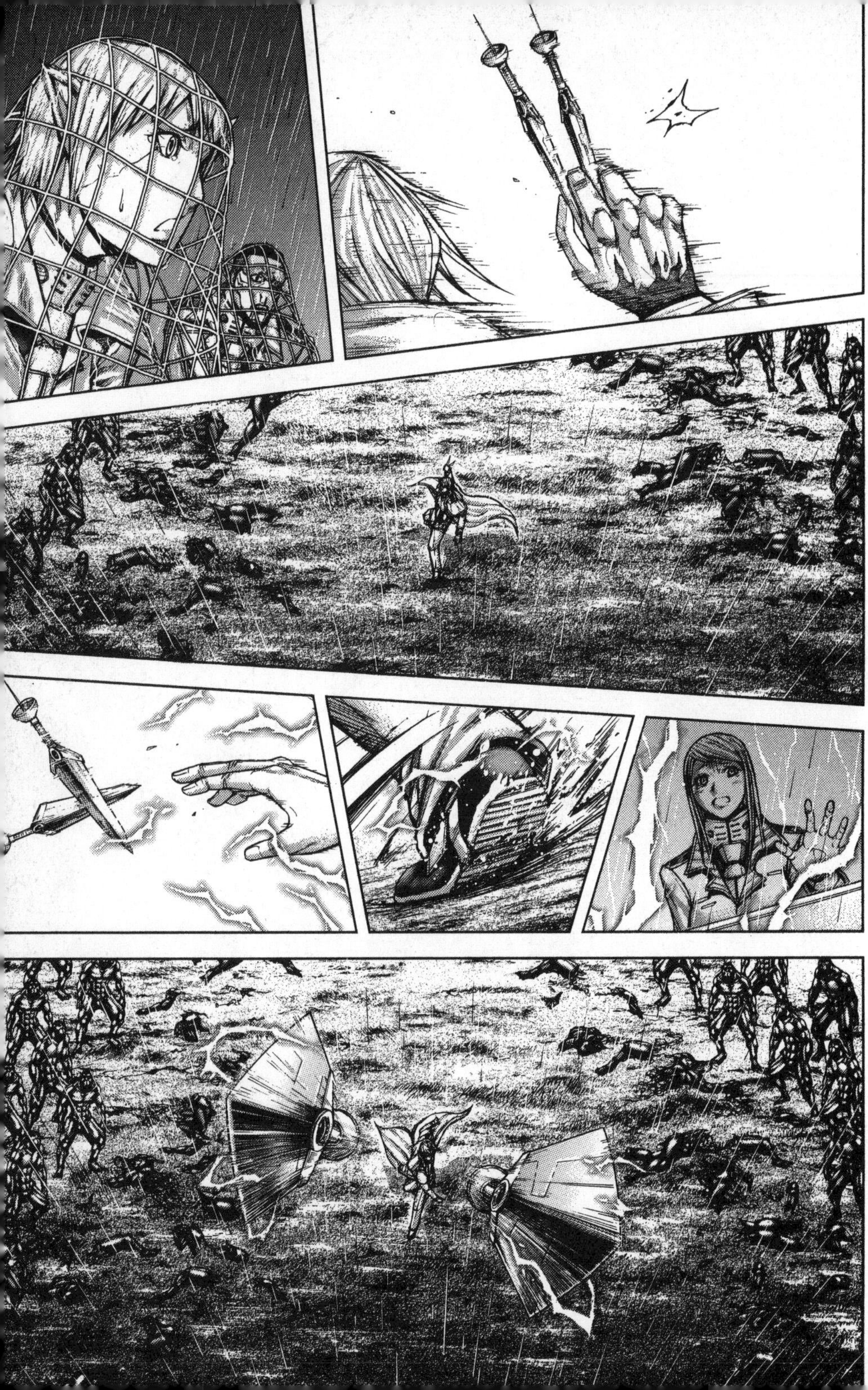

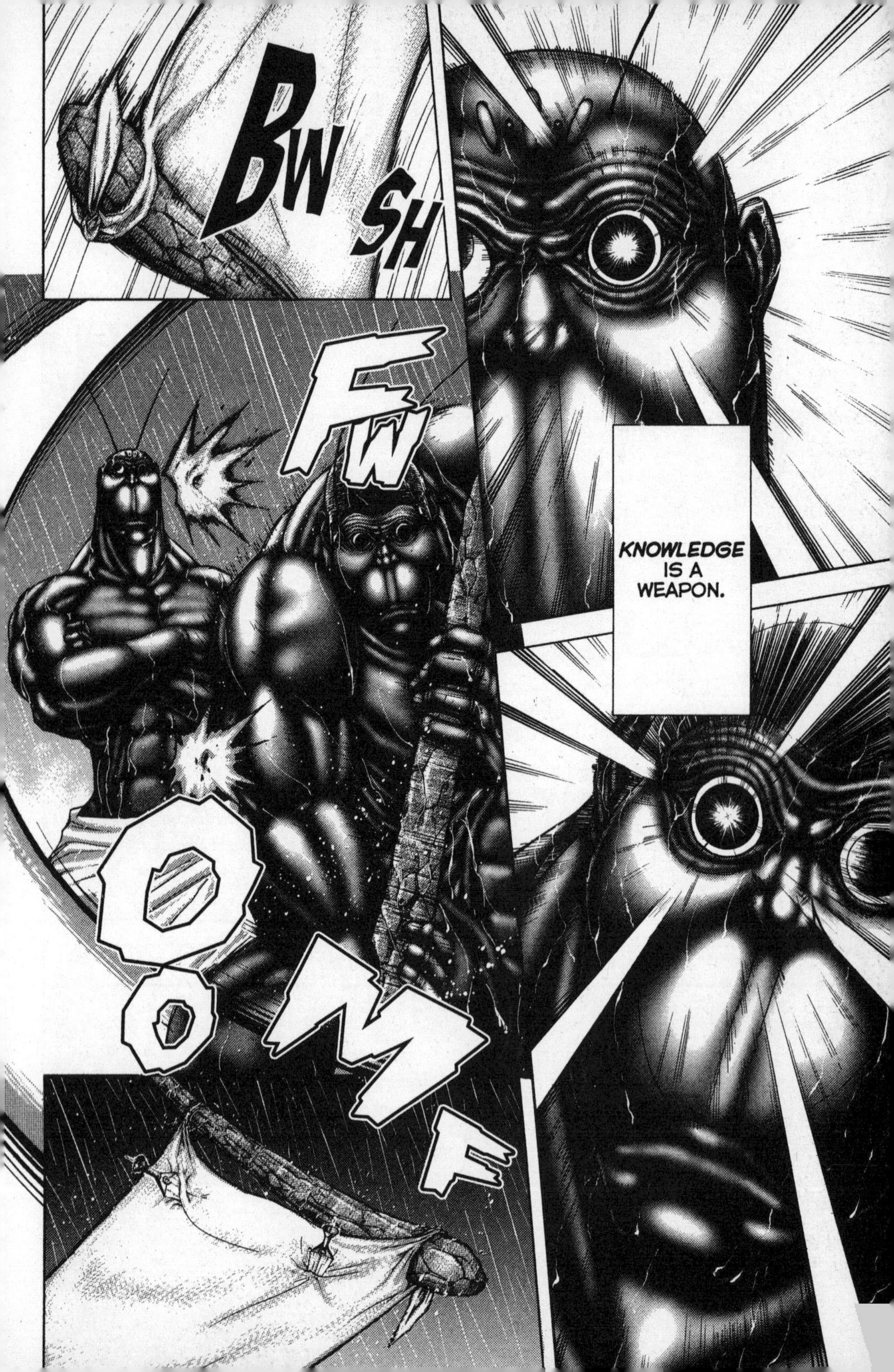
KNOWLEDGE IS A WEAPON.
BWSH
FWOOMF

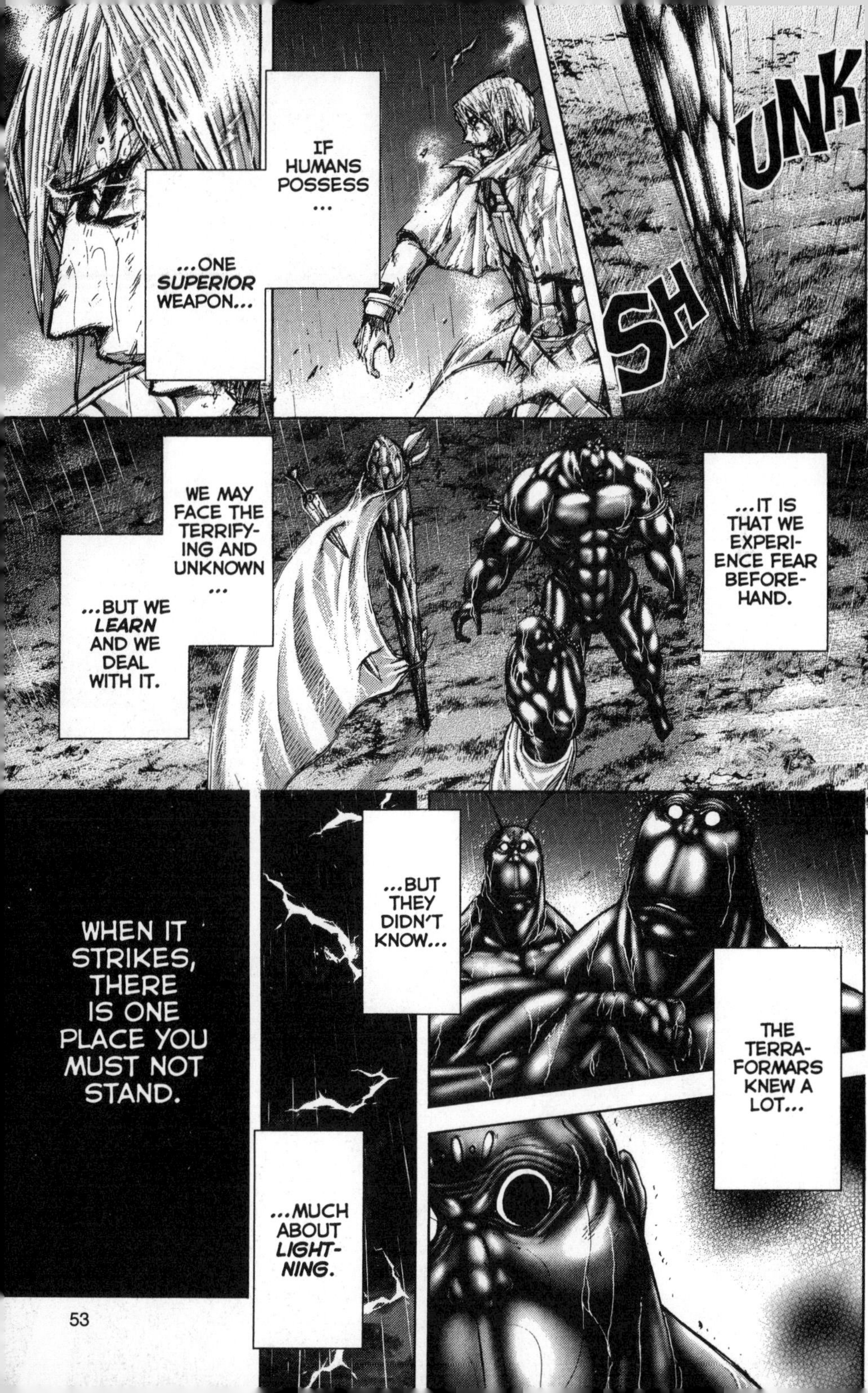
SHUNK
IF HUMANS POSSESS ...
...ONE *SUPERIOR* WEAPON...
...IT IS THAT WE EXPERIENCE FEAR BEFOREHAND.
WE MAY FACE THE TERRIFYING AND UNKNOWN ...
...BUT WE *LEARN* AND WE DEAL WITH IT.
THE TERRAFORMARS KNEW A LOT...
...BUT THEY DIDN'T KNOW...
...MUCH ABOUT *LIGHTNING*.
WHEN IT STRIKES, THERE IS ONE PLACE YOU MUST NOT STAND.

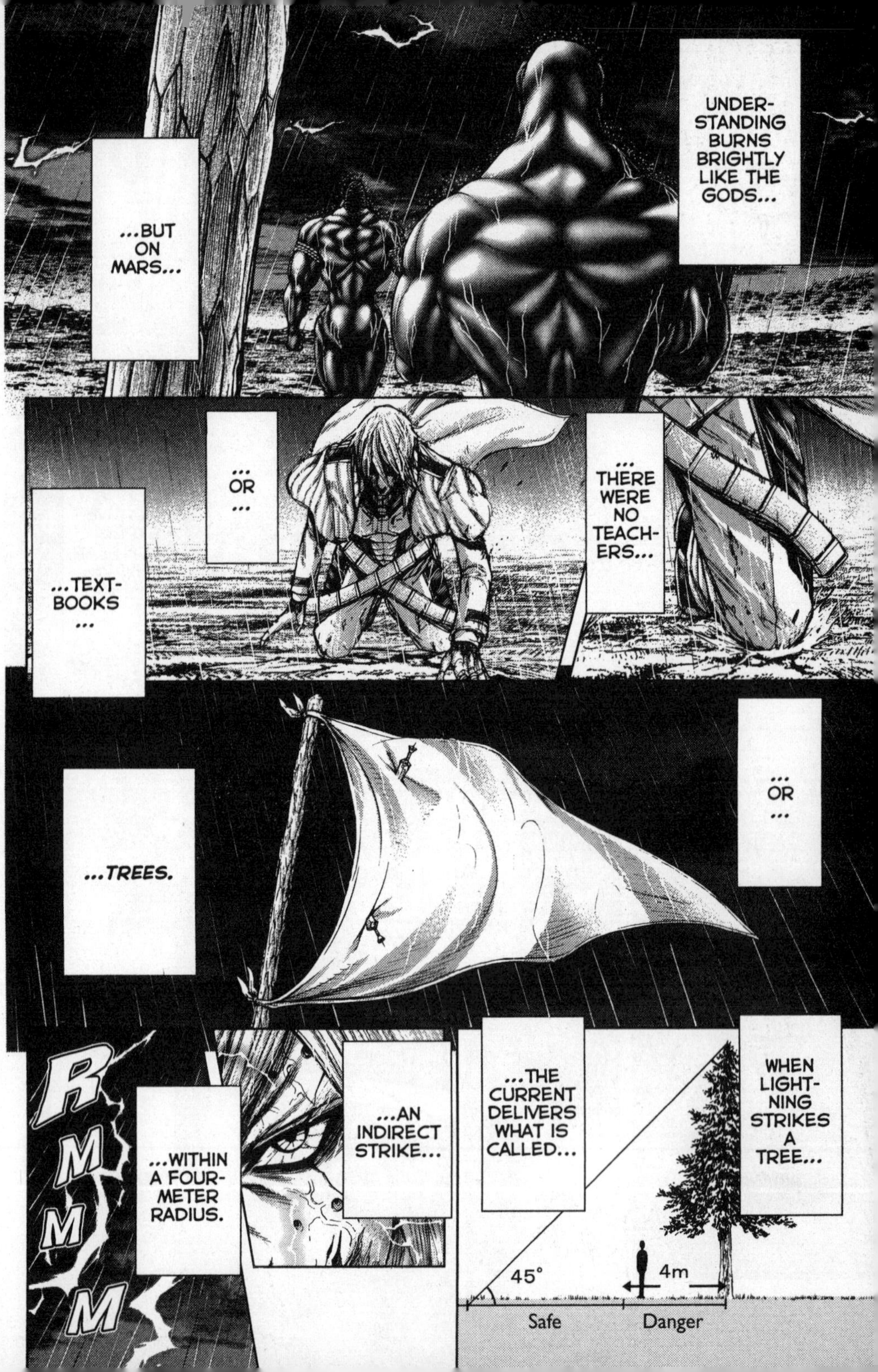
UNDERSTANDING BURNS BRIGHTLY LIKE THE GODS...
...BUT ON MARS...
...THERE WERE NO TEACHERS...
...OR...
...TEXTBOOKS...
...OR...
...TREES.
WHEN LIGHTNING STRIKES A TREE...
...THE CURRENT DELIVERS WHAT IS CALLED...
45°
4m
Safe
Danger
...AN INDIRECT STRIKE...
...WITHIN A FOUR-METER RADIUS.
RMMM

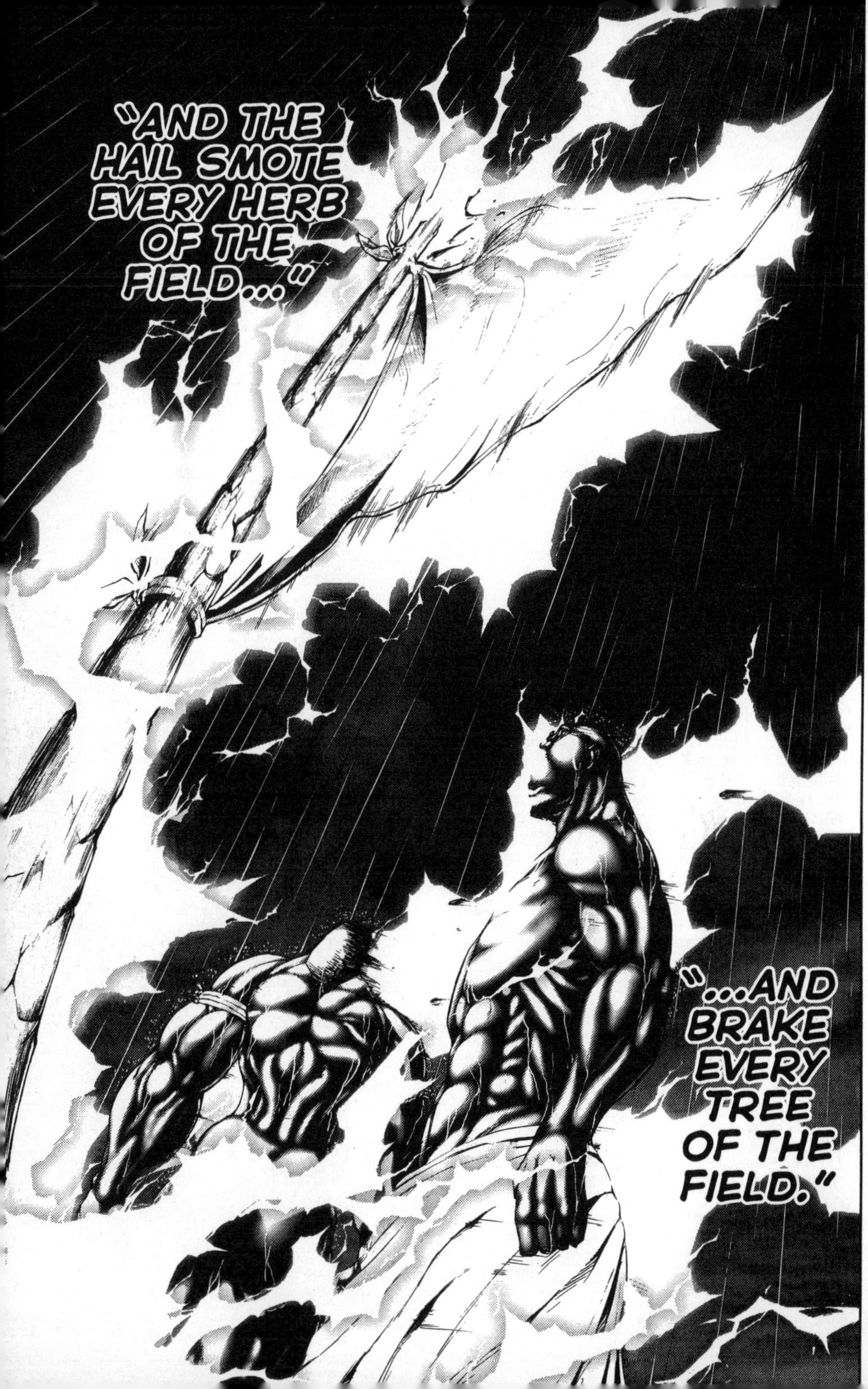
"AND THE HAIL SMOTE EVERY HERB OF THE FIELD..."
"...AND BRAKE EVERY TREE OF THE FIELD."

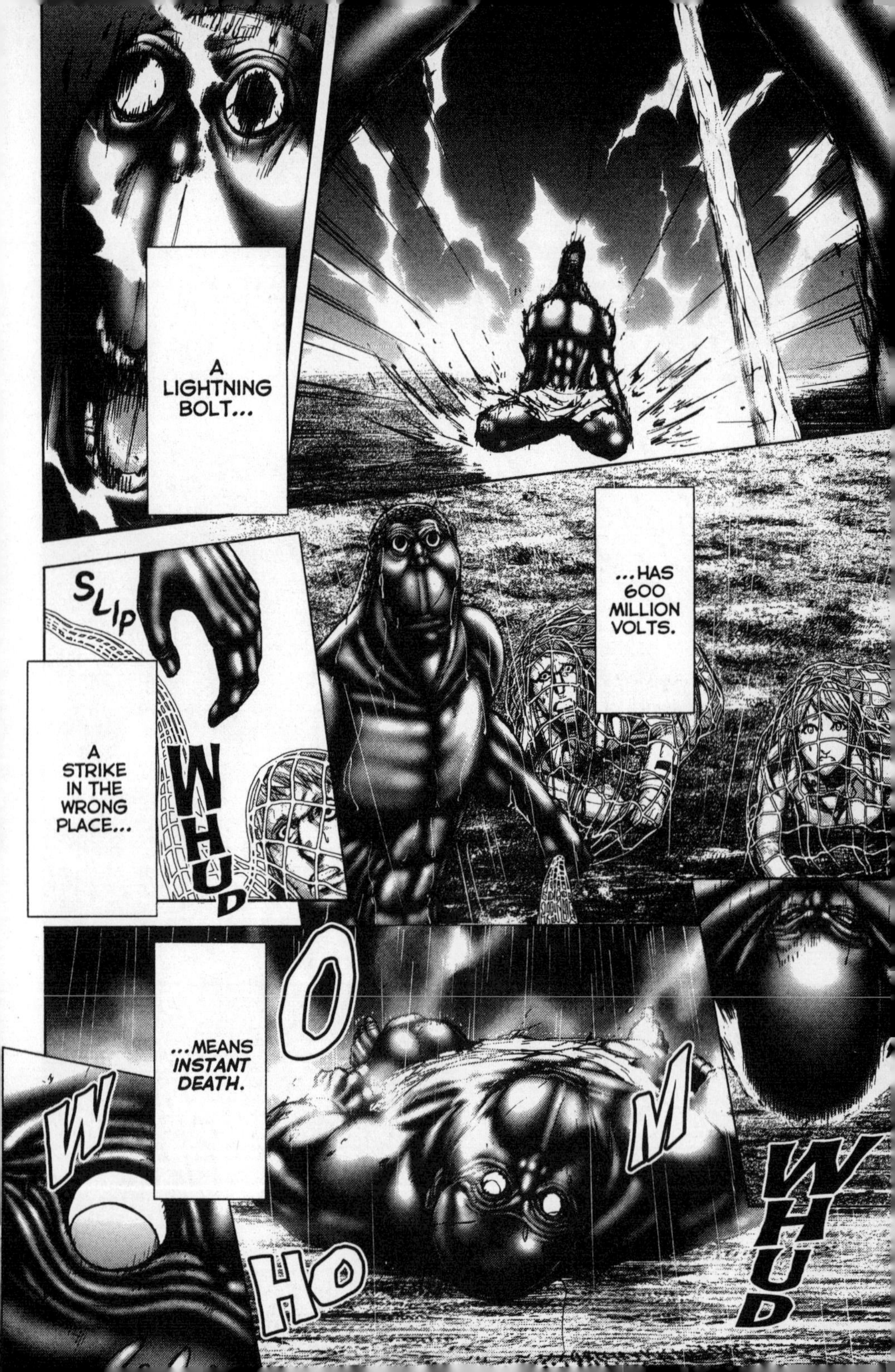
A LIGHTNING BOLT...
...HAS 600 MILLION VOLTS.
SLIP
A STRIKE IN THE WRONG PLACE...
WHUD
WHUD
...MEANS INSTANT DEATH.
WHOOM

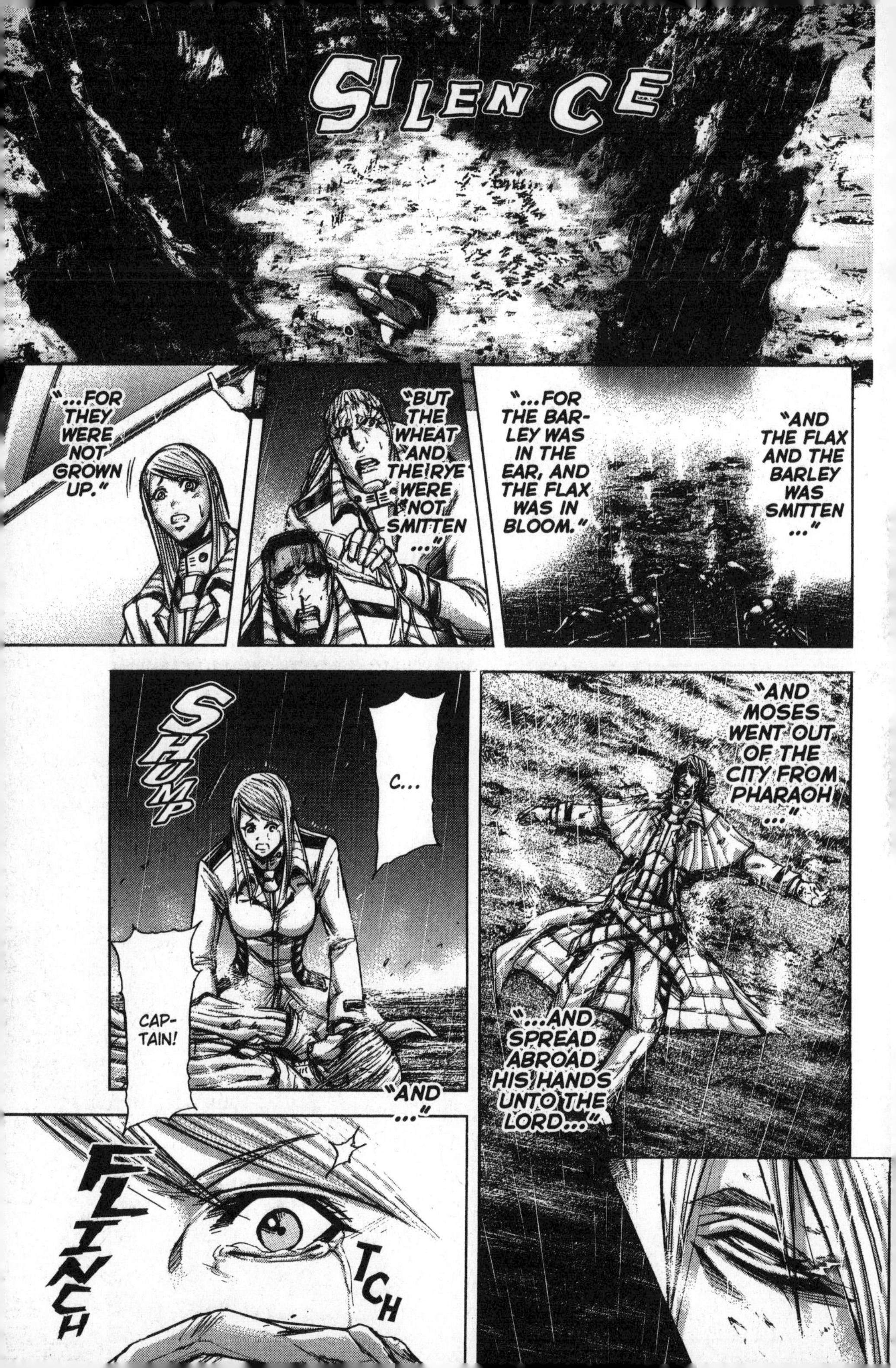
SILENCE
"AND THE FLAX AND THE BARLEY WAS SMITTEN ..."
"...FOR THE BAR-LEY WAS IN THE EAR, AND THE FLAX WAS IN BLOOM."
"BUT THE WHEAT AND THE RYE WERE NOT SMITTEN ..."
"...FOR THEY WERE NOT GROWN UP."
"AND MOSES WENT OUT OF THE CITY FROM PHARAOH ..."
"...AND SPREAD ABROAD HIS HANDS UNTO THE LORD..."
C...
SHUMP
CAP-TAIN!
"AND ..."
FLINCH
TCH

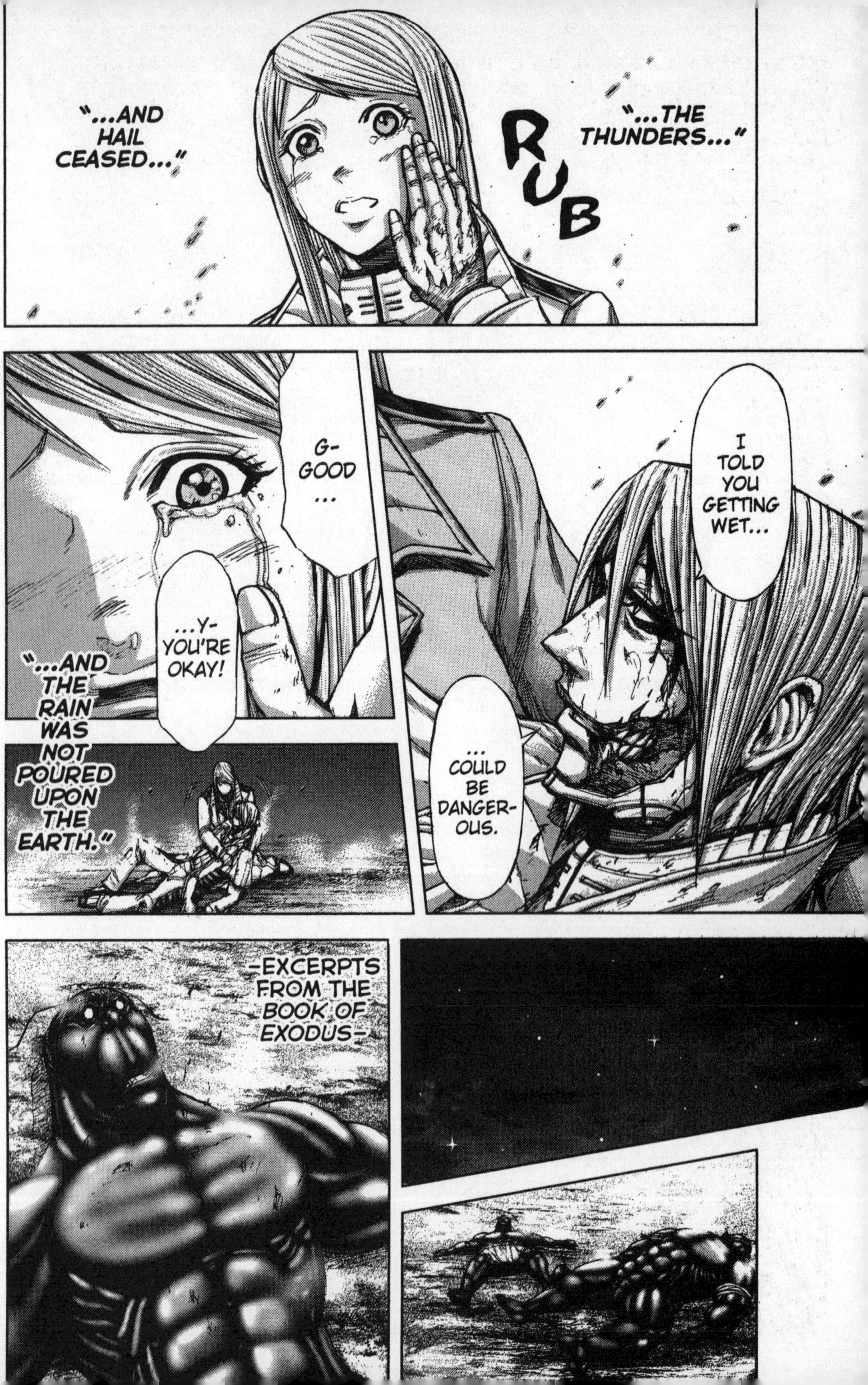
"...THE THUNDERS..."
RUB
"...AND HAIL CEASED..."
I TOLD YOU GETTING WET...
...COULD BE DANGER-OUS.
G-GOOD...
...Y-YOU'RE OKAY!
"...AND THE RAIN WAS NOT POURED UPON THE EARTH."
-EXCERPTS FROM THE BOOK OF EXODUS-

TERRA FORMARS

Character

Adolf Reinhard ♂

Germany 27 yrs. 180 cm 88kg

M.A.R.S. Ranking: 2

Operation base: Electric Eel

Favorite Food: His wife's curry
          (originally: stuffed cabbage)
Dislikes: Garbage can lids with tight springs
Eye Color: Light Green Blood Type: O
DOB: December 25 (Capricorn)
Skills: Cooking

When he was 7, both his parents joined the Bugs 2 Project. They died during the mission, leaving him orphaned. The army took him and used him for M.O. Operation experiments. His body was strengthened with treehopper DNA (the army developed this technology based on their experiments). He went to school, but was sworn to secrecy, under observation, and subjected to physical tests. Though he may have been injected with alcohol, he never had a drink until he met Captain Komachi.

Isabella R. Leon ♀

Brazil 19 yrs. 174.5 cm 61kg

M.A.R.S. Ranking: 13

Operation base: Roick

Favorite Foods: Fruit, Soy milk
Dislikes: Treating avocados and tomatoes like fruit
Eye Color: Cobalt Blue Blood Type: O
DOB: November 21 (Scorpio)
Skill: Singing and voice mimicry

Born in a rural area to poor agricultural laborers. To earn money, she worked as a maid in the farm owner's mansion, but when the owner's son grew violent with her, she fought back and seriously injured him.

According to Eva, she smells sweet because she's always eating fruit with one hand. D Cup.

CHAPTER 34: HOLY BLOOD

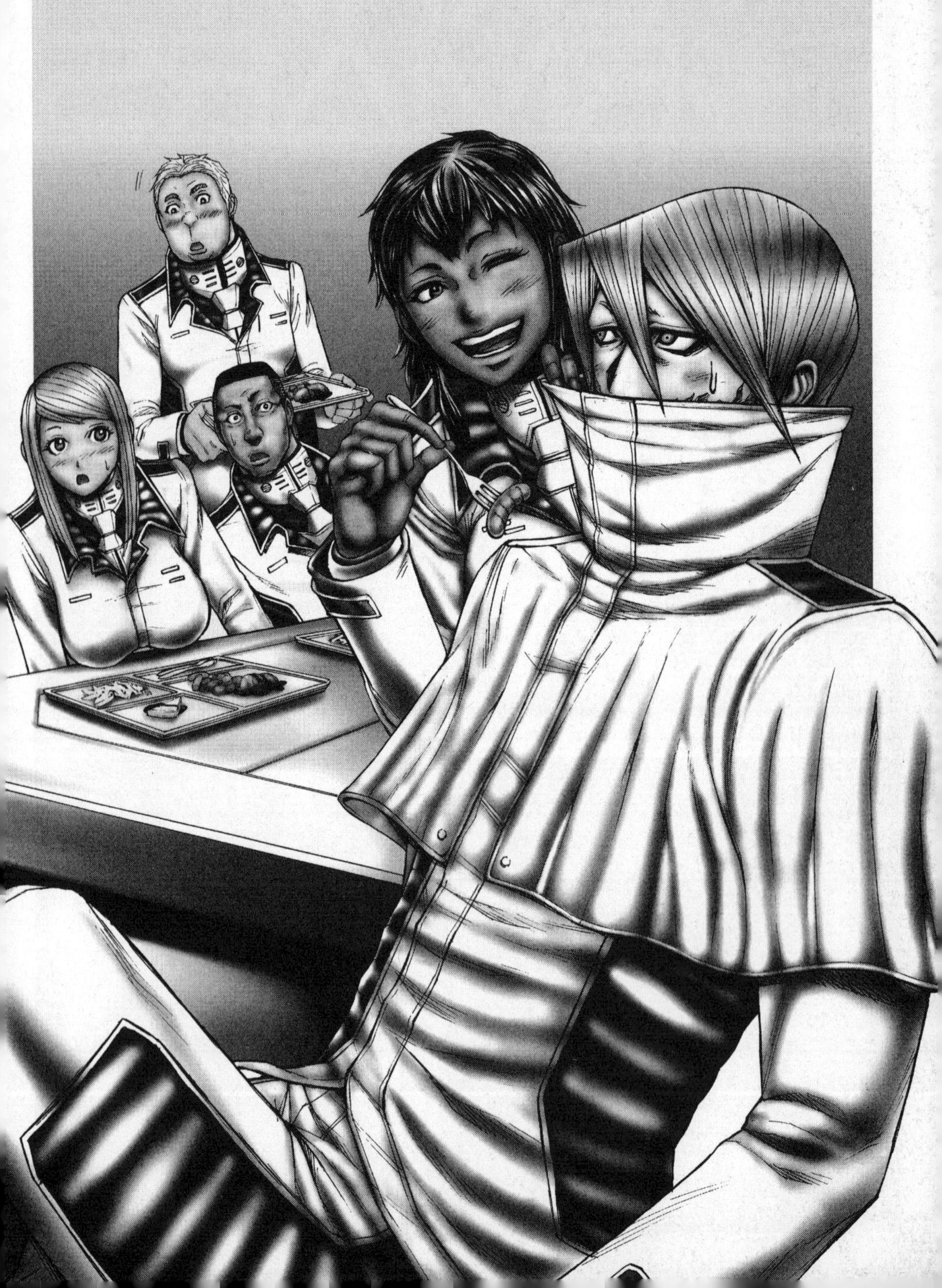

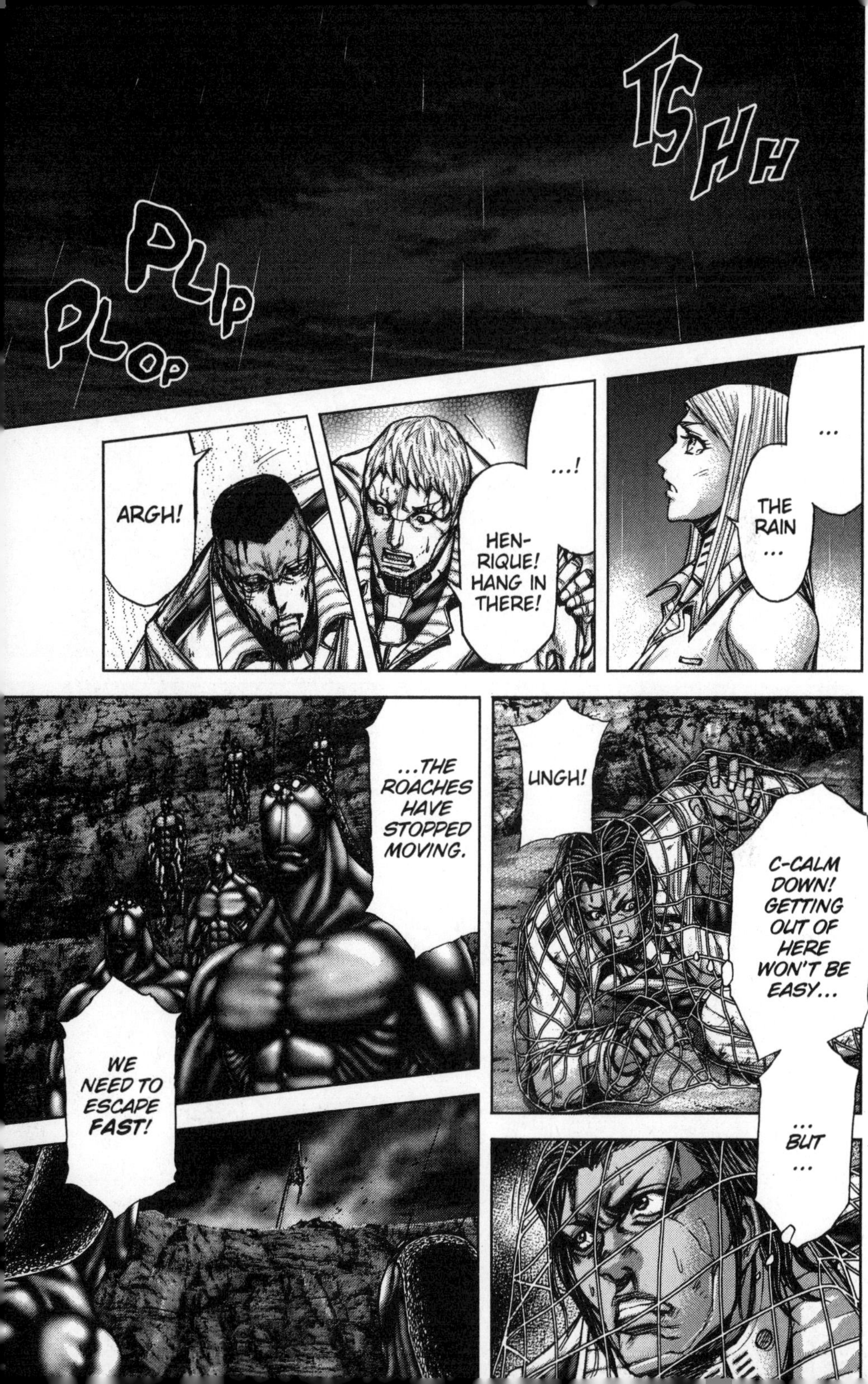
TSHH
PLIP PLOP
... THE RAIN ...
...!
HEN-RIQUE! HANG IN THERE!
ARGH!
UNGH!
C-CALM DOWN! GETTING OUT OF HERE WON'T BE EASY...
...THE ROACHES HAVE STOPPED MOVING.
... BUT ...
WE NEED TO ESCAPE FAST!

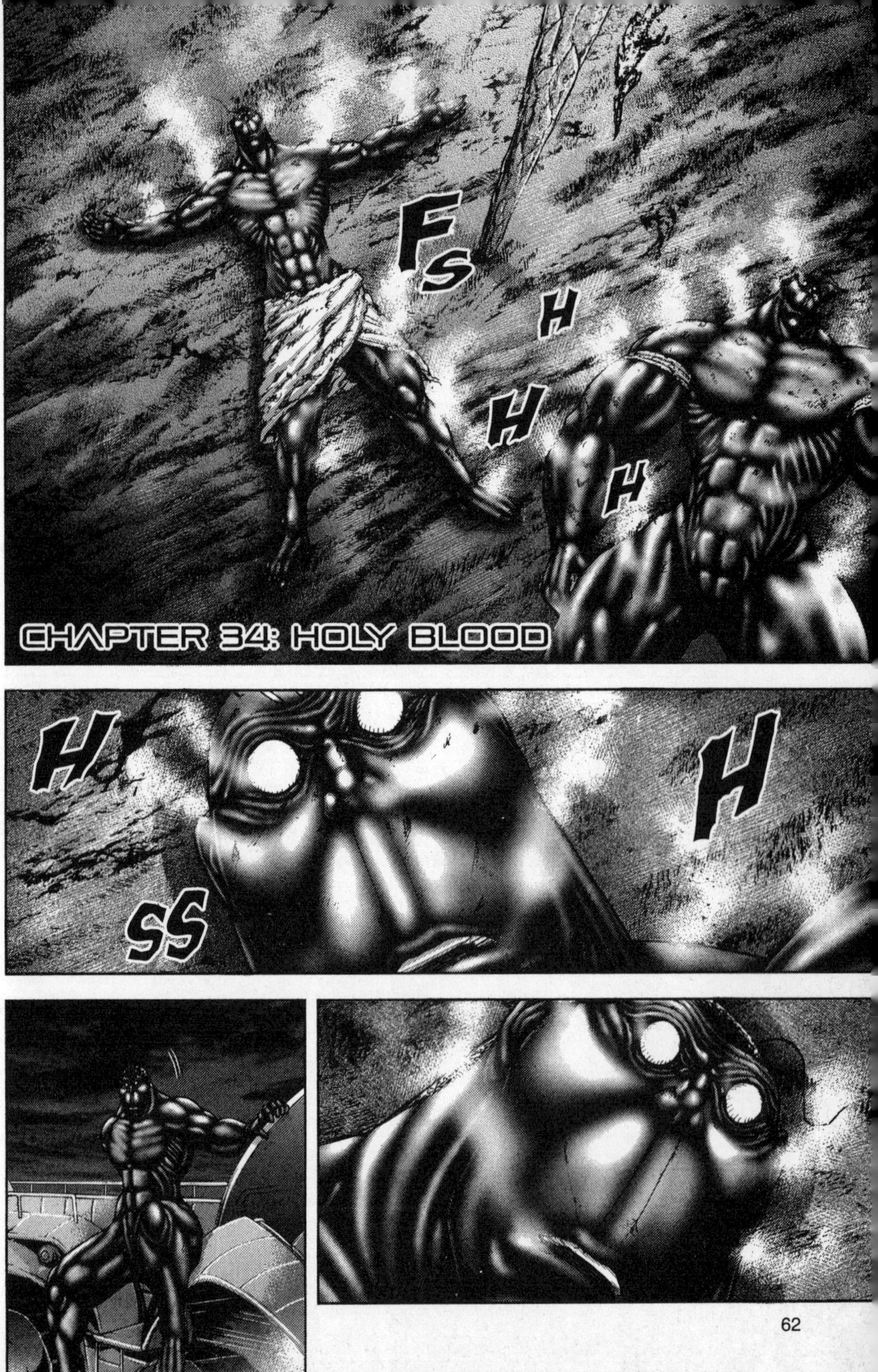
CHAPTER 34: HOLY BLOOD
FS
H
H
H
H
H
SS

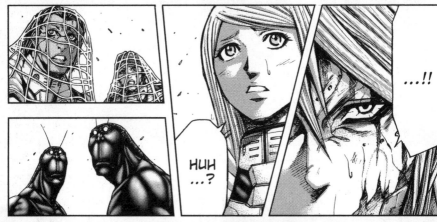

HUH
...?

...!!

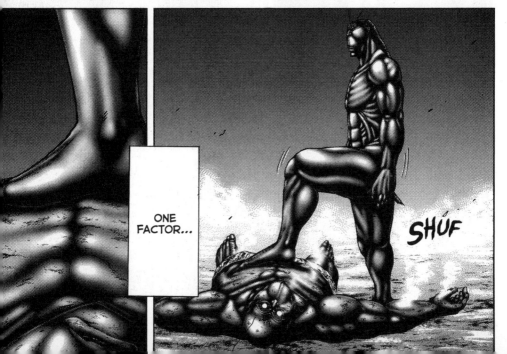

ONE
FACTOR...

SHUF

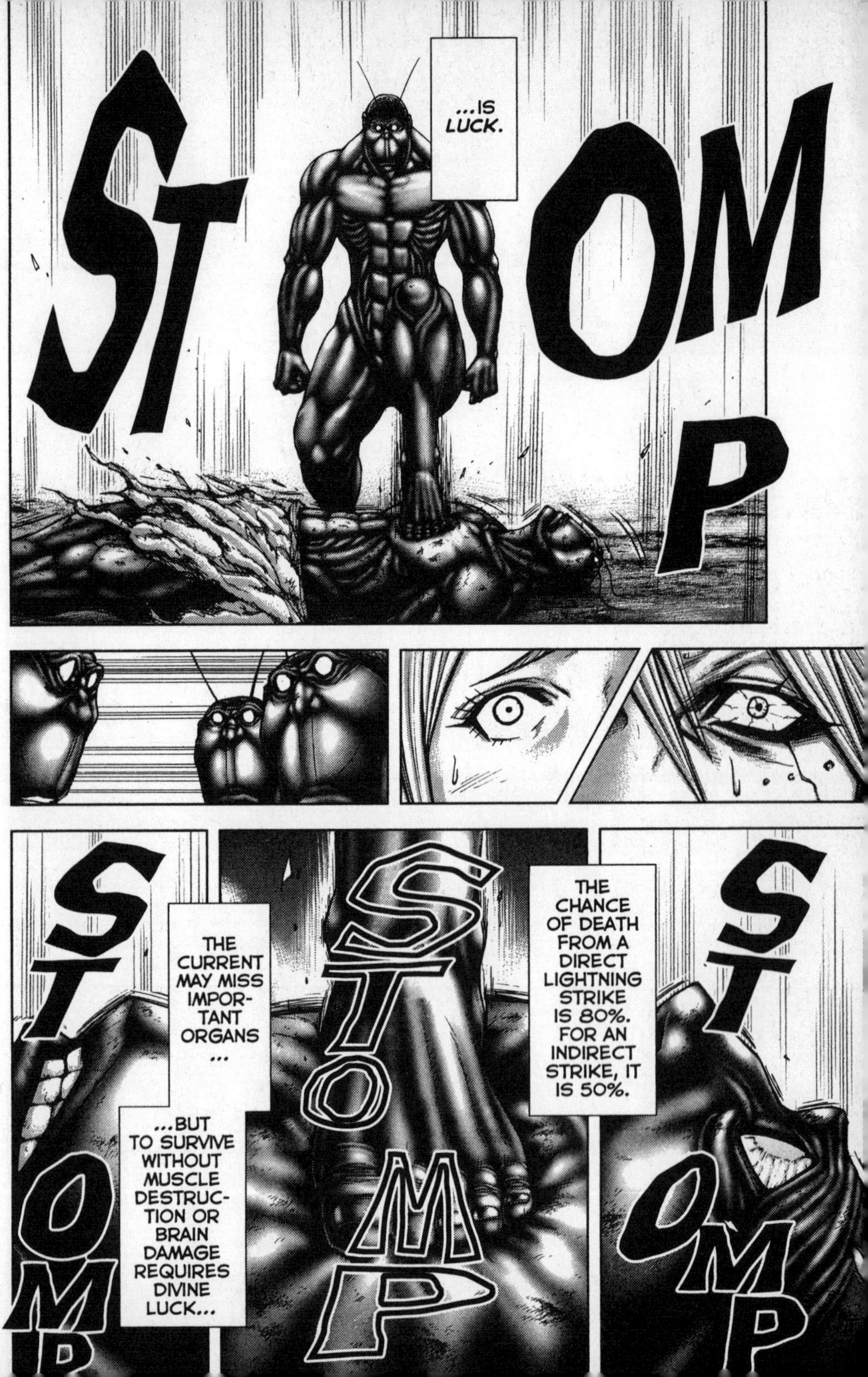
STOMP
...IS LUCK.
STOMP
THE CHANCE OF DEATH FROM A DIRECT LIGHTNING STRIKE IS 80%. FOR AN INDIRECT STRIKE, IT IS 50%.
STOMP
THE CURRENT MAY MISS IMPOR-TANT ORGANS ...
...BUT TO SURVIVE WITHOUT MUSCLE DESTRUC-TION OR BRAIN DAMAGE REQUIRES DIVINE LUCK...
STOMP

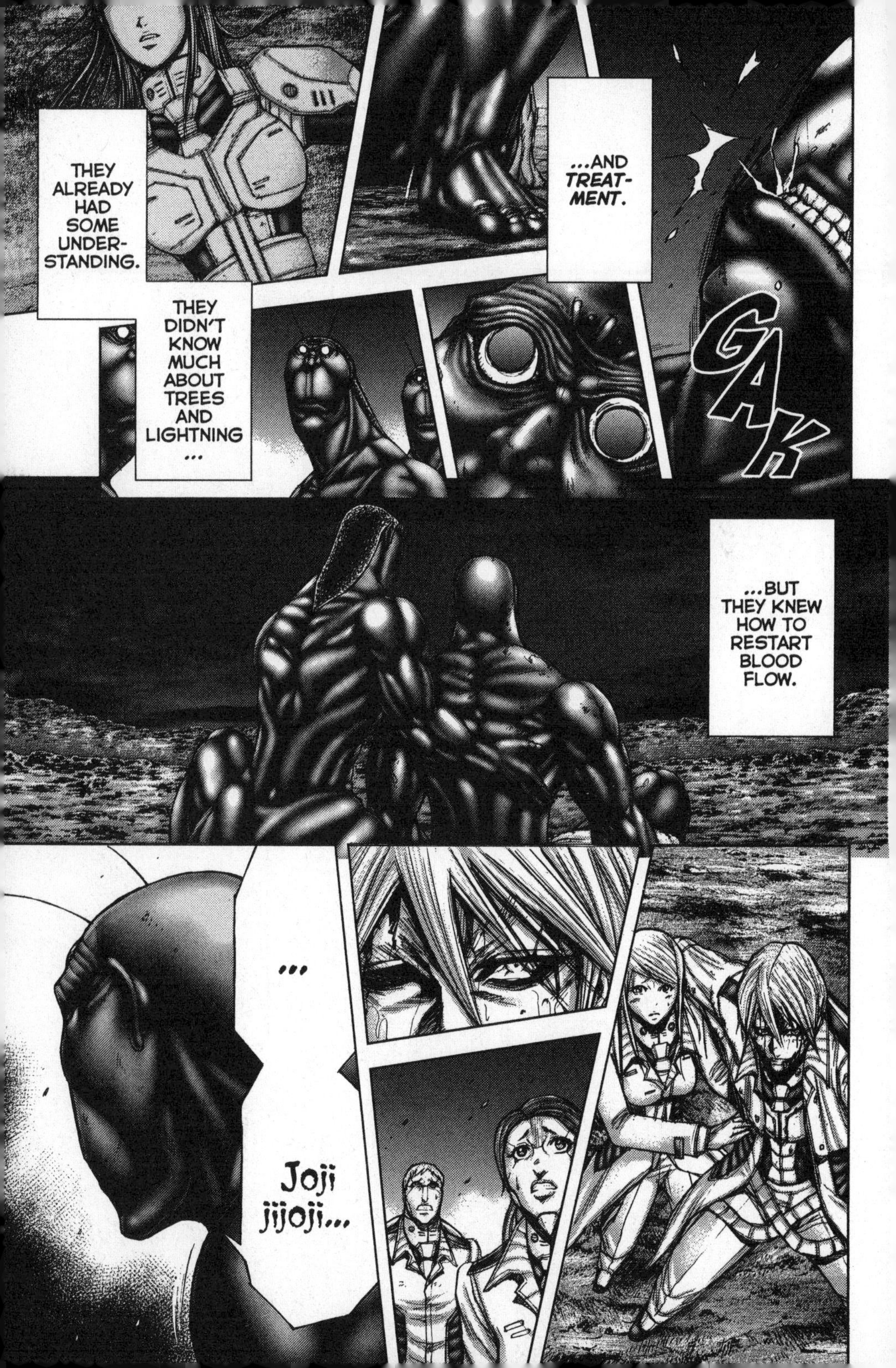
GAK
...AND TREATMENT.
THEY ALREADY HAD SOME UNDERSTANDING.
THEY DIDN'T KNOW MUCH ABOUT TREES AND LIGHTNING...
...BUT THEY KNEW HOW TO RESTART BLOOD FLOW.
...
Joji jijoji...

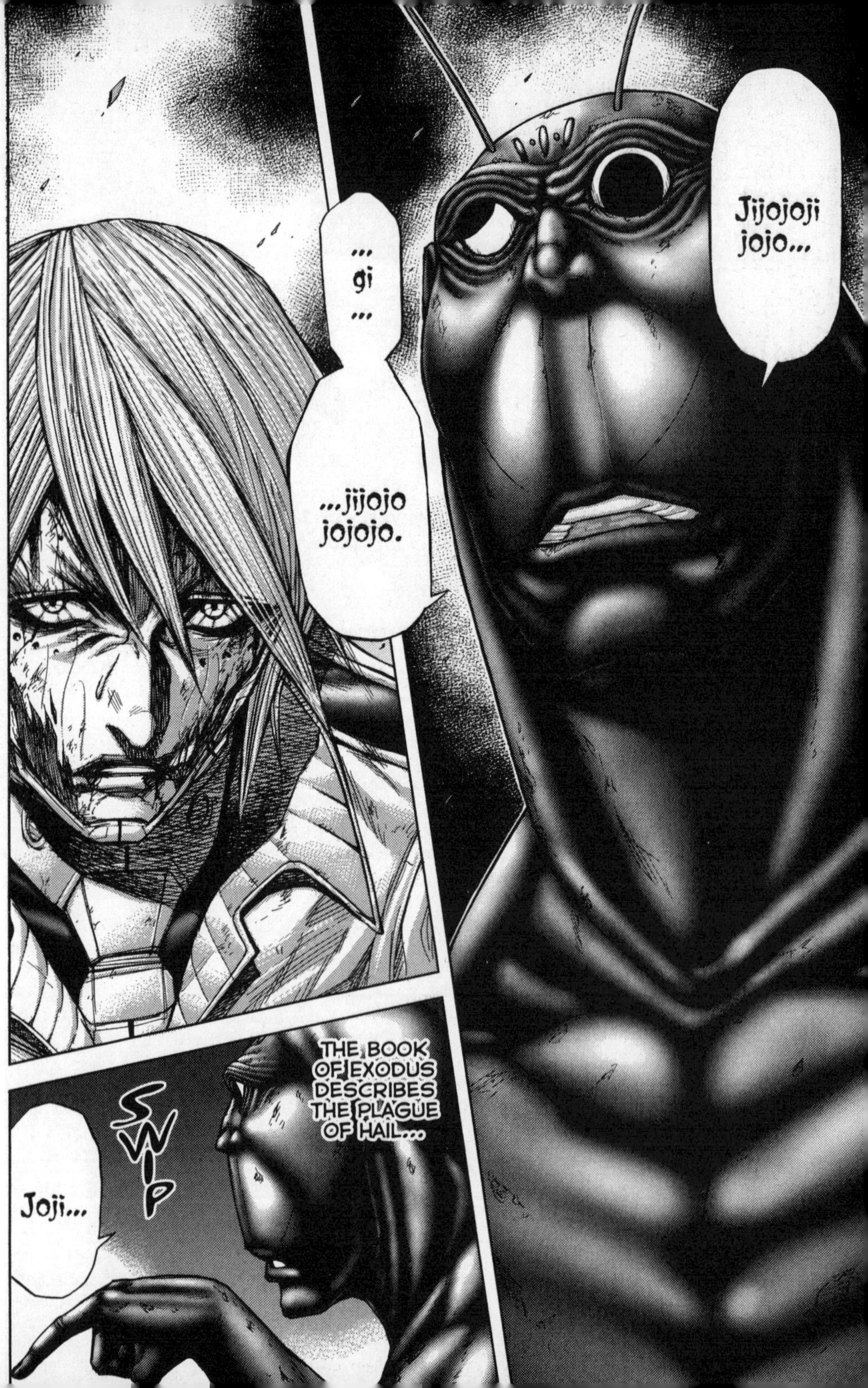
Jijojoji jojo...
...gi...
...jijojo jojojo.
THE BOOK OF EXODUS DESCRIBES THE PLAGUE OF HAIL...
SWIP
Joji...

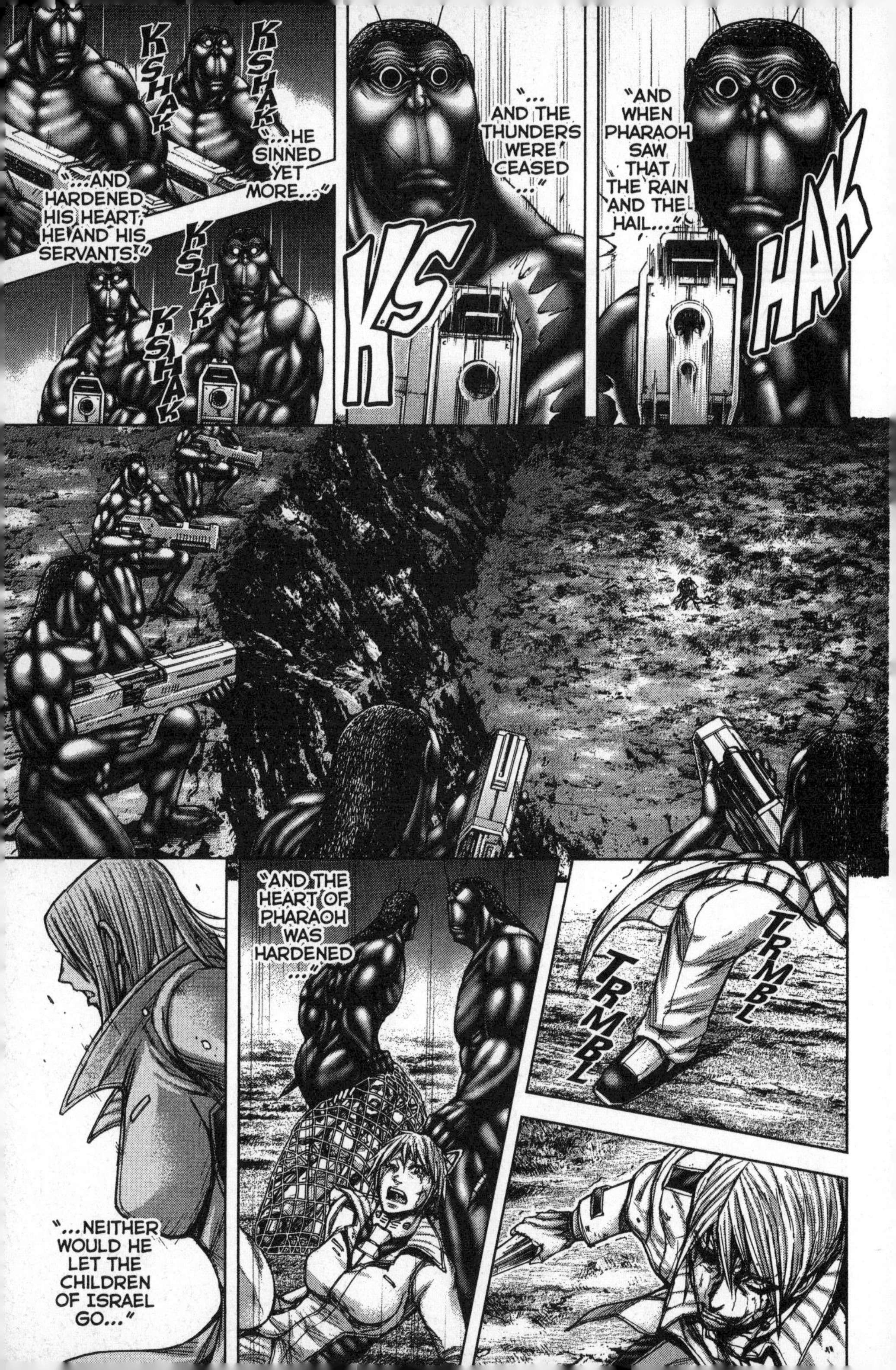
"AND WHEN PHARAOH SAW THAT THE RAIN AND THE HAIL..."
HAK
"...AND THE THUNDERS WERE CEASED..."
KS
KSHAK
KSHAK
"...HE SINNED YET MORE..."
"...AND HARDENED HIS HEART, HE AND HIS SERVANTS."
KSHAK
KSHAK
TRMBL
TRMBL
"AND THE HEART OF PHARAOH WAS HARDENED..."
"...NEITHER WOULD HE LET THE CHILDREN OF ISRAEL GO..."

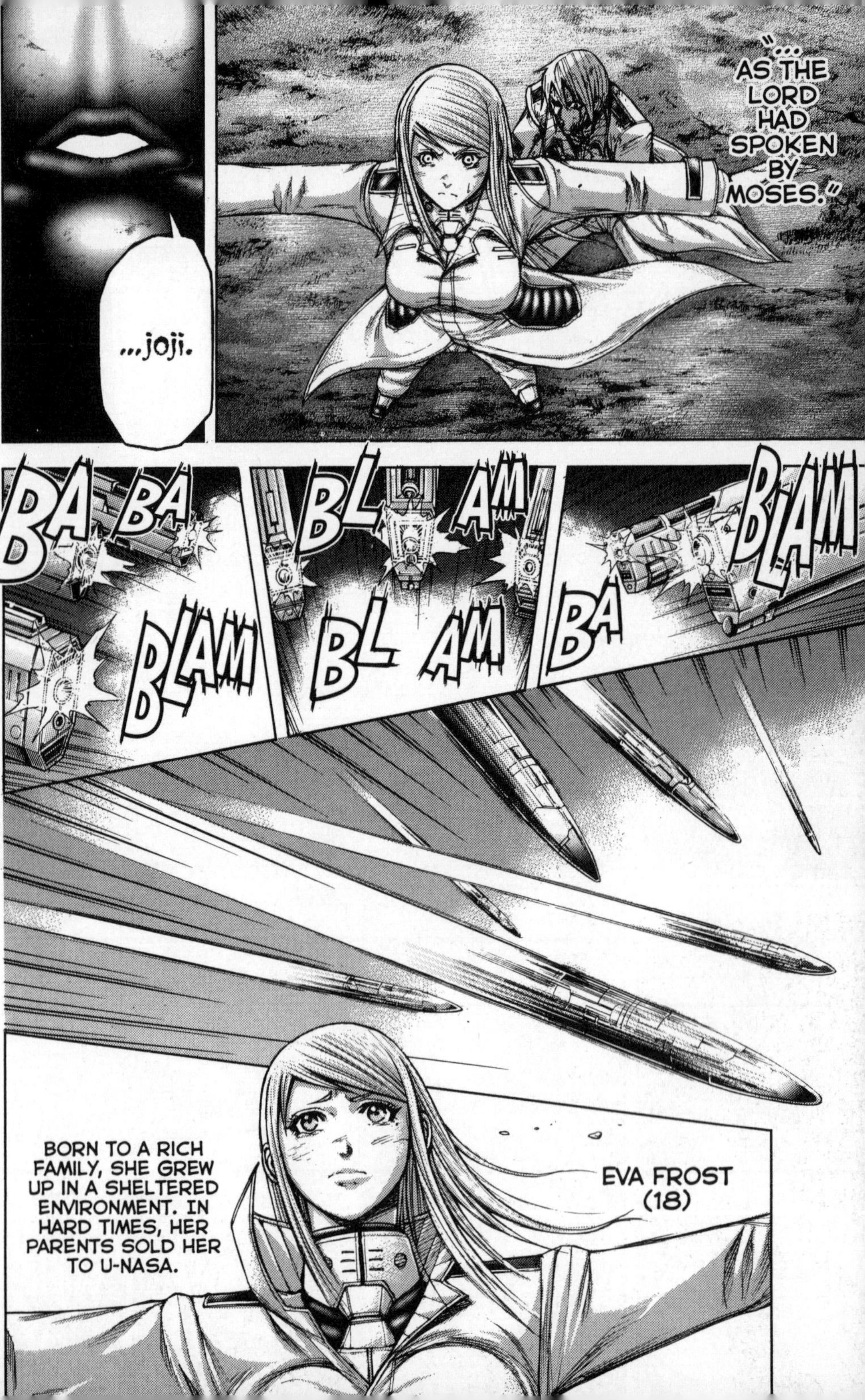
"... AS THE LORD HAD SPOKEN BY MOSES."
...joji.
BLAM
BA
BL AM
BL AM
BA BA
BLAM
EVA FROST (18)
BORN TO A RICH FAMILY, SHE GREW UP IN A SHELTERED ENVIRONMENT. IN HARD TIMES, HER PARENTS SOLD HER TO U-NASA.

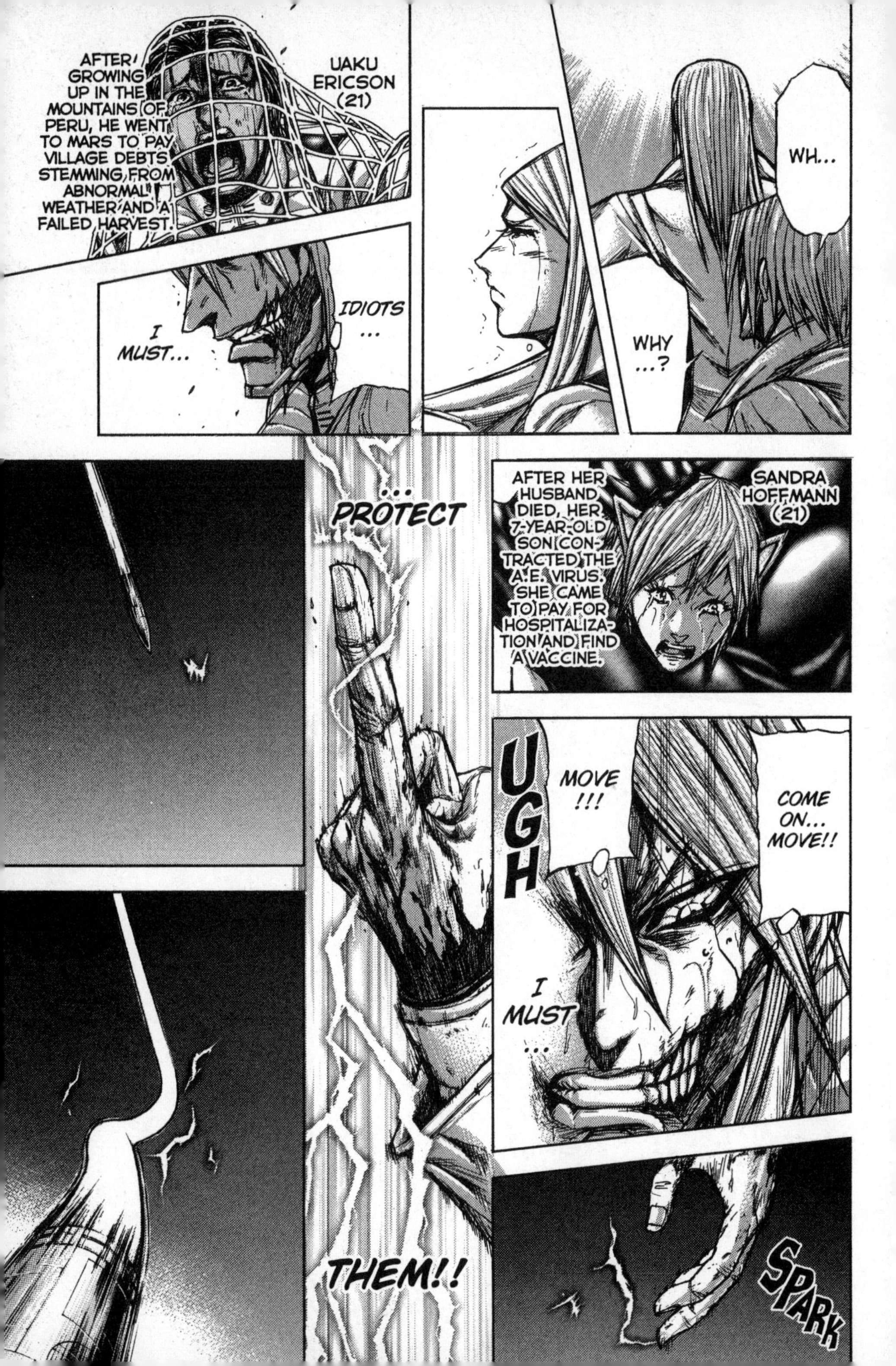
WH...
WHY ...?
UAKU ERICSON (21)
AFTER GROWING UP IN THE MOUNTAINS OF PERU, HE WENT TO MARS TO PAY VILLAGE DEBTS STEMMING FROM ABNORMAL WEATHER AND A FAILED HARVEST.
IDIOTS ...
I MUST...
SANDRA HOFFMANN (21)
AFTER HER HUSBAND DIED, HER 7-YEAR-OLD SON CONTRACTED THE A.E. VIRUS. SHE CAME TO PAY FOR HOSPITALIZATION AND FIND A VACCINE.
COME ON... MOVE!!
MOVE !!!
UGH
I MUST ...
SPARK
... PROTECT
THEM!!

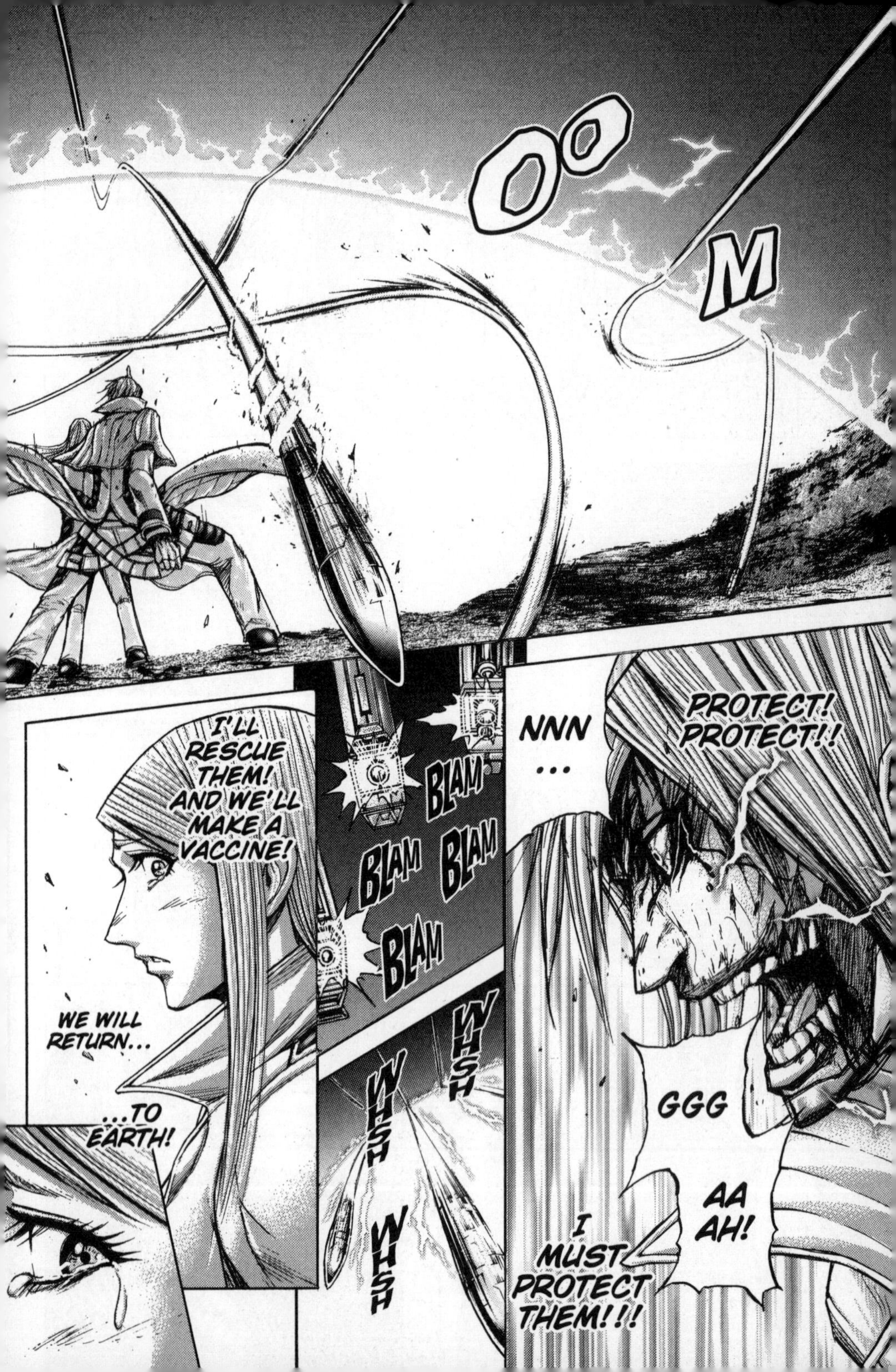
OOM
PROTECT! PROTECT!!
NNN...
GGG
AAAH!
I MUST PROTECT THEM!!!
BLAM
BLAM
BLAM
BLAM
WHSH
WHSH
WHSH
I'LL RESCUE THEM! AND WE'LL MAKE A VACCINE!
WE WILL RETURN...
...TO EARTH!

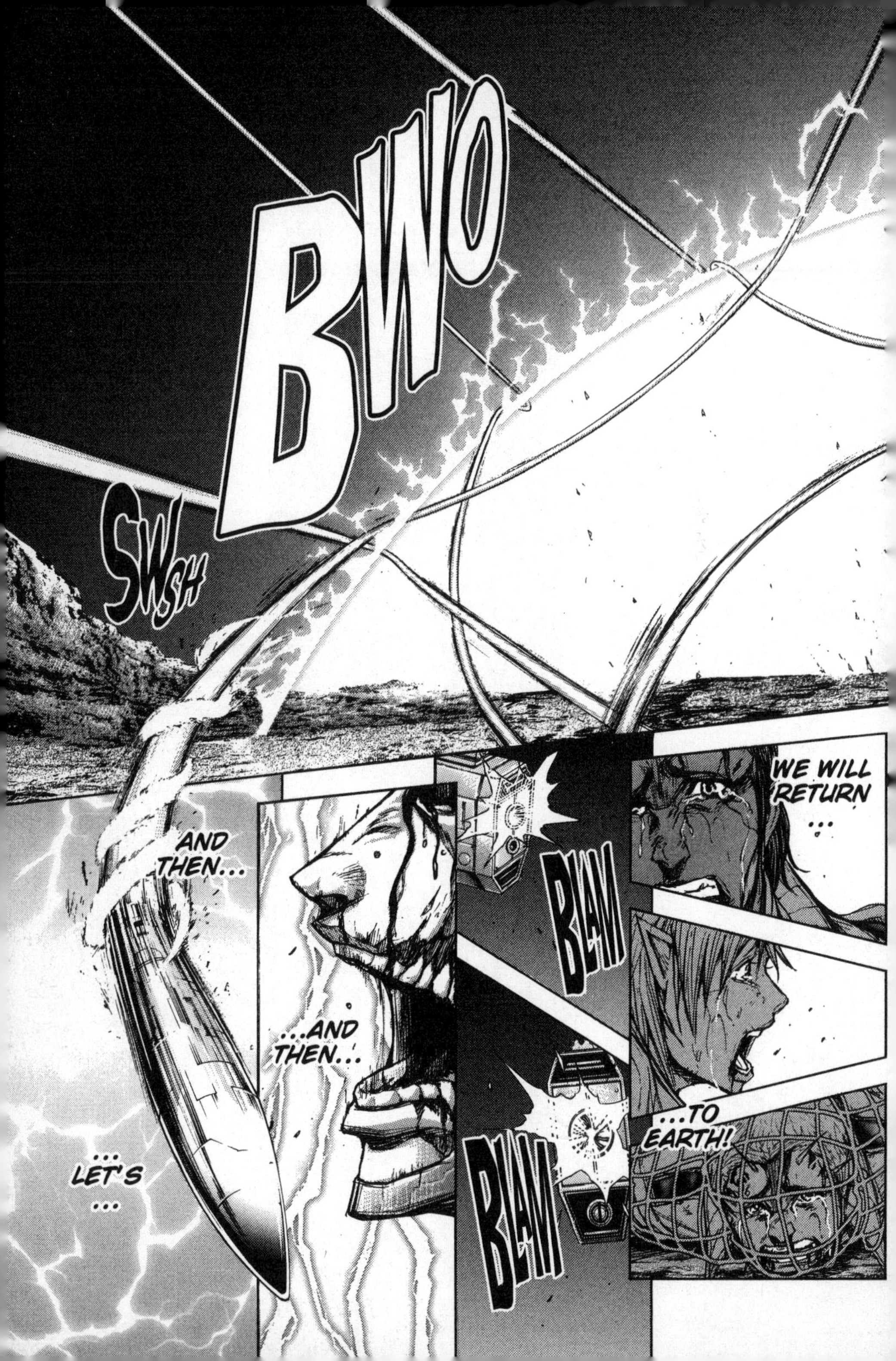
BWO
SWSH
WE WILL RETURN ...
...TO EARTH!
BLAM
BLAM
AND THEN...
...AND THEN...
... LET'S ...

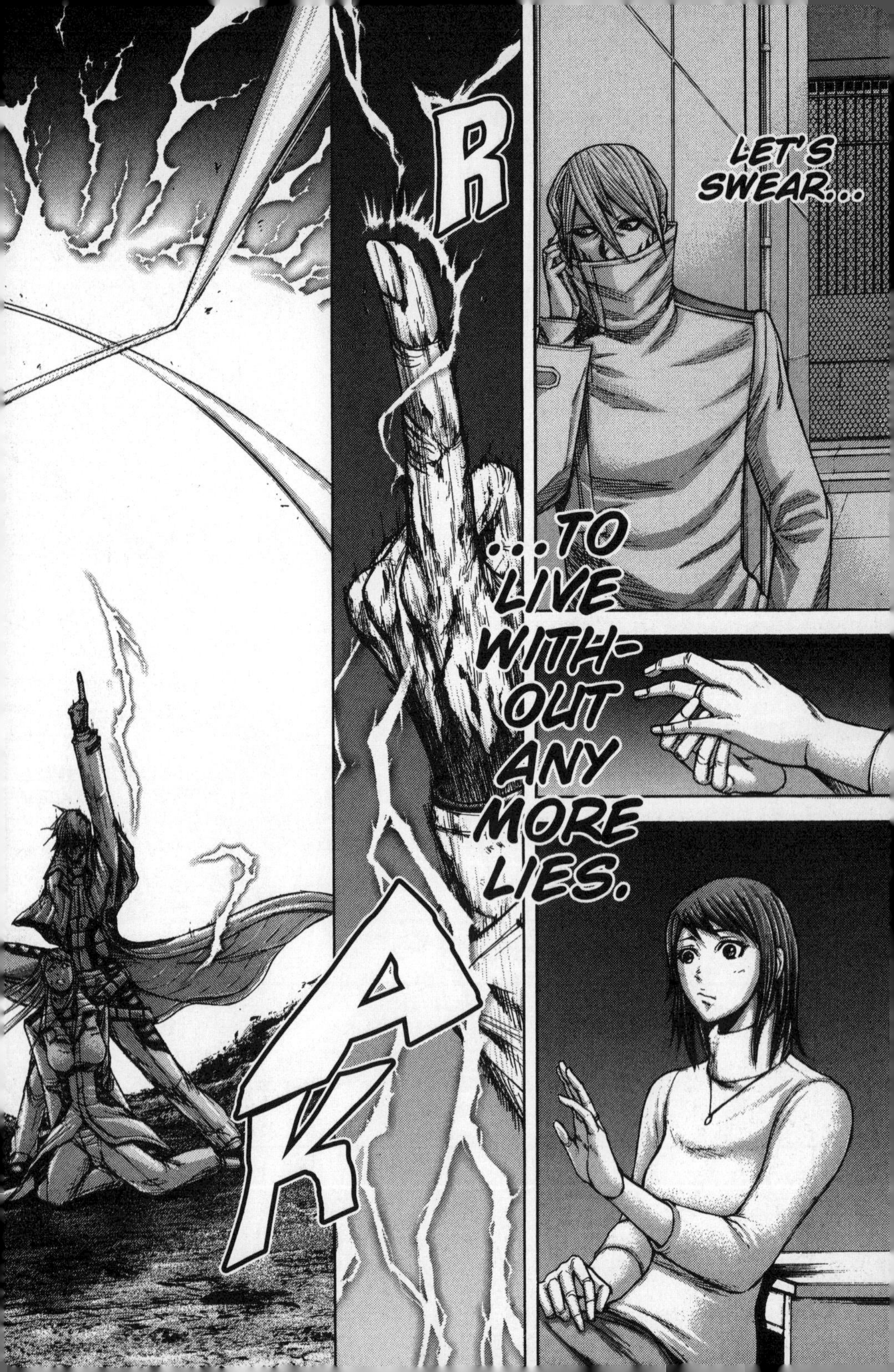
LET'S SWEAR...
...TO LIVE WITH-OUT ANY MORE LIES.
RAK

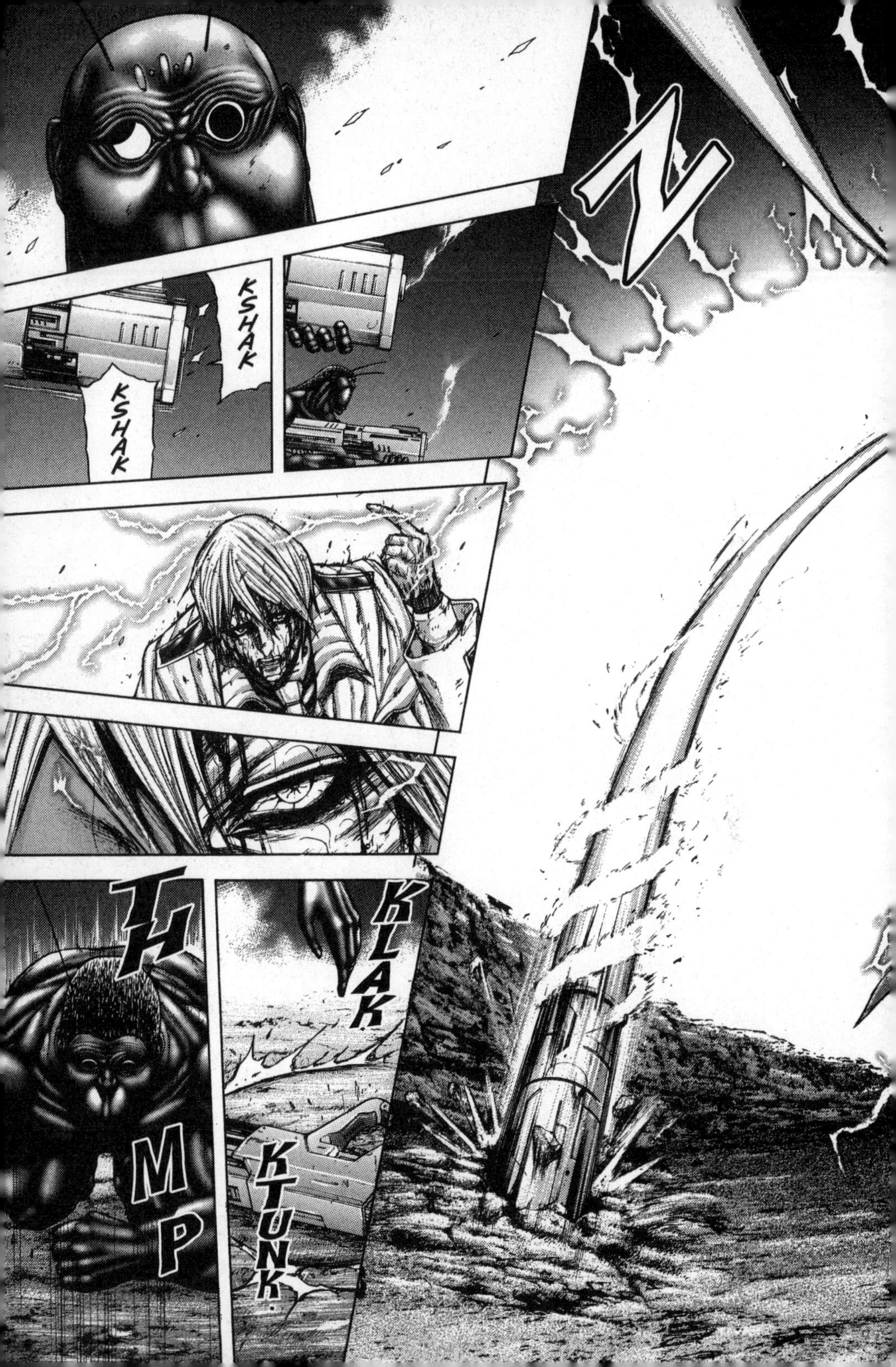
Z
KSHAK
KSHAK
KLAK
KTUNK.
THMP

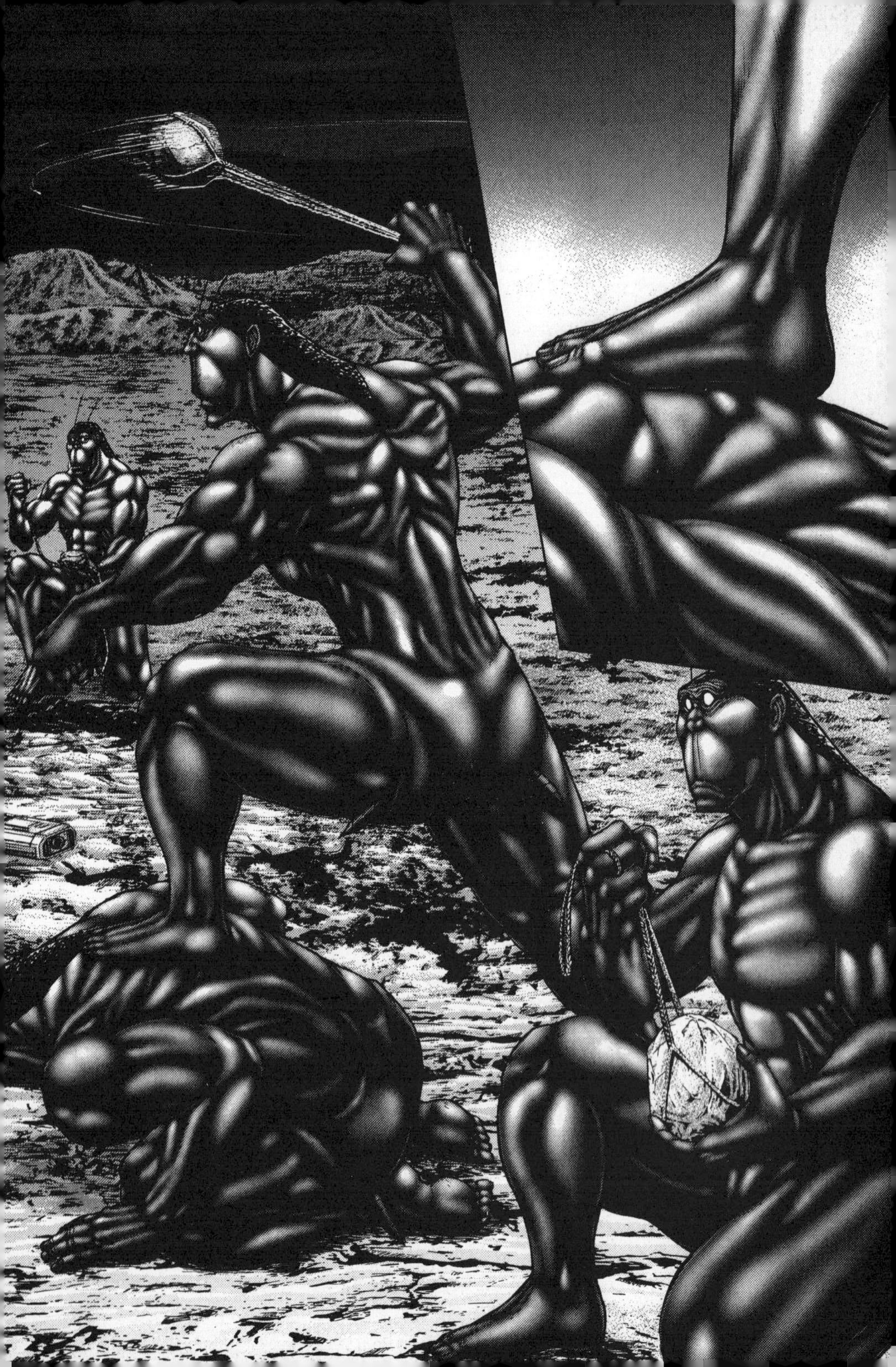

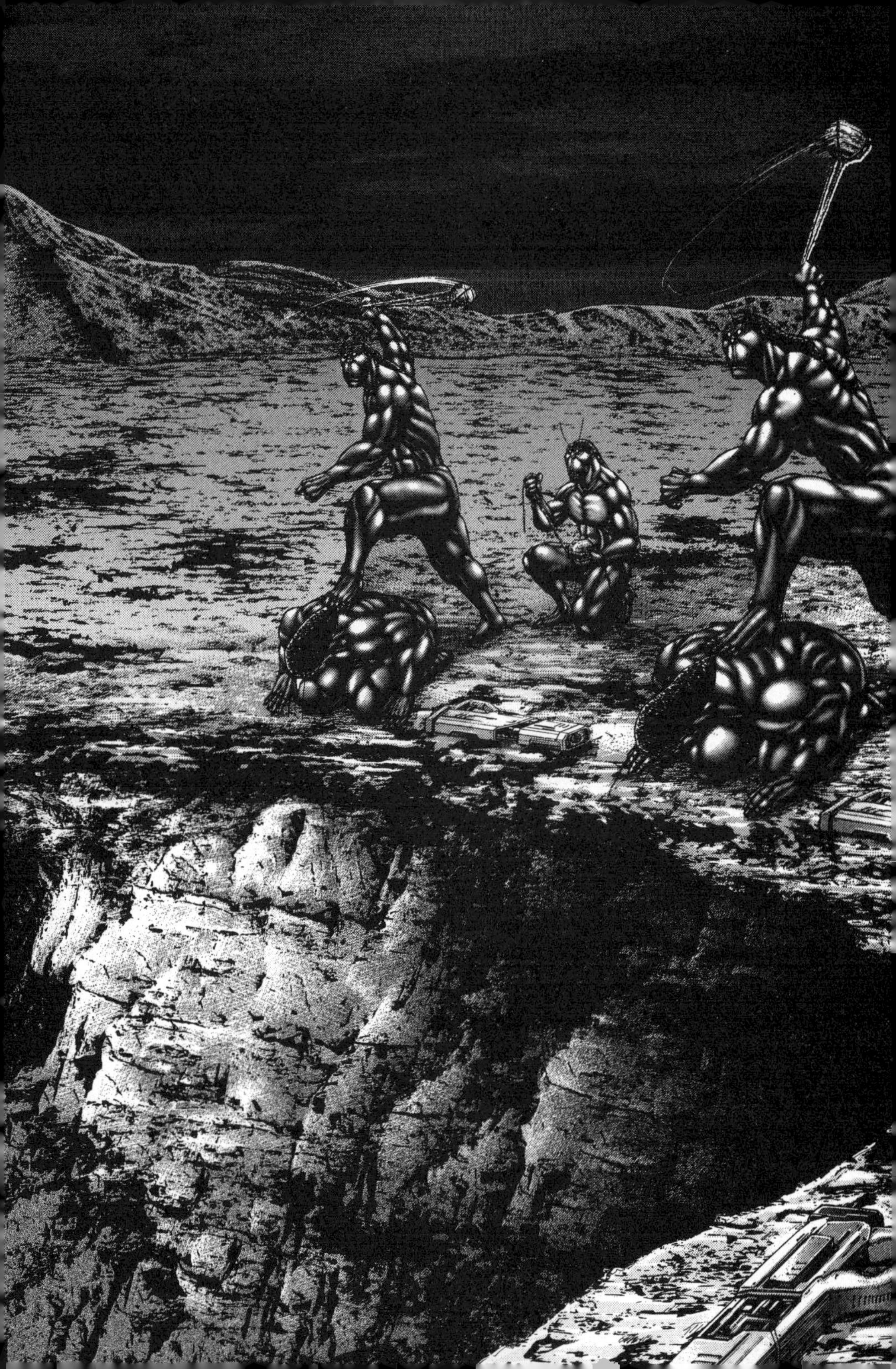

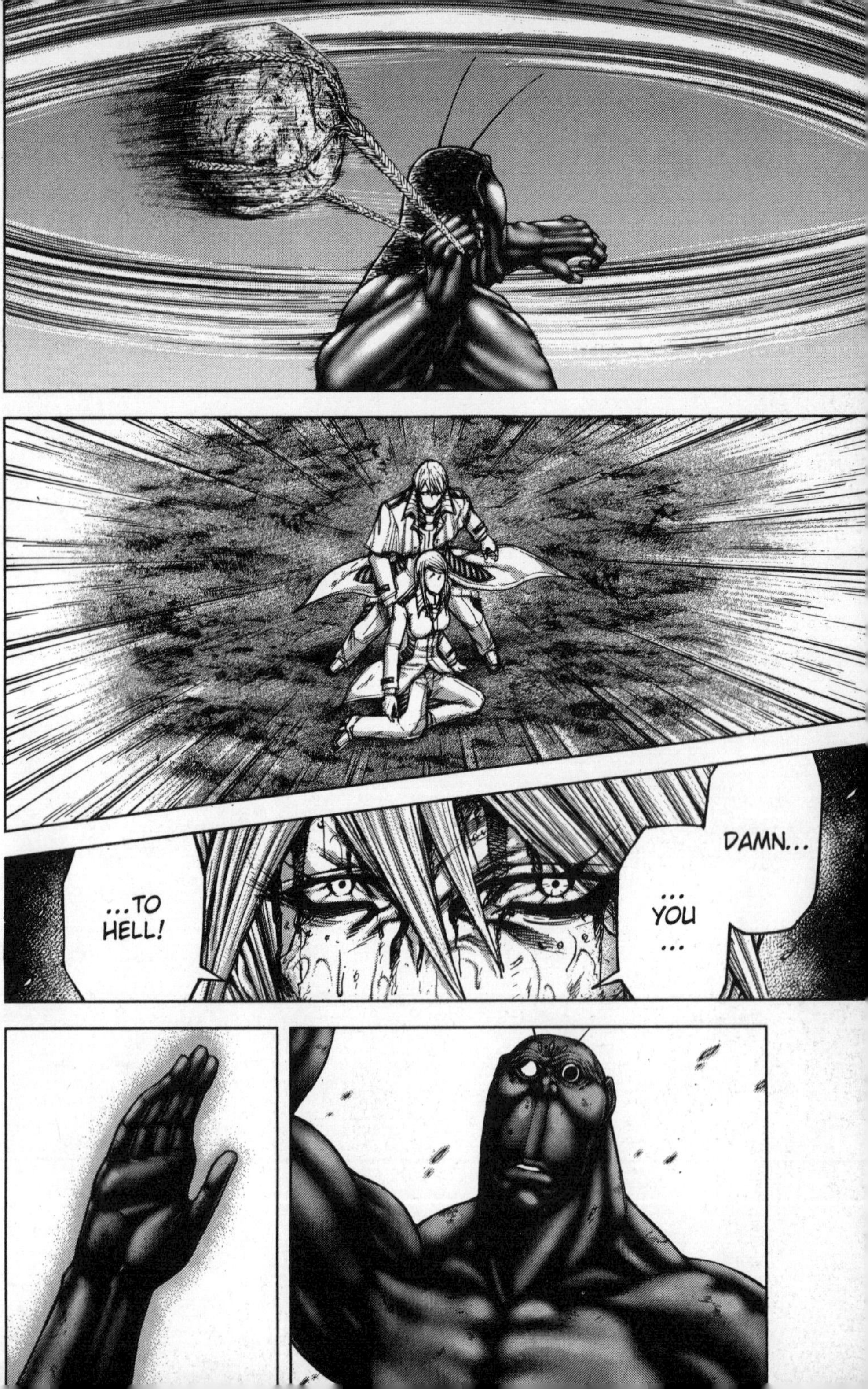
DAMN...
...
YOU
...
...TO
HELL!

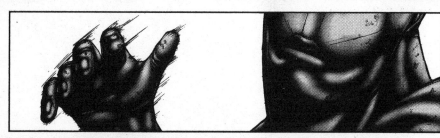

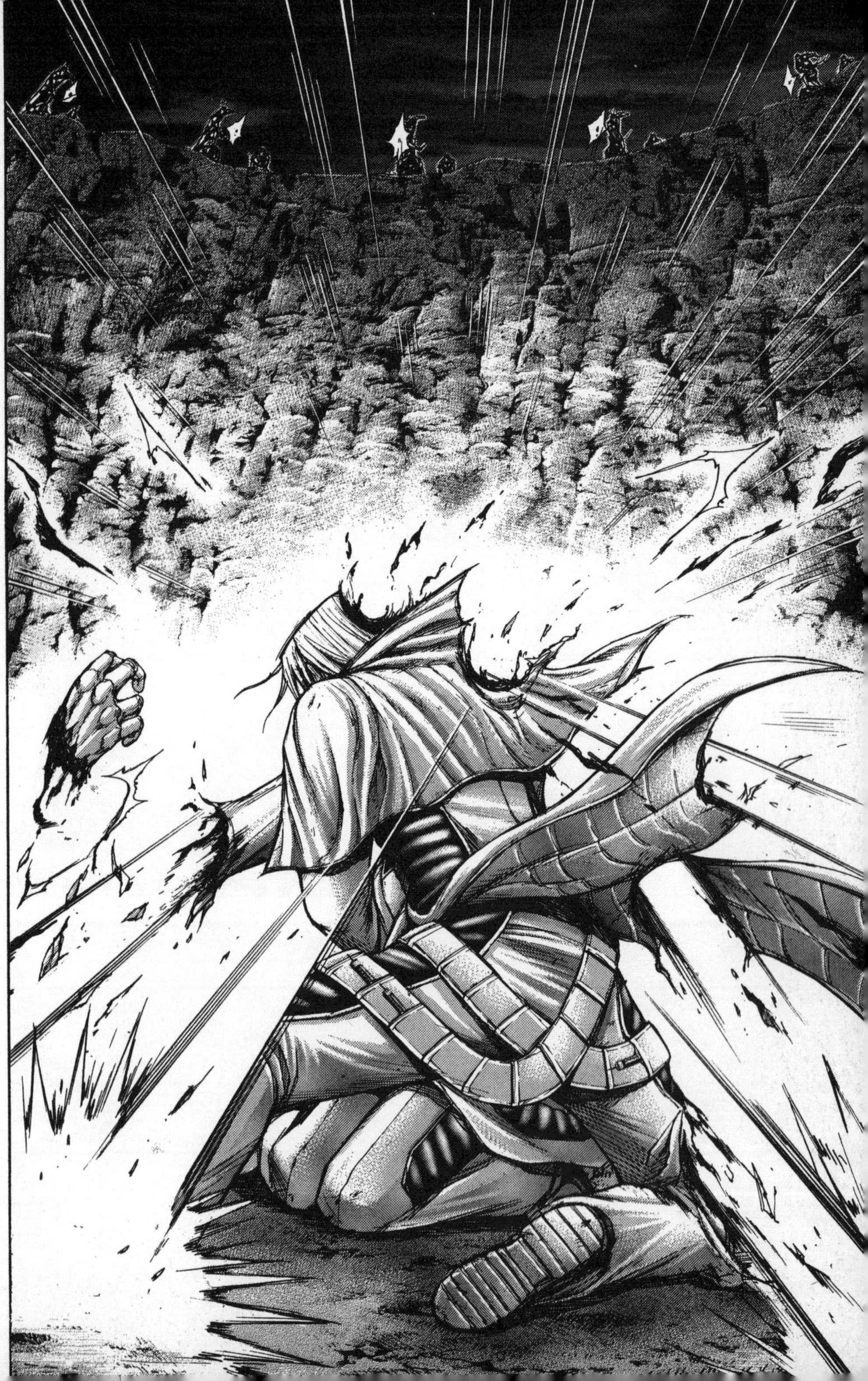

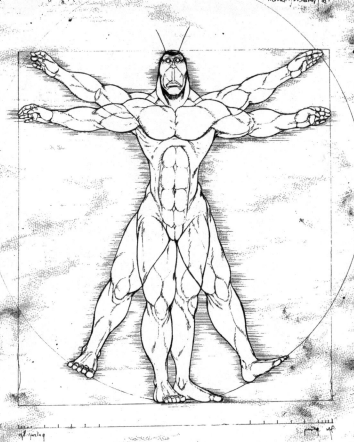

CHAPTER 35: DESIRE

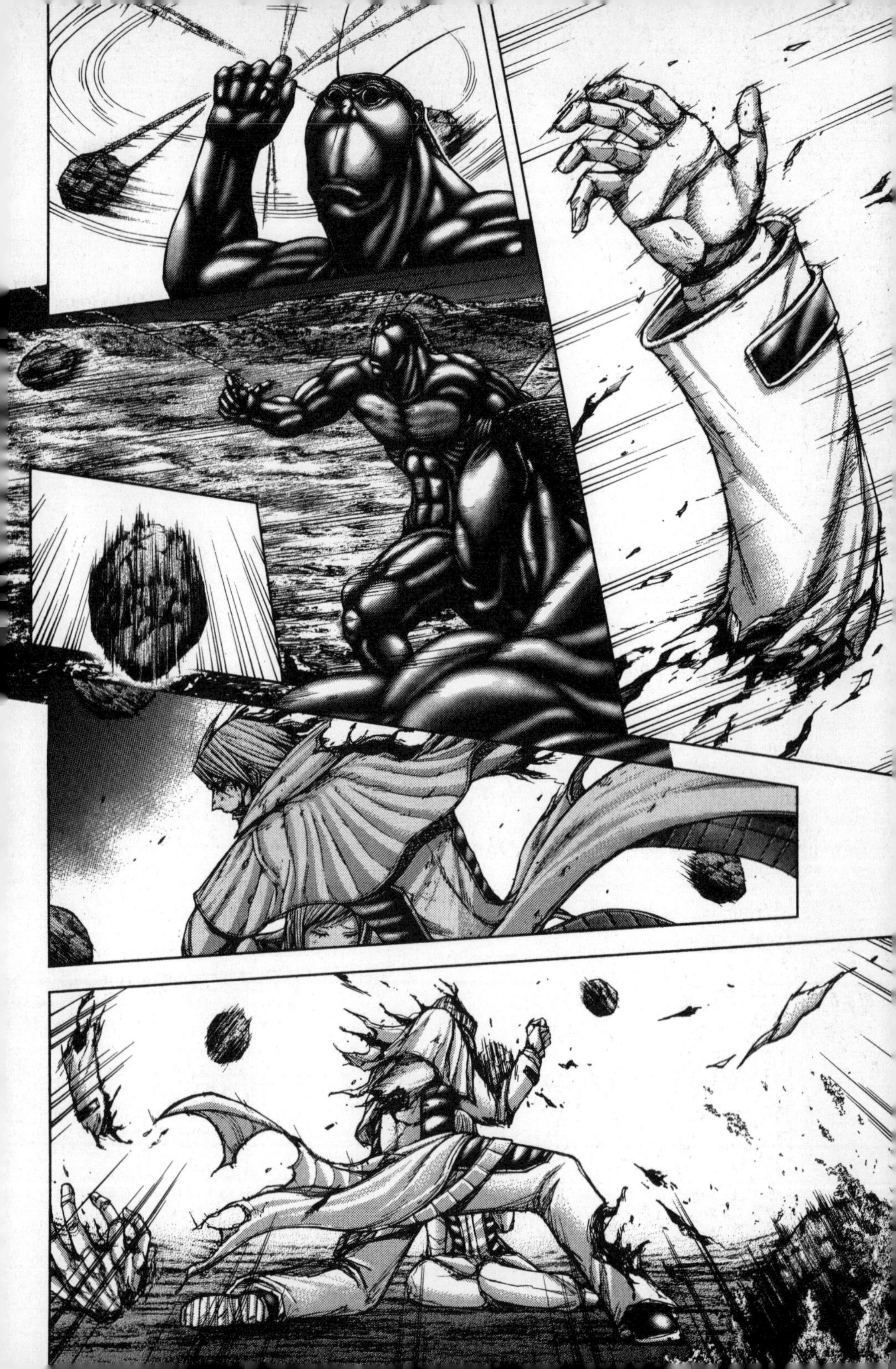

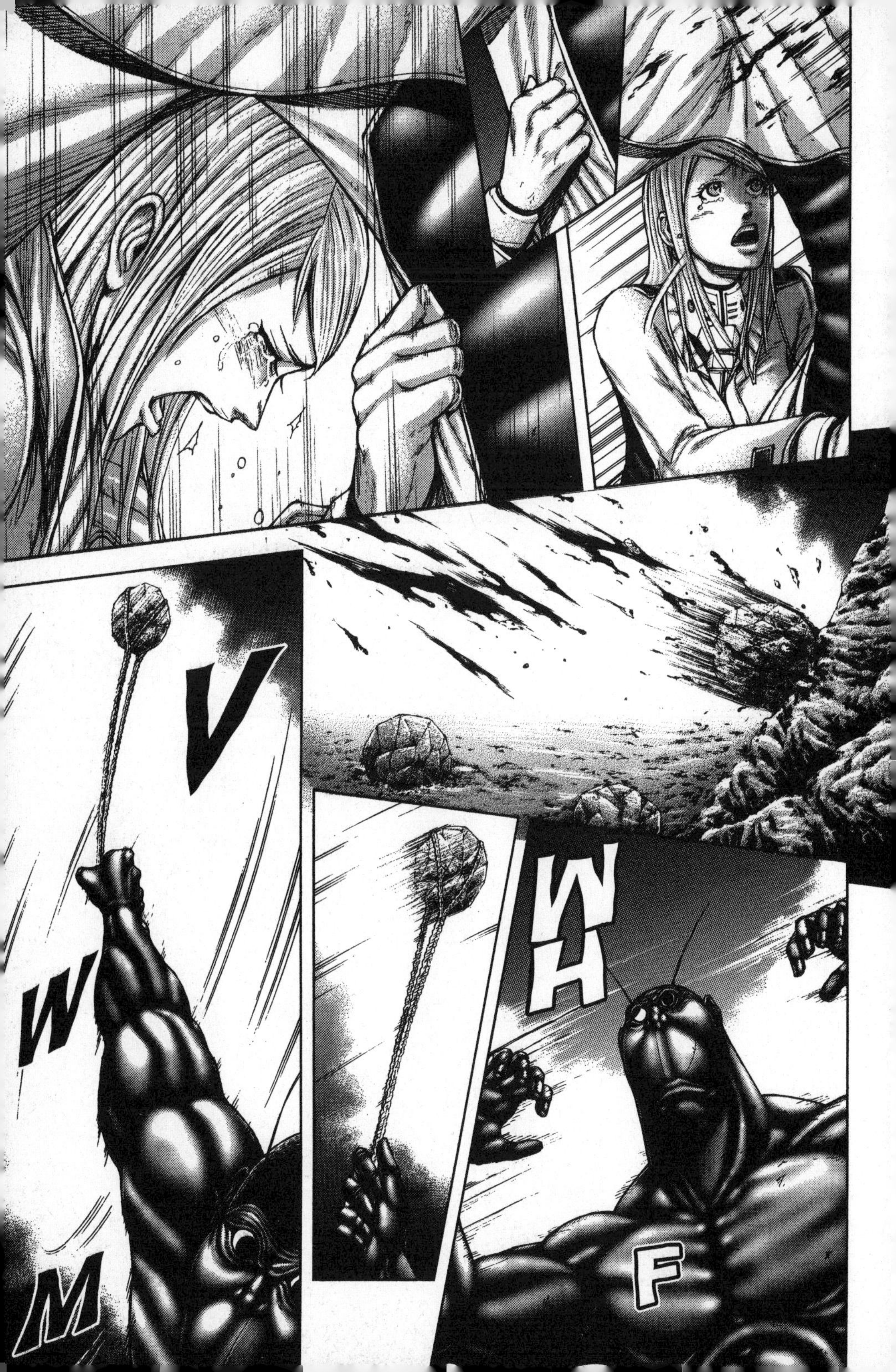
WHA
F
V
W
M

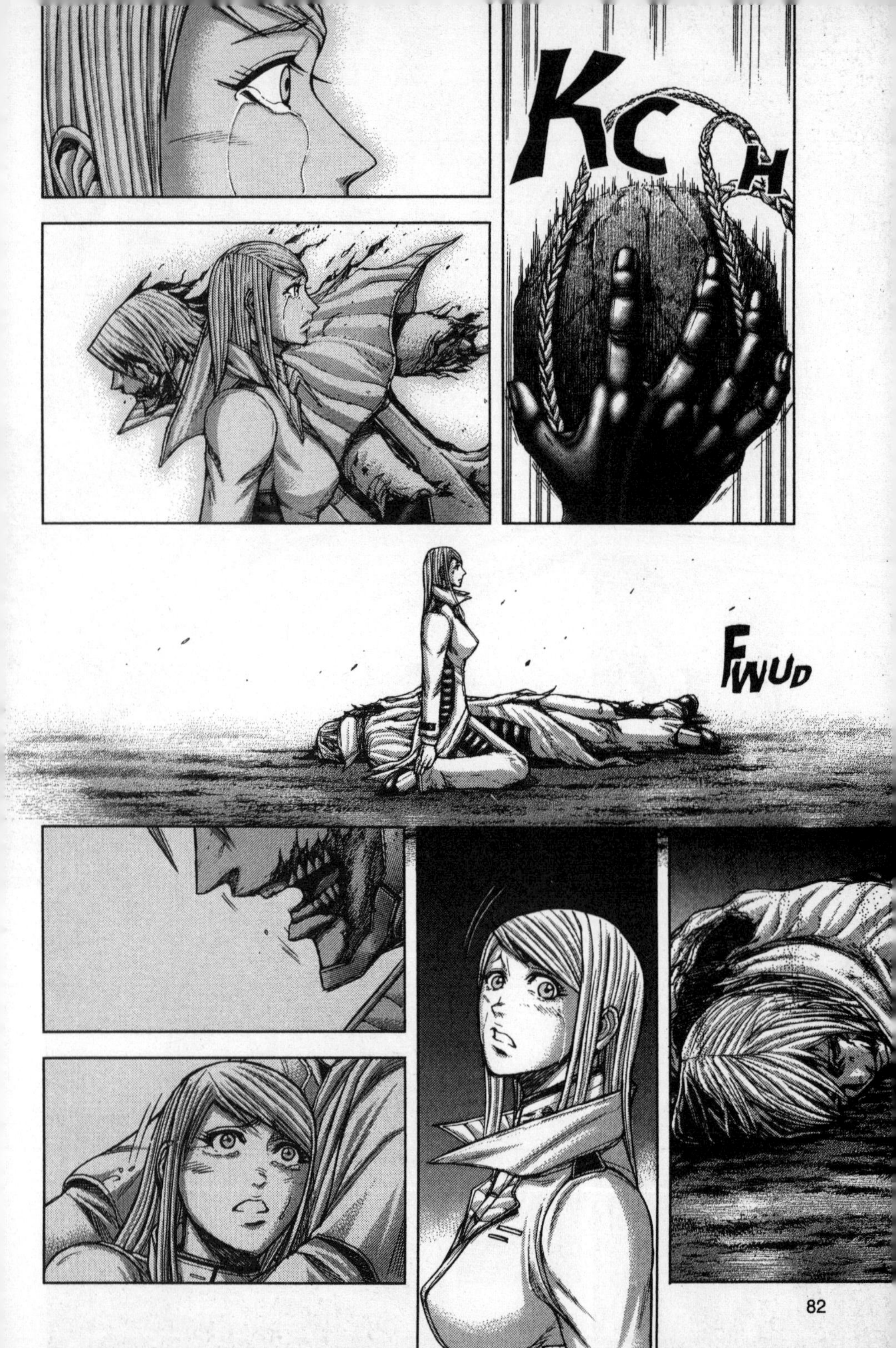
KCH
FWUD

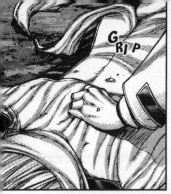

GRIP

NGH
...

ADOLF
...

I CAN'T DO IT...

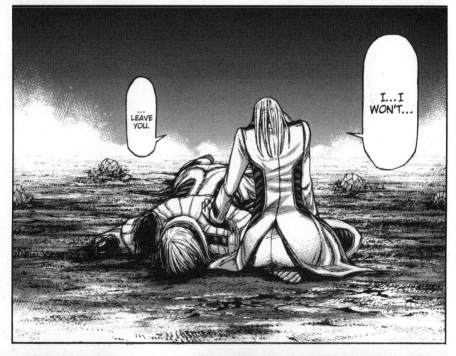

...LEAVE YOU.

I...I WON'T...

HP

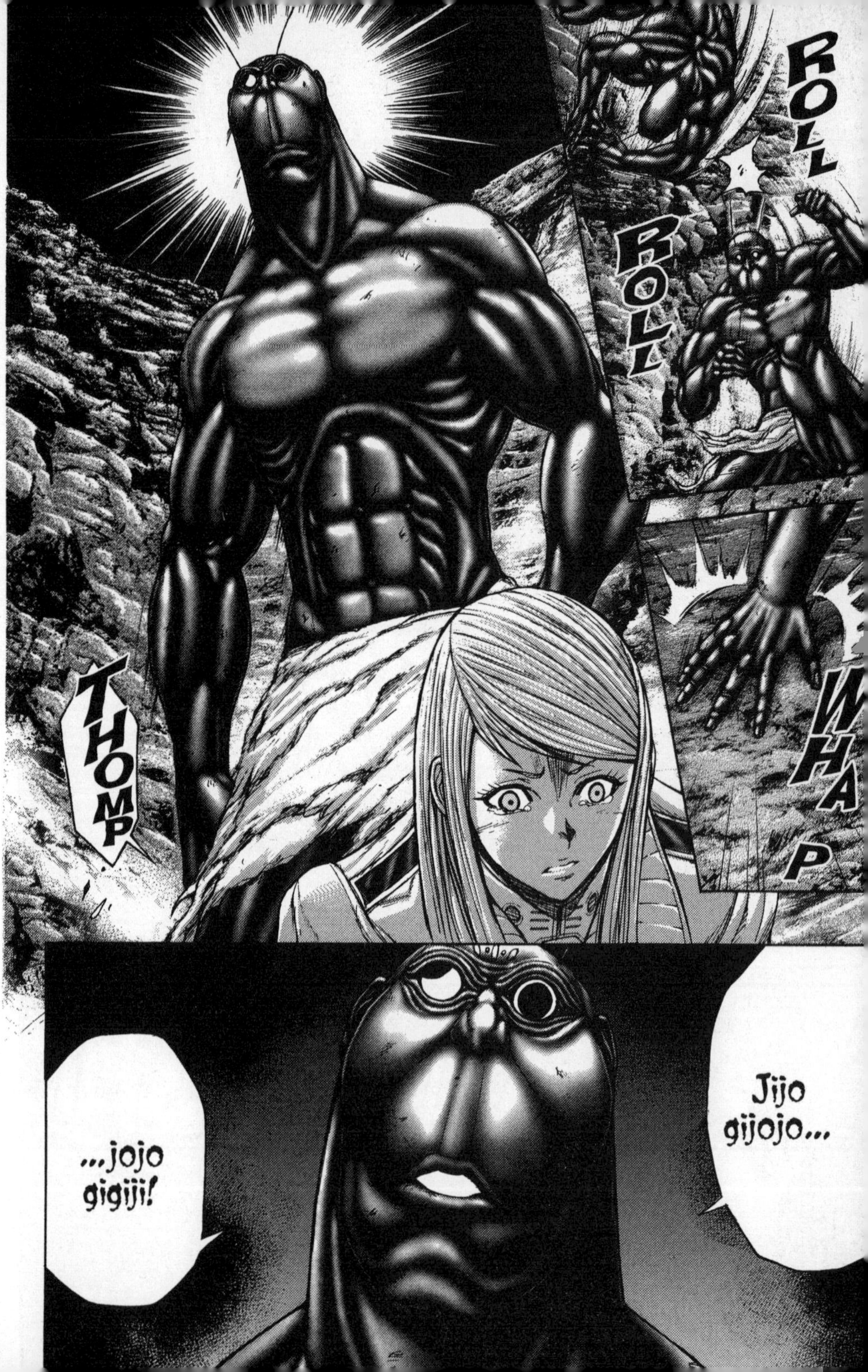
ROLL
ROLL
WHAP
THOMP
Jijo gijojo...
...jojo gigiji!

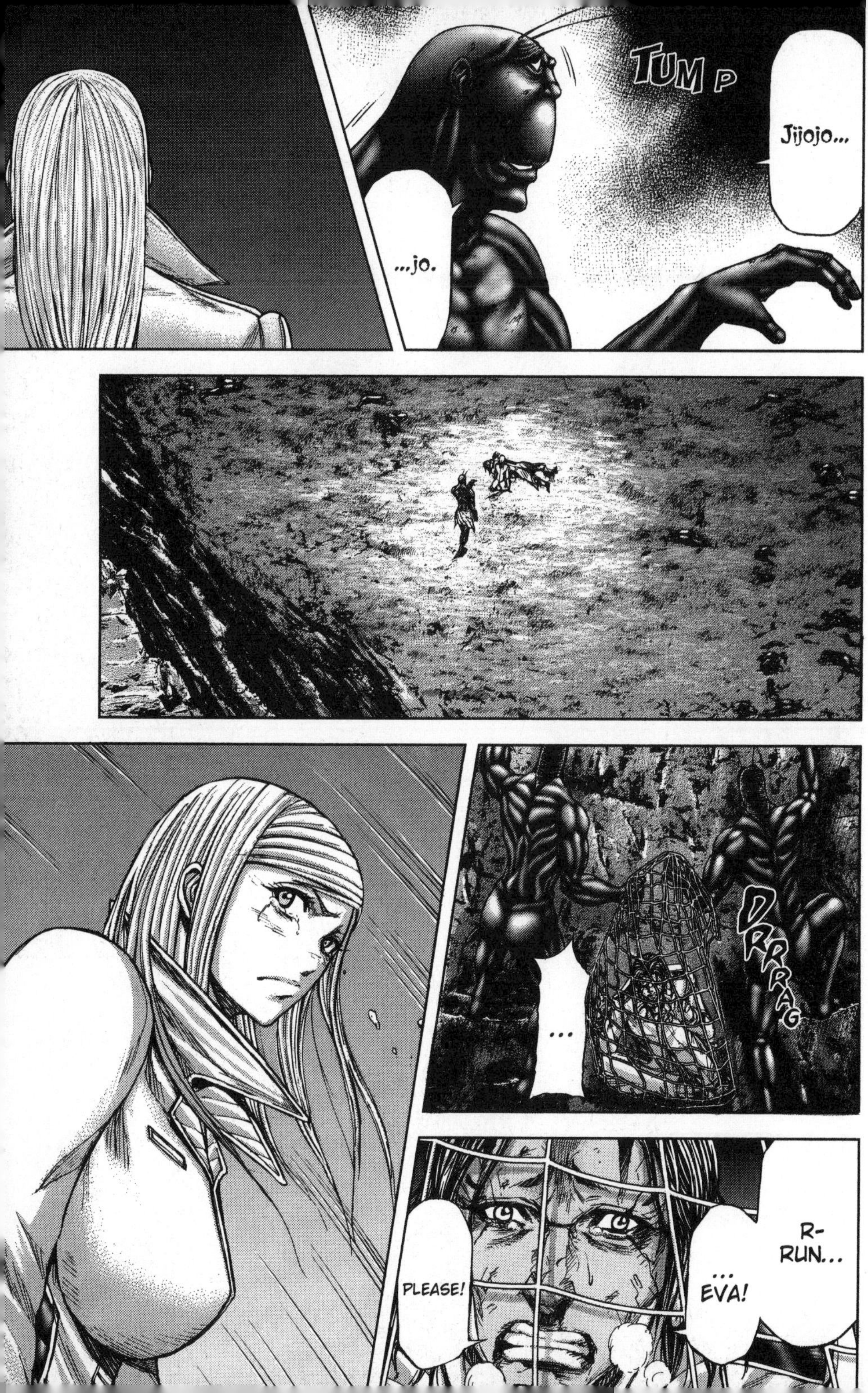
TUMP
Jijojo...
...jo.
DRRRAG
...
R-RUN...
...EVA!
PLEASE!

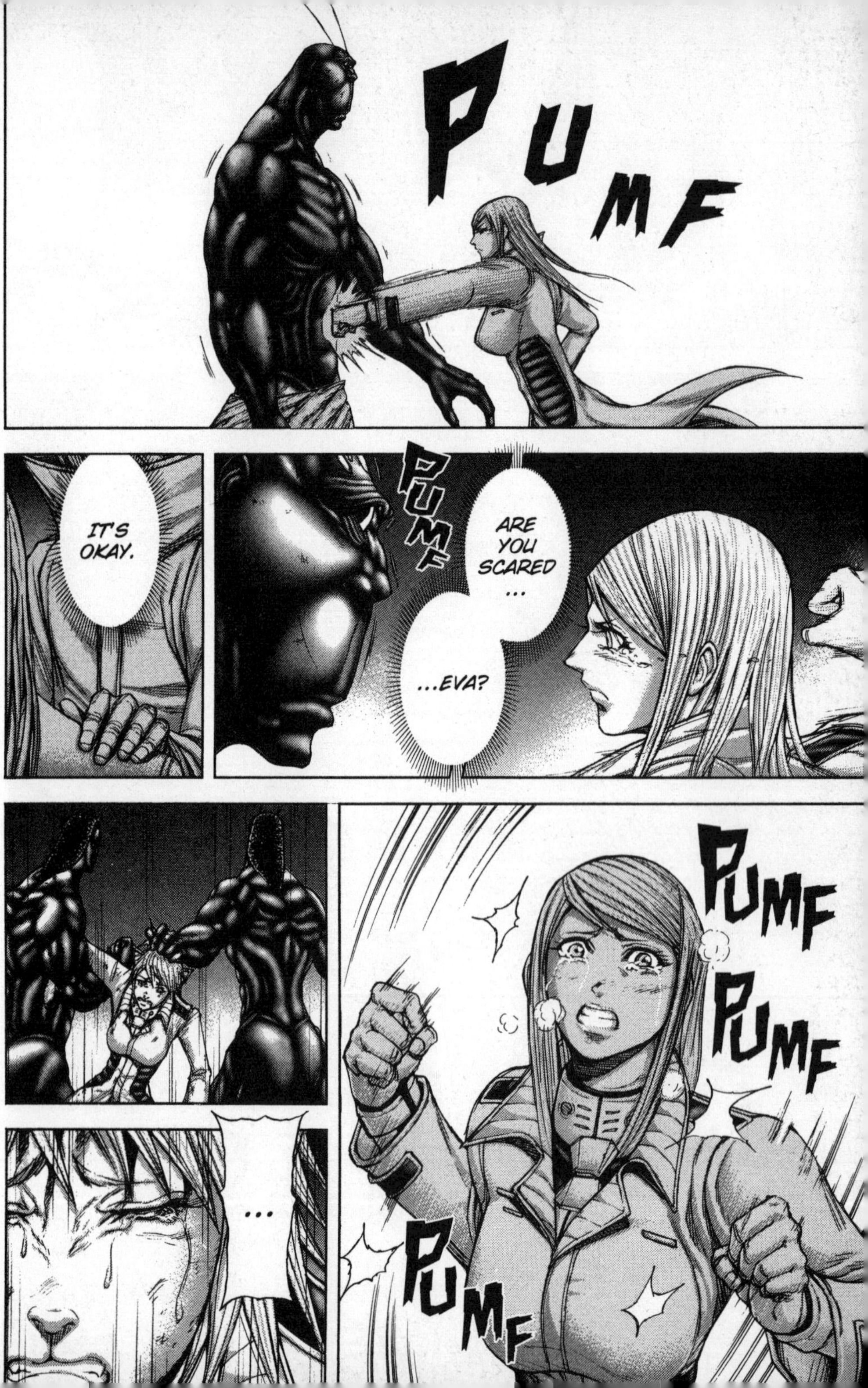
PUMF
PUMF
ARE YOU SCARED ...
...EVA?
IT'S OKAY.
PUMF
PUMF
PUMF
...

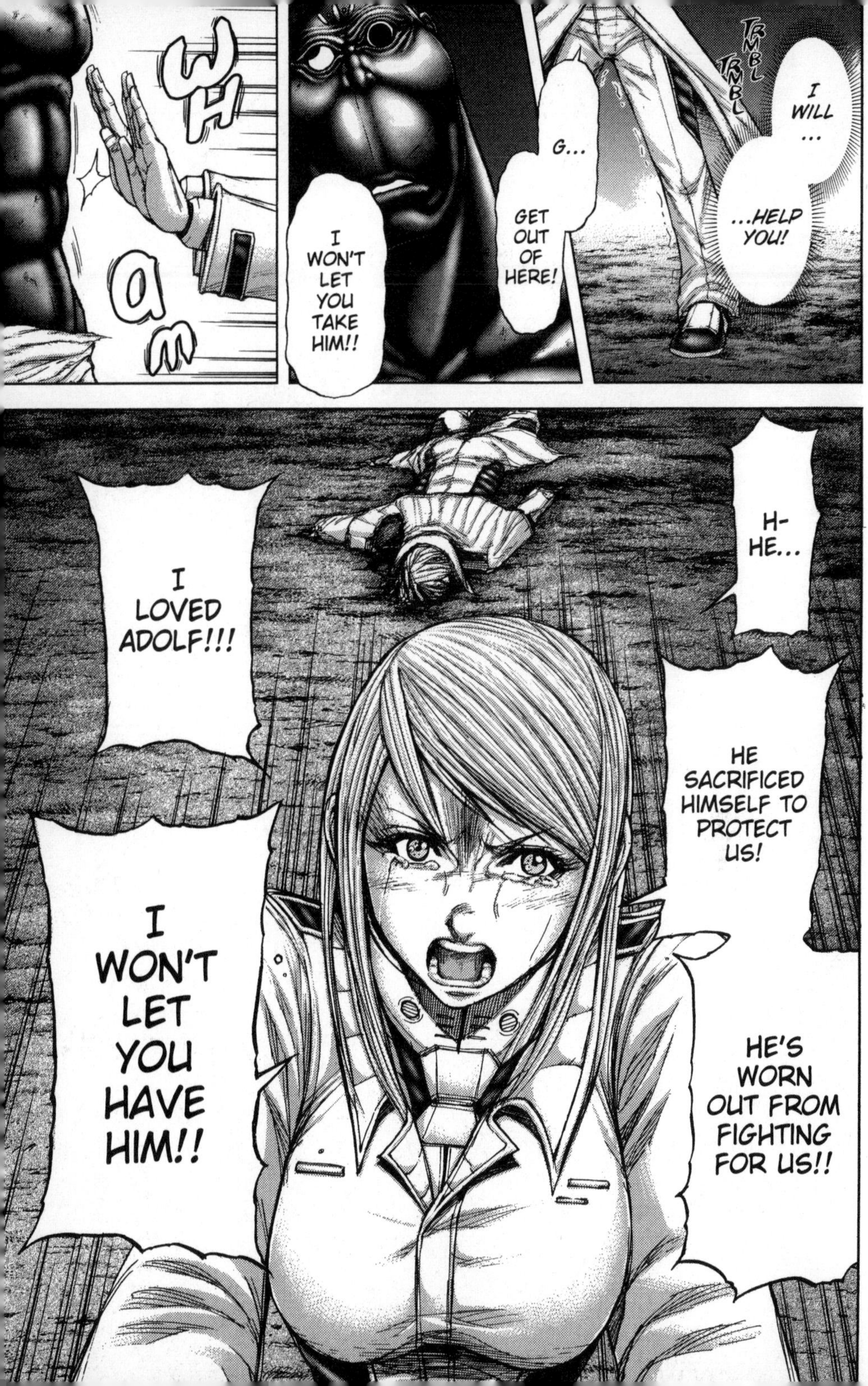
TRMBL TRMBL
I WILL...
...HELP YOU!
G...
GET OUT OF HERE!
I WON'T LET YOU TAKE HIM!!
WHAM
H-HE...
HE SACRIFICED HIMSELF TO PROTECT US!
HE'S WORN OUT FROM FIGHTING FOR US!!
I LOVED ADOLF!!!
I WON'T LET YOU HAVE HIM!!

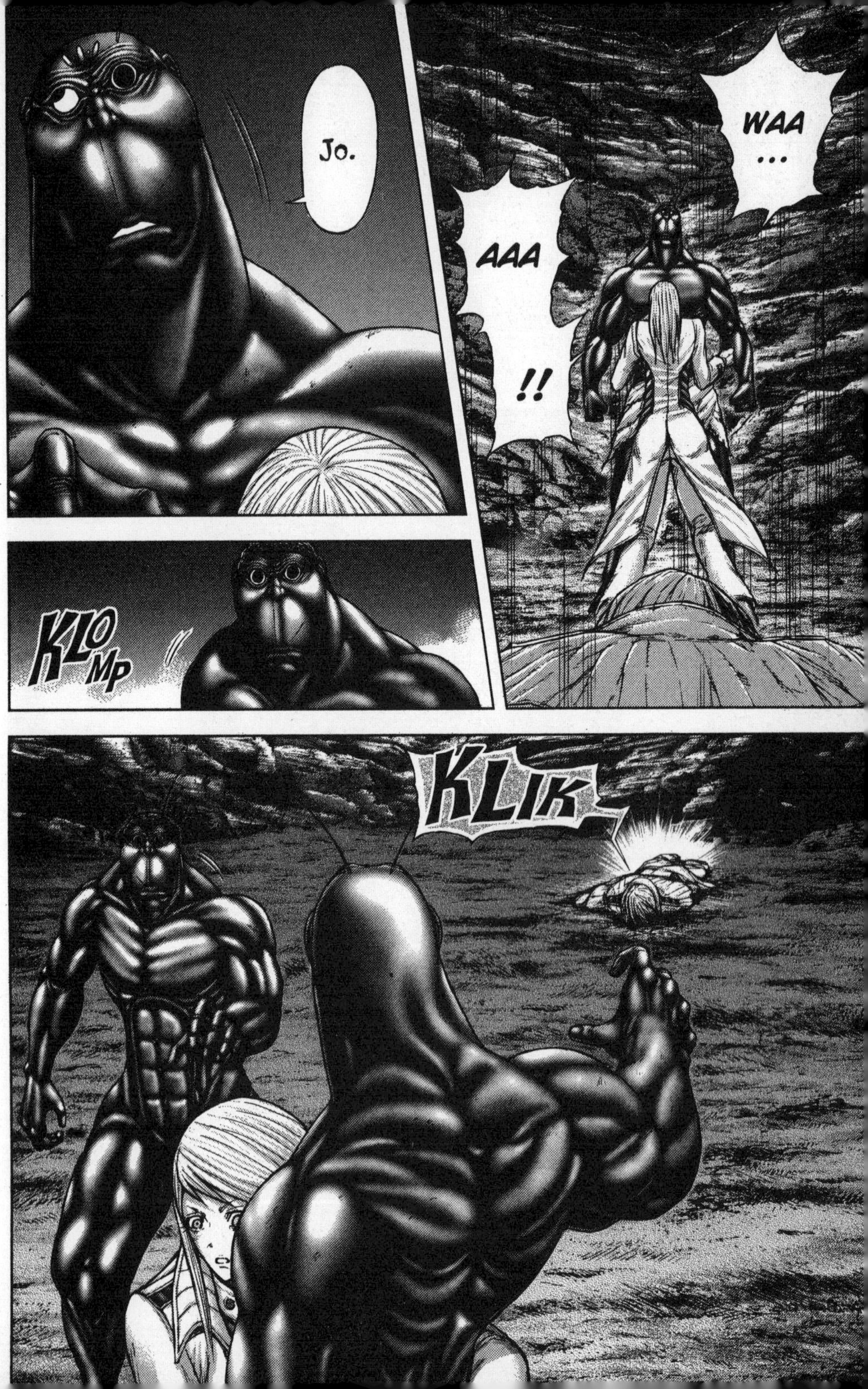
WAA ...
AAA !!
Jo.
KLOMP
KLIK

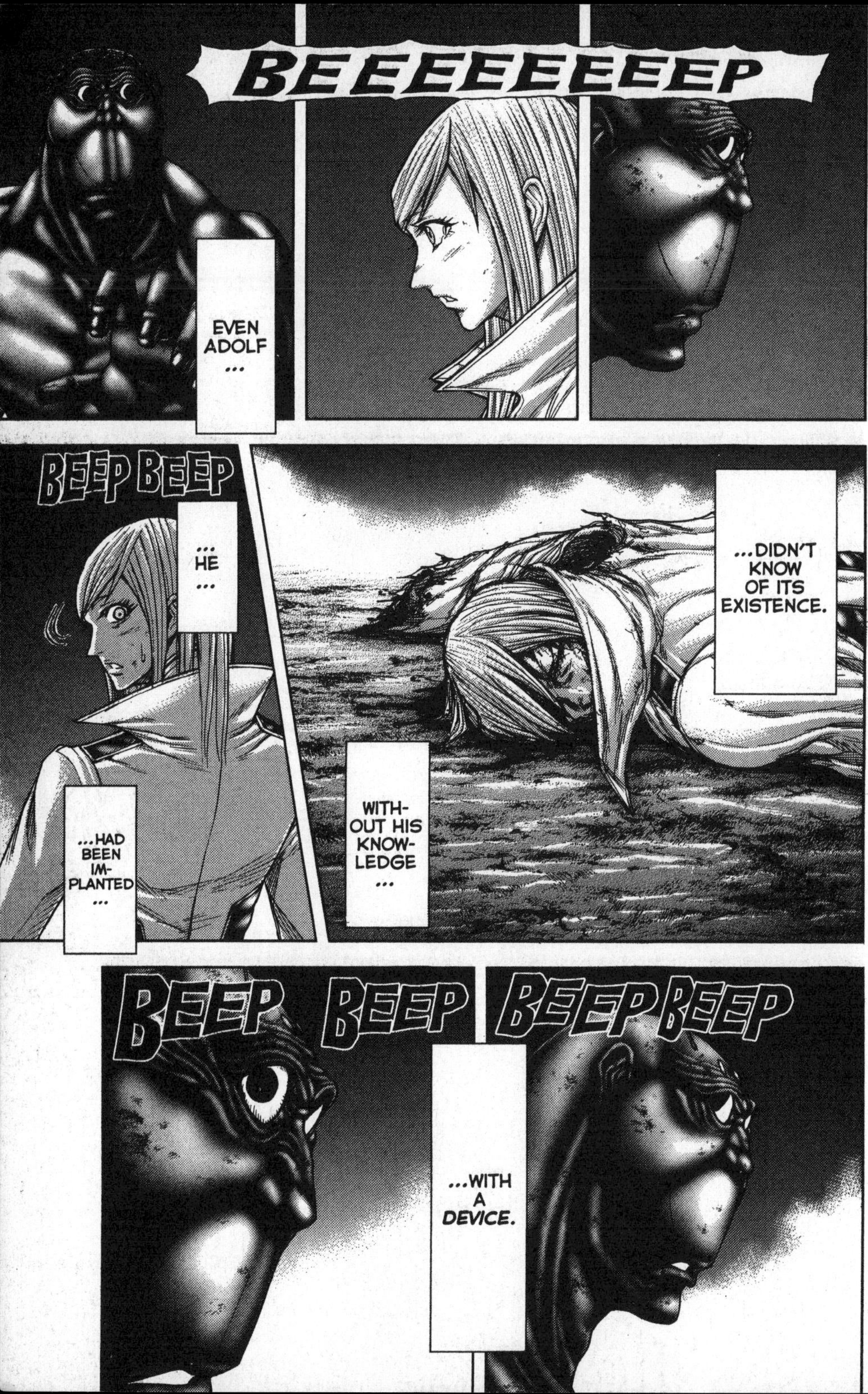
BEEEEEEEEP
EVEN ADOLF ...
BEEP BEEP
... HE ...
... DIDN'T KNOW OF ITS EXISTENCE.
WITH-OUT HIS KNOW-LEDGE ...
... HAD BEEN IM-PLANTED ...
BEEP BEEP BEEP BEEP
... WITH A *DEVICE*.

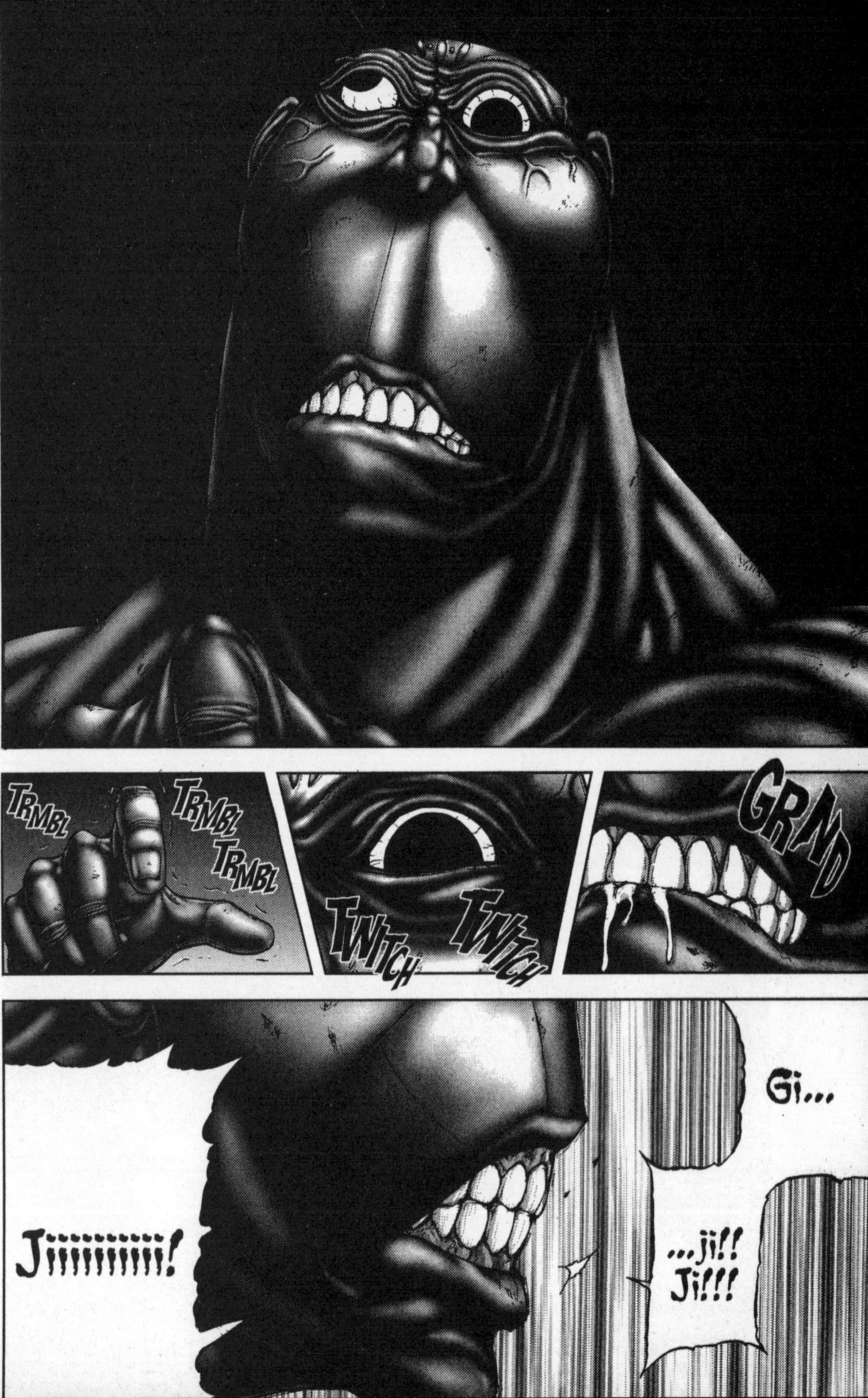
GRND
TWITCH
TWITCH
TRMBL
TRMBL
TRMBL
Gi...
...ji!!
Ji!!!
Jiiiiiiiiii!

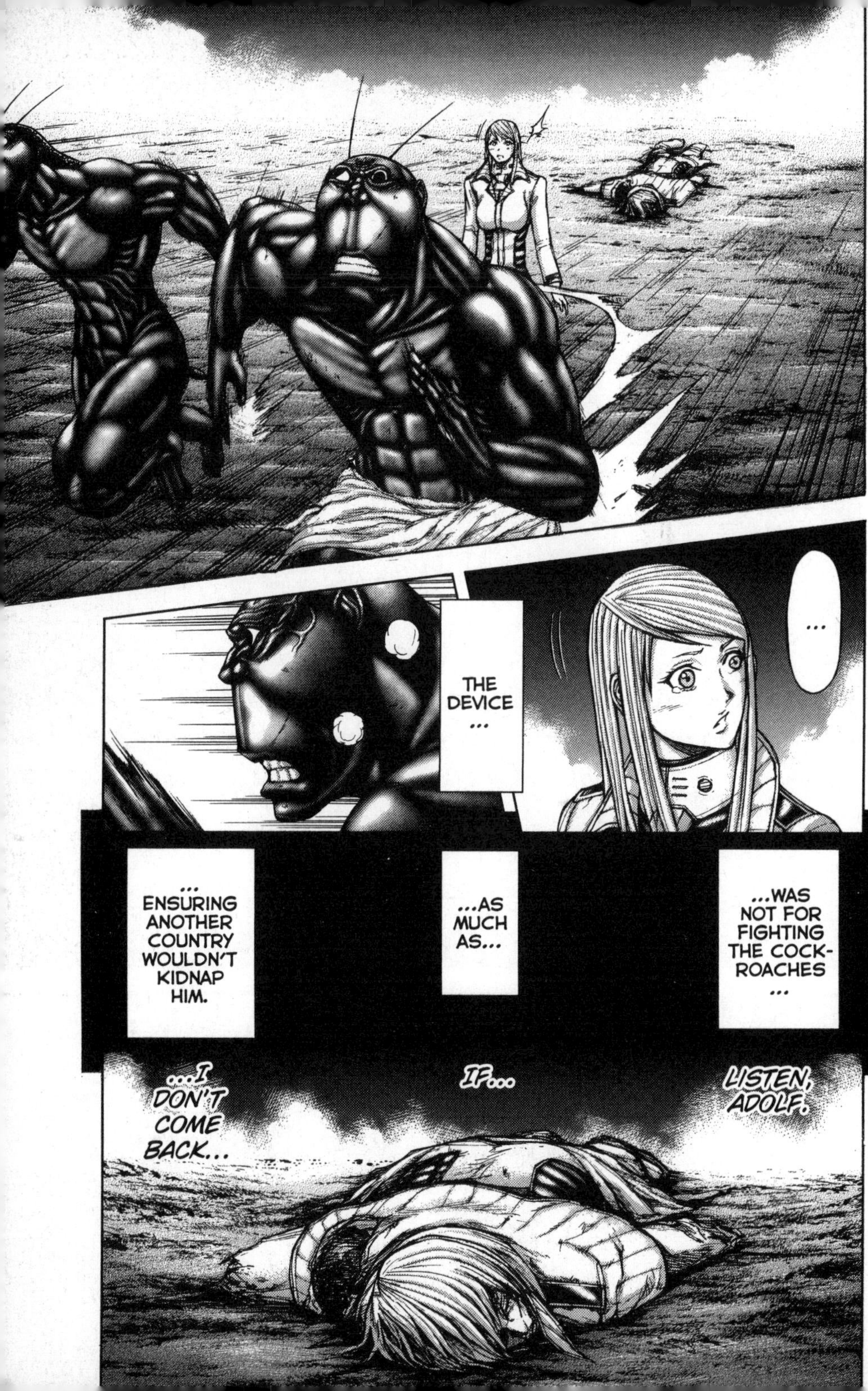
...
THE DEVICE ...
...WAS NOT FOR FIGHTING THE COCK-ROACHES ...
...AS MUCH AS...
... ENSURING ANOTHER COUNTRY WOULDN'T KIDNAP HIM.
LISTEN, ADOLF.
IF...
...I DON'T COME BACK...

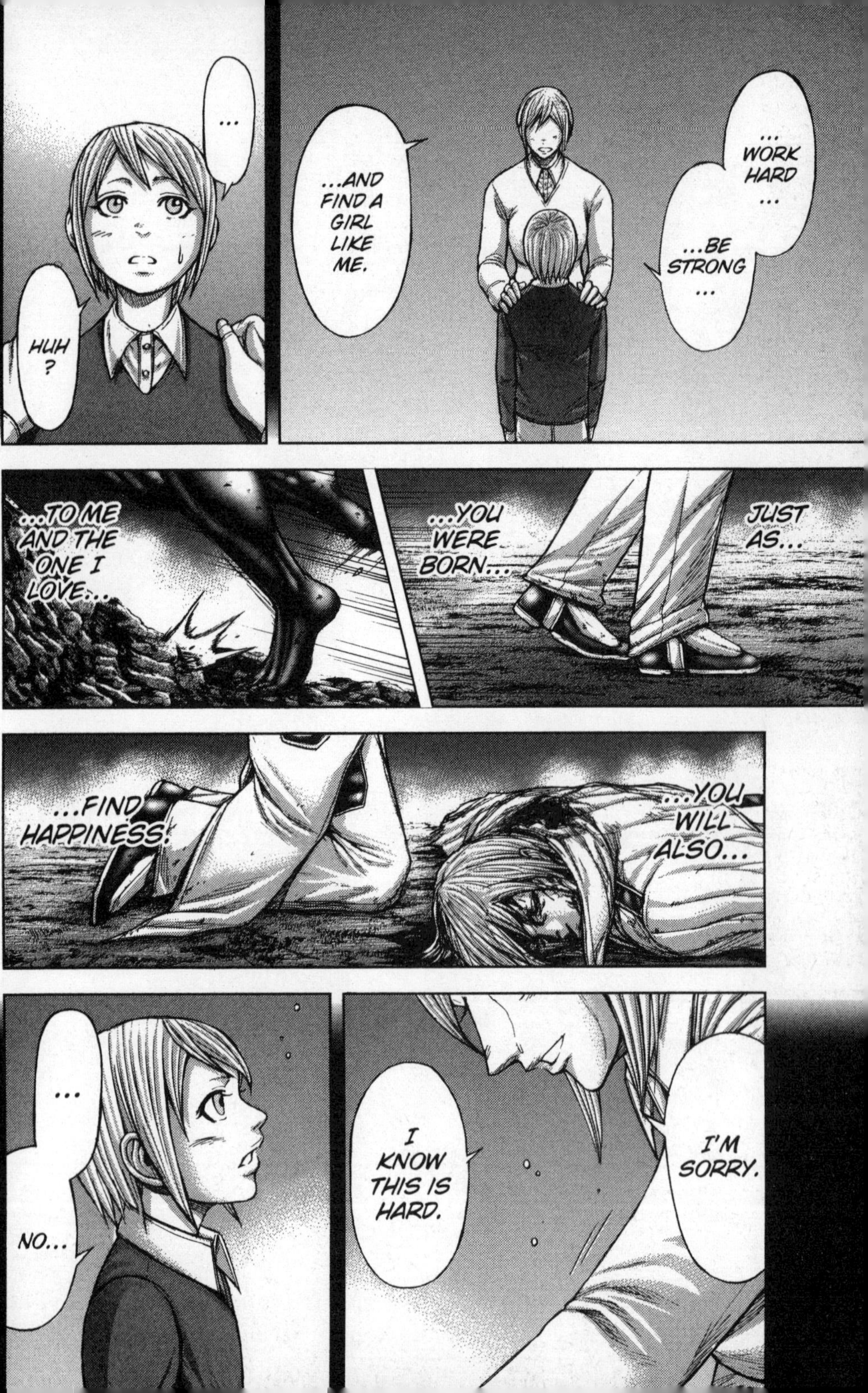
...WORK HARD...
...BE STRONG...
...AND FIND A GIRL LIKE ME.
...
HUH?
JUST AS...
...YOU WERE BORN...
...TO ME AND THE ONE I LOVE...
...YOU WILL ALSO...
...FIND HAPPINESS.
I'M SORRY.
I KNOW THIS IS HARD.
...
NO...

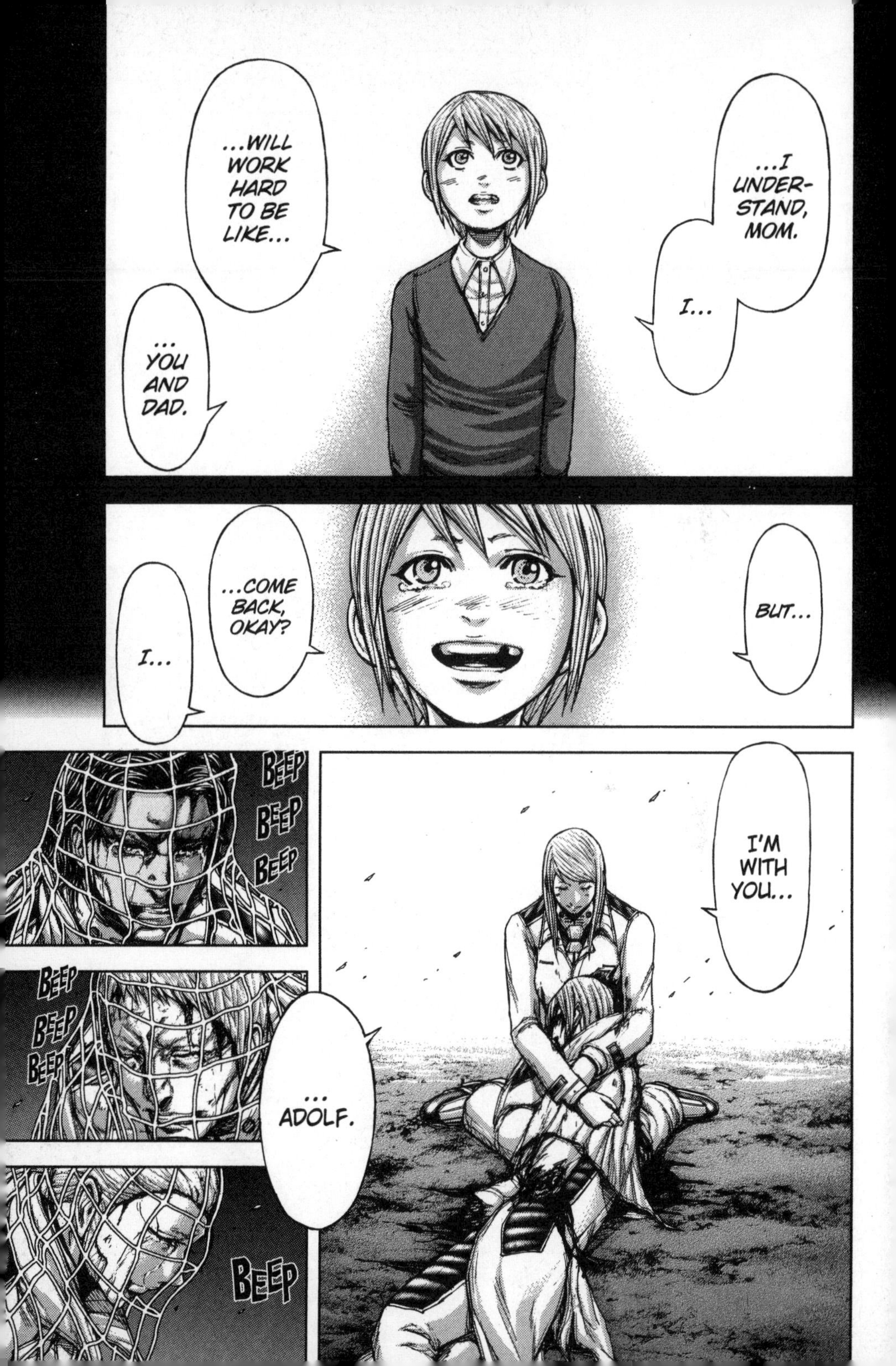
...I UNDER-STAND, MOM.
I...
...WILL WORK HARD TO BE LIKE...
...YOU AND DAD.
BUT...
...COME BACK, OKAY?
I...
I'M WITH YOU...
...ADOLF.
BEEP BEEP BEEP
BEEP BEEP BEEP
BEEP

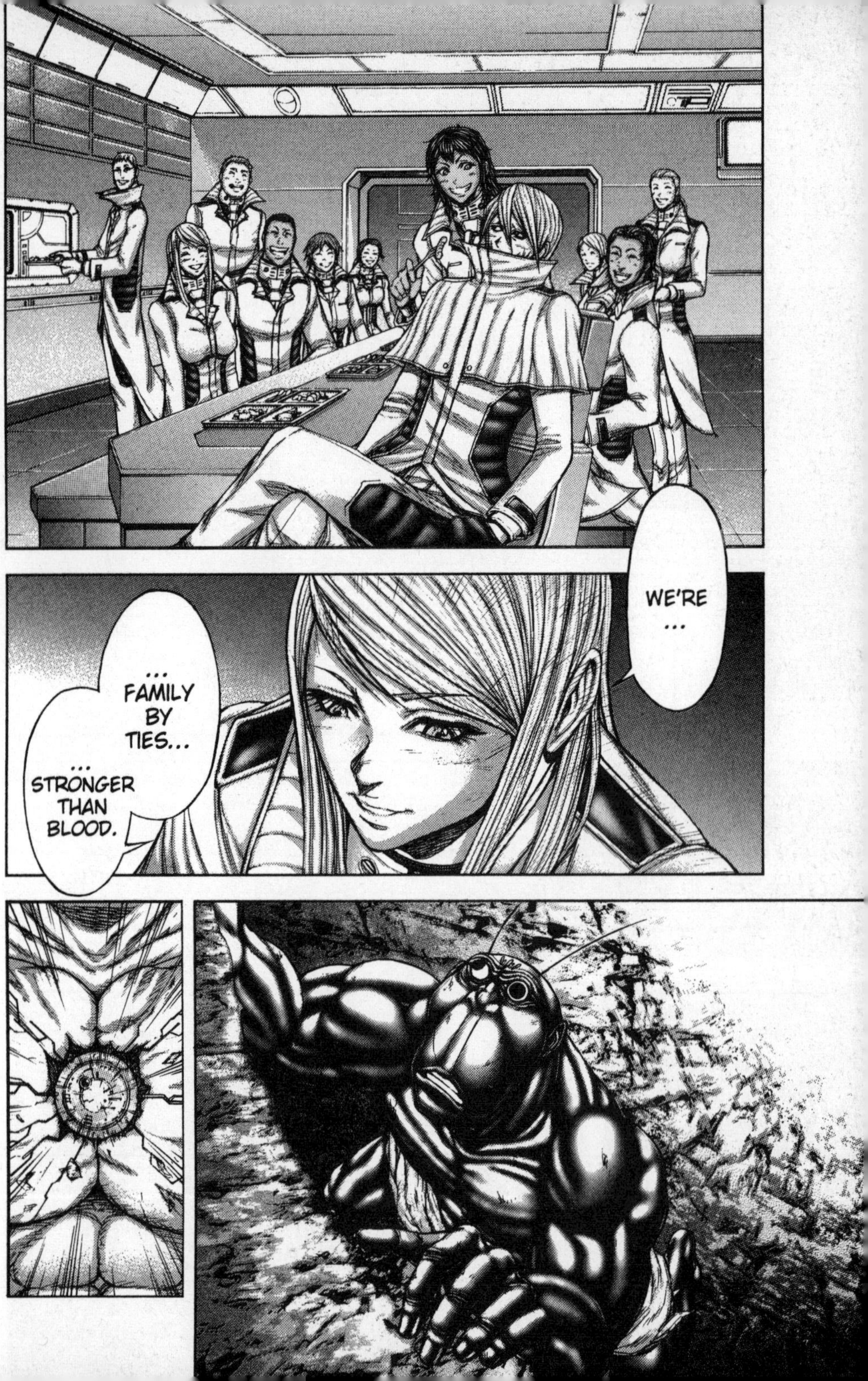
WE'RE ...
... FAMILY BY TIES... ... STRONGER THAN BLOOD.

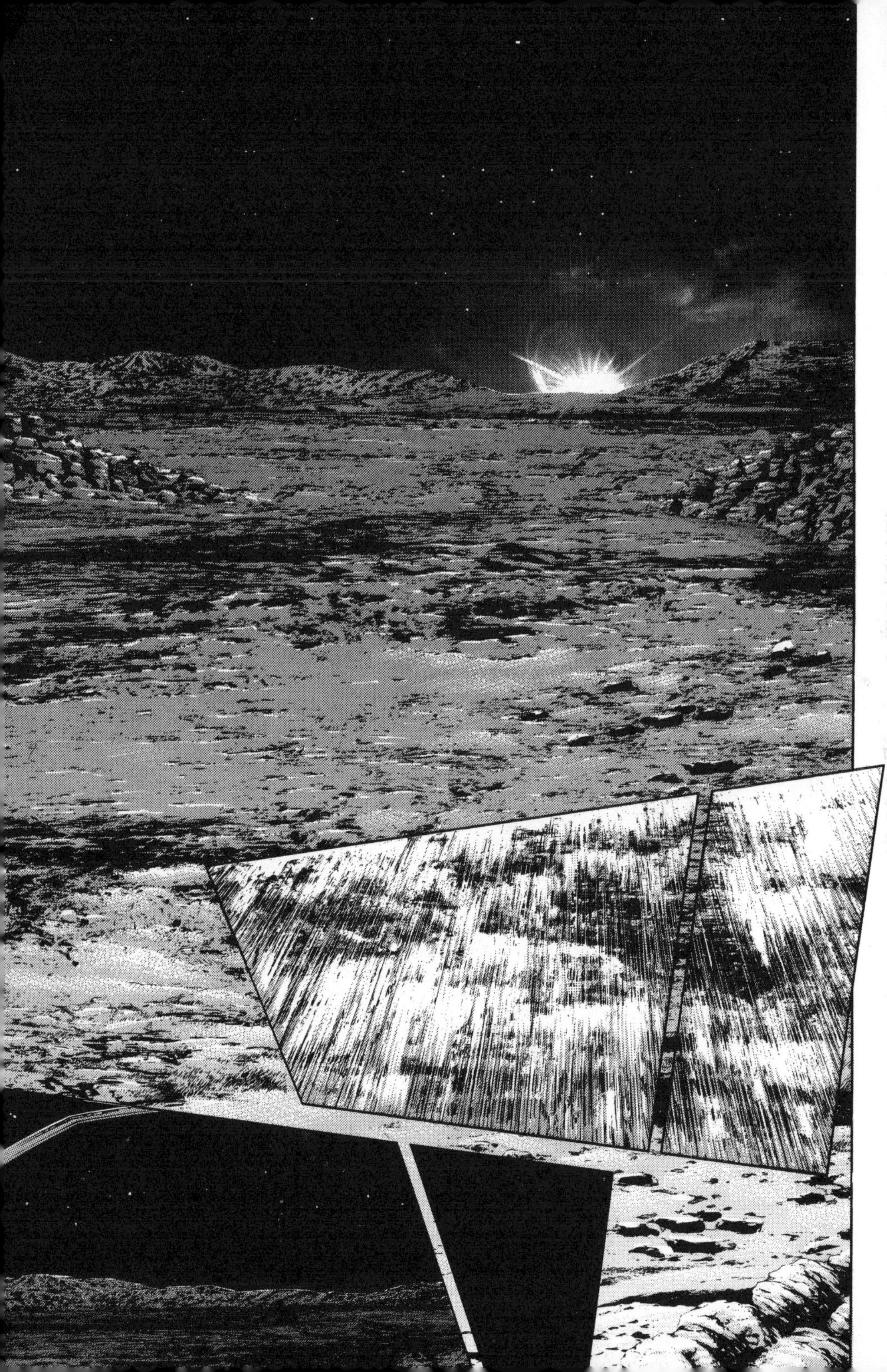

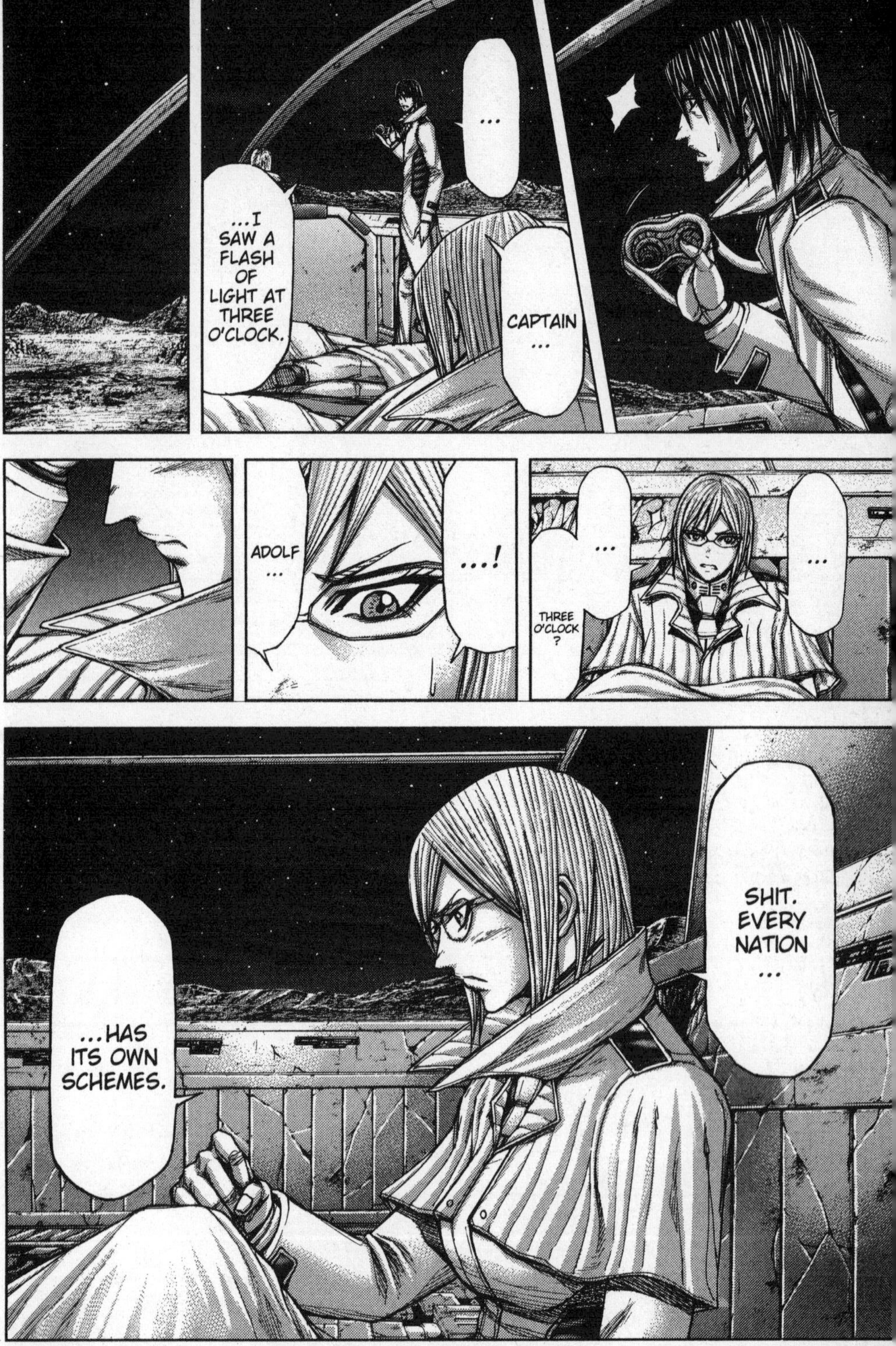
...
CAPTAIN ...
...I SAW A FLASH OF LIGHT AT THREE O'CLOCK.
...
...
THREE O'CLOCK ?
...!
ADOLF ...
SHIT. EVERY NATION ...
...HAS ITS OWN SCHEMES.

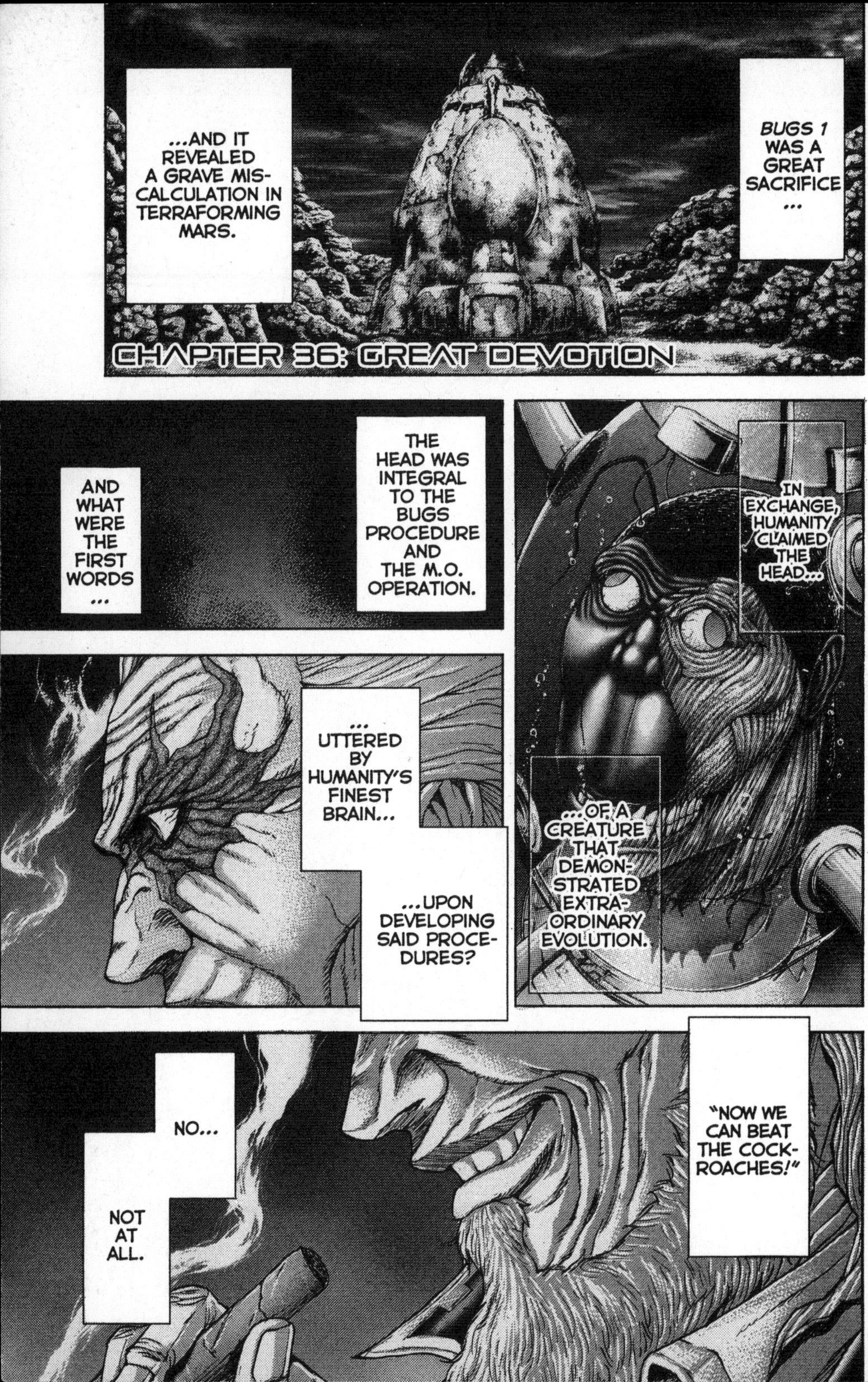
BUGS 1 WAS A GREAT SACRIFICE...
...AND IT REVEALED A GRAVE MIS-CALCULATION IN TERRAFORMING MARS.
CHAPTER 36: GREAT DEVOTION
IN EXCHANGE, HUMANITY CLAIMED THE HEAD...
...OF A CREATURE THAT DEMON-STRATED EXTRA-ORDINARY EVOLUTION.
THE HEAD WAS INTEGRAL TO THE BUGS PROCEDURE AND THE M.O. OPERATION.
AND WHAT WERE THE FIRST WORDS...
...UTTERED BY HUMANITY'S FINEST BRAIN...
...UPON DEVELOPING SAID PROCE-DURES?
"NOW WE CAN BEAT THE COCK-ROACHES!"
NO...
NOT AT ALL.

CHAPTER 36: GREAT DEVOTION

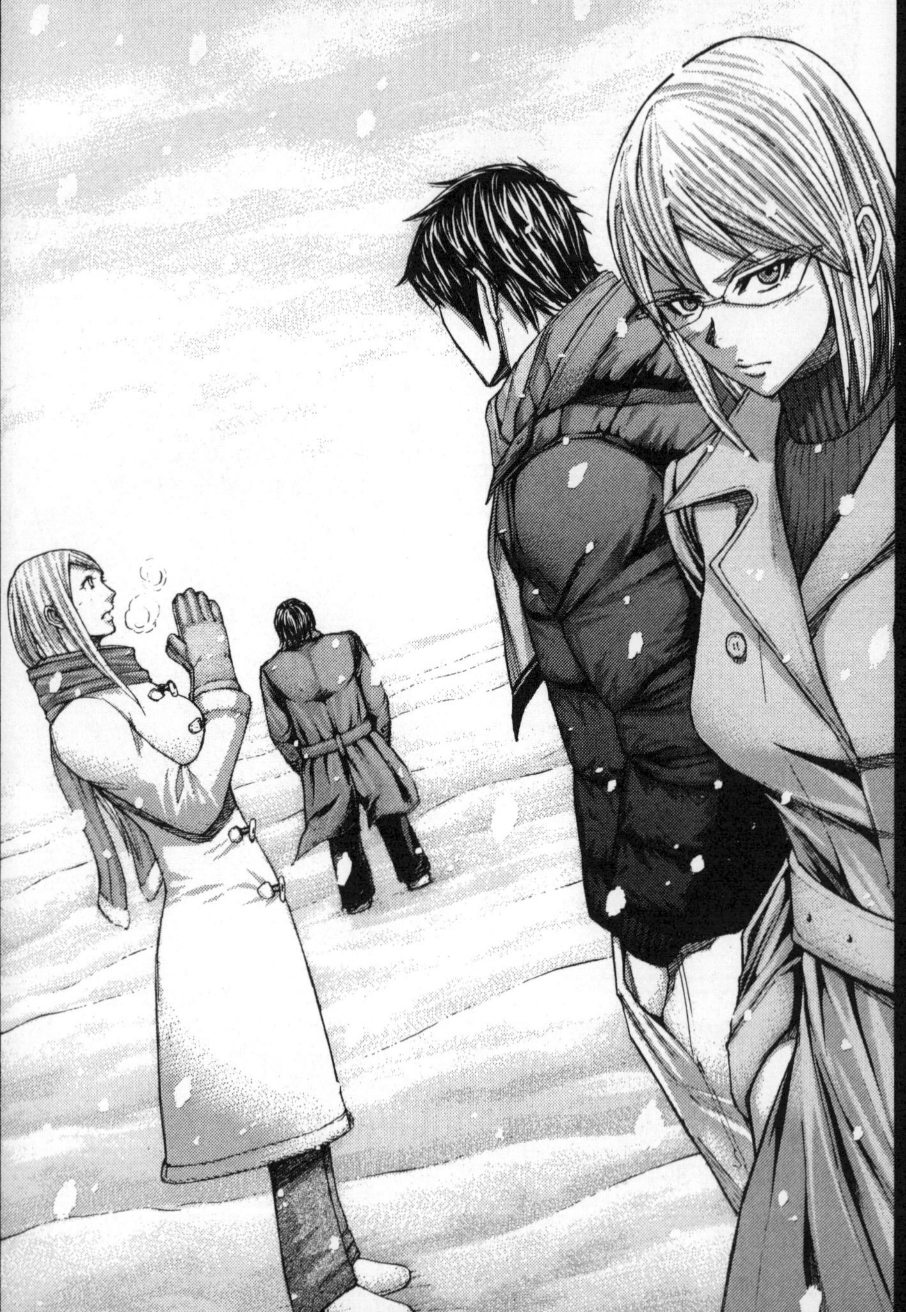

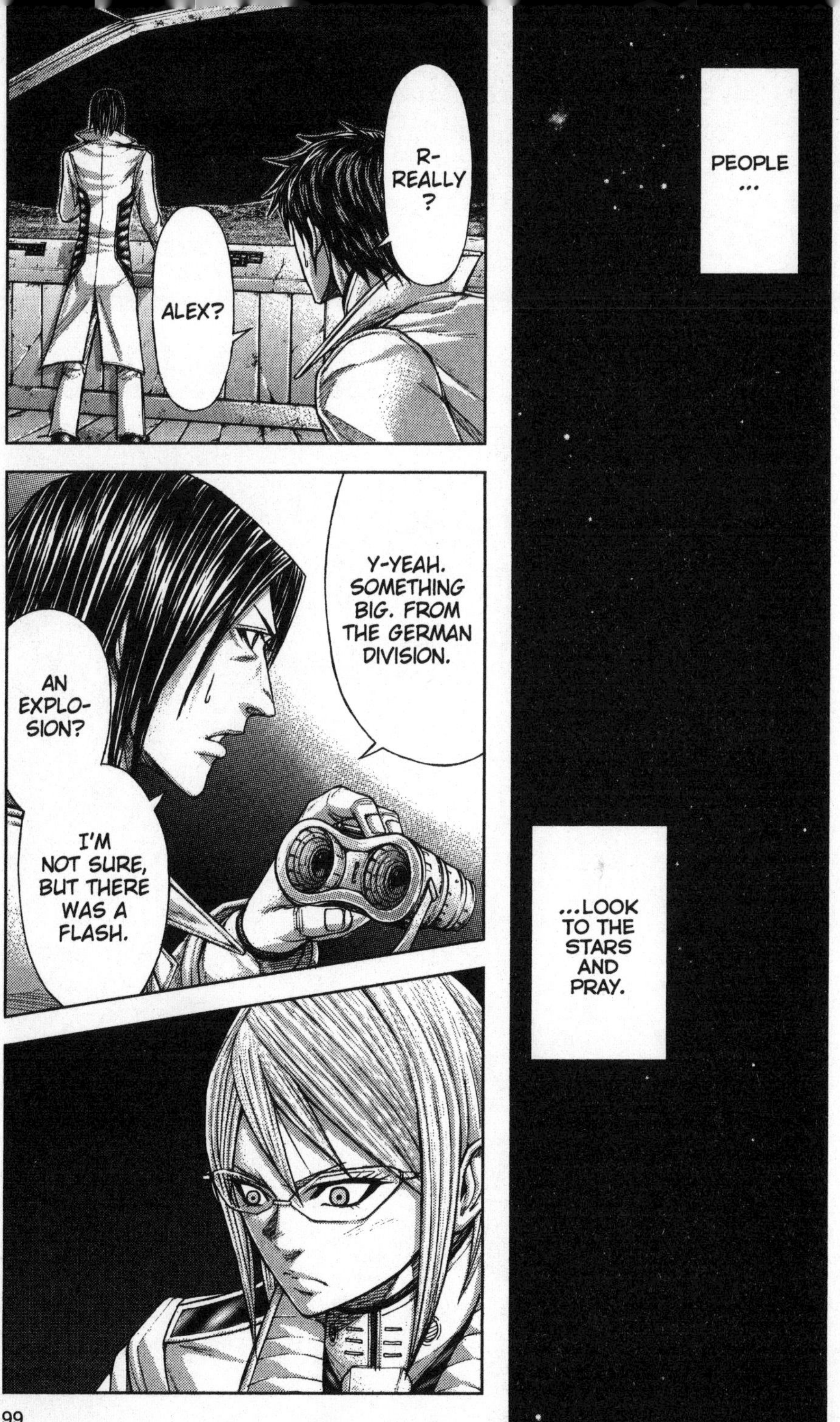
PEOPLE ...
...LOOK TO THE STARS AND PRAY.
R-REALLY?
ALEX?
Y-YEAH. SOMETHING BIG. FROM THE GERMAN DIVISION.
AN EXPLOSION?
I'M NOT SURE, BUT THERE WAS A FLASH.

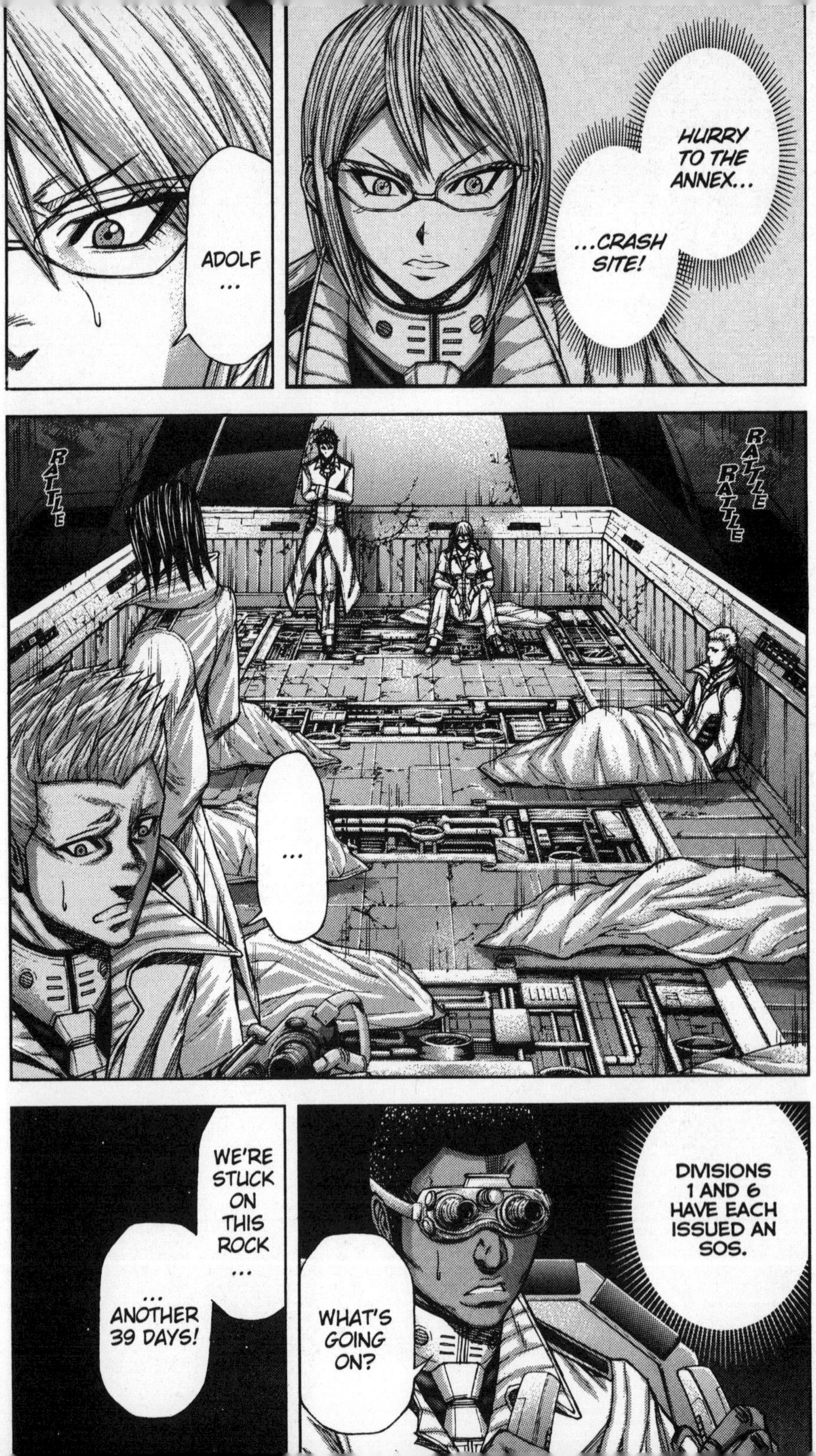
HURRY TO THE ANNEX...
...CRASH SITE!
ADOLF ...
RATTLE RATTLE
RATTLE
...
DIVISIONS 1 AND 6 HAVE EACH ISSUED AN SOS.
WHAT'S GOING ON?
WE'RE STUCK ON THIS ROCK ...
... ANOTHER 39 DAYS!

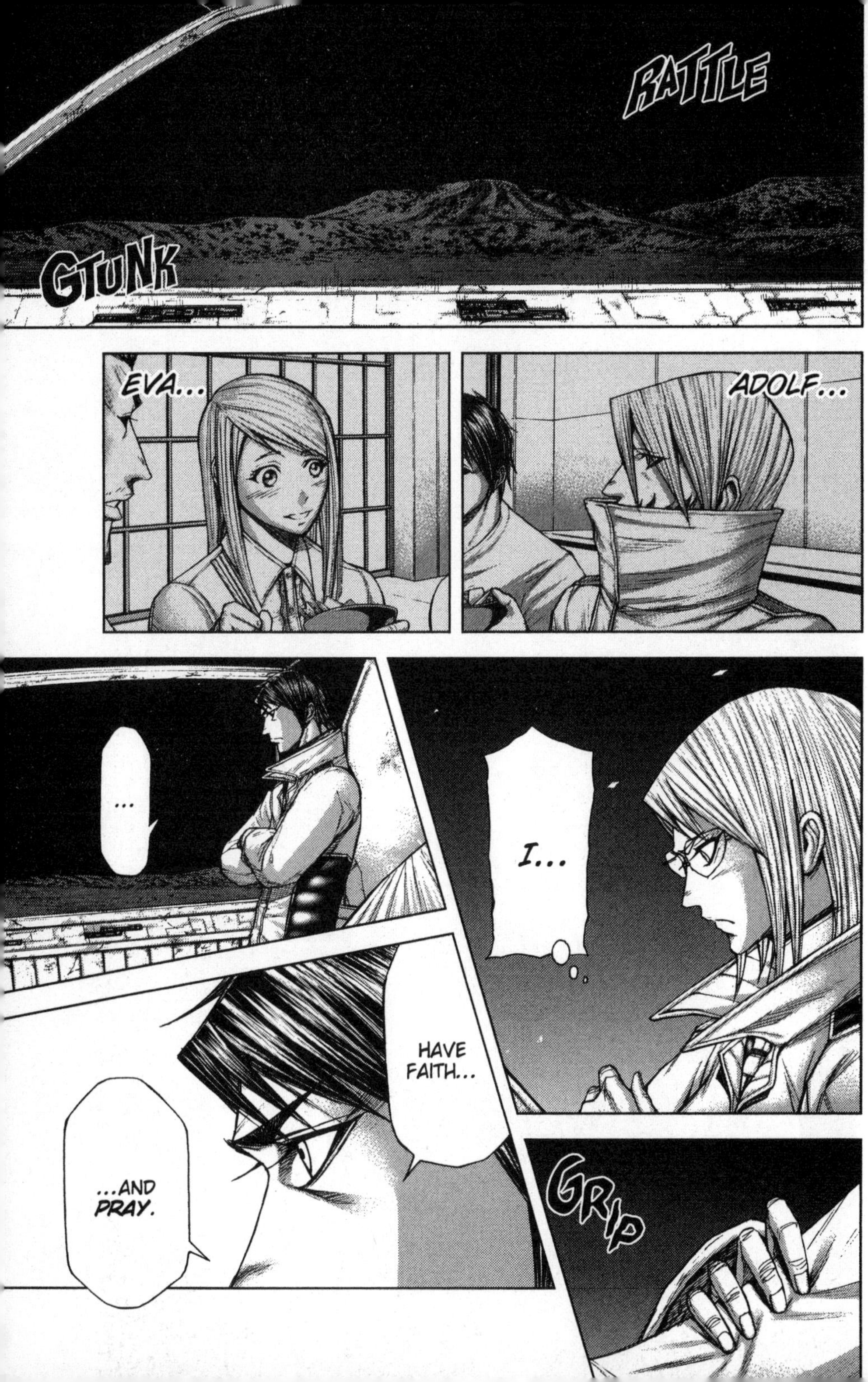
RATTLE
GTUNK
ADOLF...
EVA...
I...
...
HAVE FAITH...
...AND PRAY.
GRIP

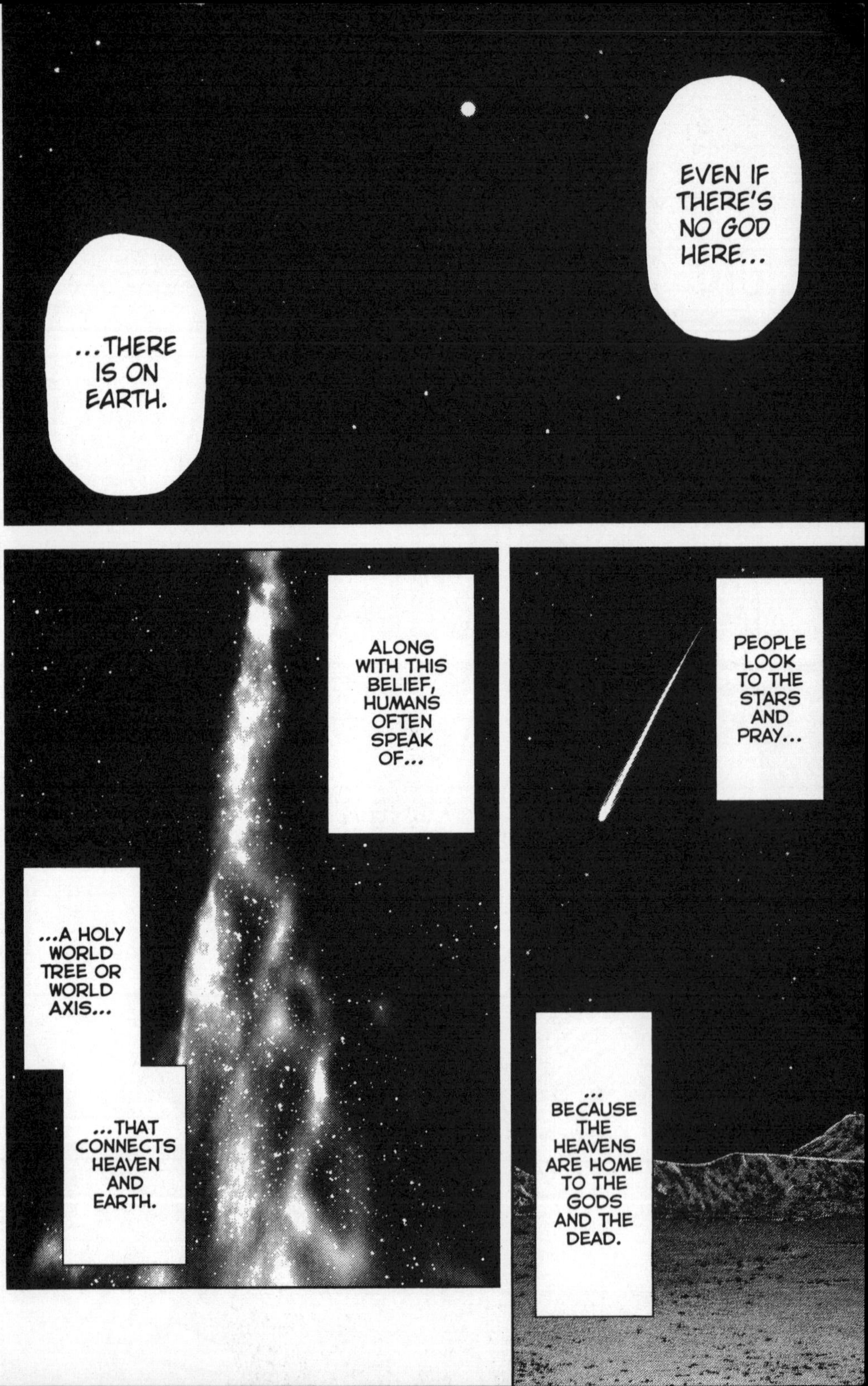
EVEN IF THERE'S NO GOD HERE...
...THERE IS ON EARTH.
PEOPLE LOOK TO THE STARS AND PRAY...
...BECAUSE THE HEAVENS ARE HOME TO THE GODS AND THE DEAD.
ALONG WITH THIS BELIEF, HUMANS OFTEN SPEAK OF...
...A HOLY WORLD TREE OR WORLD AXIS...
...THAT CONNECTS HEAVEN AND EARTH.

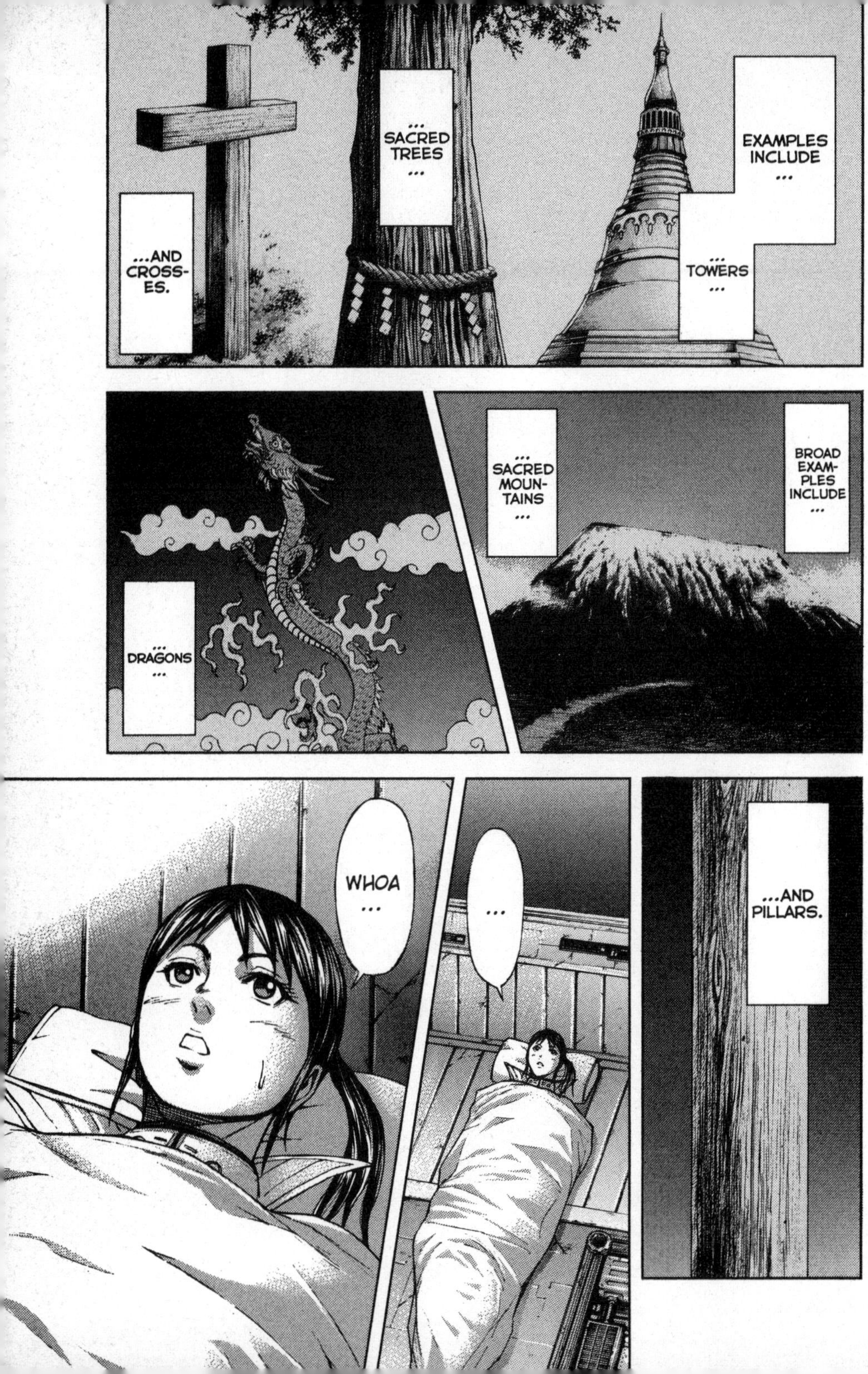
EXAMPLES INCLUDE ...
... TOWERS ...
... SACRED TREES ...
...AND CROSS-ES.
BROAD EXAM-PLES INCLUDE ...
... SACRED MOUN-TAINS ...
... DRAGONS ...
...AND PILLARS.
...
WHOA ...

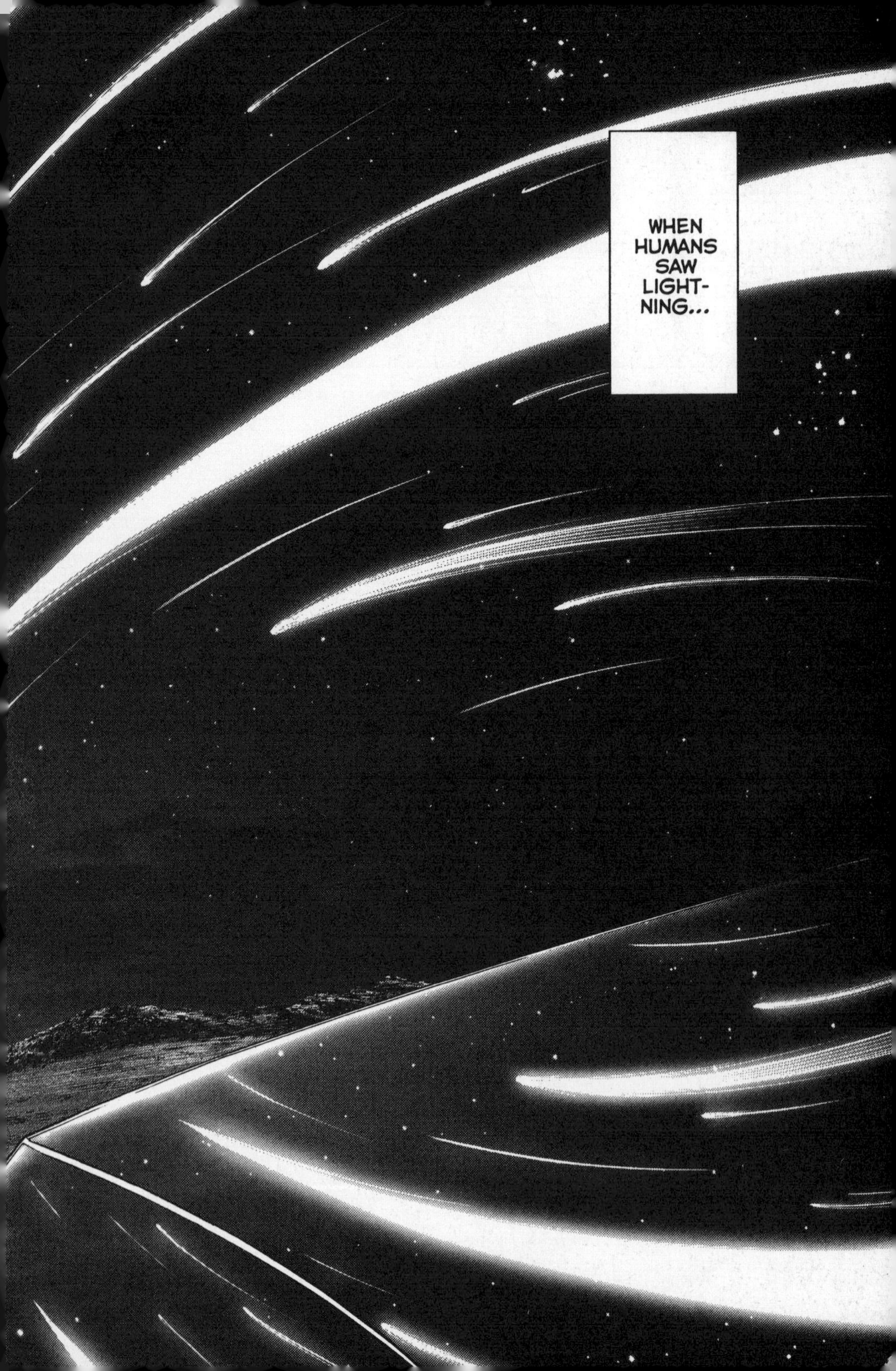
WHEN HUMANS SAW LIGHTNING...

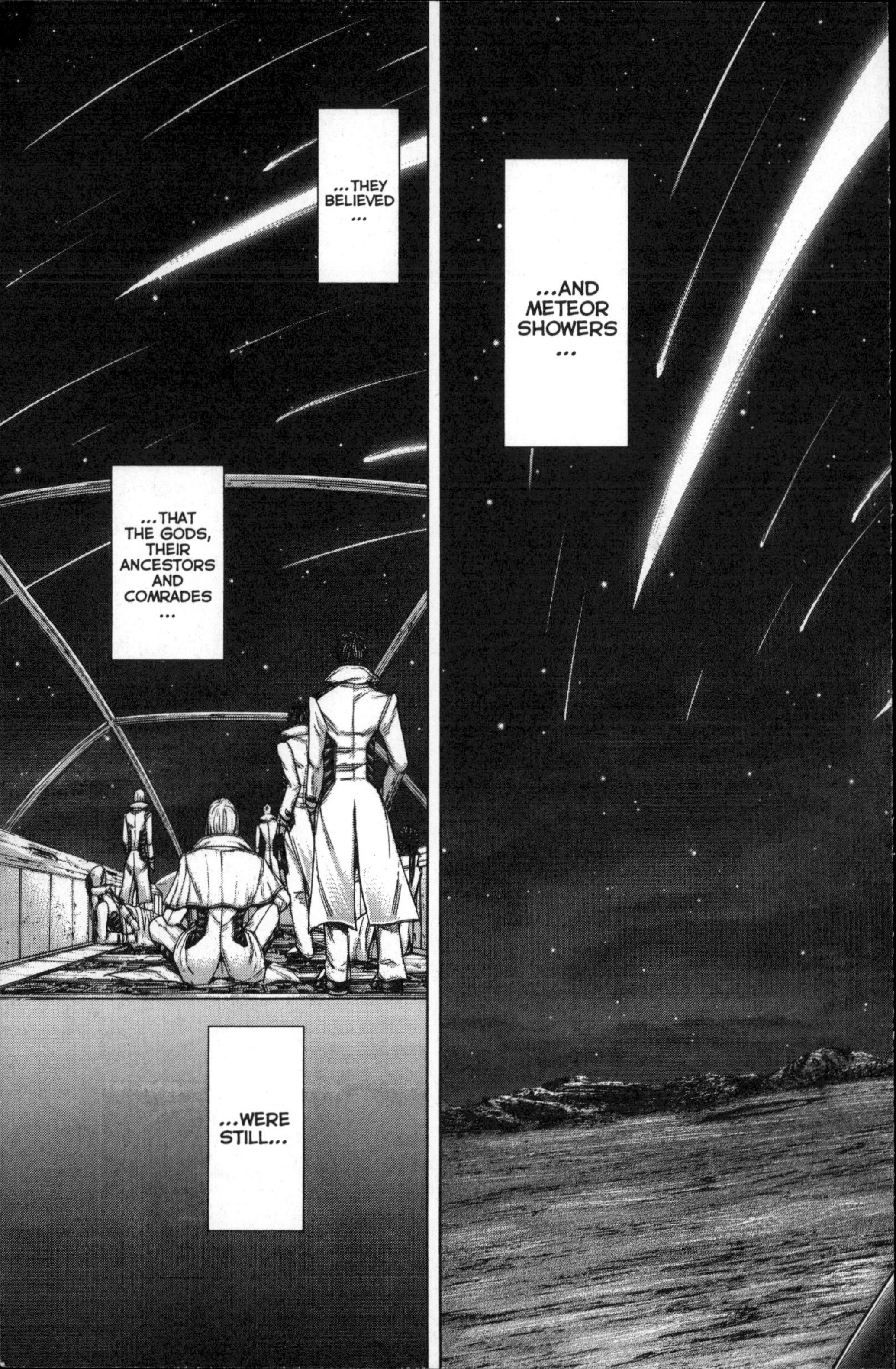
...AND METEOR SHOWERS...
...THEY BELIEVED...
...THAT THE GODS, THEIR ANCESTORS AND COMRADES...
...WERE STILL...

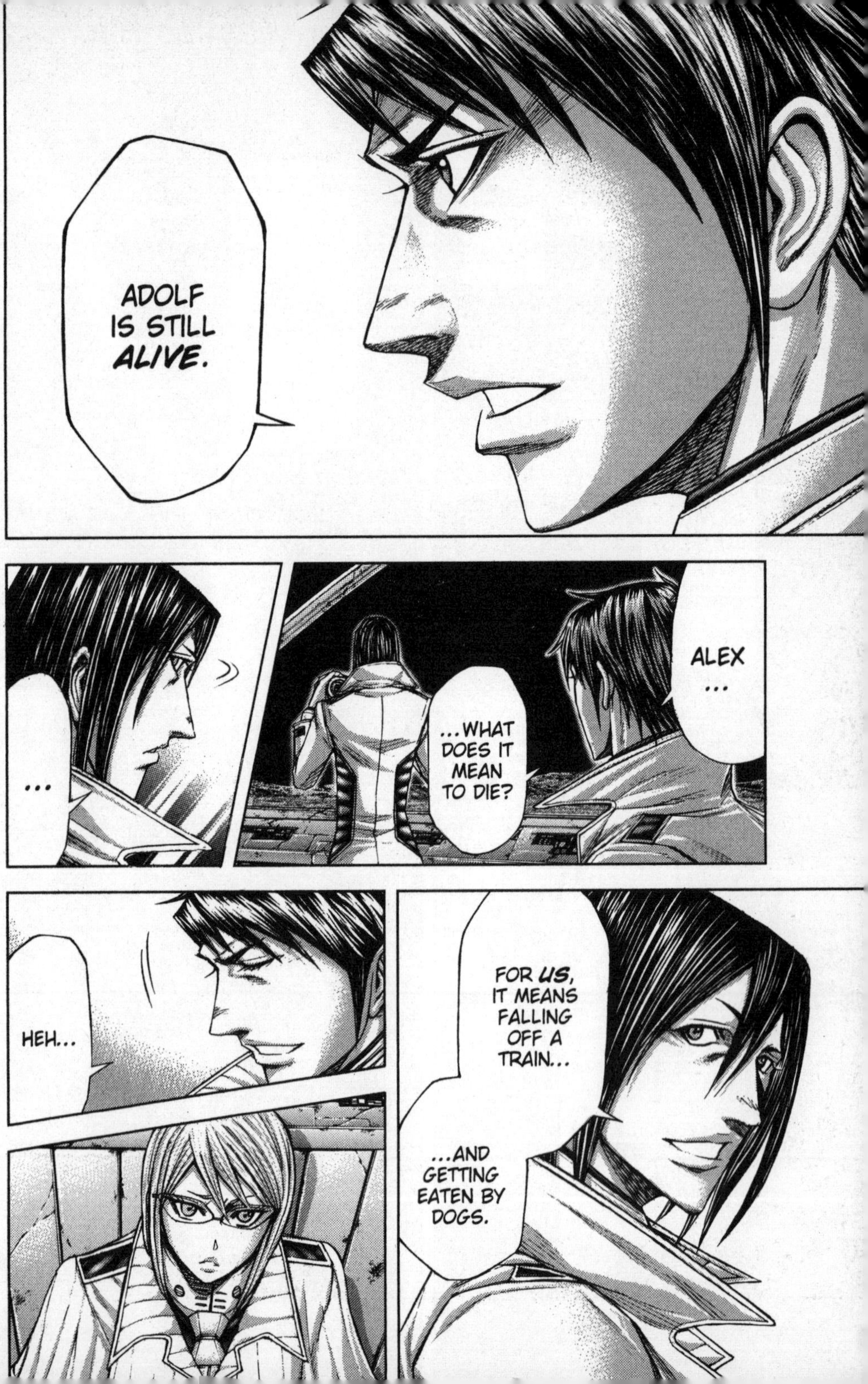
ADOLF IS STILL ALIVE.
ALEX ...
...WHAT DOES IT MEAN TO DIE?
...
FOR US, IT MEANS FALLING OFF A TRAIN...
...AND GETTING EATEN BY DOGS.
HEH...

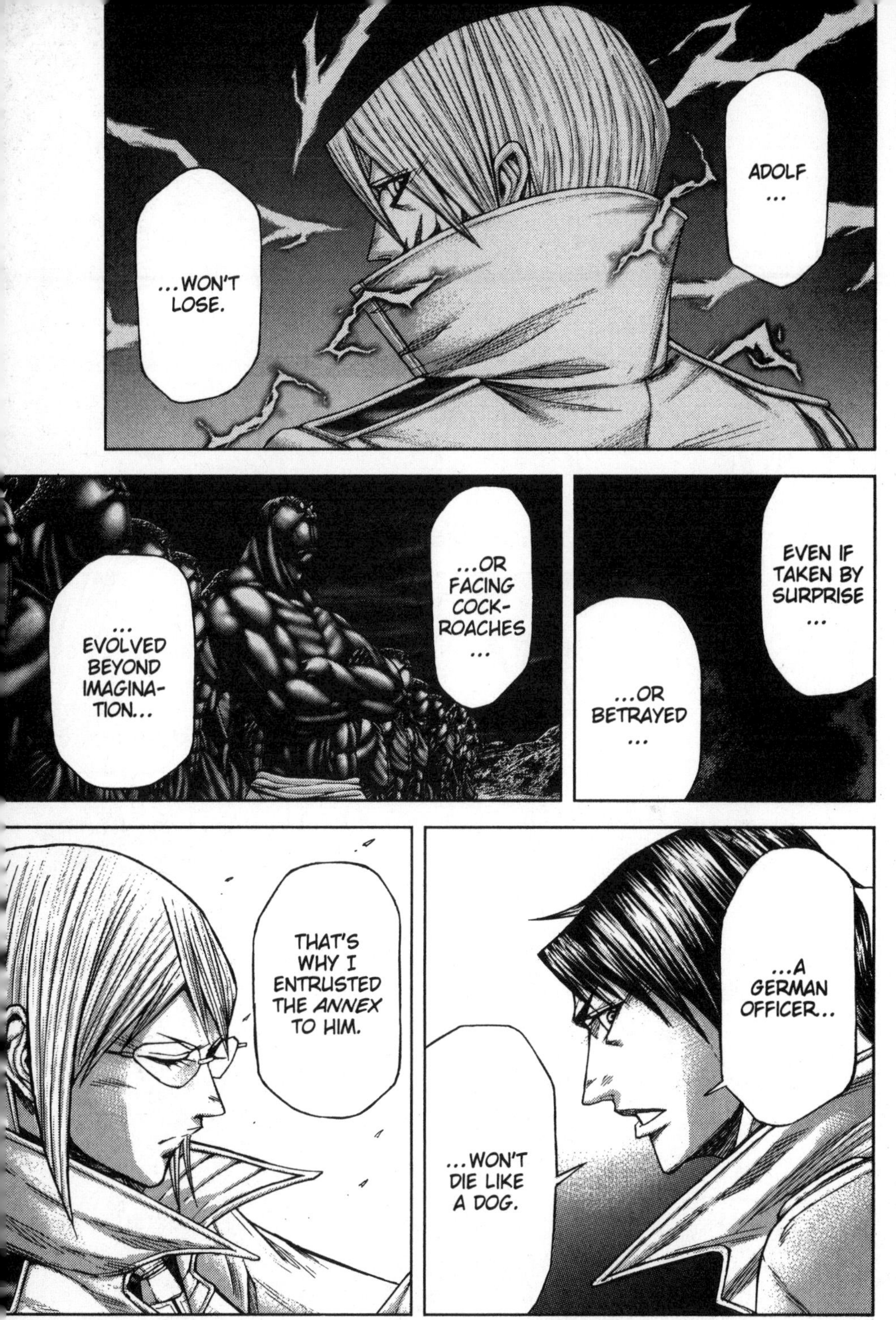
ADOLF ...
...WON'T LOSE.
EVEN IF TAKEN BY SURPRISE ...
...OR BETRAYED ...
...OR FACING COCK-ROACHES ...
... EVOLVED BEYOND IMAGINA-TION...
...A GERMAN OFFICER...
...WON'T DIE LIKE A DOG.
THAT'S WHY I ENTRUSTED THE *ANNEX* TO HIM.

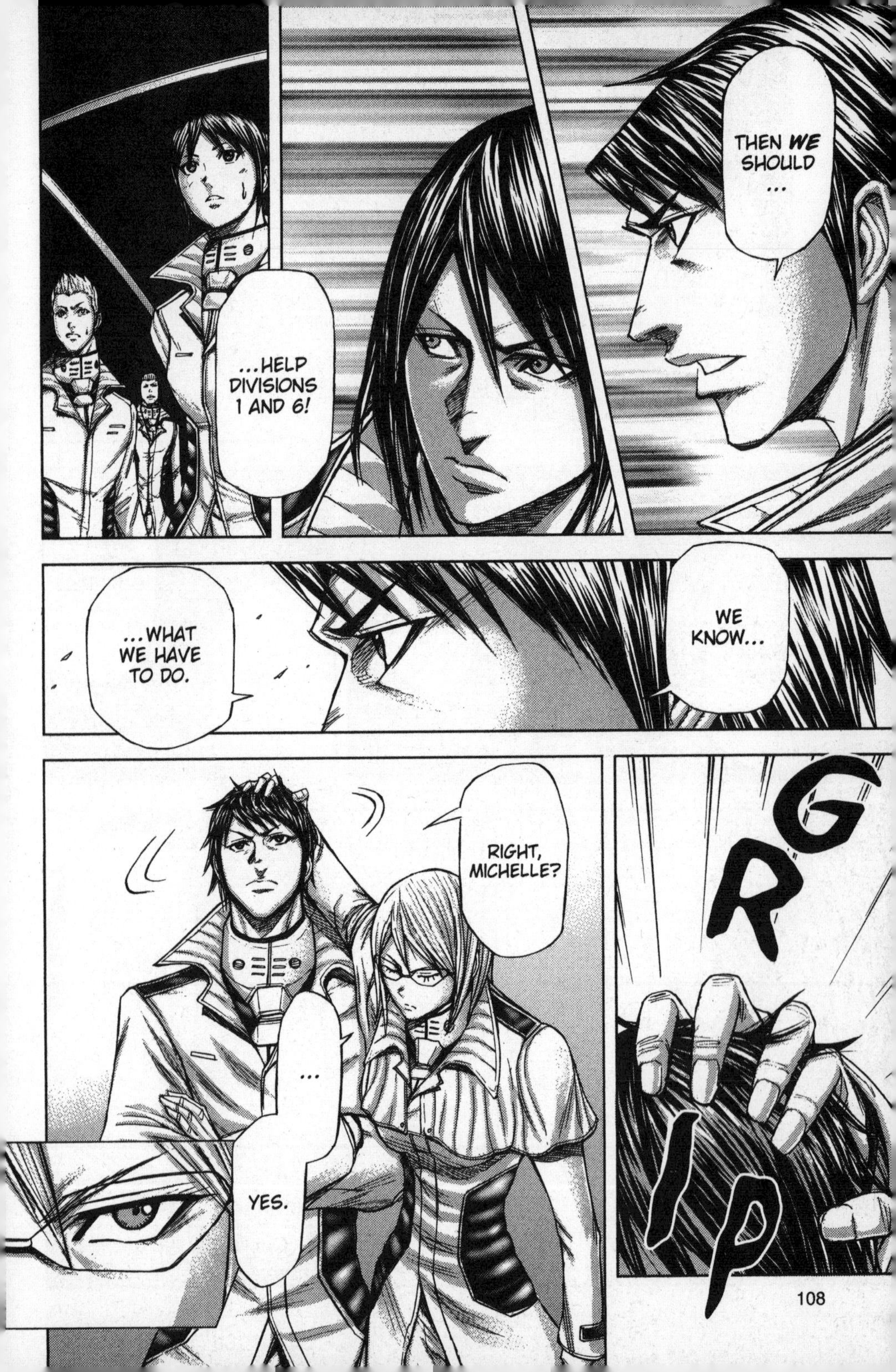

THEN *WE* SHOULD ...
...HELP DIVISIONS 1 AND 6!
WE KNOW...
...WHAT WE HAVE TO DO.
GRIP
RIGHT, MICHELLE?
...
YES.

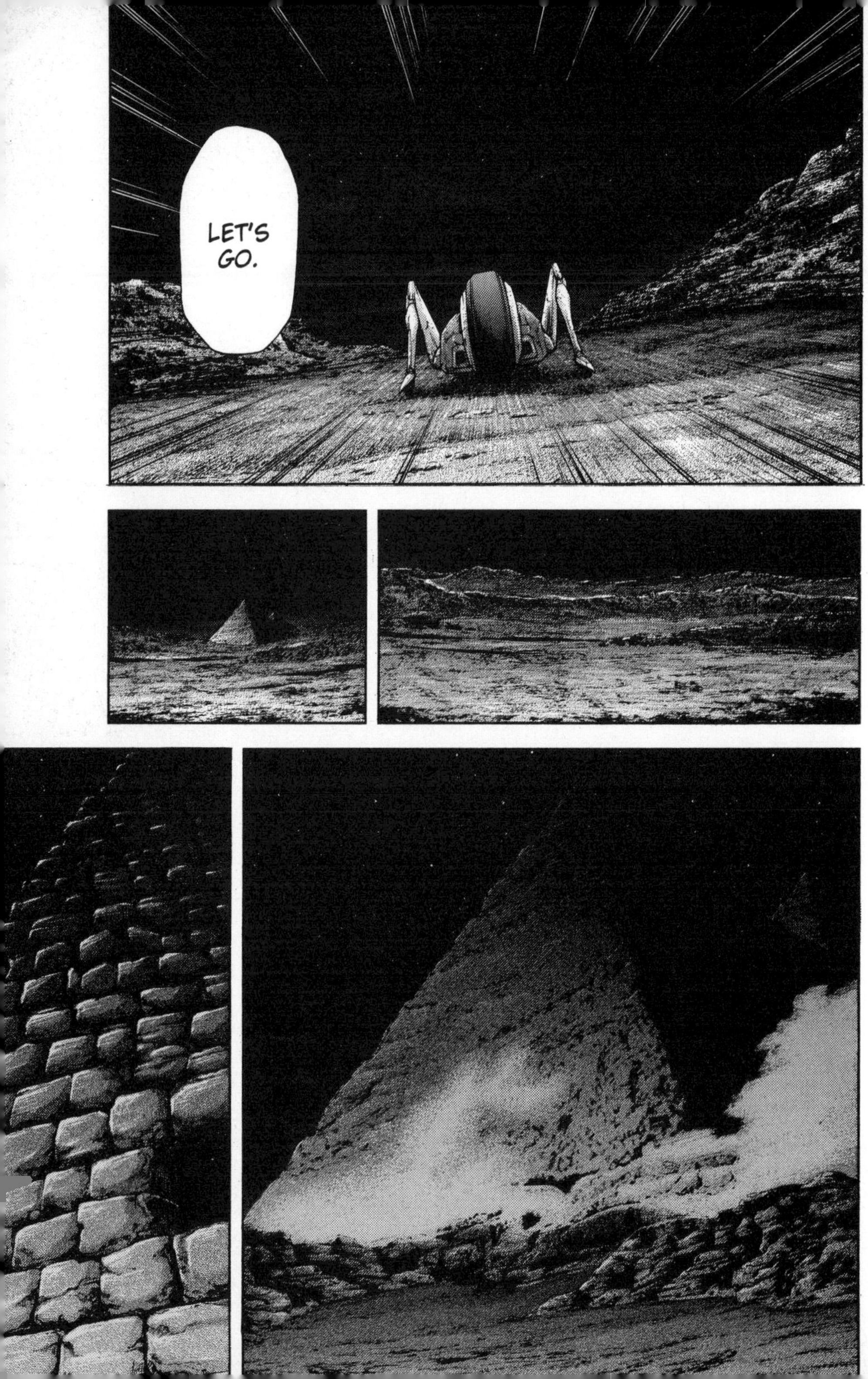
LET'S GO.

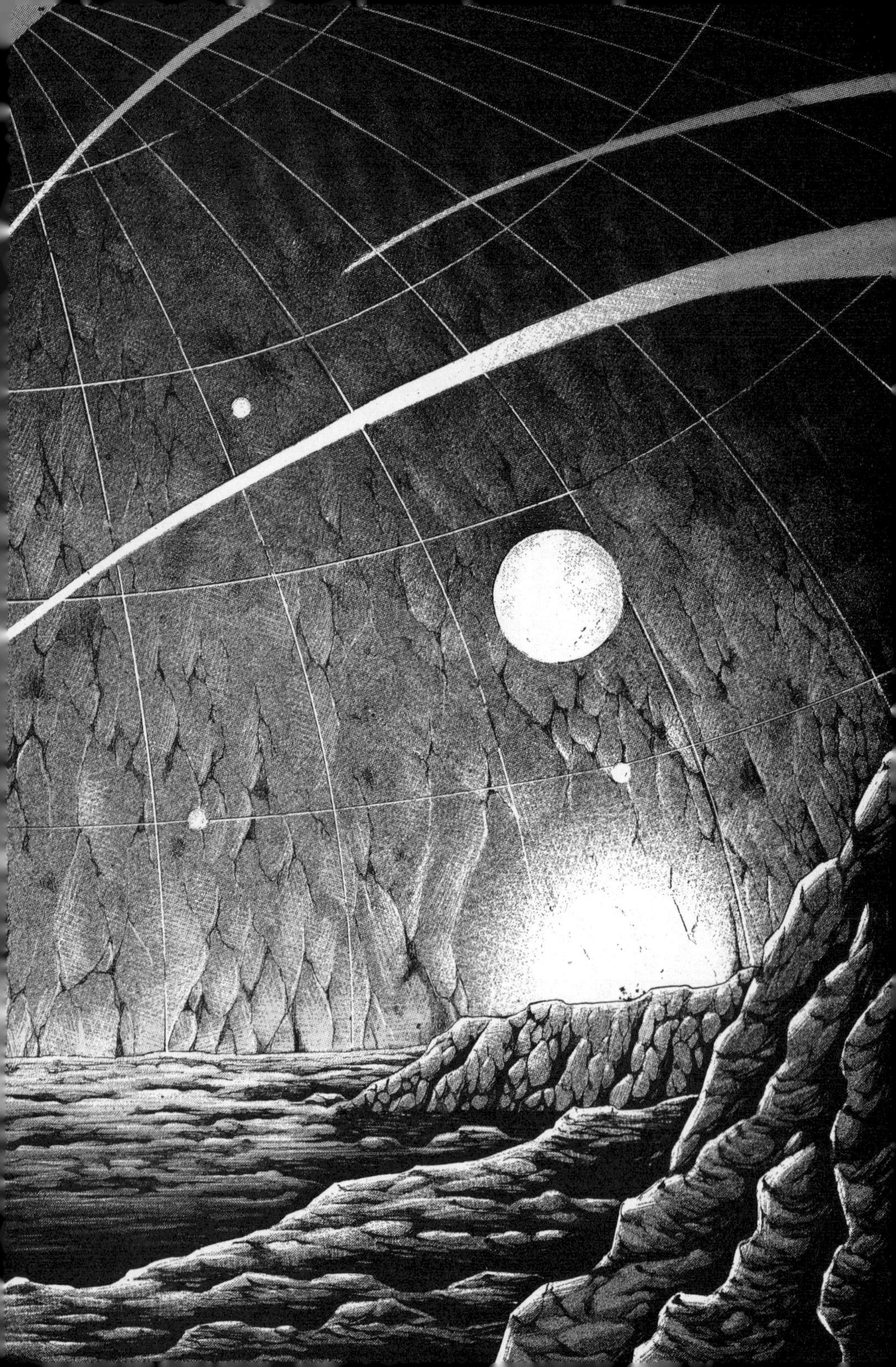

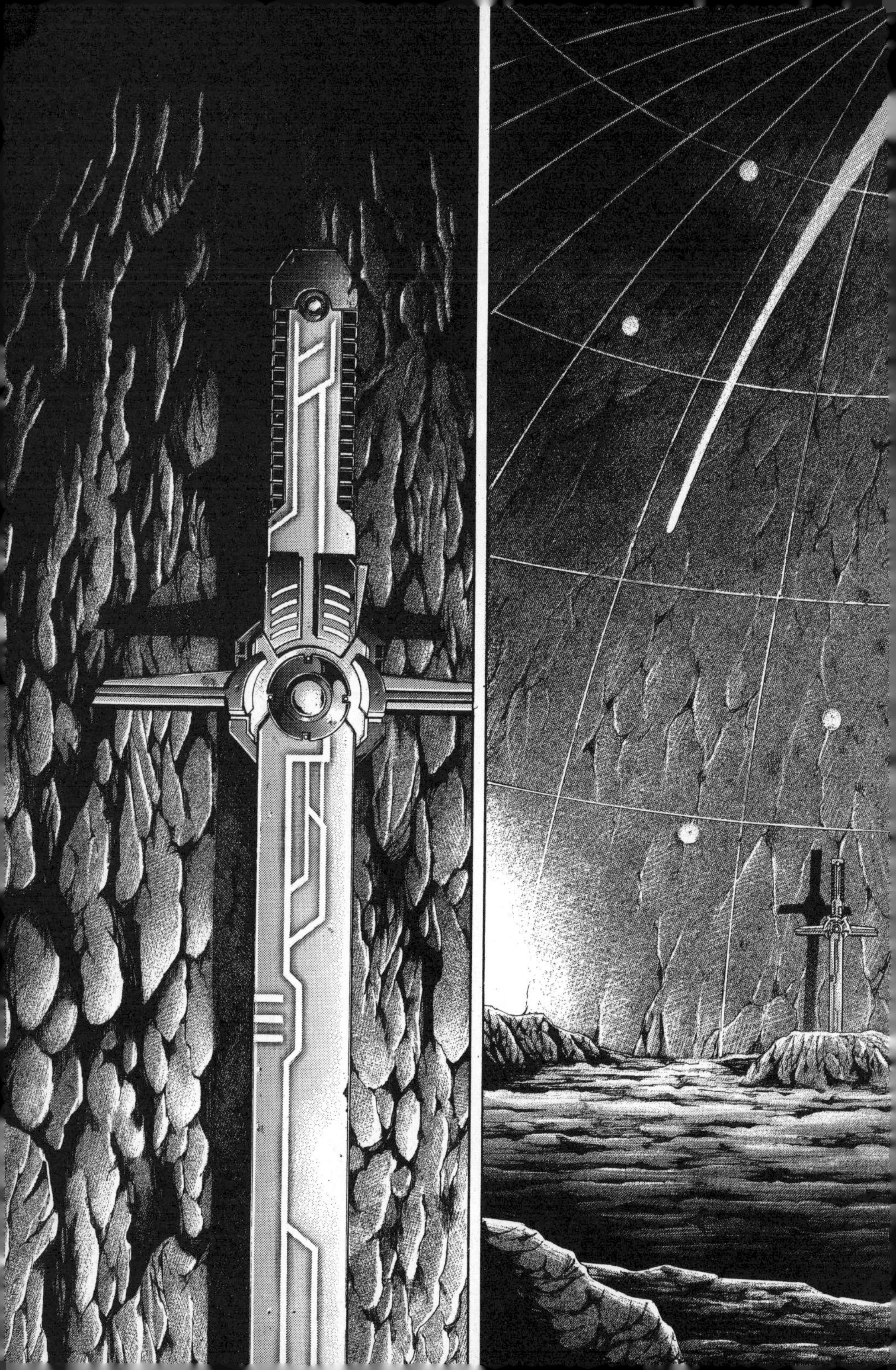

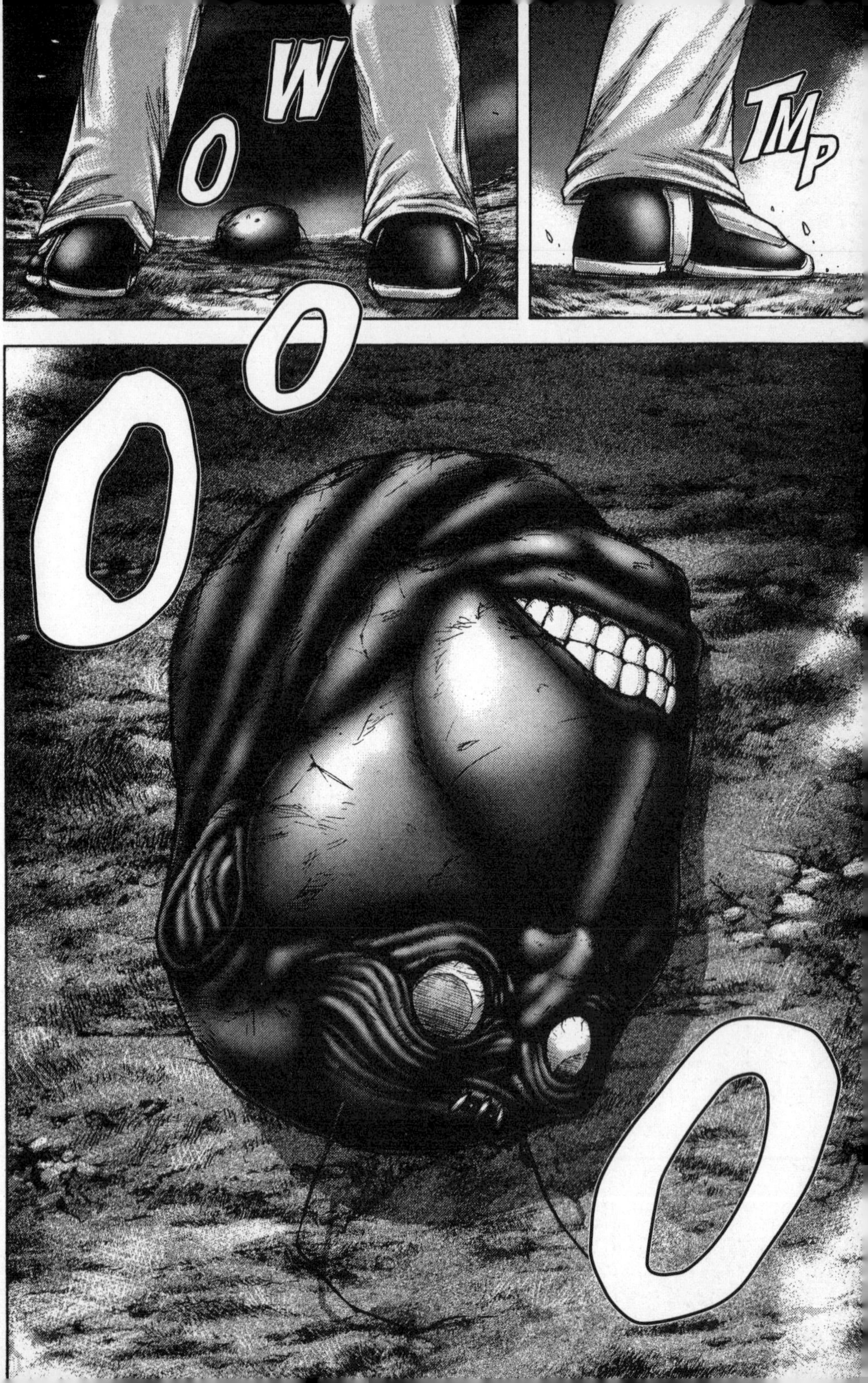
TMP
WOOOO

THE GERMAN DIVISION...

ADOLF...

THAT GIRL...

EVA...

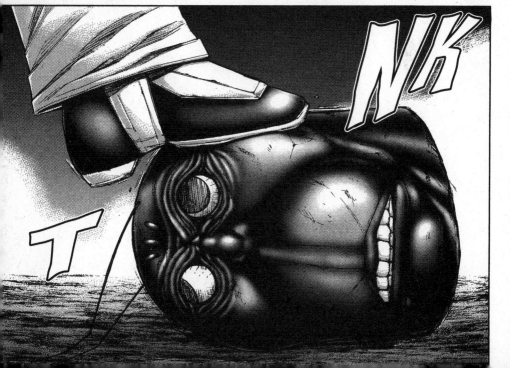

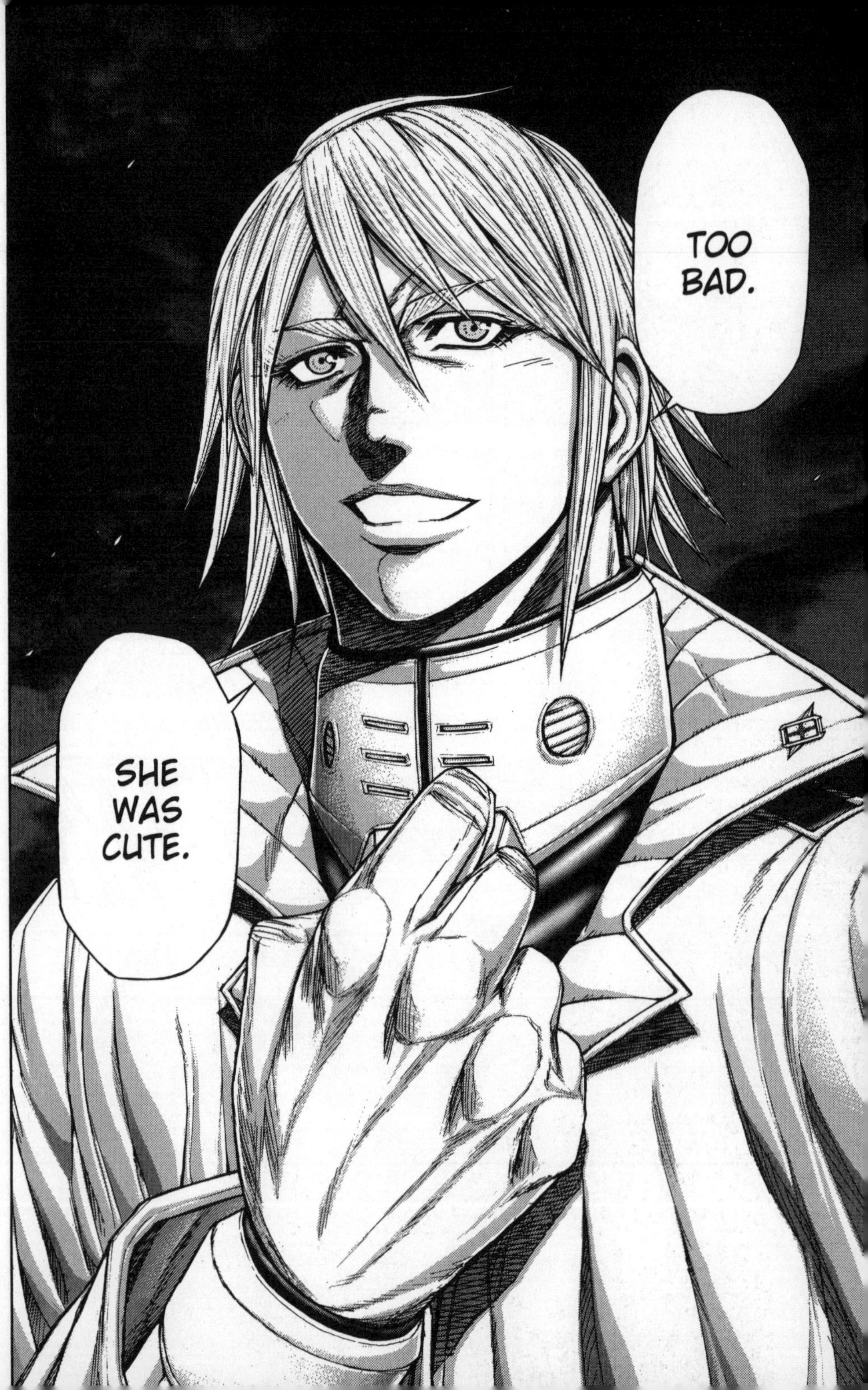
TOO BAD.
SHE WAS CUTE.

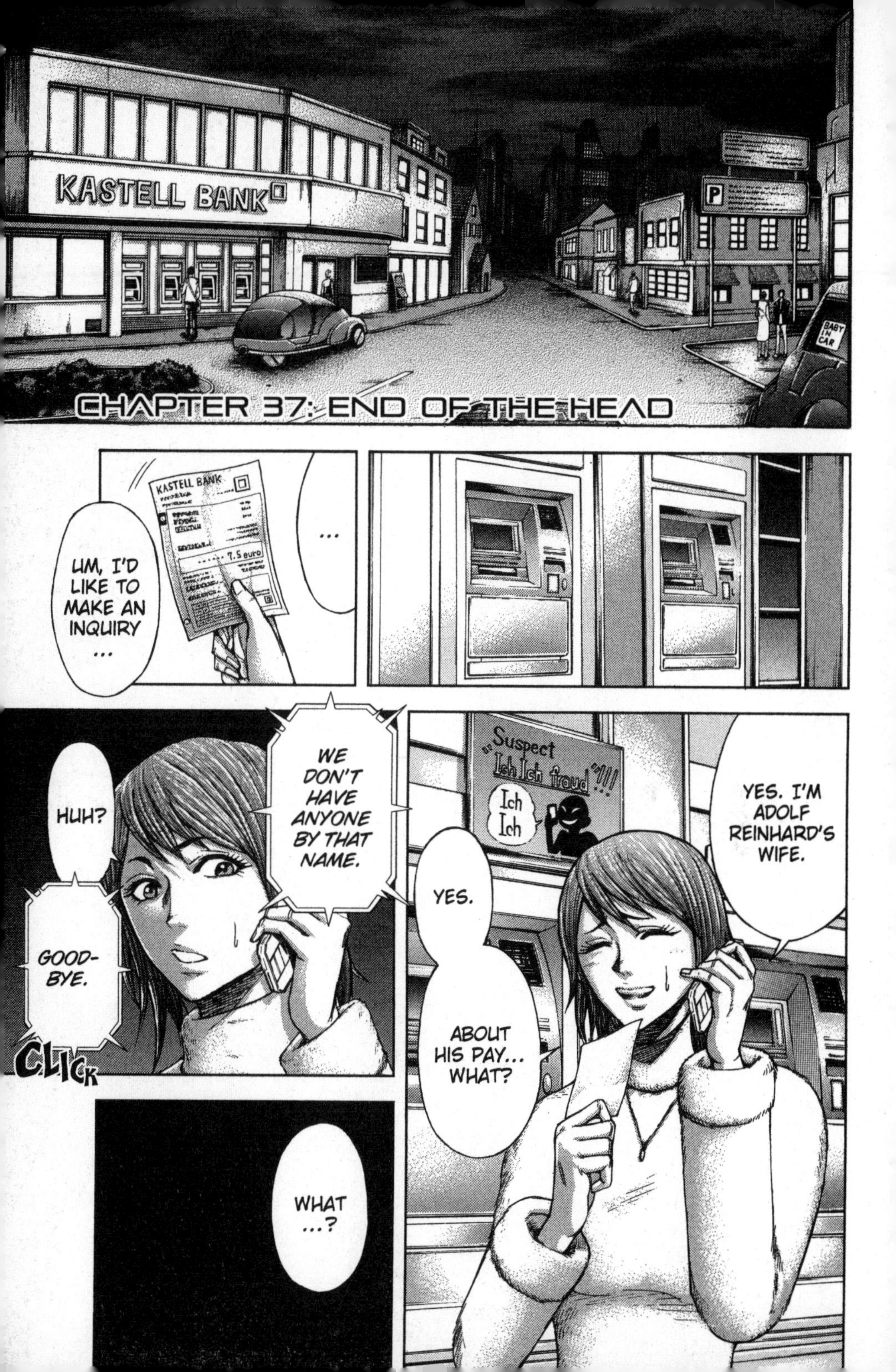
KASTELL BANK
CHAPTER 37: END OF THE HEAD
...
KASTELL BANK
7.5 euro
UM, I'D LIKE TO MAKE AN INQUIRY...
"Suspect Ich Ich fraud"!!!
Ich Ich
YES. I'M ADOLF REINHARD'S WIFE.
YES.
ABOUT HIS PAY... WHAT?
WE DON'T HAVE ANYONE BY THAT NAME.
HUH?
GOOD-BYE.
CLICK
WHAT...?

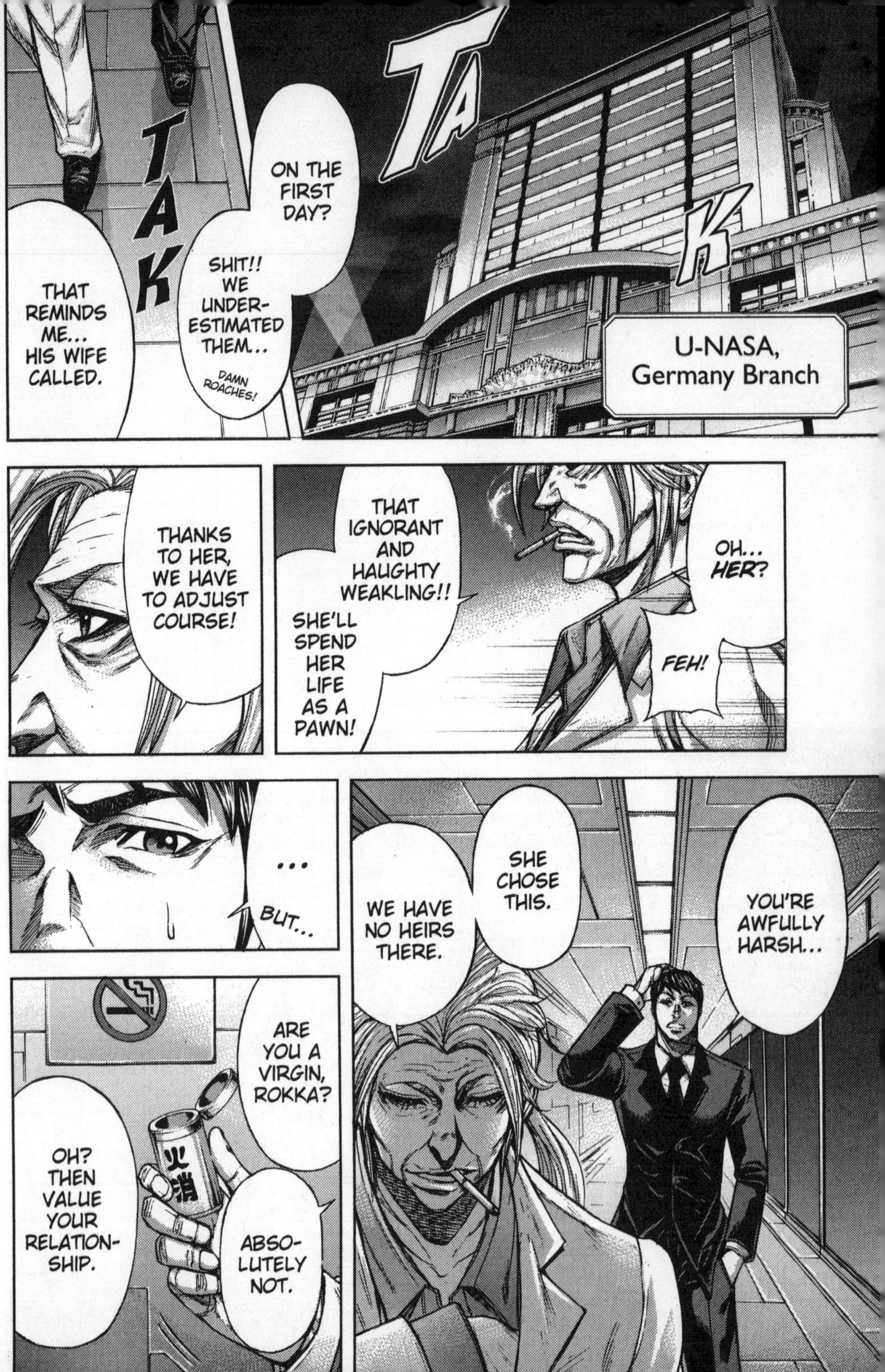
U-NASA, Germany Branch
TAK
TAK
ON THE FIRST DAY?
SHIT!! WE UNDER-ESTIMATED THEM...
DAMN ROACHES!
THAT REMINDS ME... HIS WIFE CALLED.
OH... HER?
FEH!
THAT IGNORANT AND HAUGHTY WEAKLING!!
SHE'LL SPEND HER LIFE AS A PAWN!
THANKS TO HER, WE HAVE TO ADJUST COURSE!
YOU'RE AWFULLY HARSH...
SHE CHOSE THIS.
WE HAVE NO HEIRS THERE.
...
BUT...
ARE YOU A VIRGIN, ROKKA?
ABSO-LUTELY NOT.
OH? THEN VALUE YOUR RELATION-SHIP.

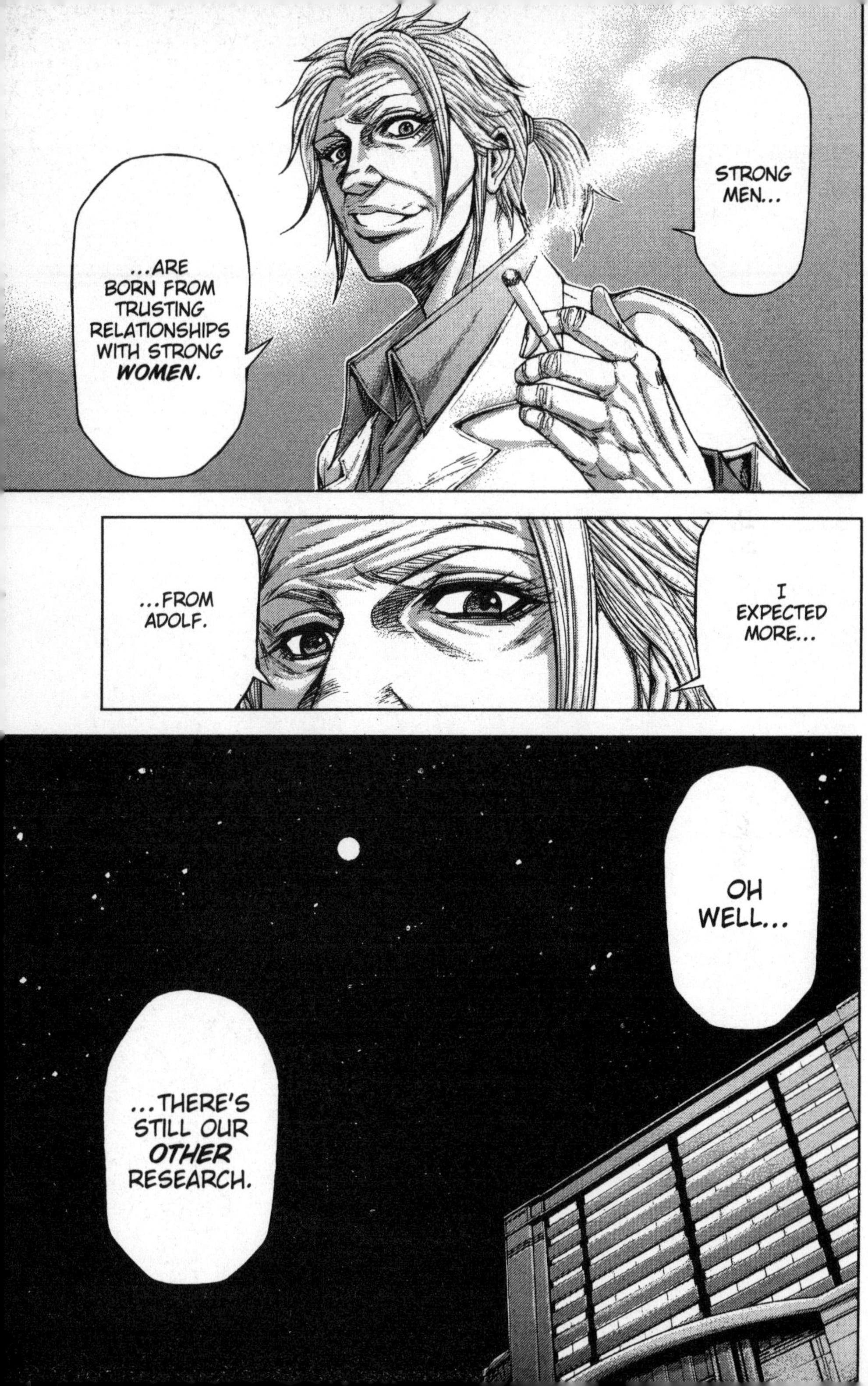
STRONG MEN...
...ARE BORN FROM TRUSTING RELATIONSHIPS WITH STRONG *WOMEN*.
I EXPECTED MORE...
...FROM ADOLF.
OH WELL...
...THERE'S STILL OUR *OTHER* RESEARCH.

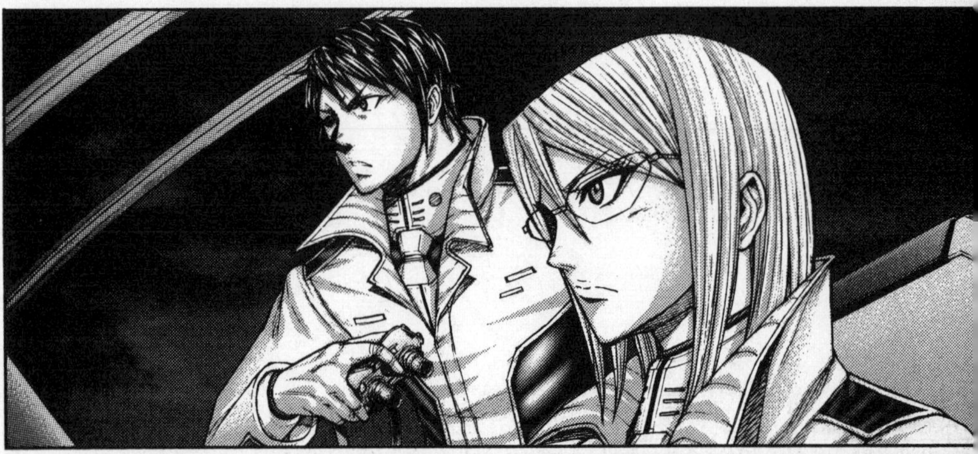

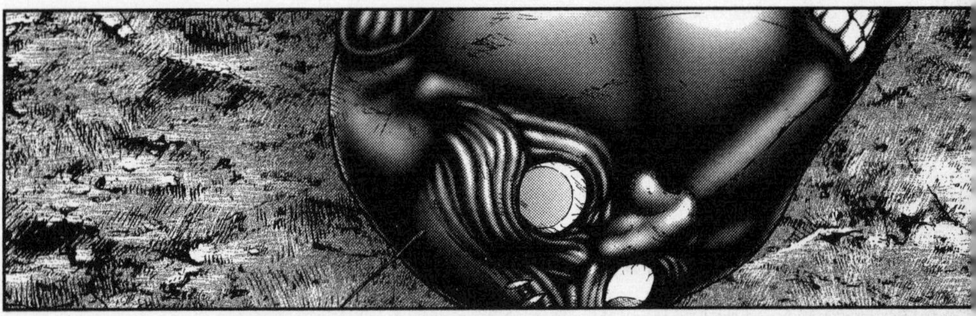

CHAPTER 37: END OF THE HEAD

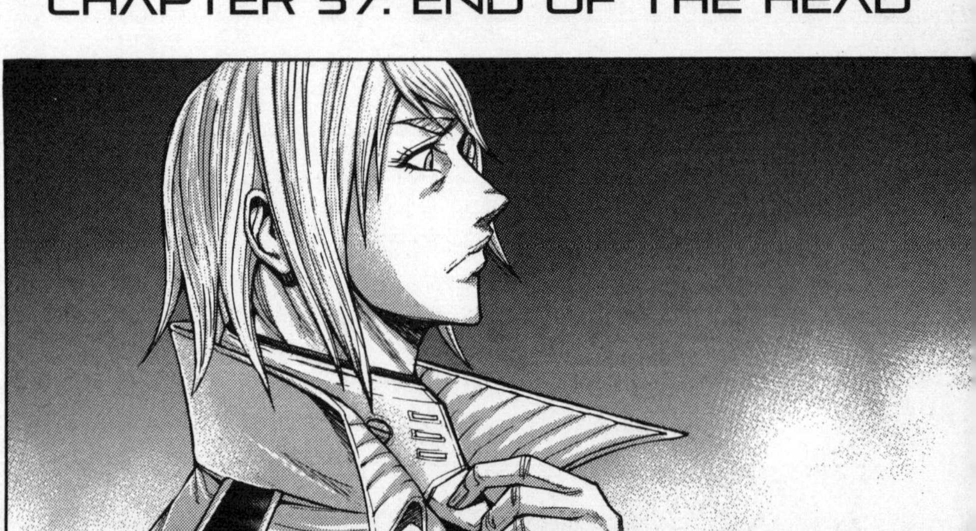

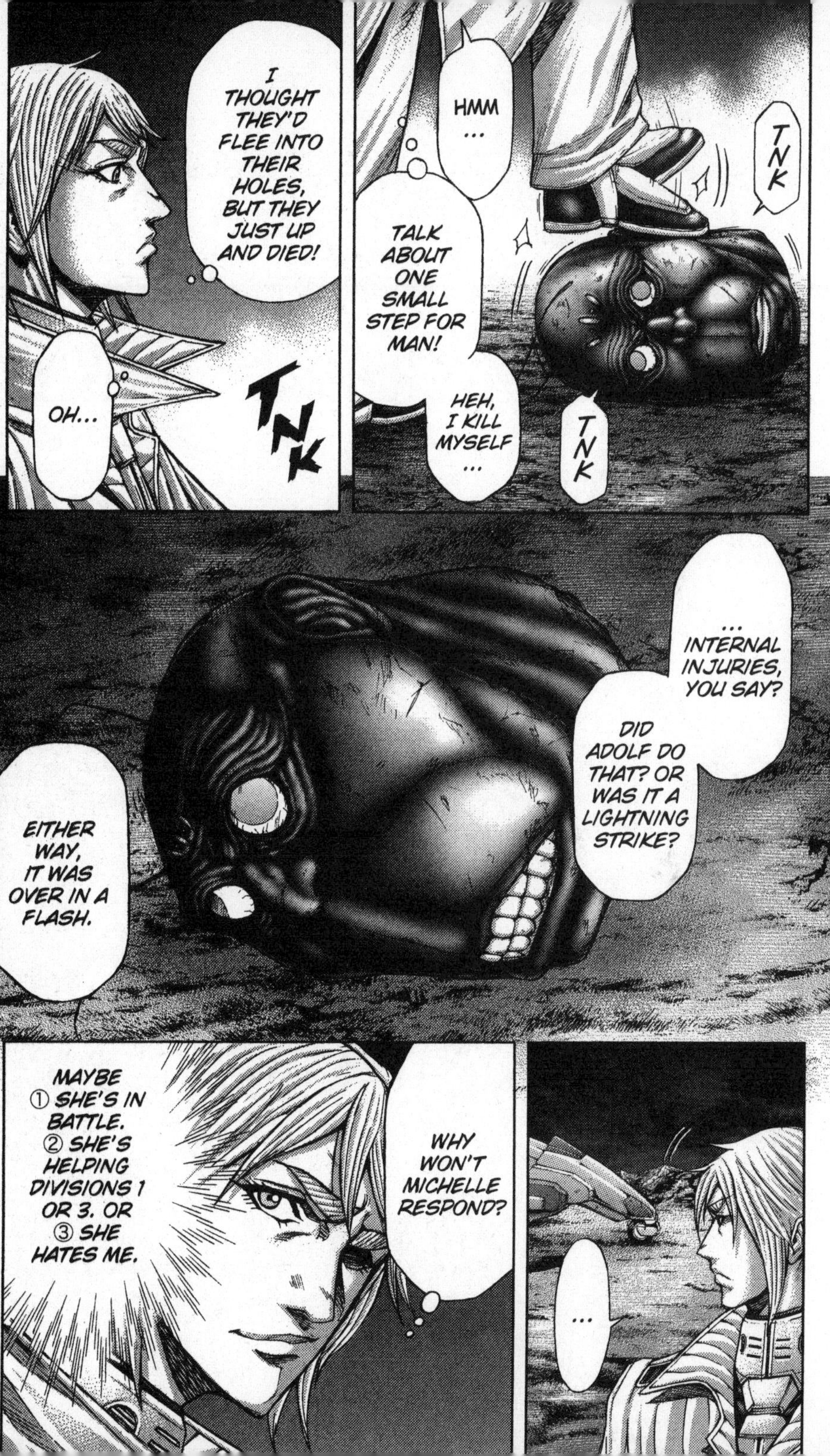
HMM ...
TNK
TALK ABOUT ONE SMALL STEP FOR MAN!
HEH, I KILL MYSELF ...
TNK
I THOUGHT THEY'D FLEE INTO THEIR HOLES, BUT THEY JUST UP AND DIED!
OH...
TNK
... INTERNAL INJURIES, YOU SAY?
DID ADOLF DO THAT? OR WAS IT A LIGHTNING STRIKE?
EITHER WAY, IT WAS OVER IN A FLASH.
...
WHY WON'T MICHELLE RESPOND?
MAYBE ① SHE'S IN BATTLE. ② SHE'S HELPING DIVISIONS 1 OR 3. OR ③ SHE HATES ME.

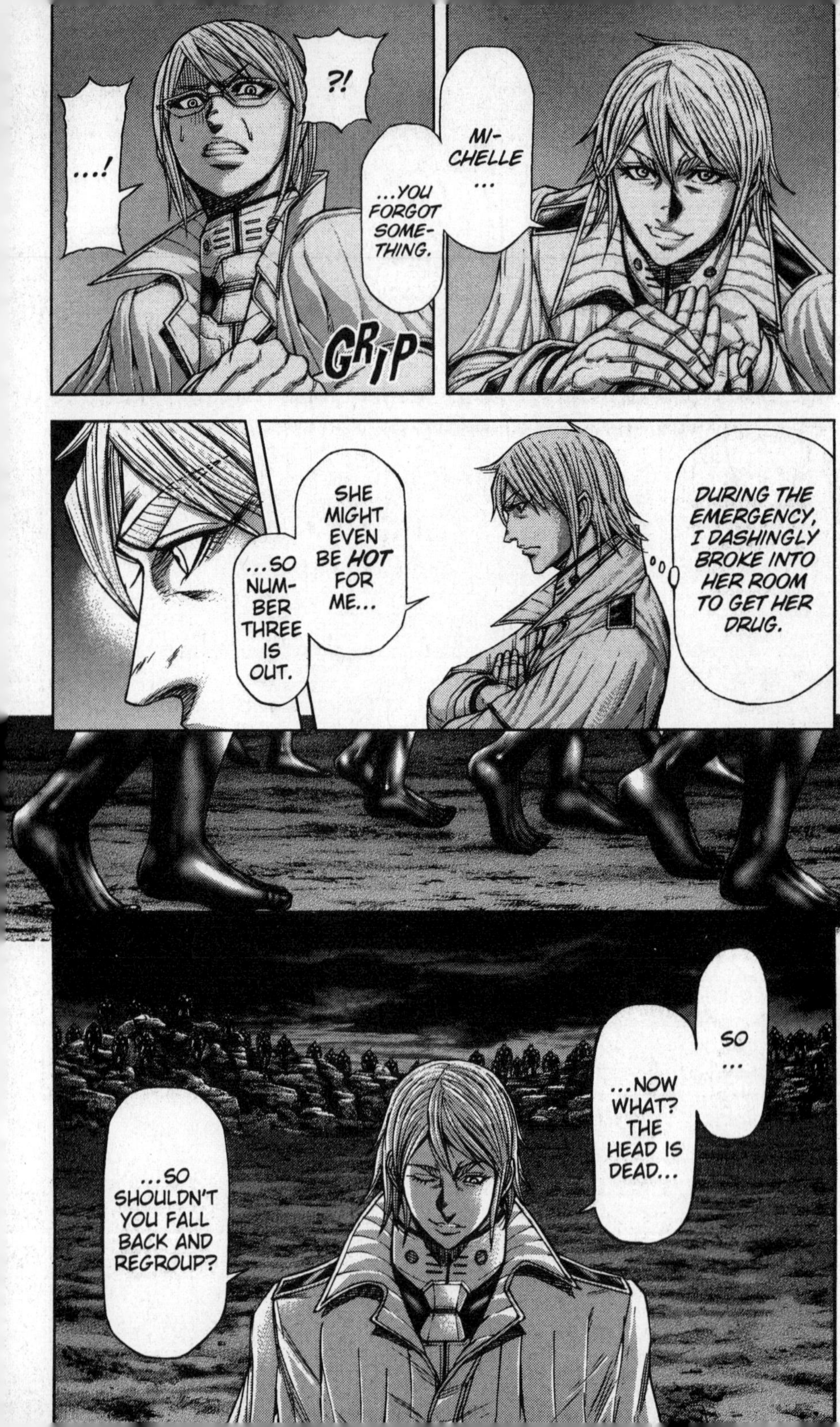
MI-CHELLE...
...YOU FORGOT SOME-THING.
?!
...!
GRIP
DURING THE EMERGENCY, I DASHINGLY BROKE INTO HER ROOM TO GET HER DRUG.
SHE MIGHT EVEN BE **HOT** FOR ME...
...SO NUMBER THREE IS OUT.
SO...
...NOW WHAT? THE HEAD IS DEAD...
...SO SHOULDN'T YOU FALL BACK AND REGROUP?

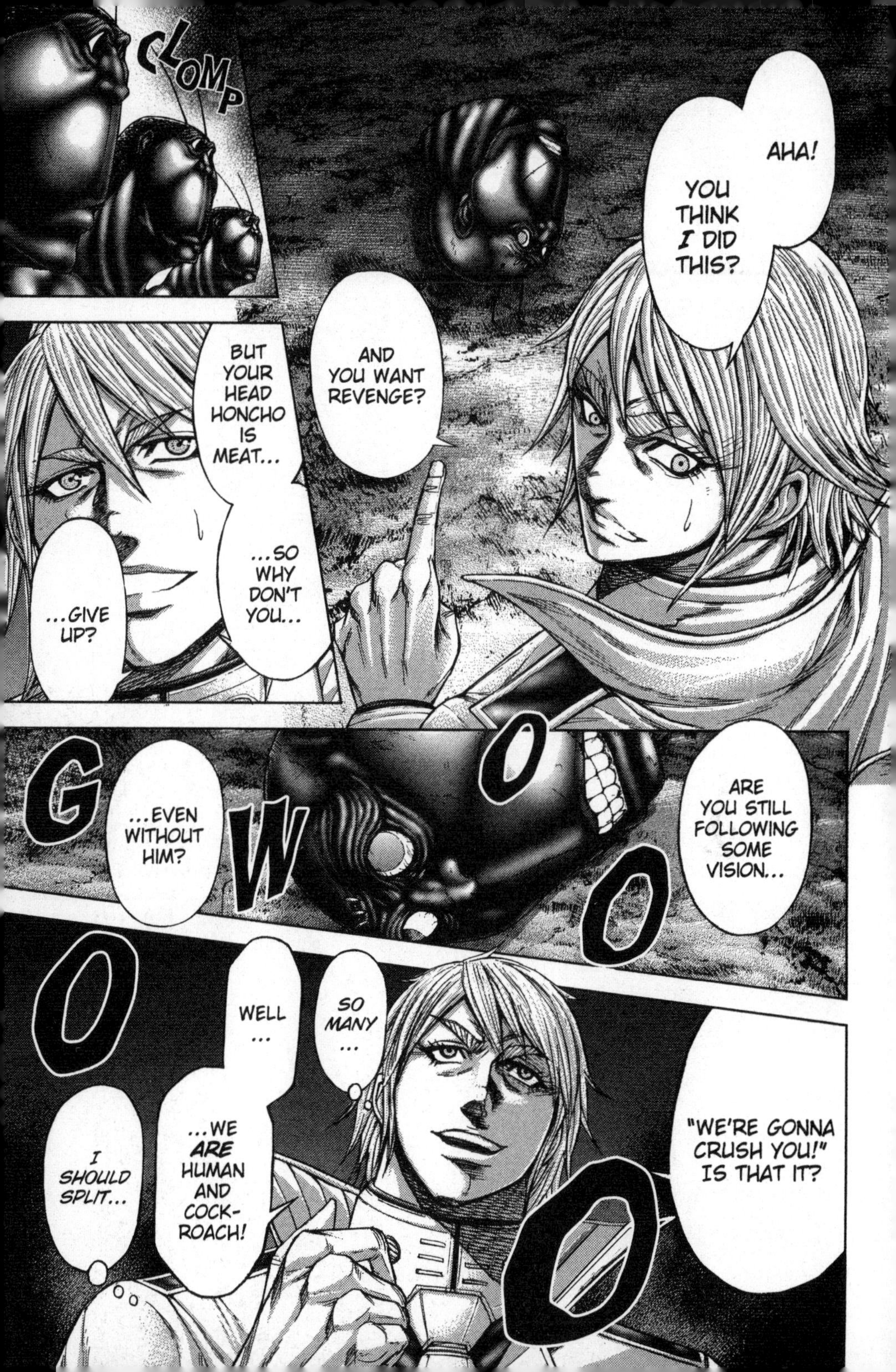
AHA!
YOU THINK *I* DID THIS?
CLOMP
AND YOU WANT REVENGE?
BUT YOUR HEAD HONCHO IS MEAT...
...SO WHY DON'T YOU...
...GIVE UP?
ARE YOU STILL FOLLOWING SOME VISION...
...EVEN WITHOUT HIM?
GOWOOOO
"WE'RE GONNA CRUSH YOU!" IS THAT IT?
SO MANY ...
WELL ...
...WE ***ARE*** HUMAN AND COCK-ROACH!
I SHOULD SPLIT...

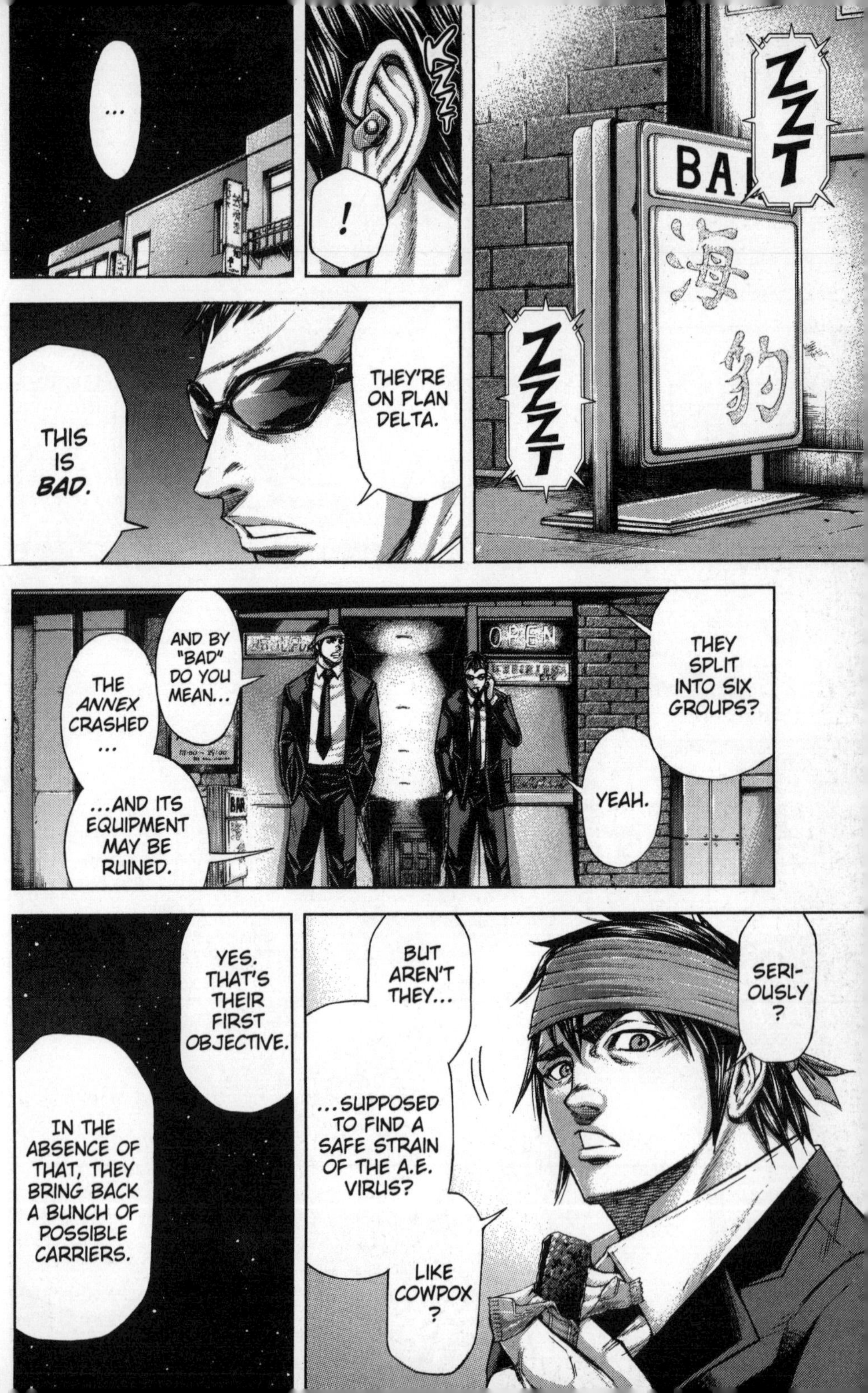
ZZZT
BA
海豹
ZZZT
ZZZT
!
...
THEY'RE ON PLAN DELTA.
THIS IS *BAD.*
THEY SPLIT INTO SIX GROUPS?
YEAH.
OPEN
AND BY "BAD" DO YOU MEAN...
THE *ANNEX* CRASHED...
...AND ITS EQUIPMENT MAY BE RUINED.
SERI-OUSLY?
BUT AREN'T THEY...
...SUPPOSED TO FIND A SAFE STRAIN OF THE A.E. VIRUS?
LIKE COWPOX?
YES. THAT'S THEIR FIRST OBJECTIVE.
IN THE ABSENCE OF THAT, THEY BRING BACK A BUNCH OF POSSIBLE CARRIERS.

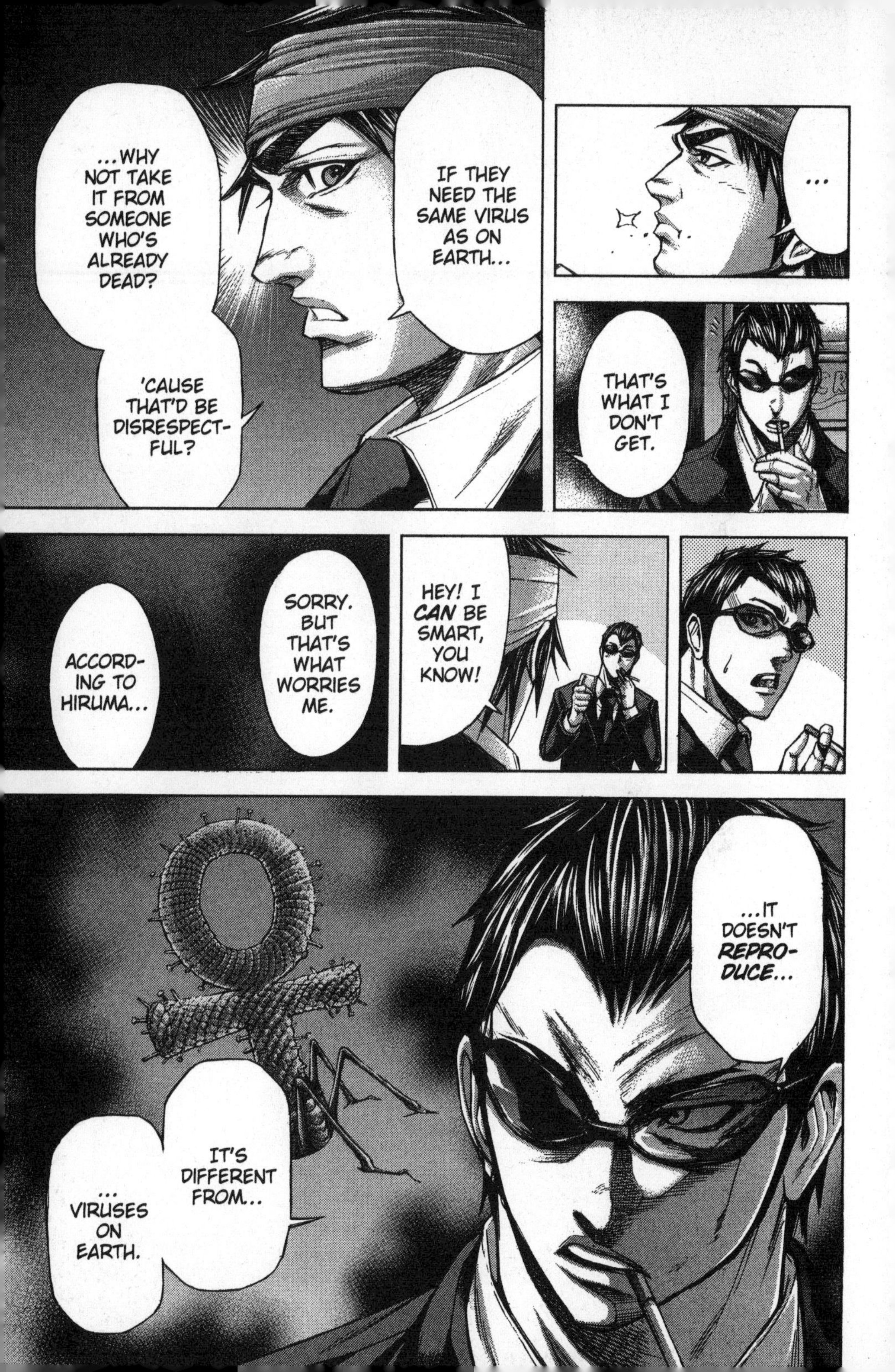
...
THAT'S WHAT I DON'T GET.
IF THEY NEED THE SAME VIRUS AS ON EARTH...
...WHY NOT TAKE IT FROM SOMEONE WHO'S ALREADY DEAD?
'CAUSE THAT'D BE DISRESPECTFUL?
HEY! I CAN BE SMART, YOU KNOW!
SORRY. BUT THAT'S WHAT WORRIES ME.
ACCORDING TO HIRUMA...
...IT DOESN'T REPRODUCE...
IT'S DIFFERENT FROM...
...VIRUSES ON EARTH.

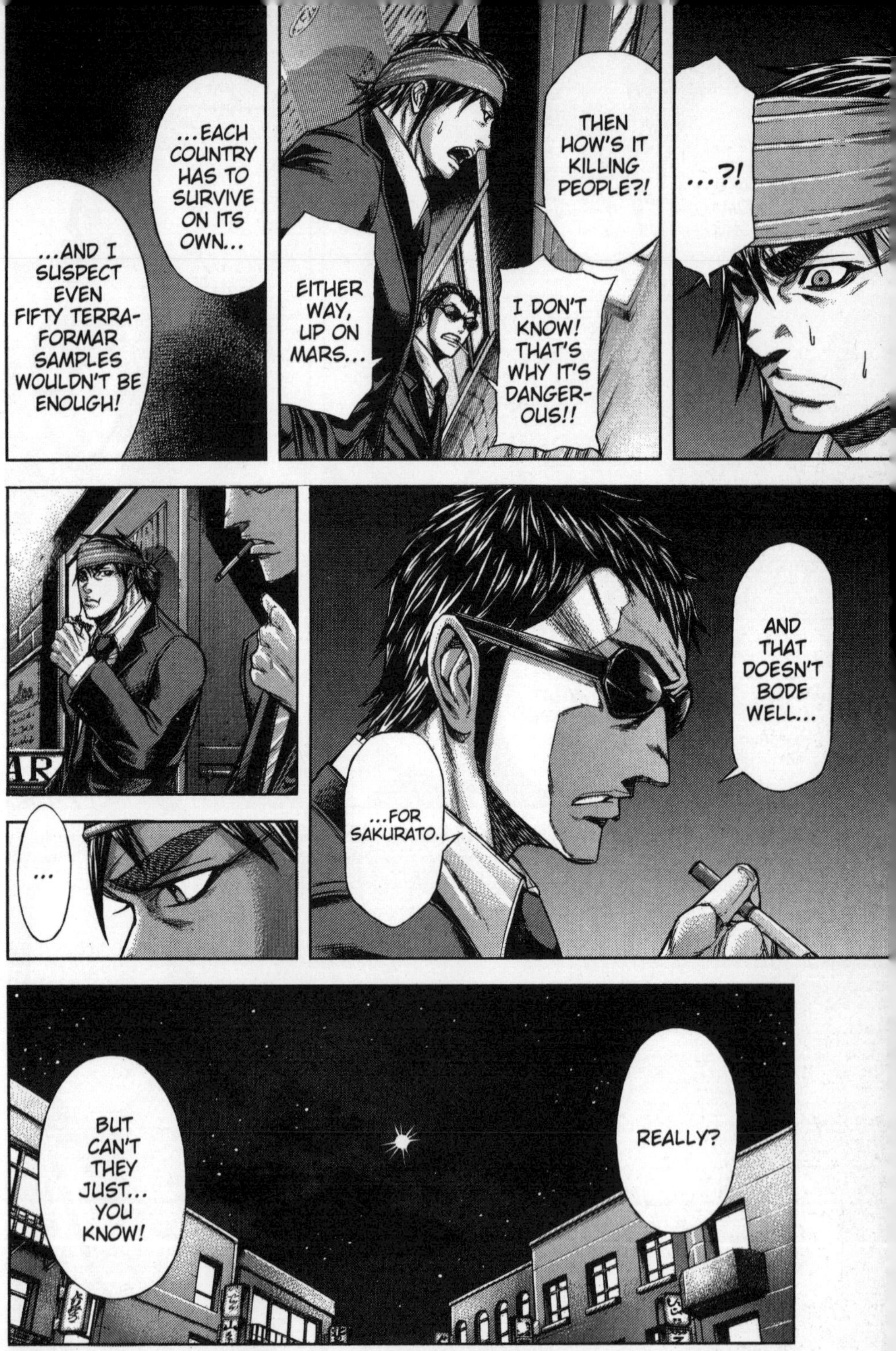
...?!
THEN HOW'S IT KILLING PEOPLE?!
I DON'T KNOW! THAT'S WHY IT'S DANGER-OUS!!
EITHER WAY, UP ON MARS...
...EACH COUNTRY HAS TO SURVIVE ON ITS OWN...
...AND I SUSPECT EVEN FIFTY TERRA-FORMAR SAMPLES WOULDN'T BE ENOUGH!
AND THAT DOESN'T BODE WELL...
...FOR SAKURATO.
...
REALLY?
BUT CAN'T THEY JUST... YOU KNOW!

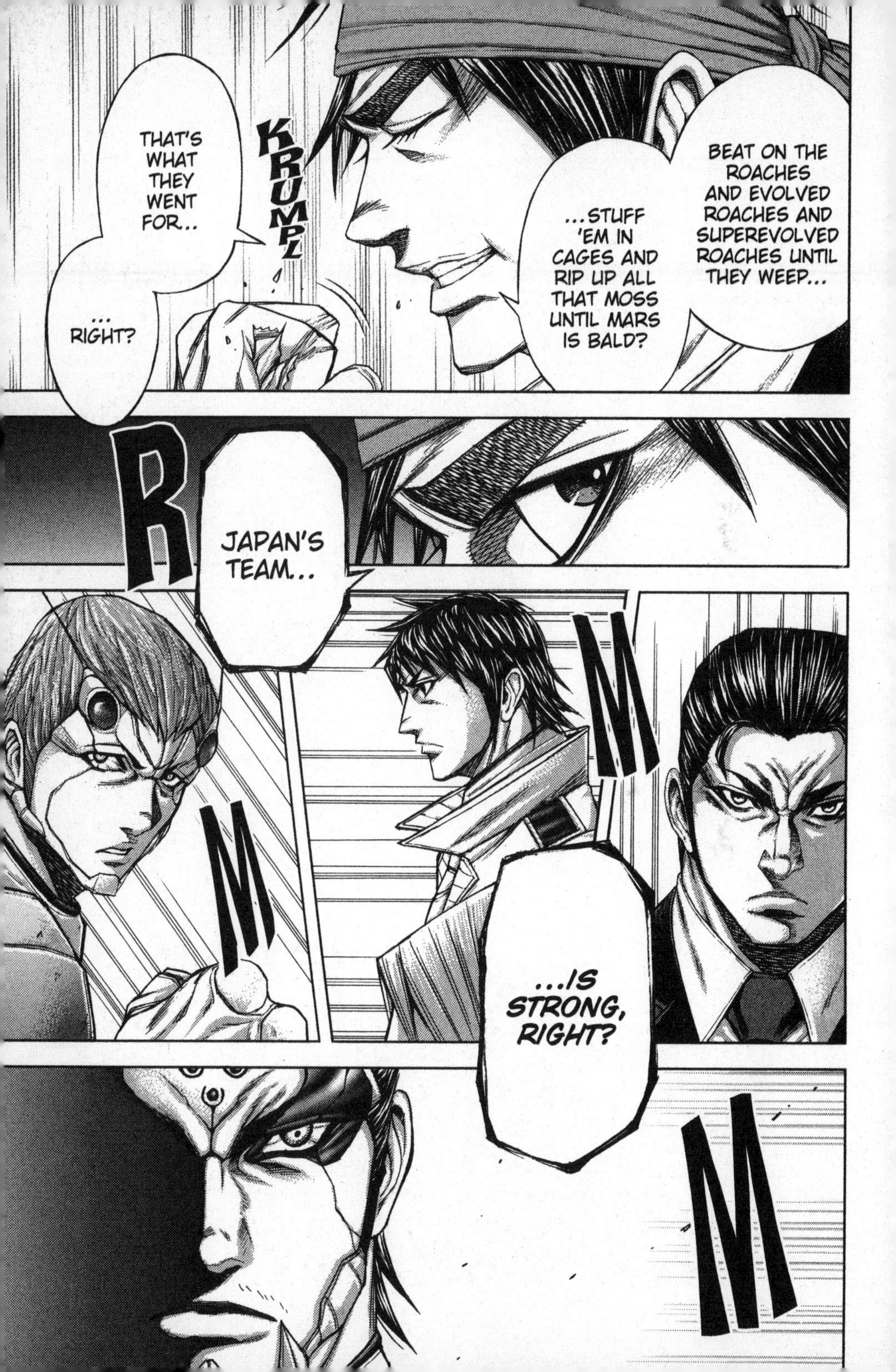
BEAT ON THE ROACHES AND EVOLVED ROACHES AND SUPEREVOLVED ROACHES UNTIL THEY WEEP...
...STUFF 'EM IN CAGES AND RIP UP ALL THAT MOSS UNTIL MARS IS BALD?
KRUMPL
THAT'S WHAT THEY WENT FOR...
...RIGHT?
JAPAN'S TEAM...
RMMM
...IS STRONG, RIGHT?

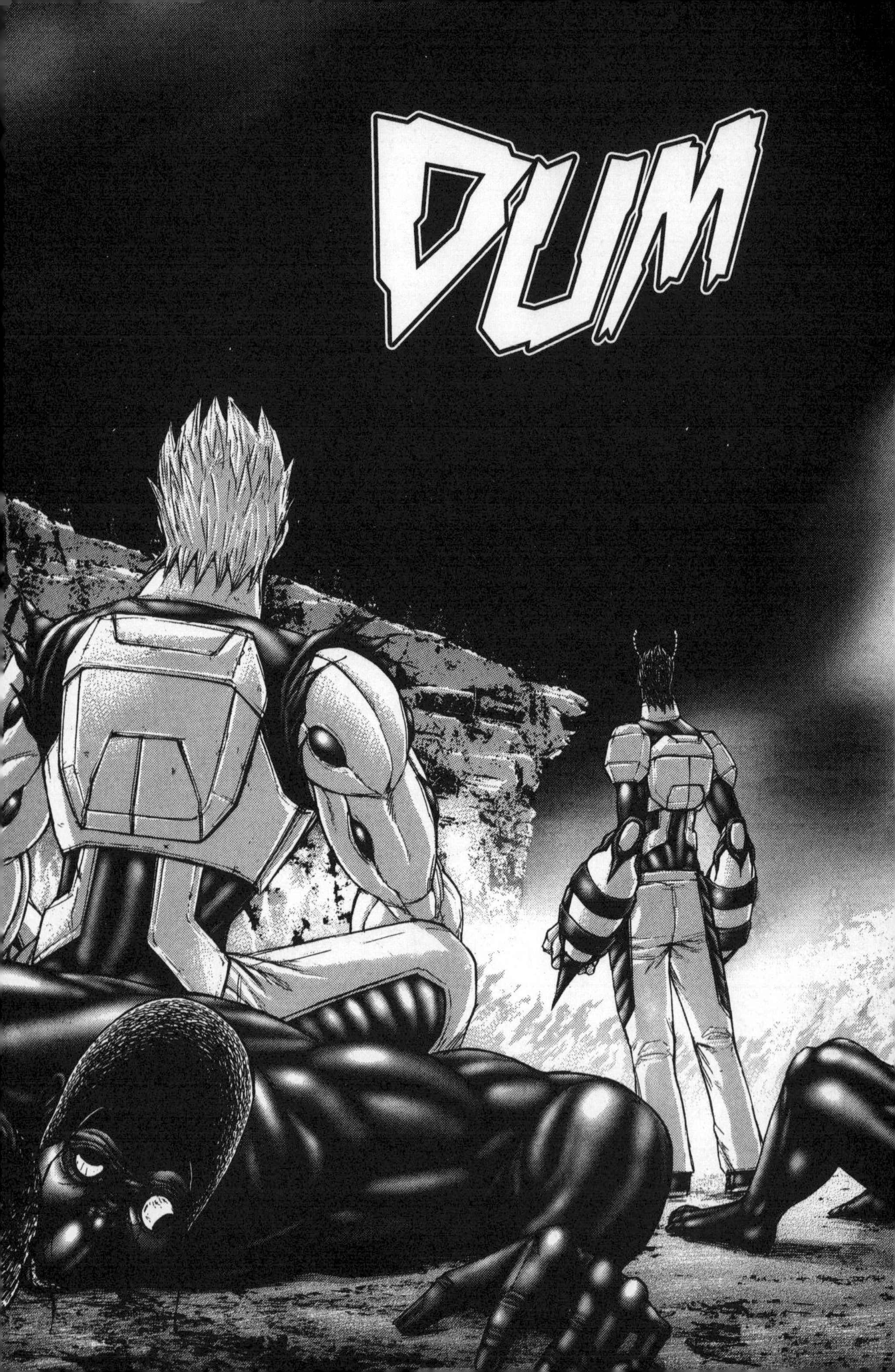
DUM

FULL

W G O

DA

O

CAP-
TAIN
...

O

...IS
THE
ENEMY
THAT
STRONG
...

...
BECAUSE
OF THE
BUGS
PROCE-
DURE?

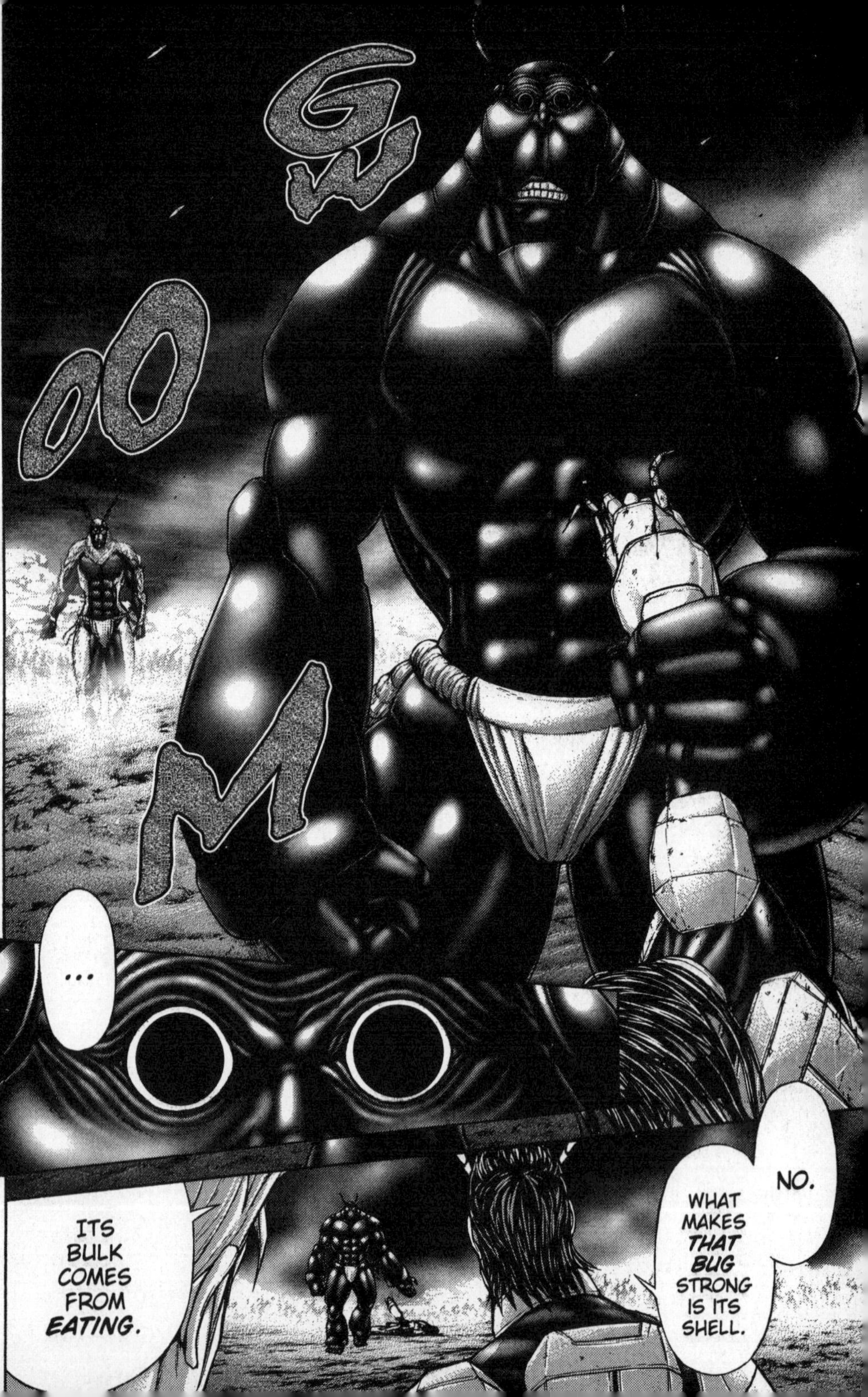
GWOOM
...
NO.
WHAT MAKES *THAT BUG* STRONG IS ITS SHELL.
ITS BULK COMES FROM *EATING*.

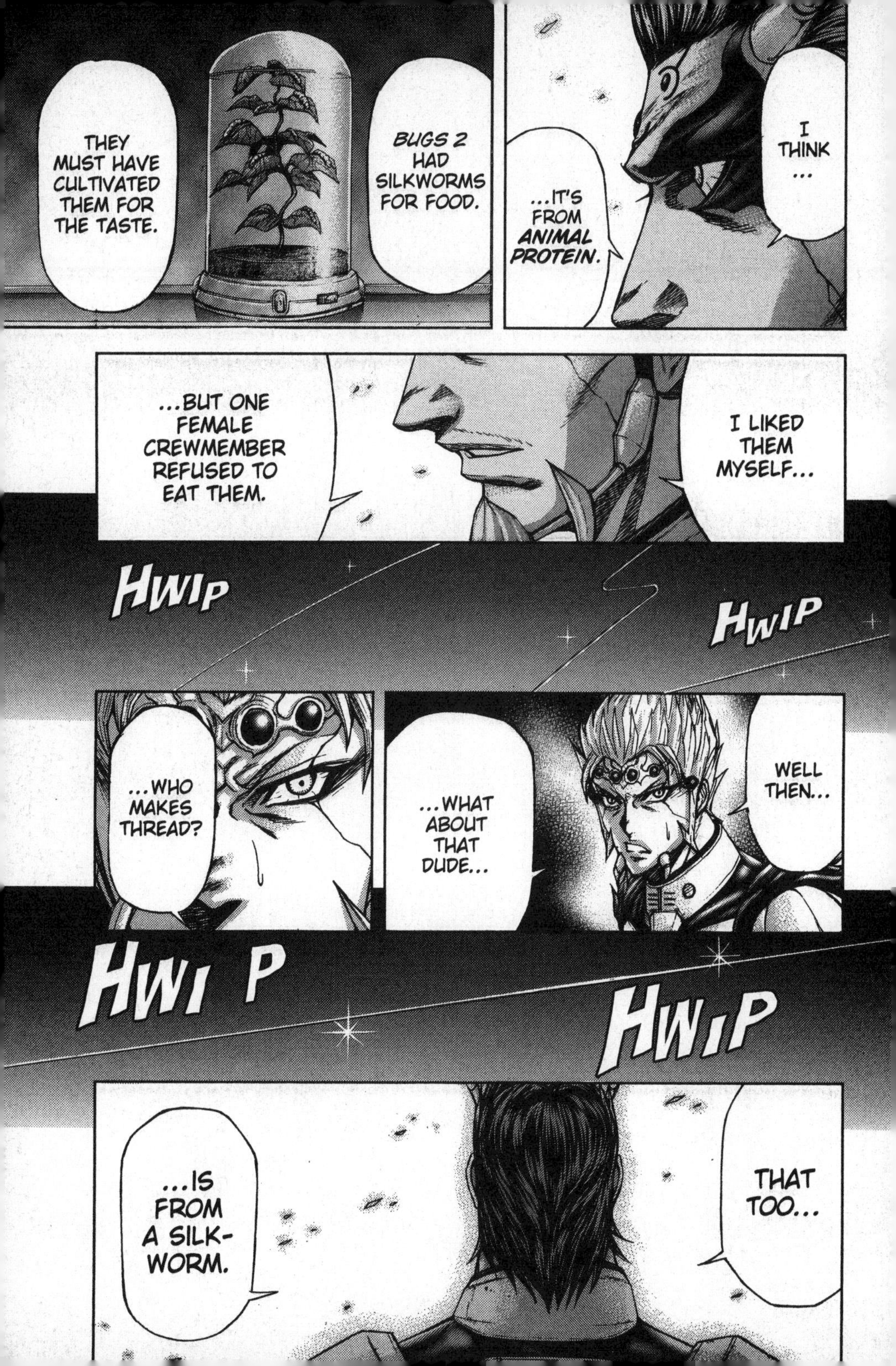
I THINK...
...IT'S FROM ANIMAL PROTEIN.
BUGS 2 HAD SILKWORMS FOR FOOD.
THEY MUST HAVE CULTIVATED THEM FOR THE TASTE.
I LIKED THEM MYSELF...
...BUT ONE FEMALE CREWMEMBER REFUSED TO EAT THEM.
HWIP
HWIP
WELL THEN...
...WHAT ABOUT THAT DUDE...
...WHO MAKES THREAD?
HWIP
HWI P
THAT TOO...
...IS FROM A SILK-WORM.

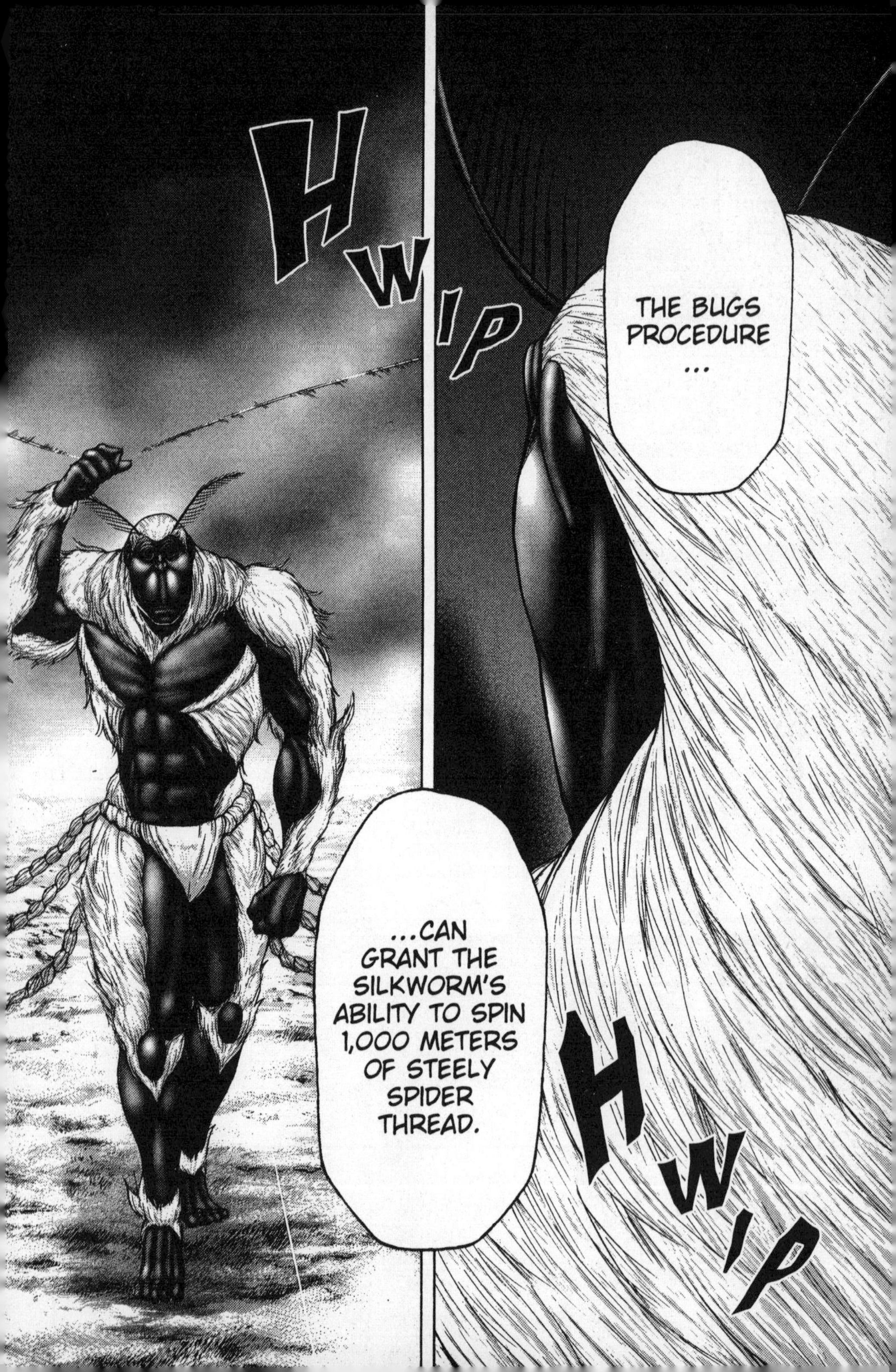
THE BUGS PROCEDURE ...
...CAN GRANT THE SILKWORM'S ABILITY TO SPIN 1,000 METERS OF STEELY SPIDER THREAD.
HWIP
HWIP

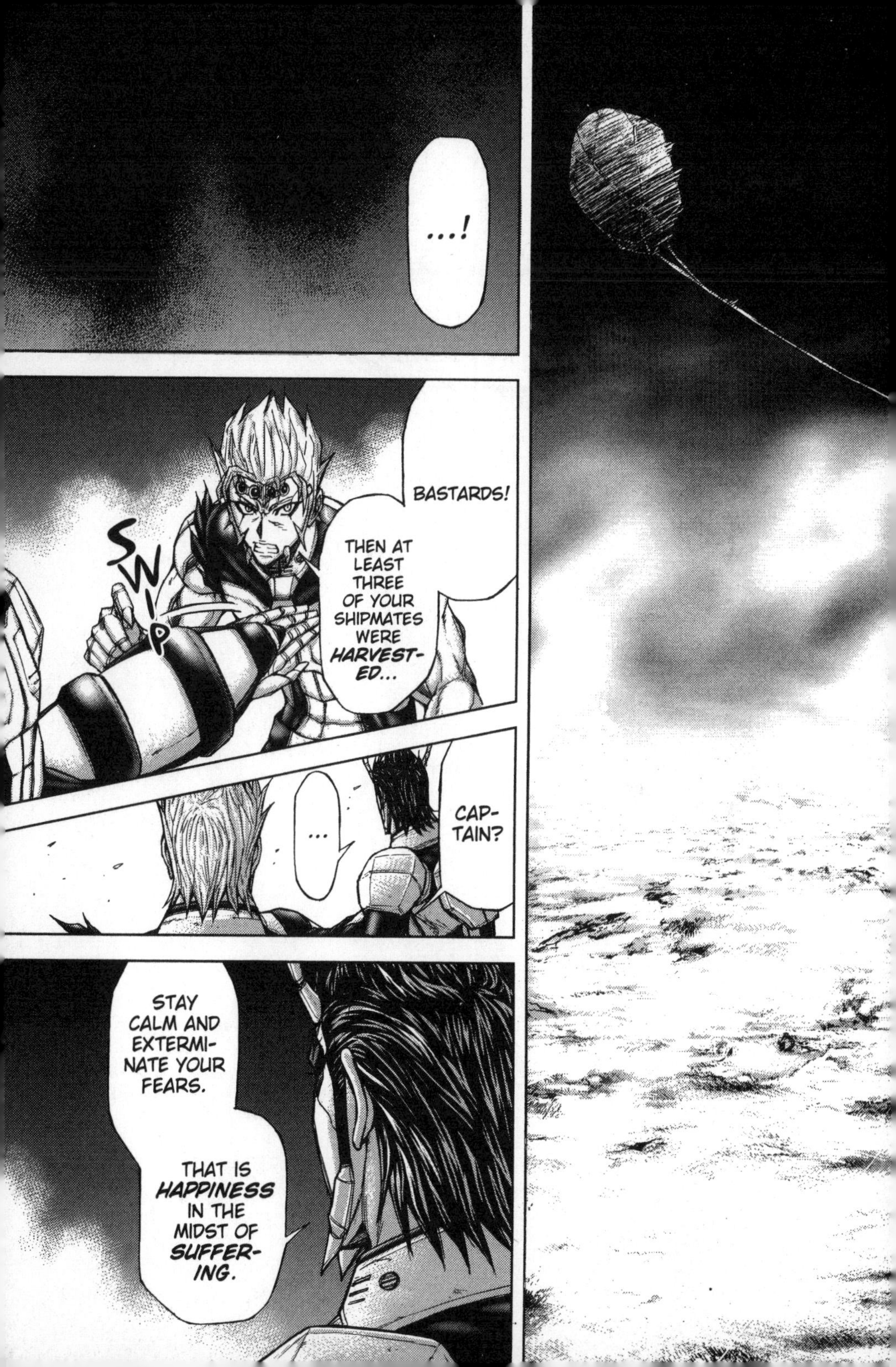
...!
BASTARDS!
THEN AT LEAST THREE OF YOUR SHIPMATES WERE HARVESTED...
SWIP
CAPTAIN?
...
STAY CALM AND EXTERMINATE YOUR FEARS.
THAT IS HAPPINESS IN THE MIDST OF SUFFERING.

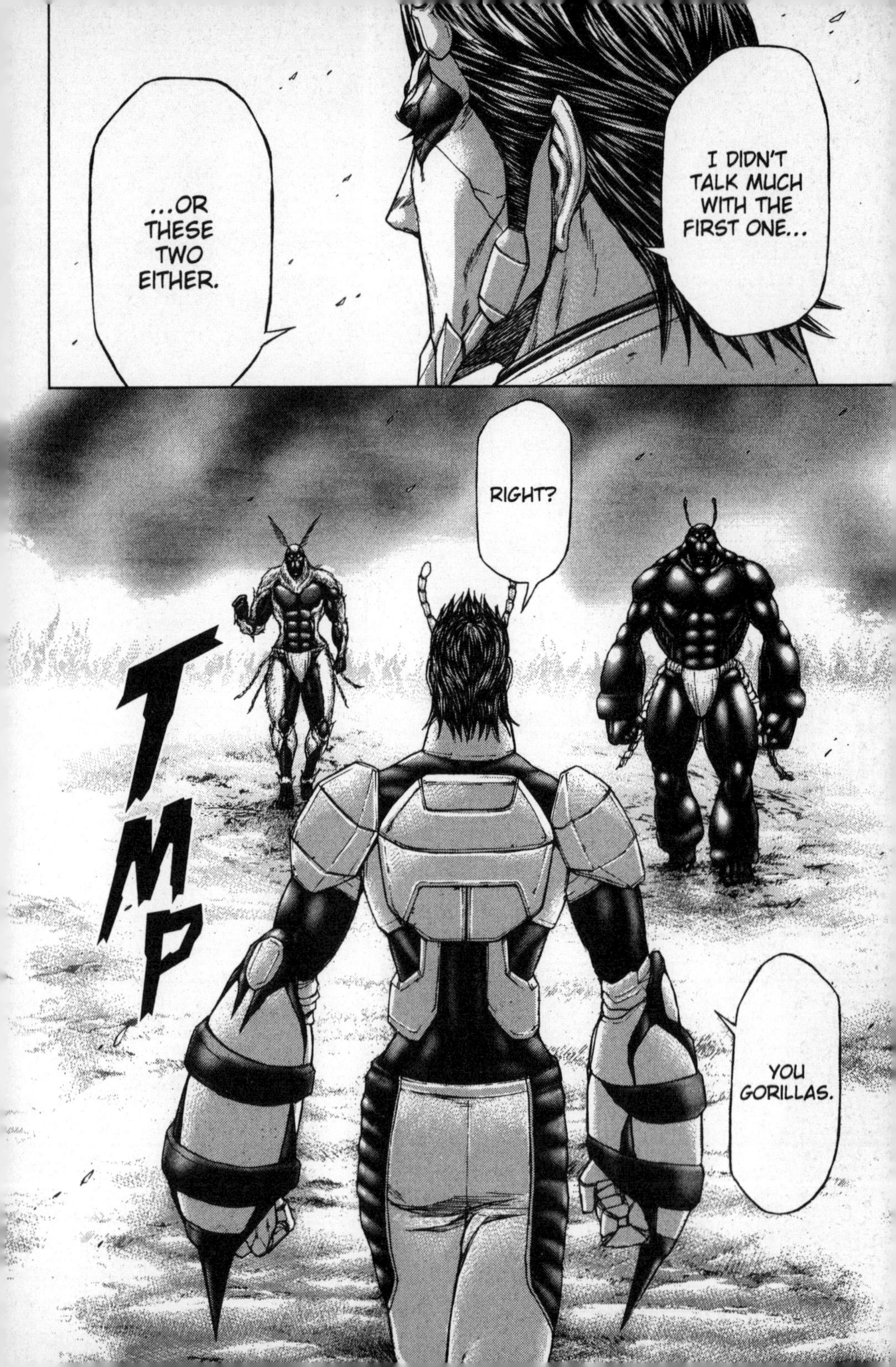
I DIDN'T TALK MUCH WITH THE FIRST ONE...
...OR THESE TWO EITHER.
RIGHT?
YOU GORILLAS.
TMP

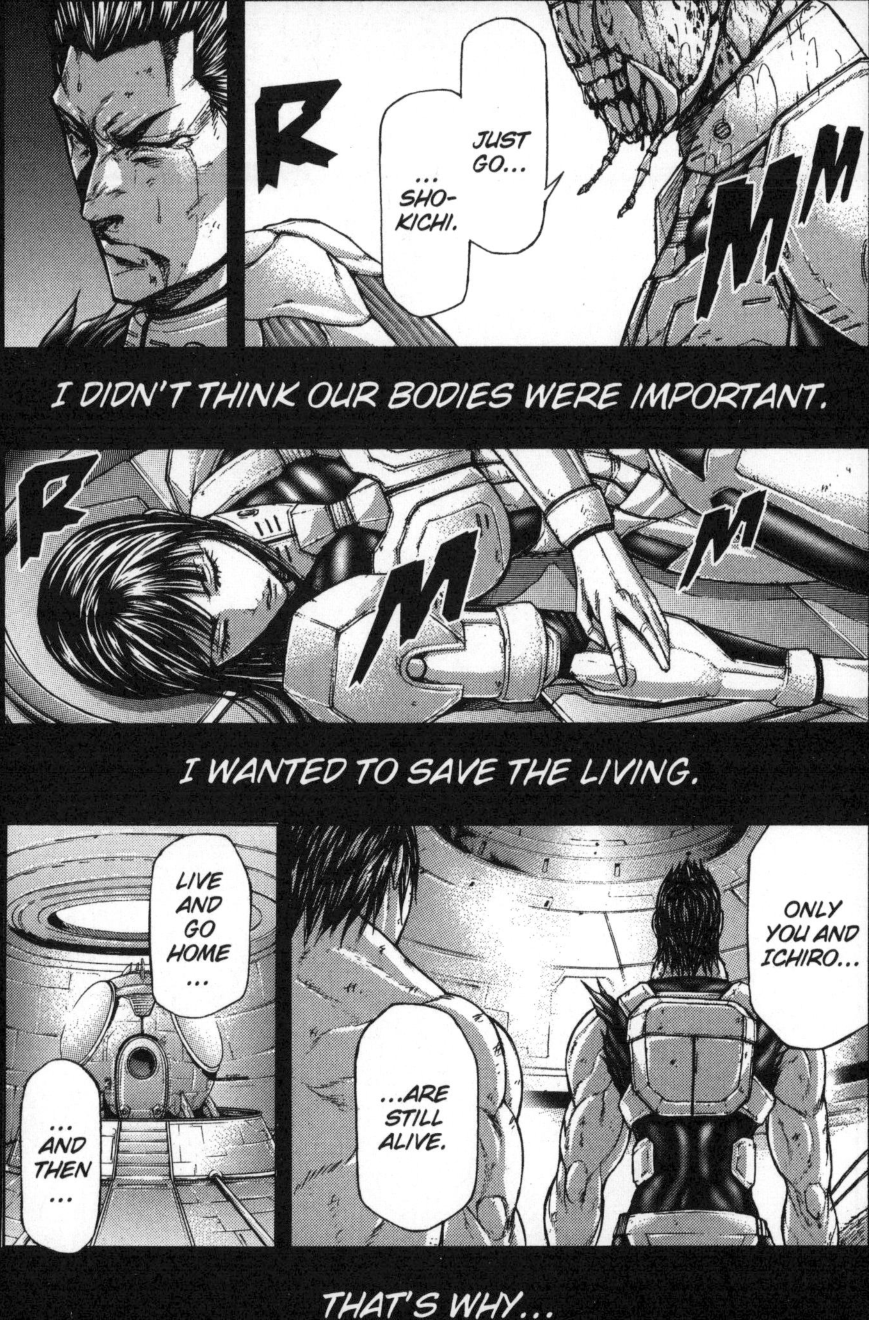
JUST GO...
...SHO-KICHI.
RMMM
I DIDN'T THINK OUR BODIES WERE IMPORTANT.
RMM
I WANTED TO SAVE THE LIVING.
ONLY YOU AND ICHIRO...
...ARE STILL ALIVE.
LIVE AND GO HOME...
...AND THEN...
THAT'S WHY...

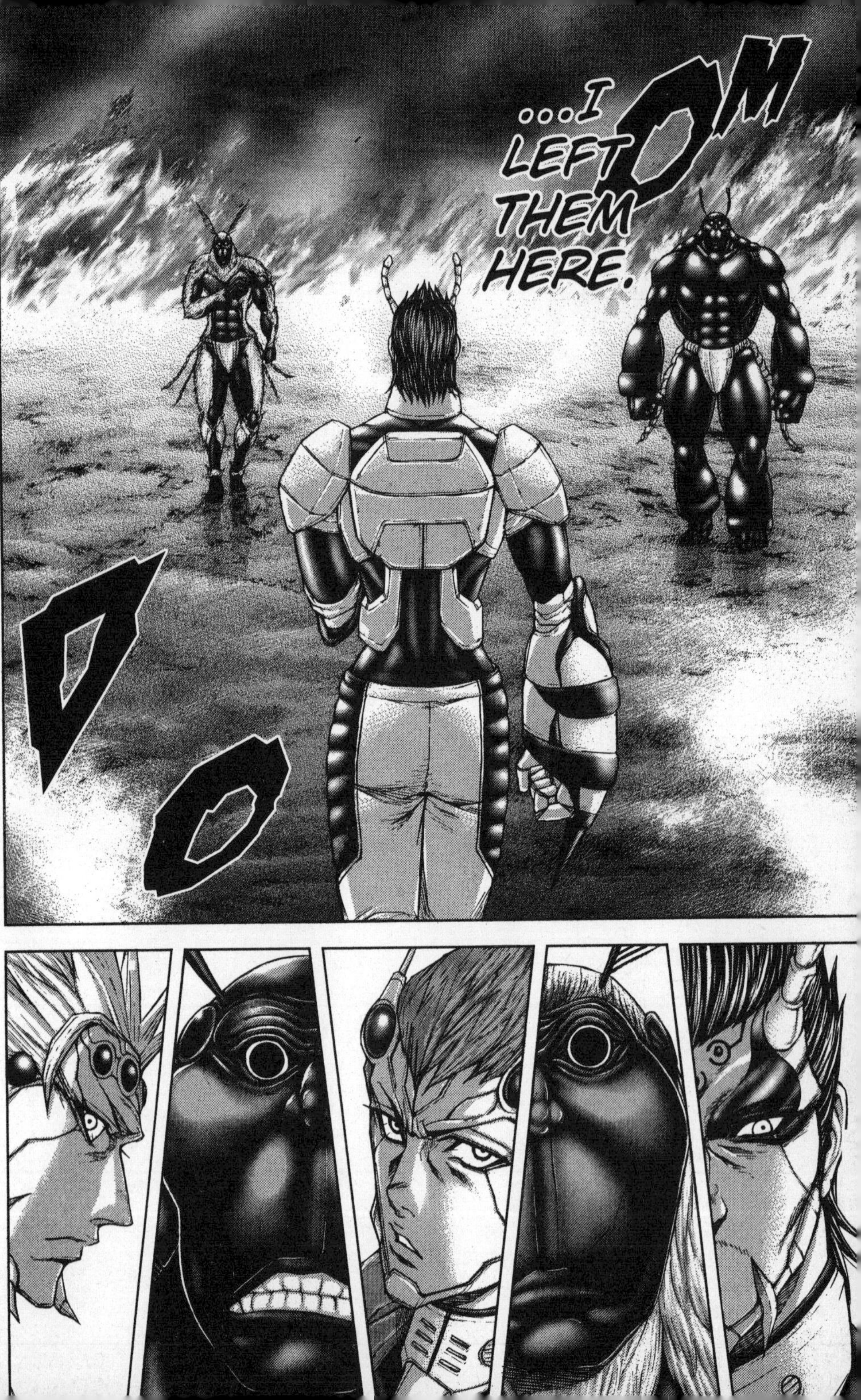
...I LEFT THEM HERE.
DOOM

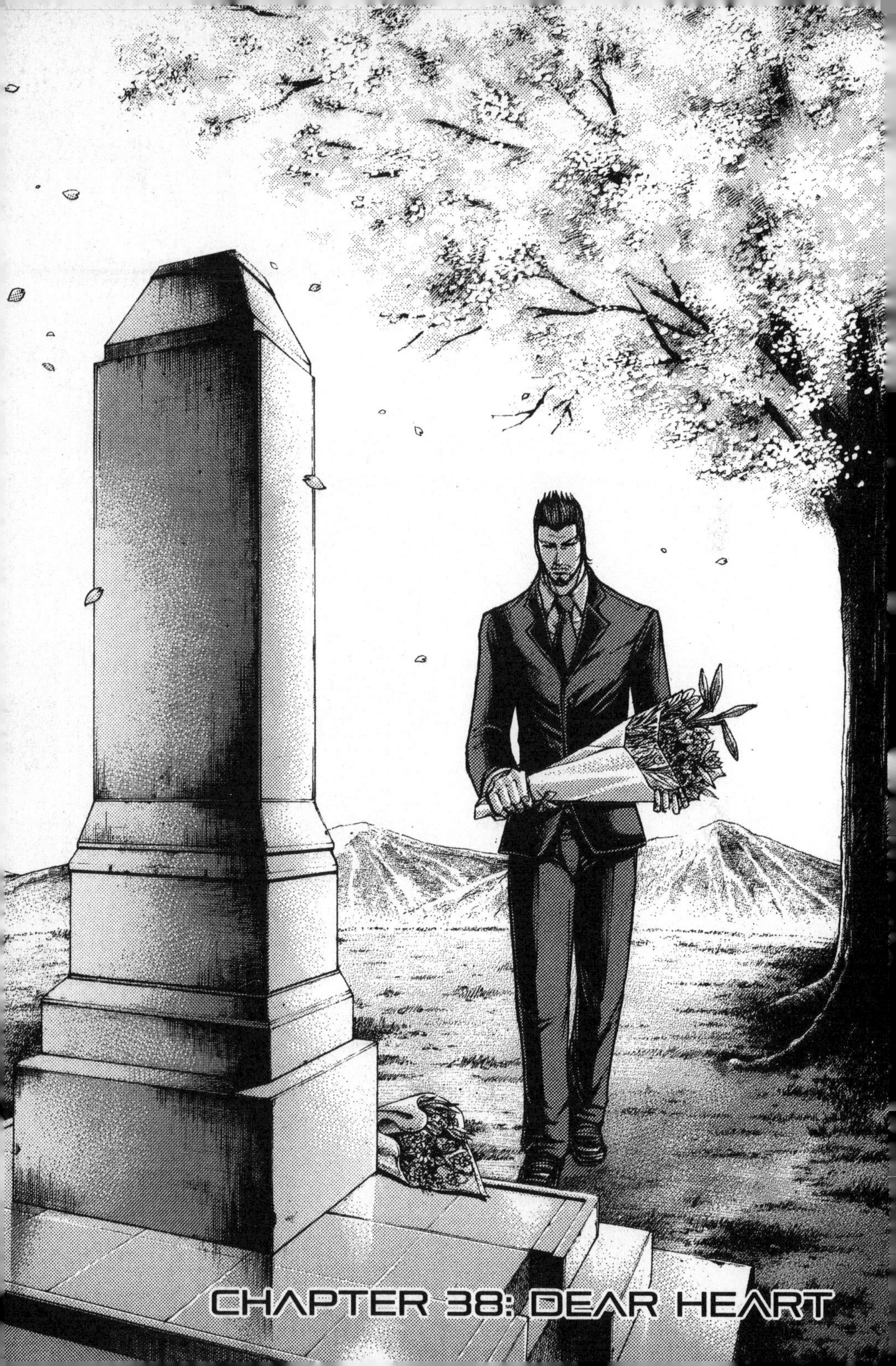
CHAPTER 38: DEAR HEART

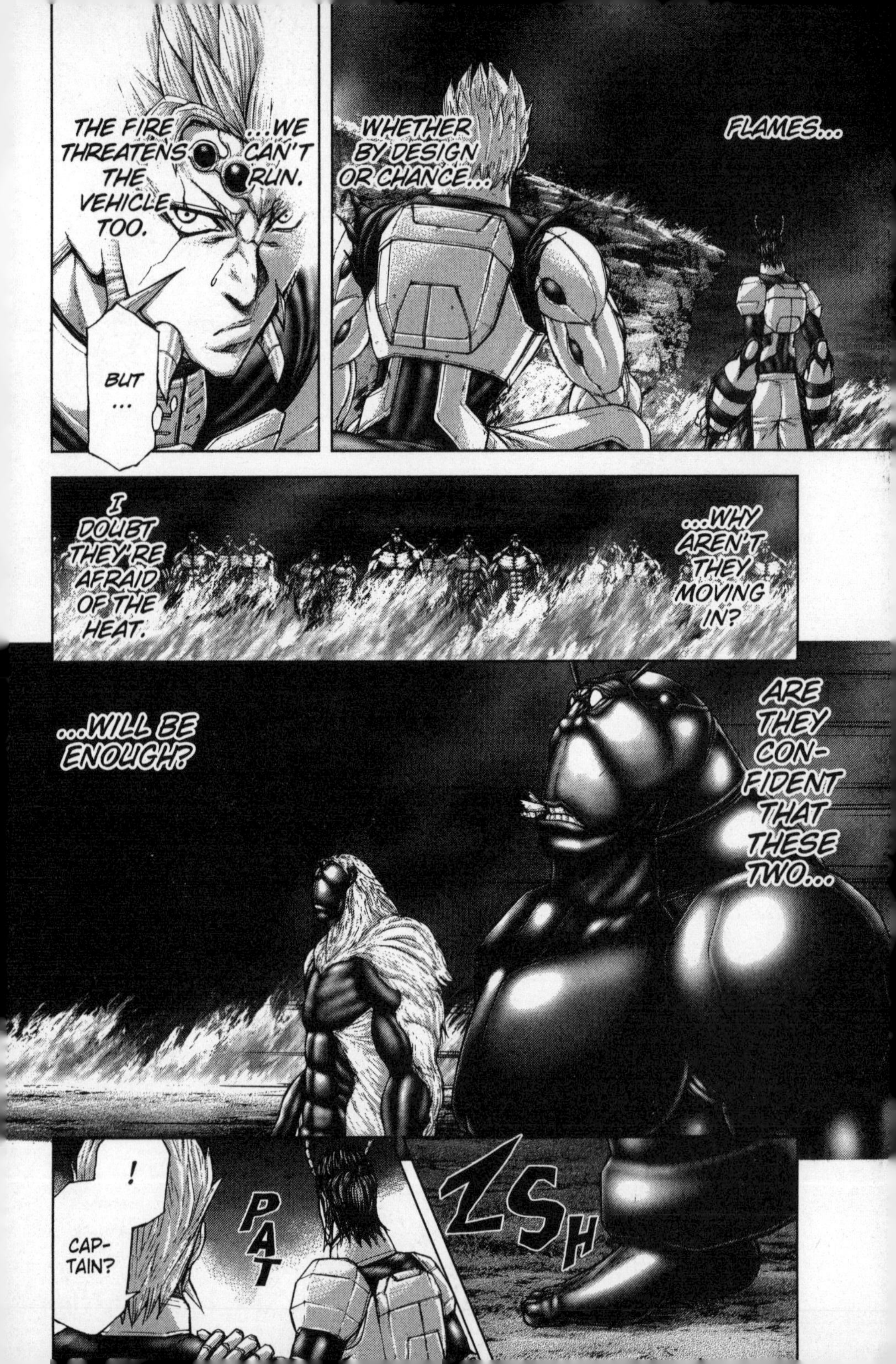
FLAMES...
WHETHER BY DESIGN OR CHANCE...
...WE CAN'T RUN.
THE FIRE THREATENS THE VEHICLE TOO.
BUT ...
...WHY AREN'T THEY MOVING IN?
I DOUBT THEY'RE AFRAID OF THE HEAT.
ARE THEY CON-FIDENT THAT THESE TWO...
...WILL BE ENOUGH?
ZSH
PAT
!
CAP-TAIN?

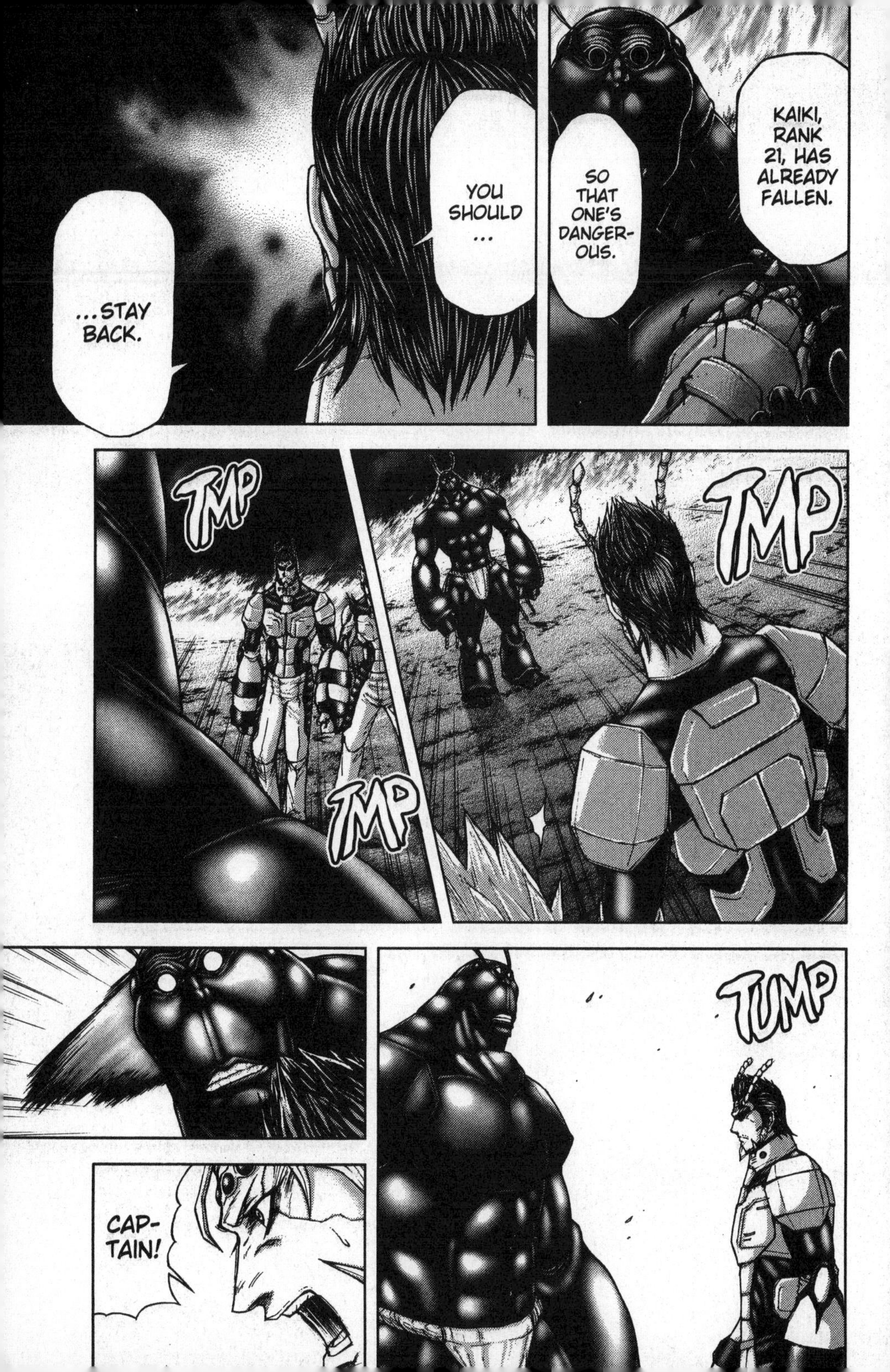
KAIKI, RANK 21, HAS ALREADY FALLEN.
SO THAT ONE'S DANGER-OUS.
YOU SHOULD ...
...STAY BACK.
TMP
TMP
TMP
TUMP
CAP-TAIN!

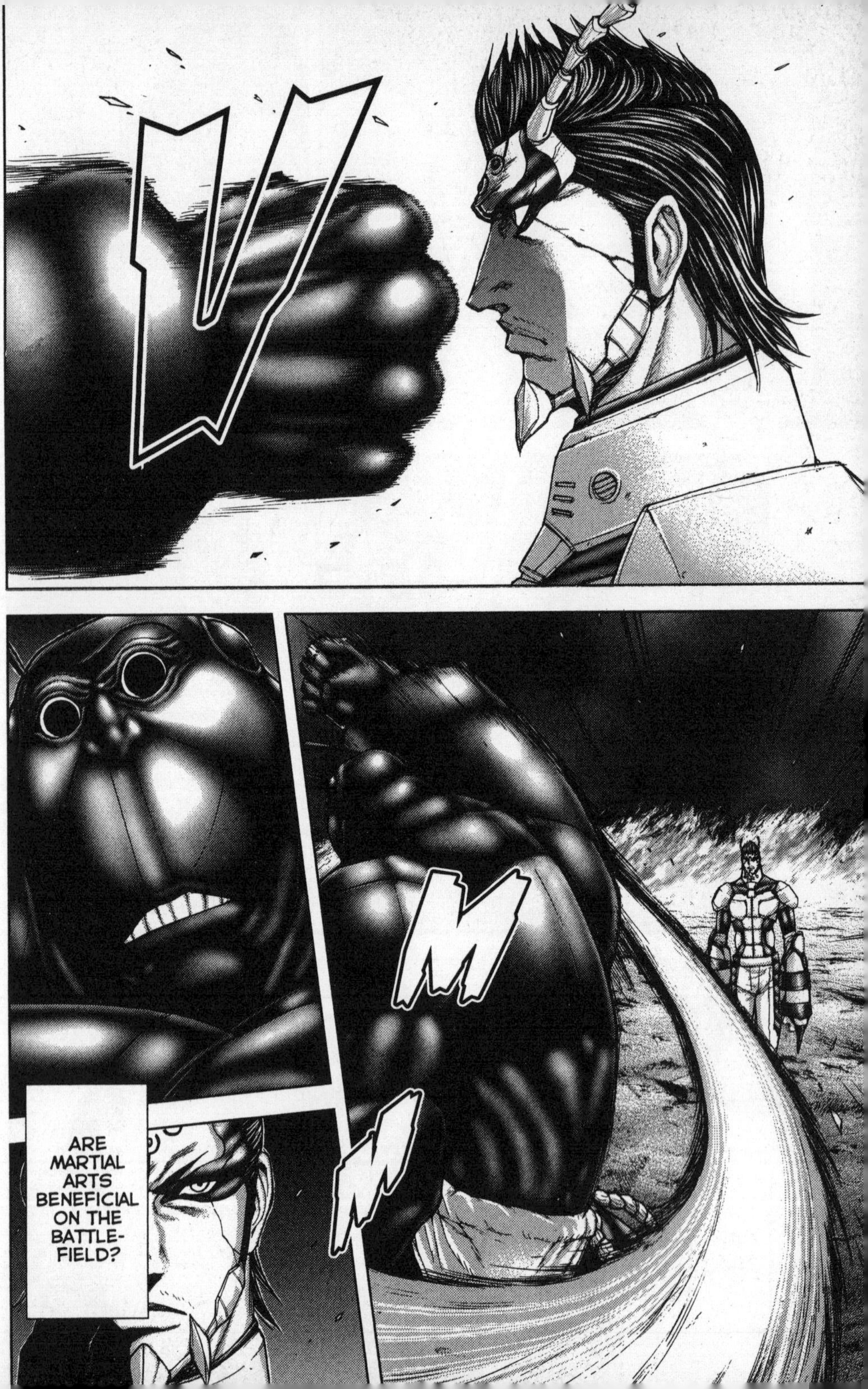
V
M
M
ARE MARTIAL ARTS BENEFICIAL ON THE BATTLE-FIELD?

THERE IS ROOM FOR DEBATE...

...BUT AT THE VERY LEAST...

...MARTIAL ARTS WERE *BORN* ON THE BATTLE-FIELD.

THEY...

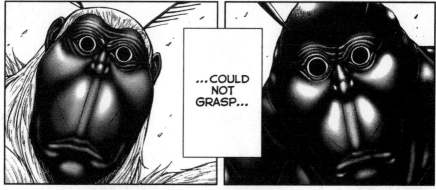

...COULD NOT GRASP...

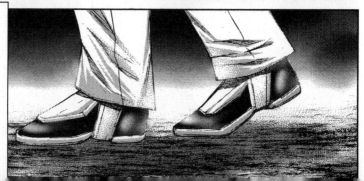

...HOW SHOKICHI KOMACHI'S 6TH-DAN FOOTWORK...

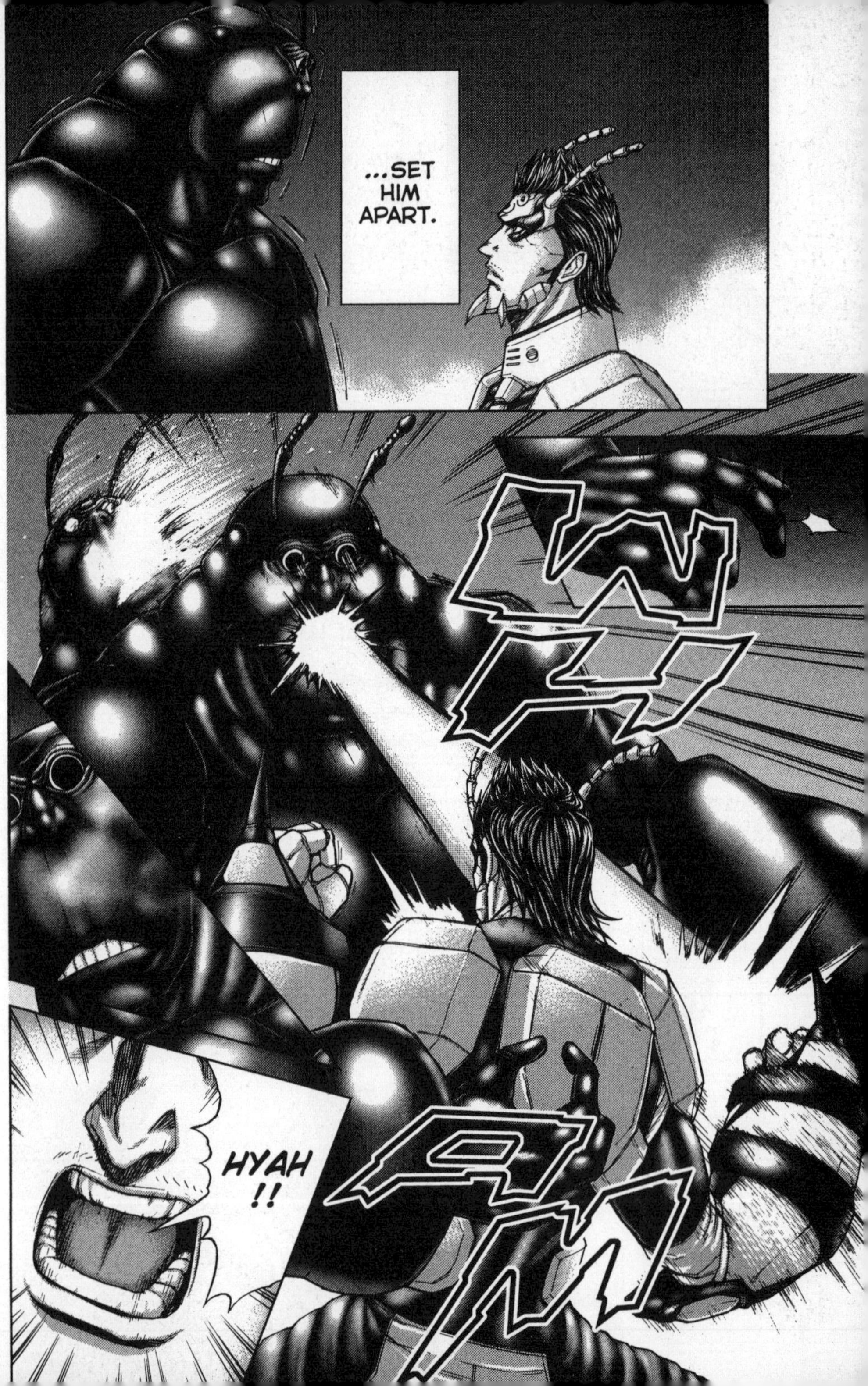
...SET HIM APART.
HYAH !!

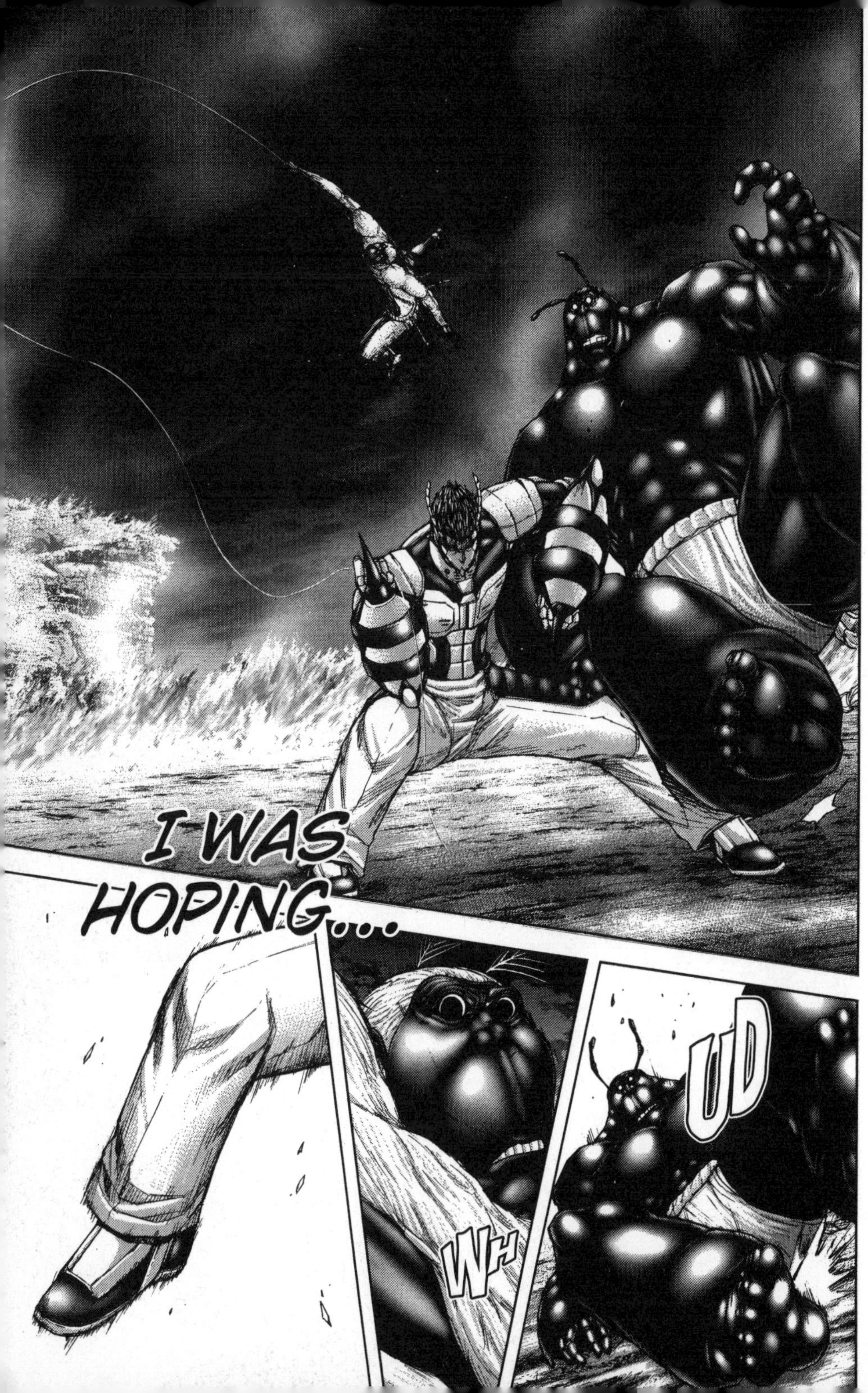
I WAS HOPING...
UD
WH

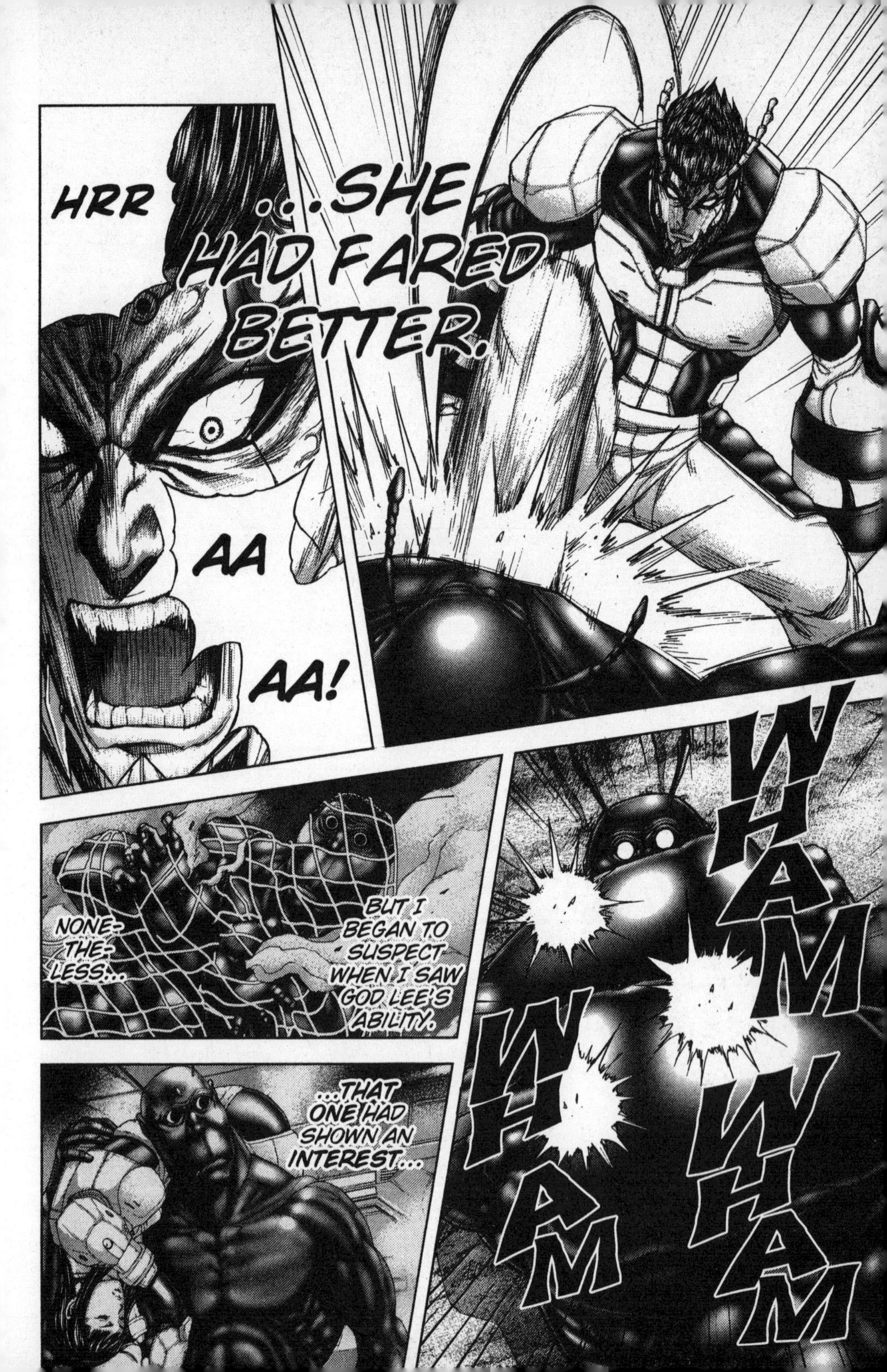
...SHE HAD FARED BETTER.
HRR
AA
AA!
WHAM
WHAM
WHAM
BUT I BEGAN TO SUSPECT WHEN I SAW GOD LEE'S ABILITY.
NONE-THE-LESS...
...THAT ONE HAD SHOWN AN INTEREST...

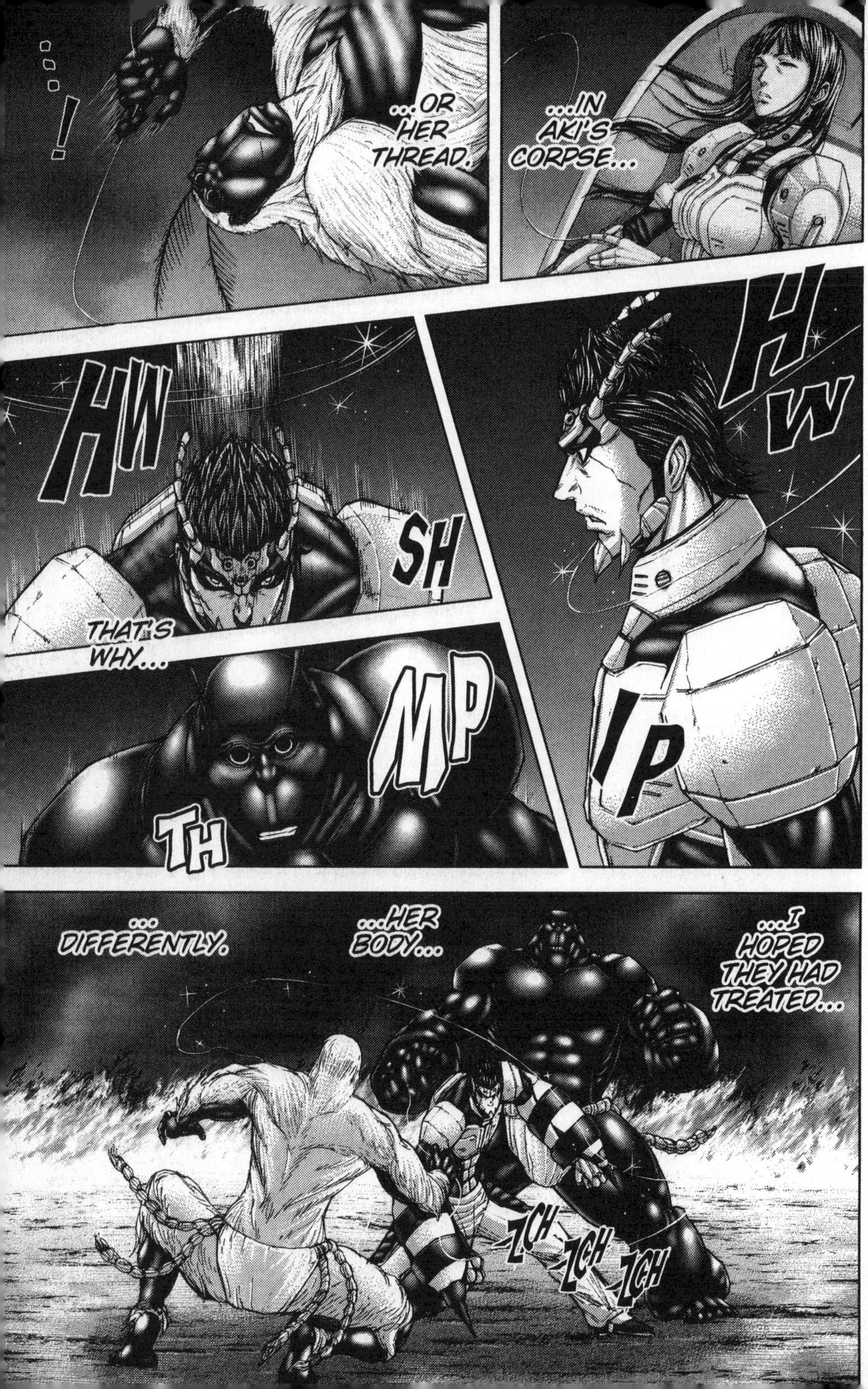
...IN AKI'S CORPSE...
...OR HER THREAD.
...!
HW
IP
HW
SH
THAT'S WHY...
MP
TH
...I HOPED THEY HAD TREATED...
...HER BODY...
...DIFFERENTLY.
ZCH
ZCH
ZCH

I AM **NOT** IN THE MOOD FOR THIS!

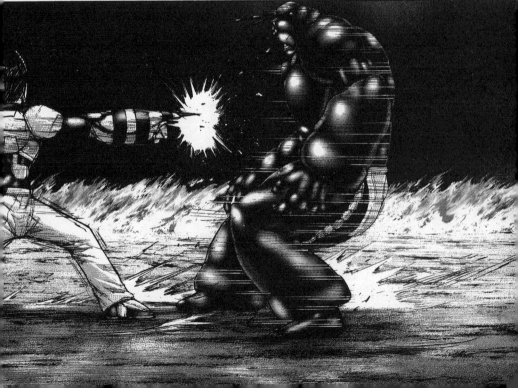

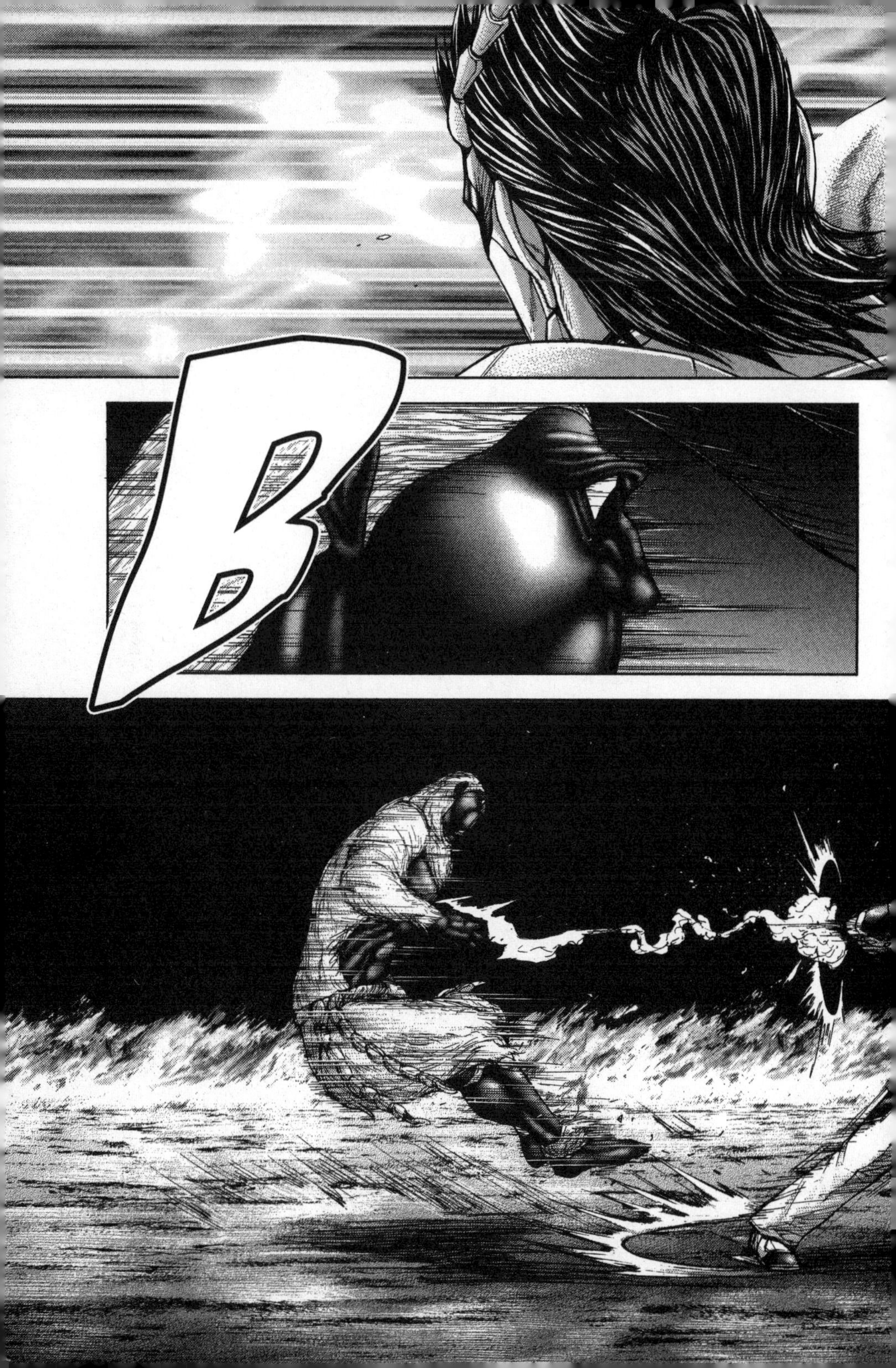
B

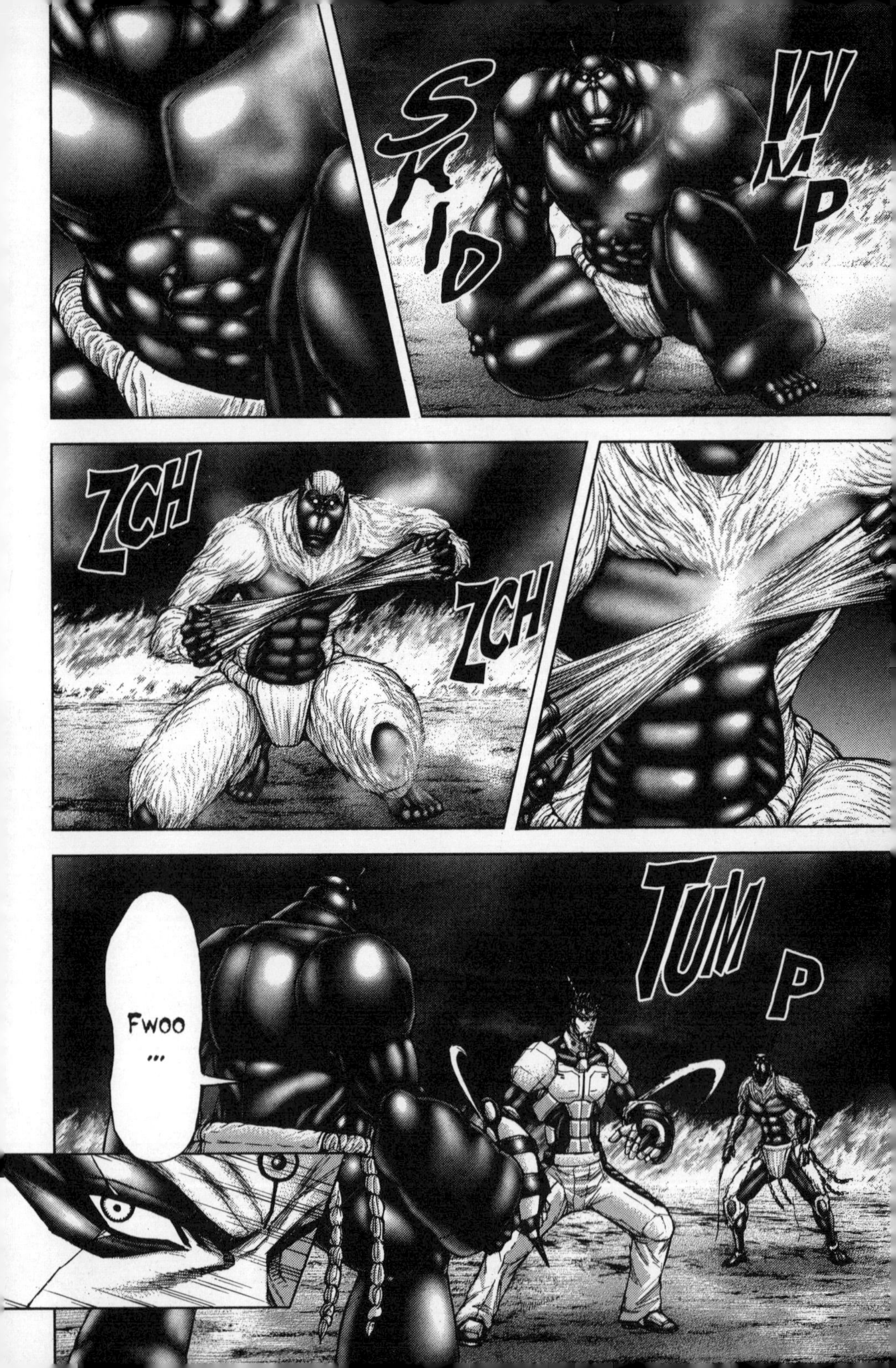
SKID
WMP
ZCH
ZCH
TUMP
Fwoo...

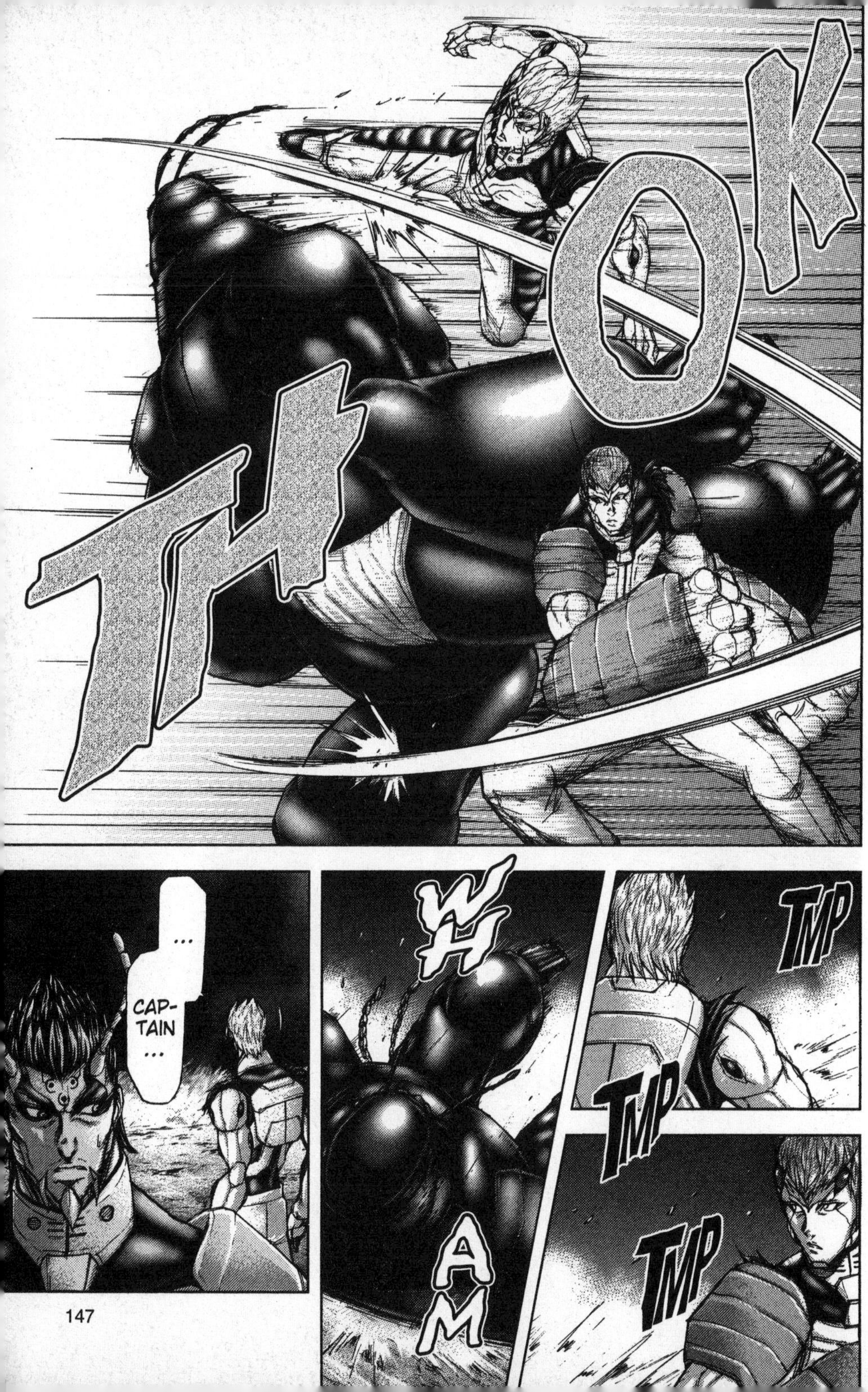
THOK
TMP
TMP
TMP
TMP
WH
AM
...
CAP-TAIN
...

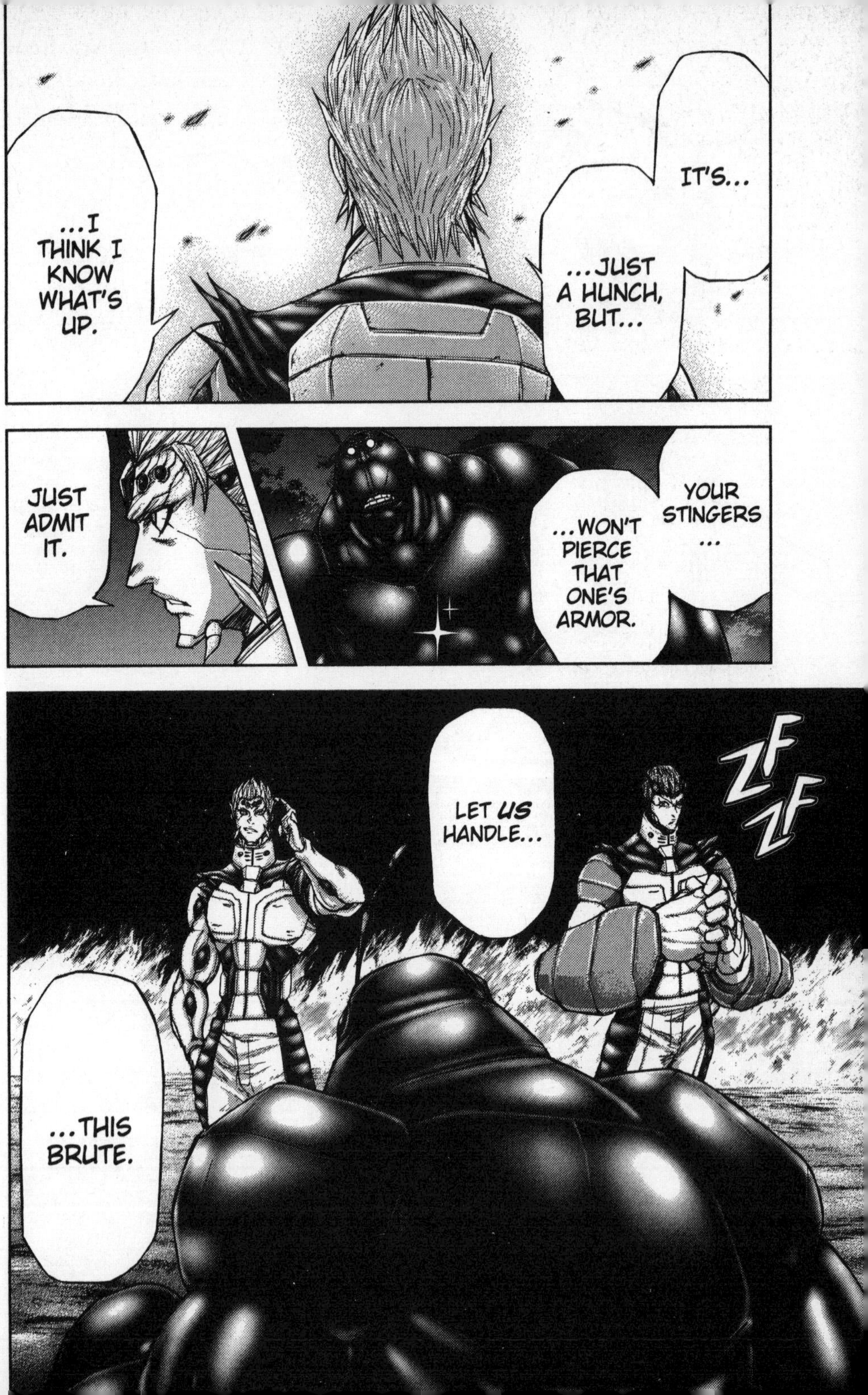
IT'S...
...JUST A HUNCH, BUT...
...I THINK I KNOW WHAT'S UP.
YOUR STINGERS...
...WON'T PIERCE THAT ONE'S ARMOR.
JUST ADMIT IT.
ZF ZF
LET US HANDLE...
...THIS BRUTE.

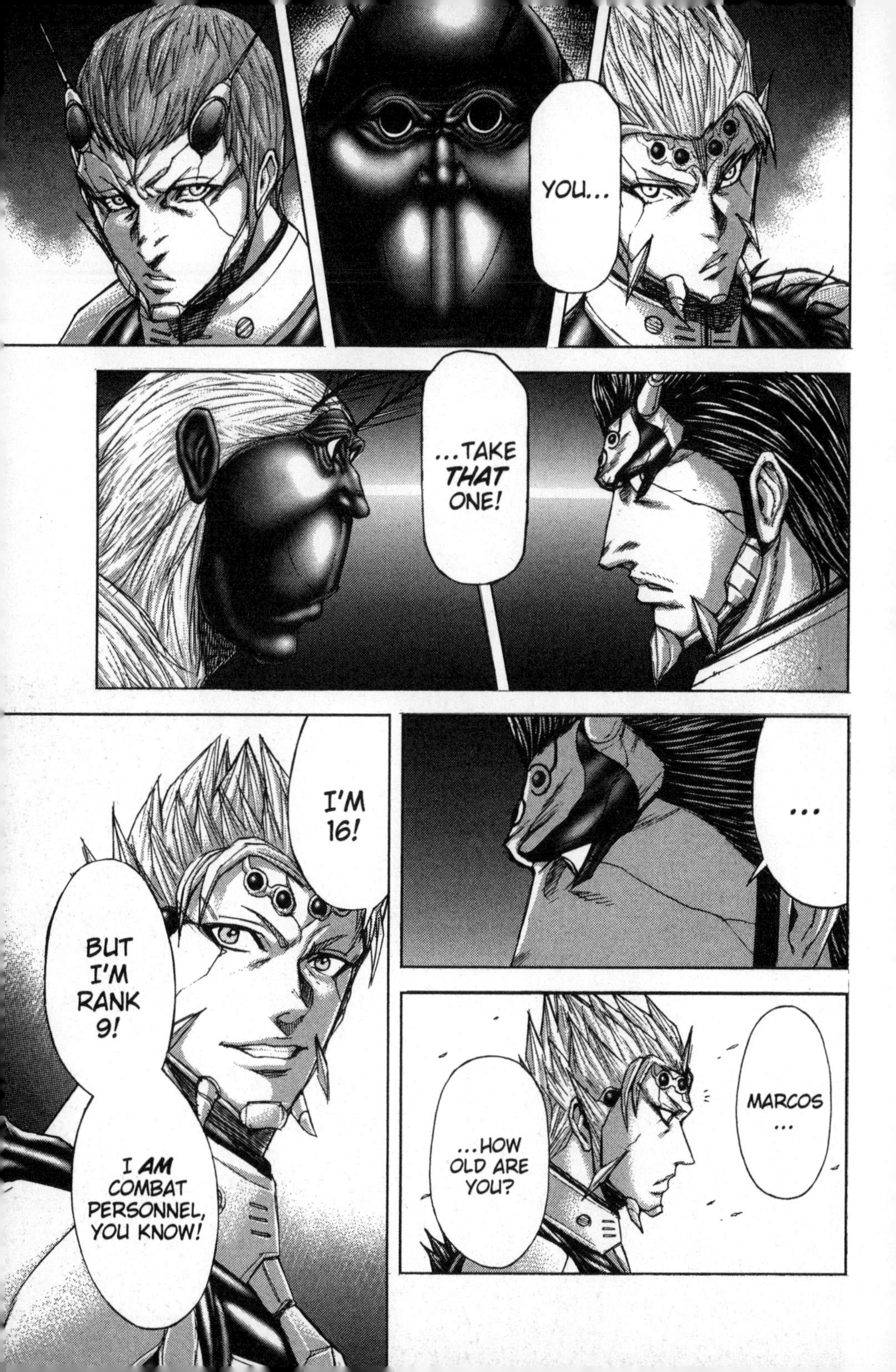
YOU...
...TAKE *THAT* ONE!
...
MARCOS...
...HOW OLD ARE YOU?
I'M 16!
BUT I'M RANK 9!
I *AM* COMBAT PERSONNEL, YOU KNOW!

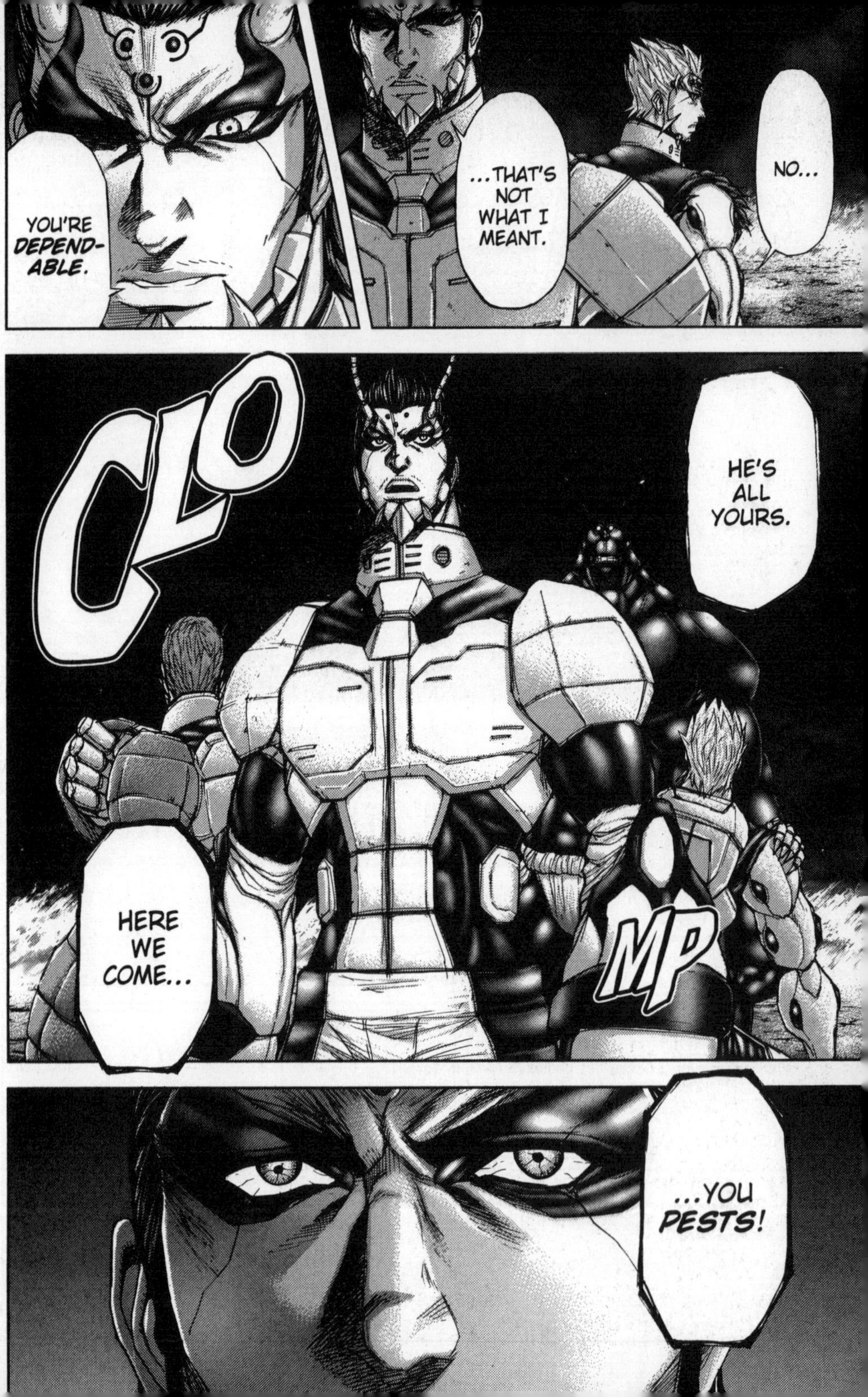
NO...
...THAT'S NOT WHAT I MEANT.
YOU'RE DEPENDABLE.
HE'S ALL YOURS.
CLO
MP
HERE WE COME...
...YOU PESTS!

TERRA FORMARS
Character

Eva Frost ♀

Germany 18 yrs. 162 cm 54kg

Favorite Foods: Grilled cow guts, fish soup
Dislikes: Using love as an excuse
Eye Color: Green Blood Type: B
DOB: June 29 (Cancer)
Something difficult to admit: She likes the
CD she borrowed from Michelle better than the one she got
from Isabella.

The only daughter of an IT millionaire living in a suburb in
northern Germany. However, her parents were extremely
fastidious and protective, so she could rarely leave the
mansion and grew up under oppressive control. When her
parents lost their wealth, they refused to let her get a job
outside and forced her into the M.O. Operation.

The first time she ever ate cow guts or fish bones was after
coming to U-NASA. When she learned that the soft, white
stuff with the weird taste floating in the pot was fish testes,
she made an impolite sound like "Bleagh!" for the first time.

She claims to wear an E cup but is actually three sizes bigger.

Jared Anderson ♂

America 25 yrs. 1681 cm 86kg

Favorite Food: Hamburgers
　　　　　　(and not thin ones)
Dislikes: Erotic manga that get serious
　　　　　after about the fourth chapter
Eye Color: Gold Blood Type: B
DOB: August 16 (Leo)
Skill: Playing bass

Raised in an average home, he volunteered for the
air force after graduating from high school and was
assigned to communications.

Out of consideration for his peers, he took his duties
seriously, but he was bad with money and couldn't
overcome his love of luxury and gambling. As his debts
grew, he joined the Annex Project.

He gets drunk easily, so he knows a lot about
non-alcoholic cocktails with impressive names.

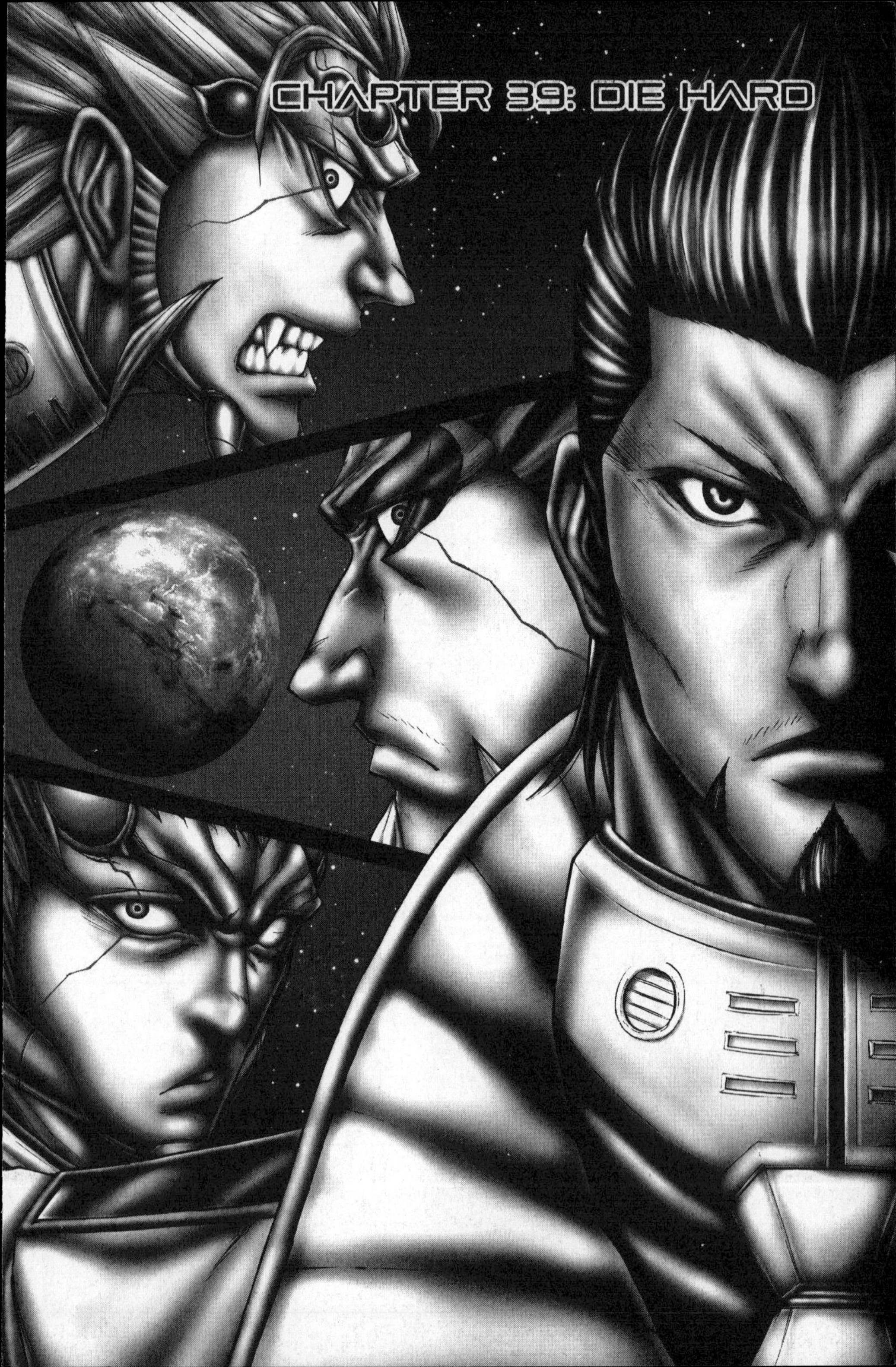
CHAPTER 39: DIE HARD

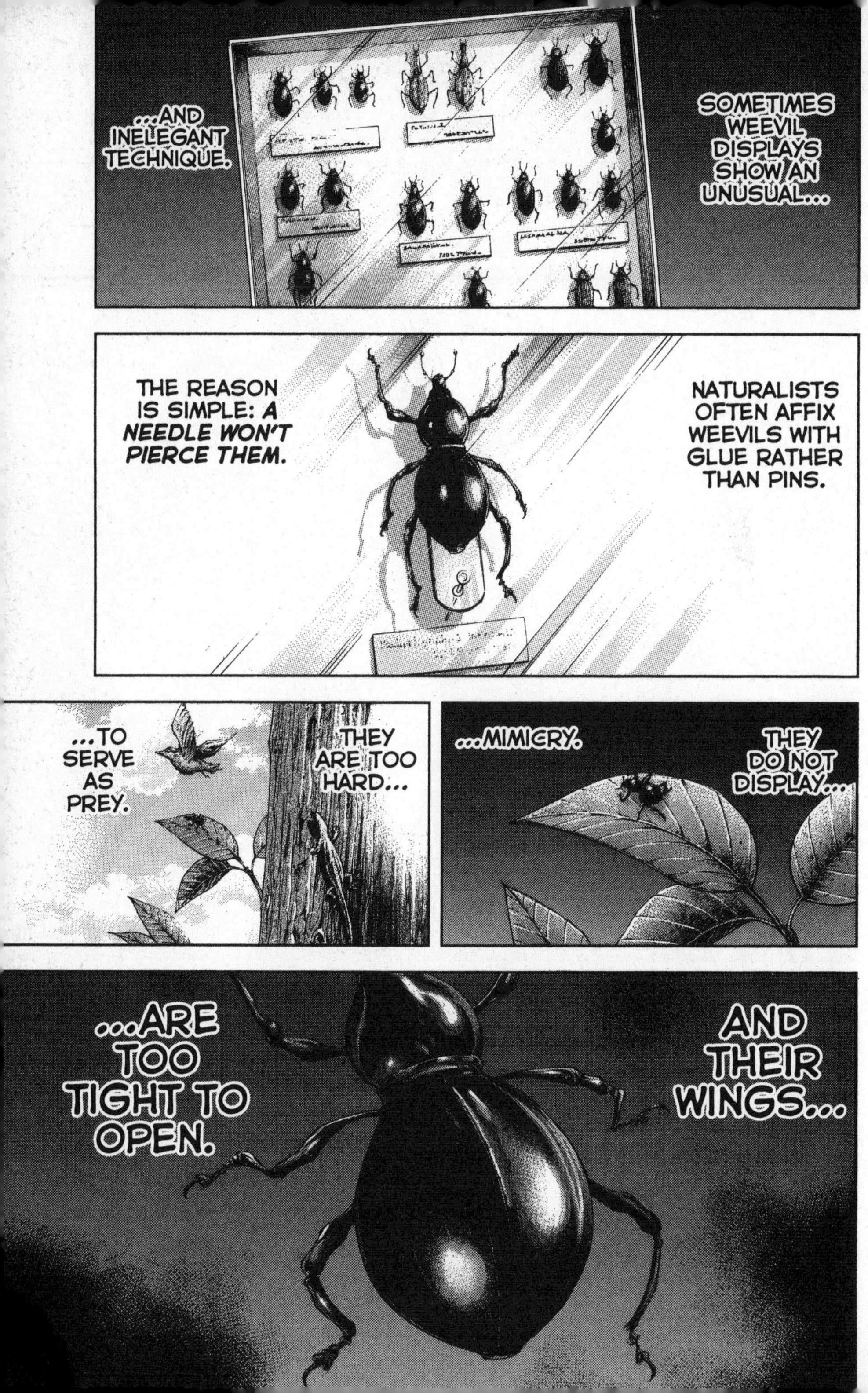
SOMETIMES WEEVIL DISPLAYS SHOW AN UNUSUAL...
...AND INELEGANT TECHNIQUE.
NATURALISTS OFTEN AFFIX WEEVILS WITH GLUE RATHER THAN PINS.
THE REASON IS SIMPLE: *A NEEDLE WON'T PIERCE THEM.*
THEY DO NOT DISPLAY...
...MIMICRY.
THEY ARE TOO HARD...
...TO SERVE AS PREY.
AND THEIR WINGS...
...ARE TOO TIGHT TO OPEN.

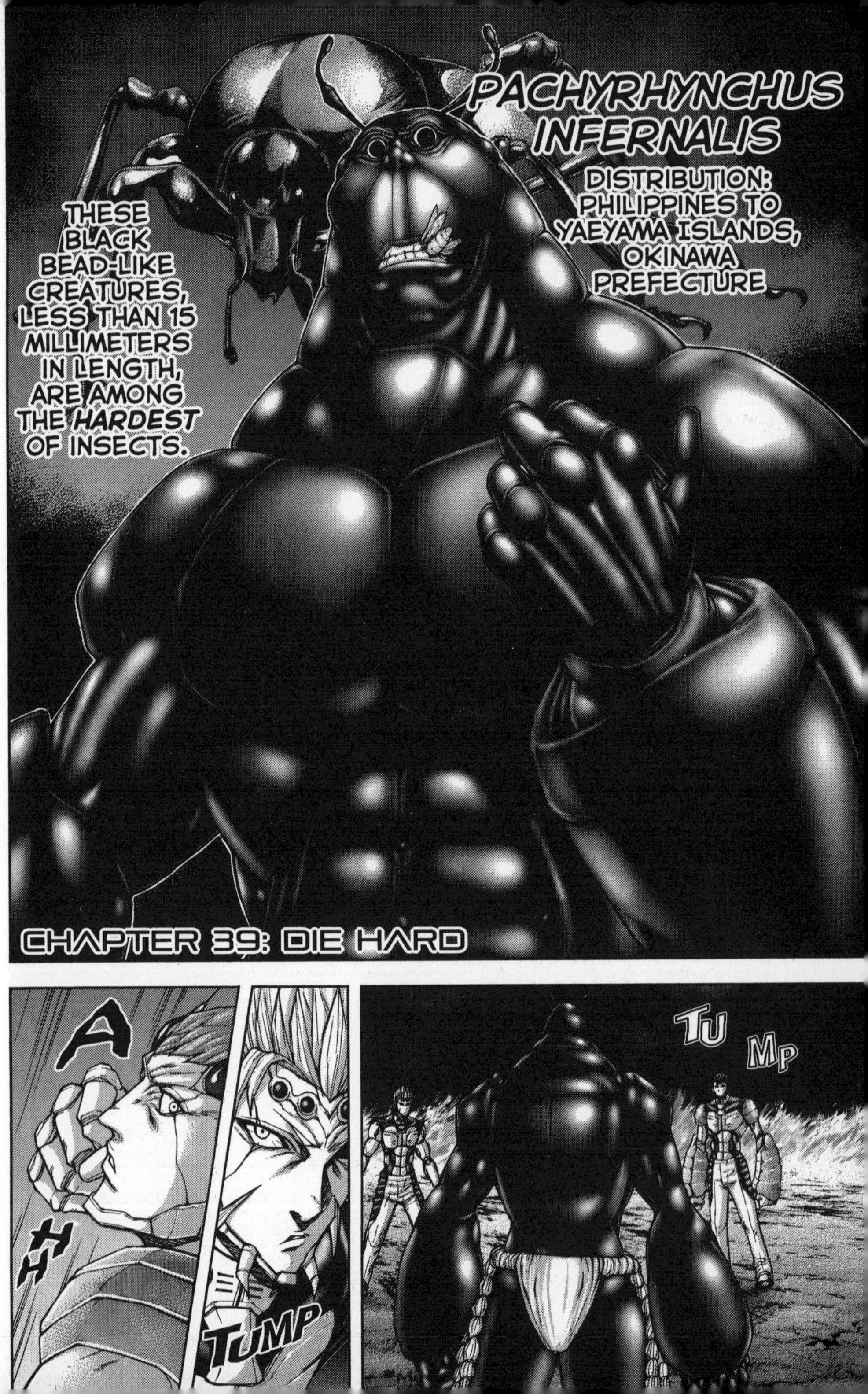
PACHYRHYNCHUS INFERNALIS
DISTRIBUTION: PHILIPPINES TO YAEYAMA ISLANDS, OKINAWA PREFECTURE
THESE BLACK BEAD-LIKE CREATURES, LESS THAN 15 MILLIMETERS IN LENGTH, ARE AMONG THE *HARDEST* OF INSECTS.
CHAPTER 39: DIE HARD
TU MP
TUMP
A
HH

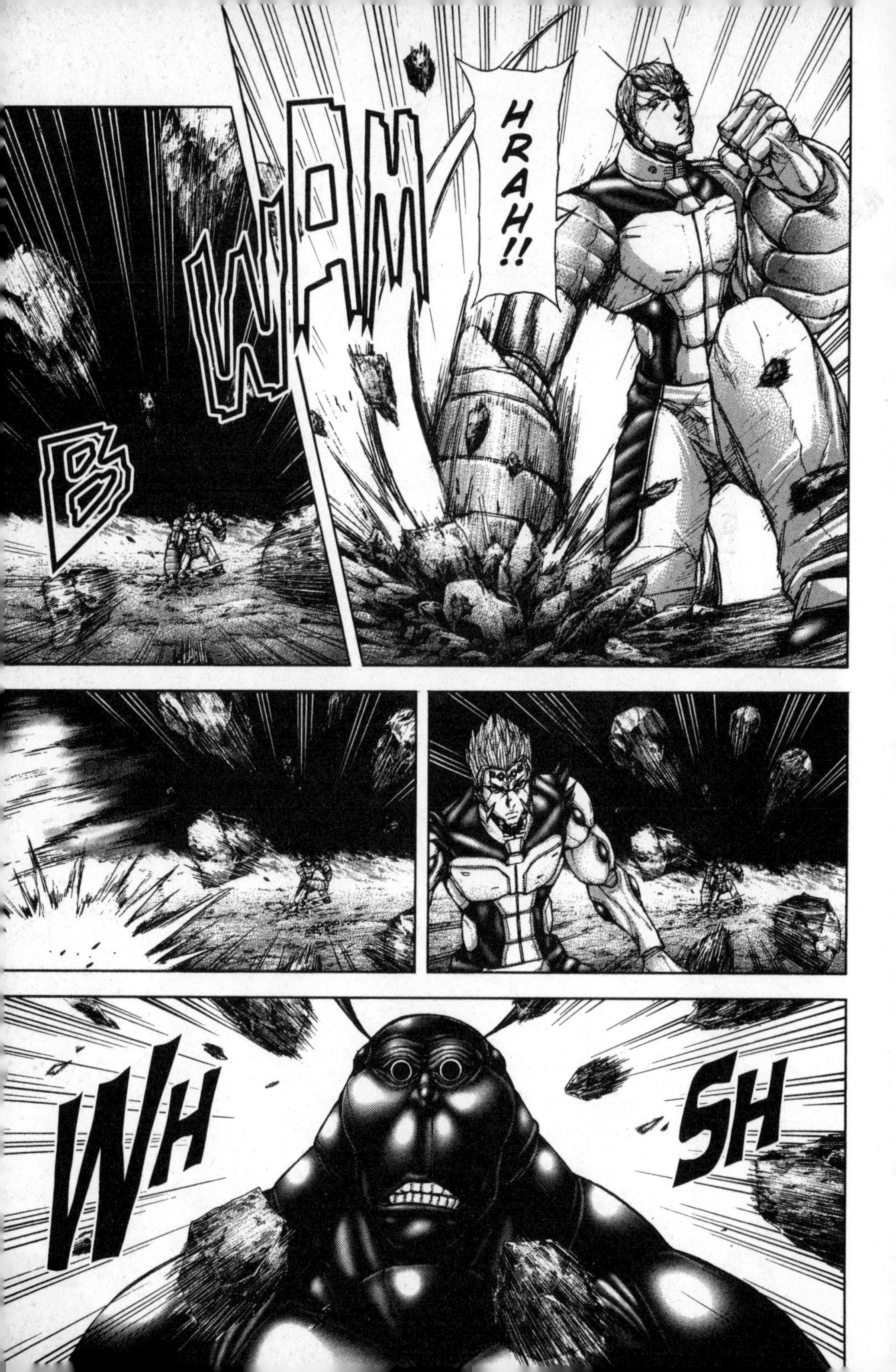

HRAH!!
WAM
B
WH
SH

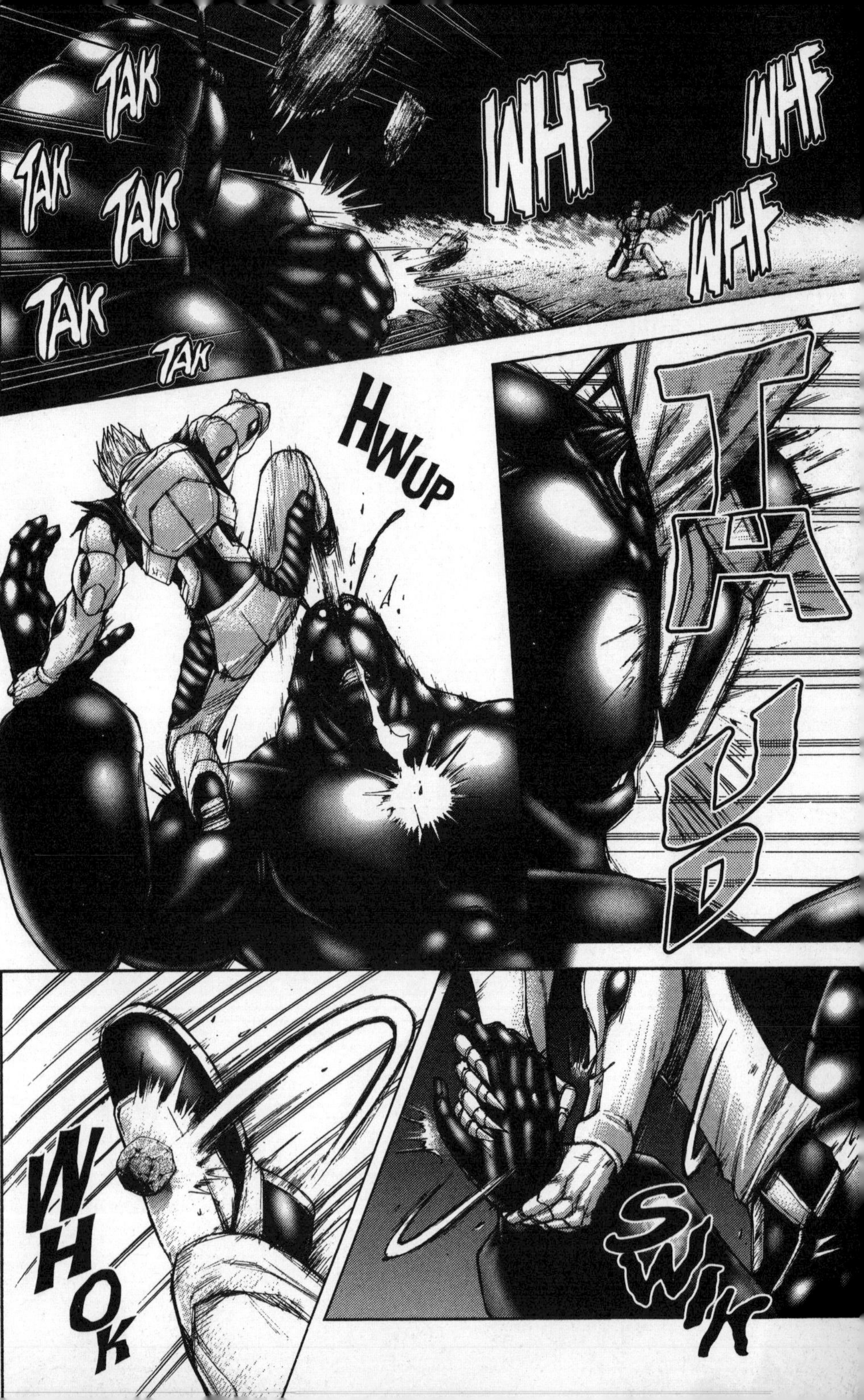
WHF
WHF
WHF
TAK
TAK
TAK
TAK
TAK
THUD
HWUP
SWIK
WHOK

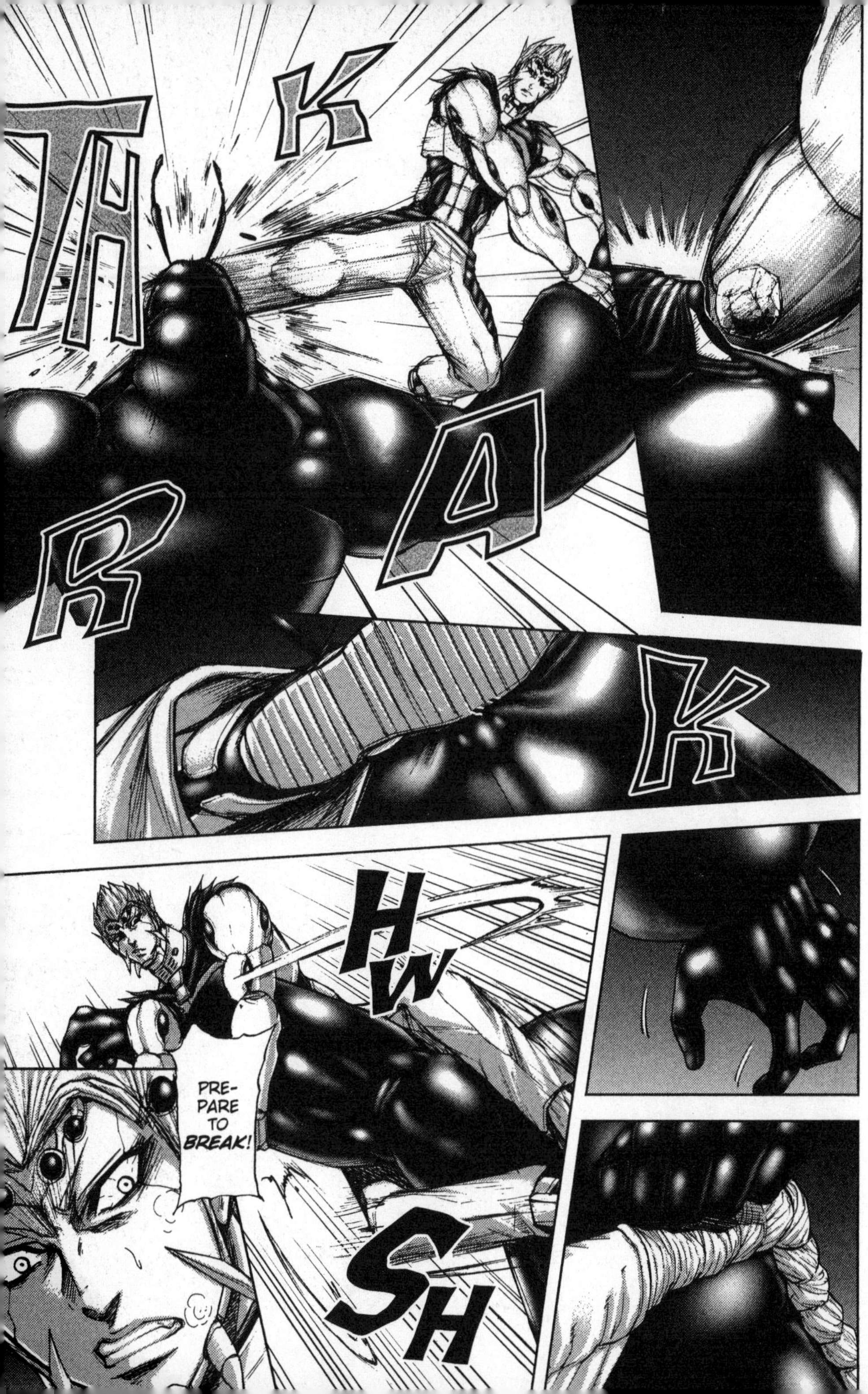
K
TH
A
R
K
HW
SH
PRE-PARE TO BREAK!

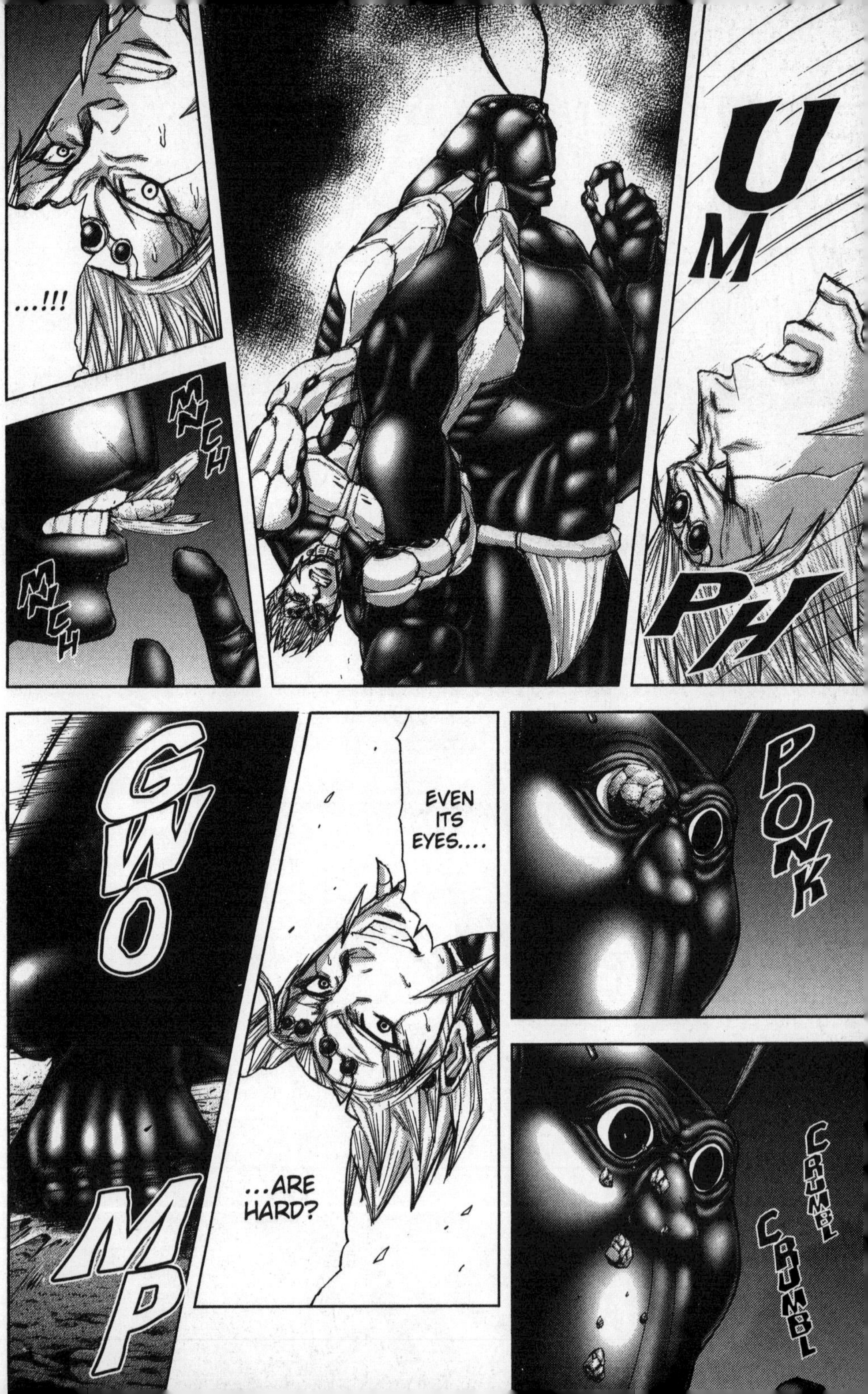
UMPH
...!!!
MNCH
MNCH
PONK
CRUMBL
CRUMBL
EVEN ITS EYES....
...ARE HARD?
GWOMP

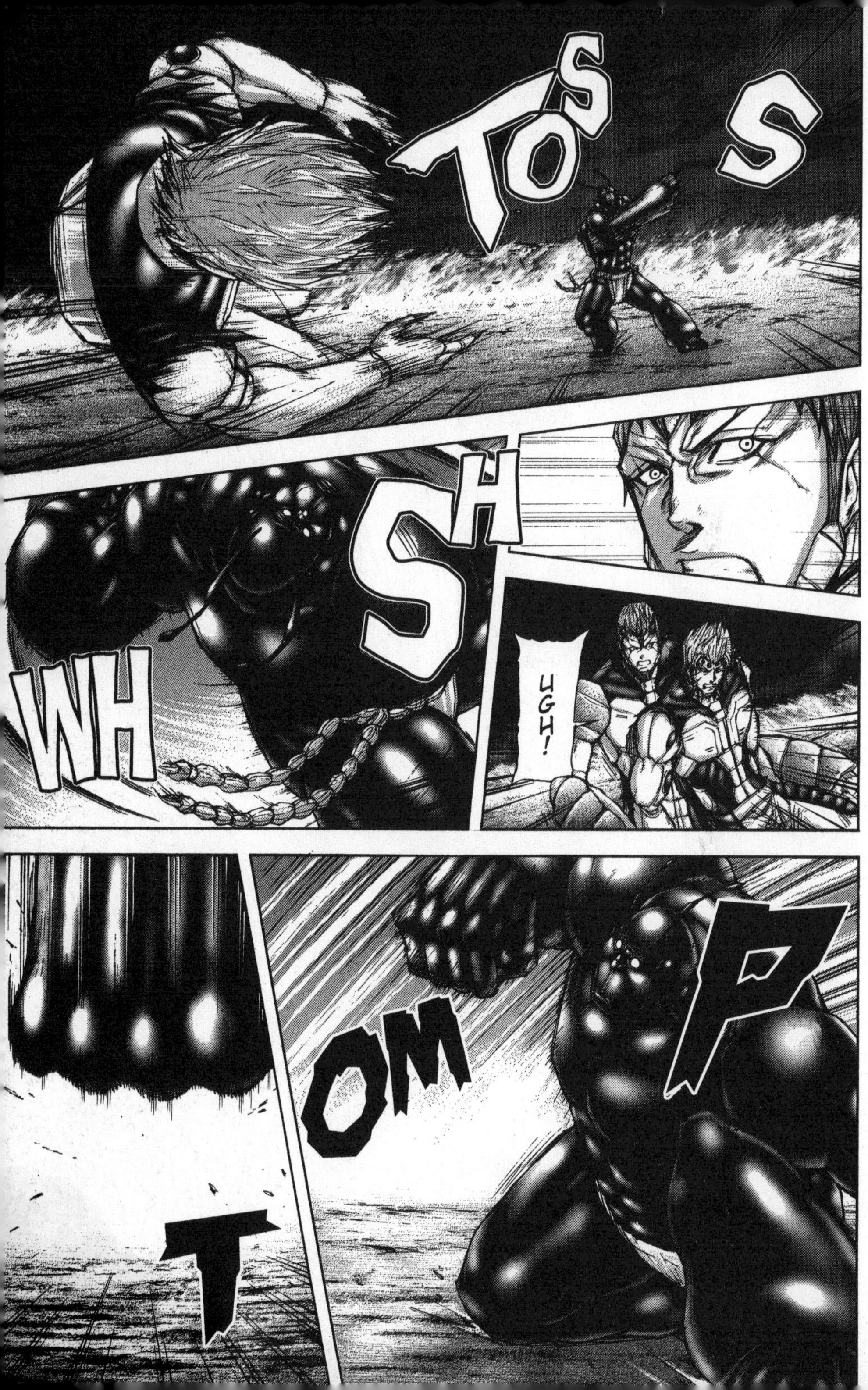
TOSS
UGH!
WHSH
TOMP

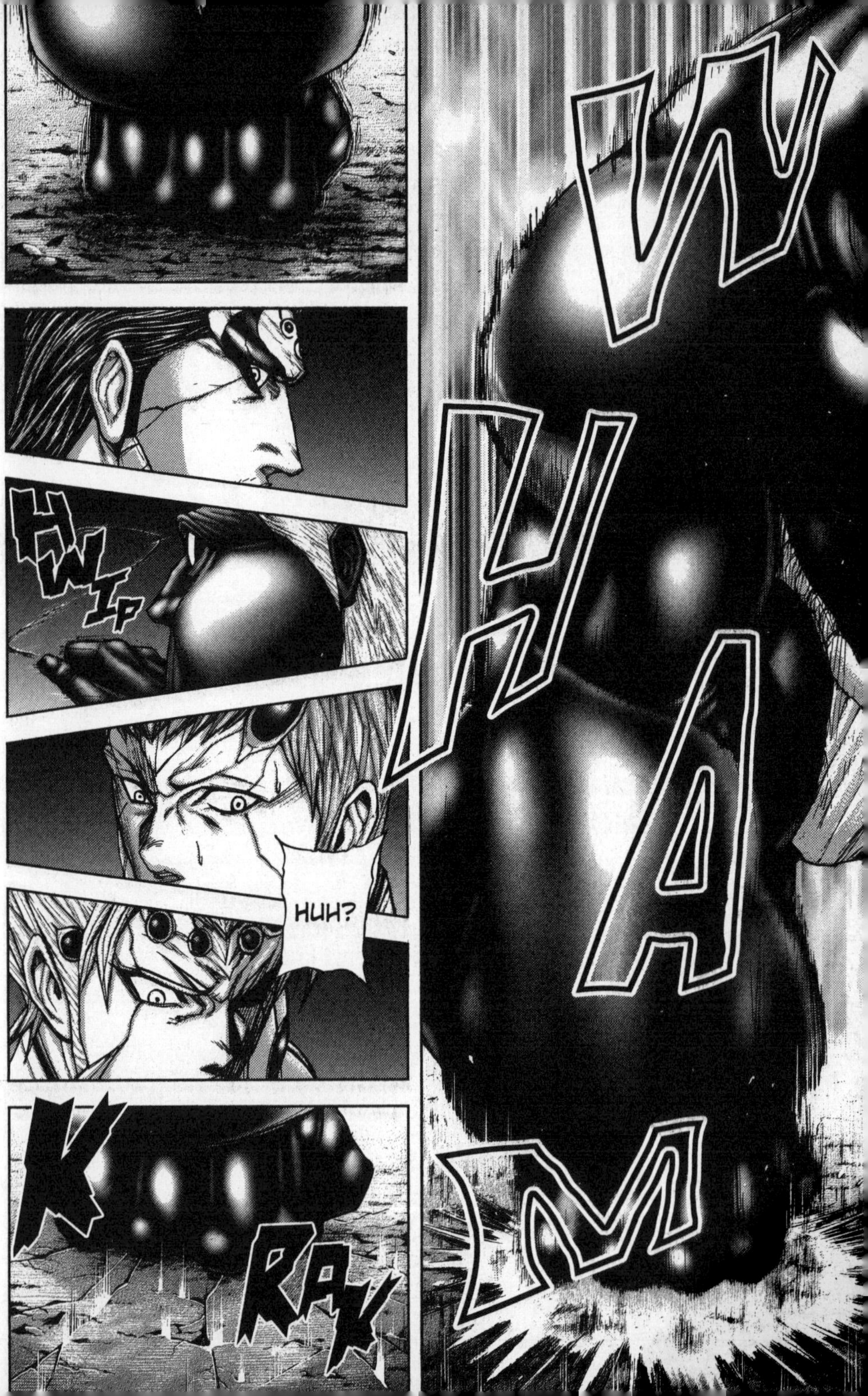
WHAM
HWIP
HUH?
KRAK

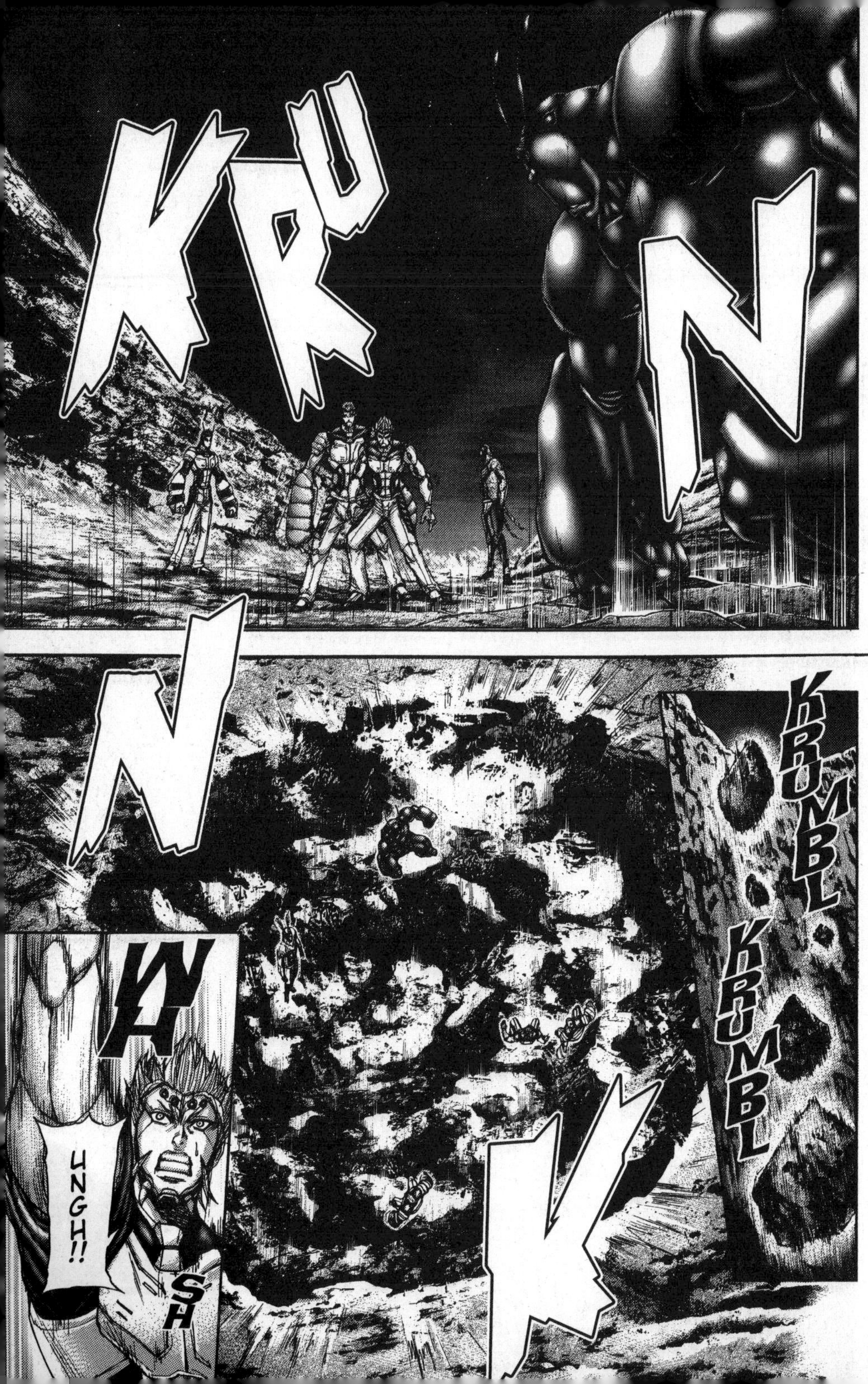
KRU
N
N
K
KRUMBL
KRUMBL
WH
UNGH!!
SH

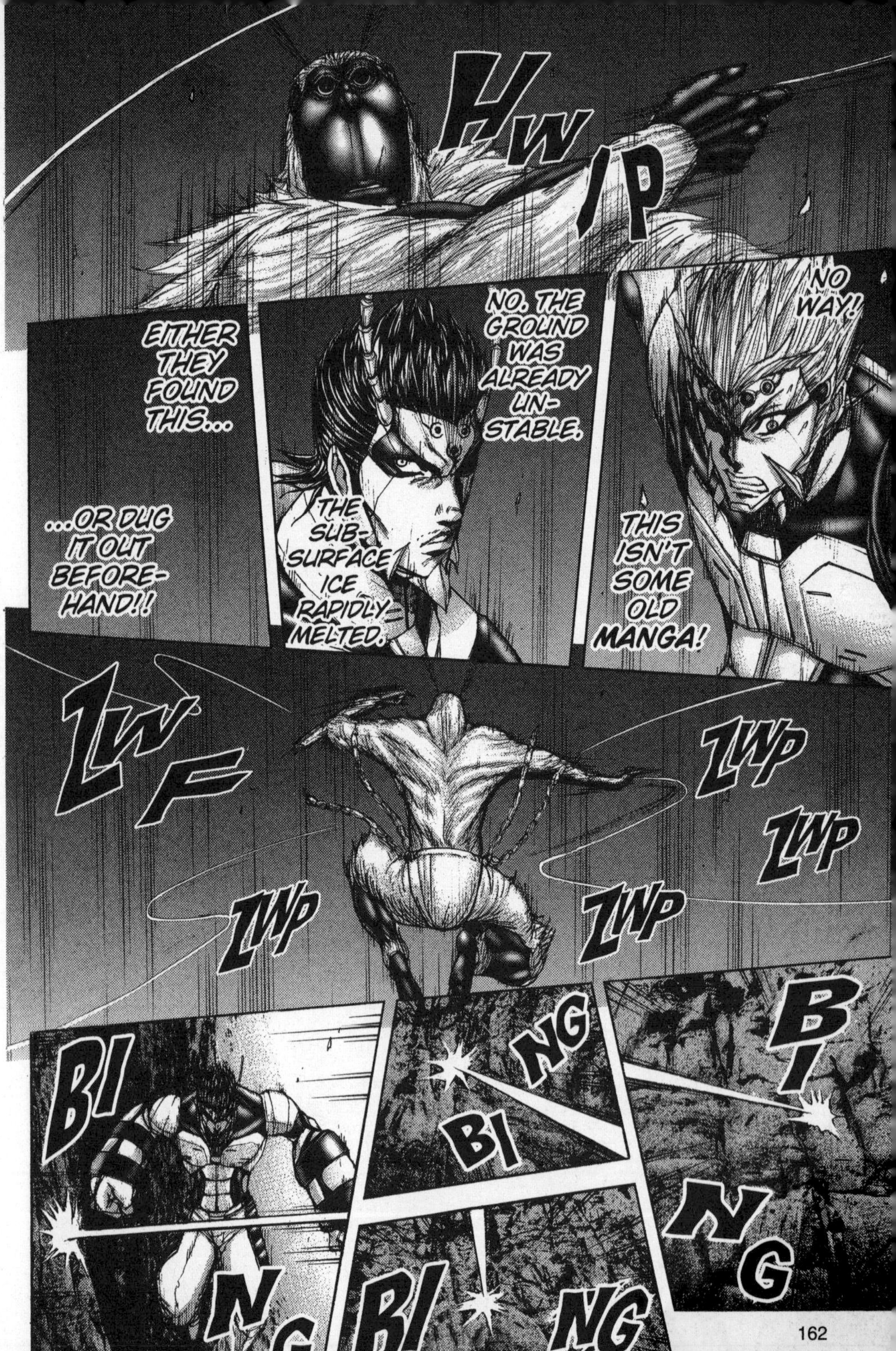
HWIP
NO WAY!
THIS ISN'T SOME OLD MANGA!
NO. THE GROUND WAS ALREADY UN-STABLE.
THE SUB-SURFACE ICE RAPIDLY MELTED.
EITHER THEY FOUND THIS...
...OR DUG IT OUT BEFORE-HAND!!
ZWP
ZWP
ZWP
ZWF
ZWP
BING
BING
BING
BING
BING

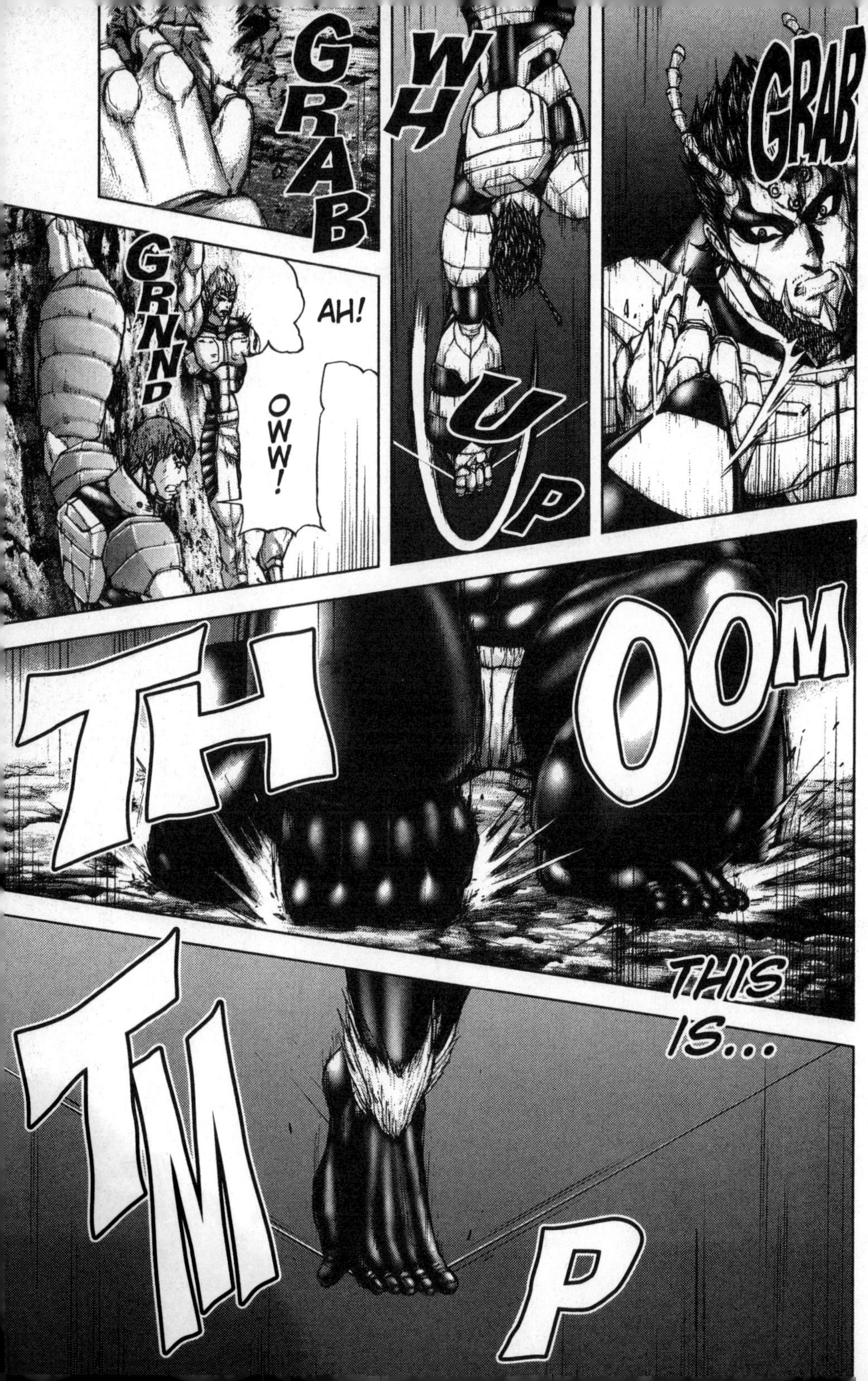
GRAB
WH
UP
GRAB
GRNND
AH!
OWW!
THOOM
THIS IS...
TMP

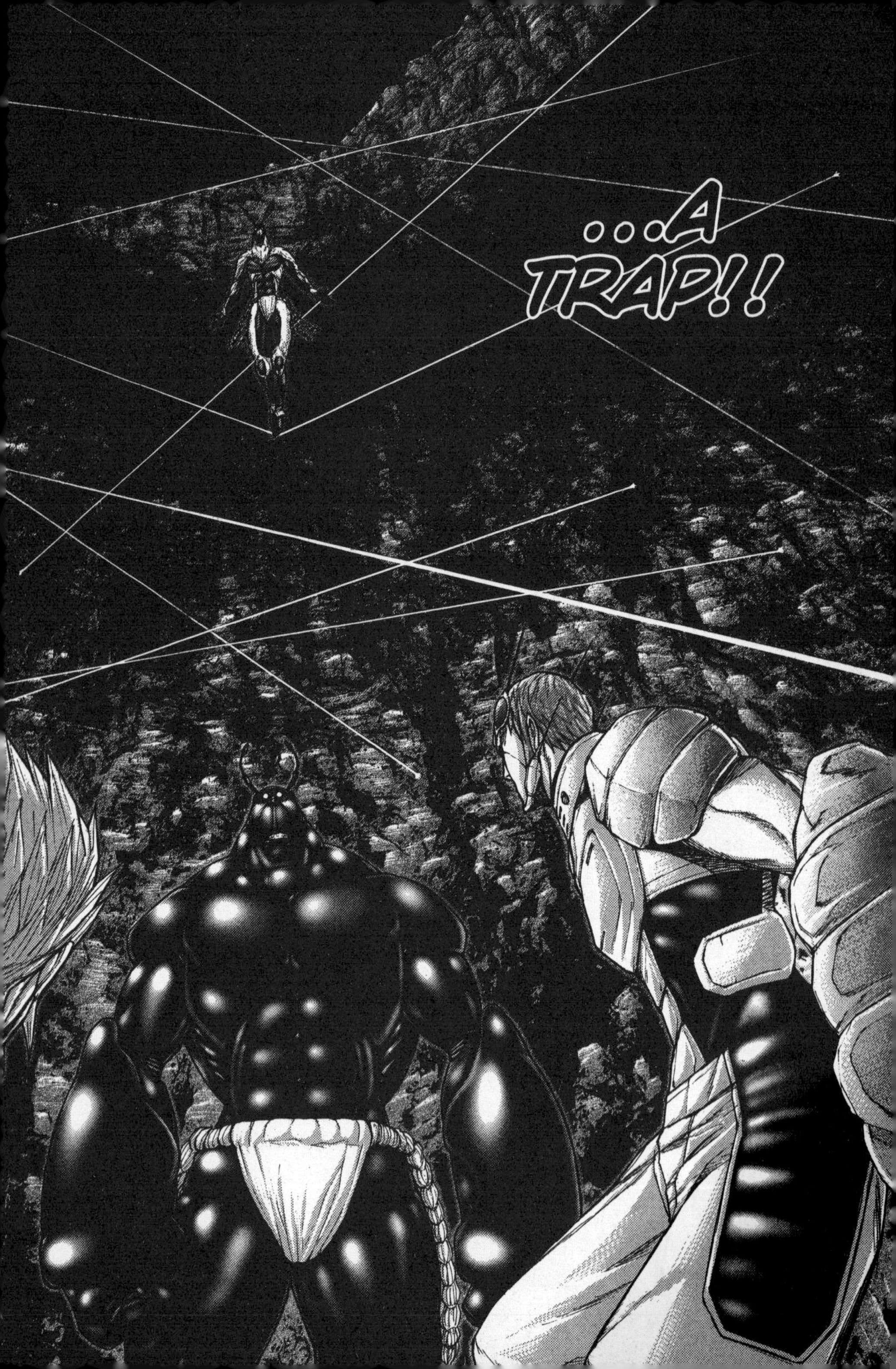
...A TRAP!!

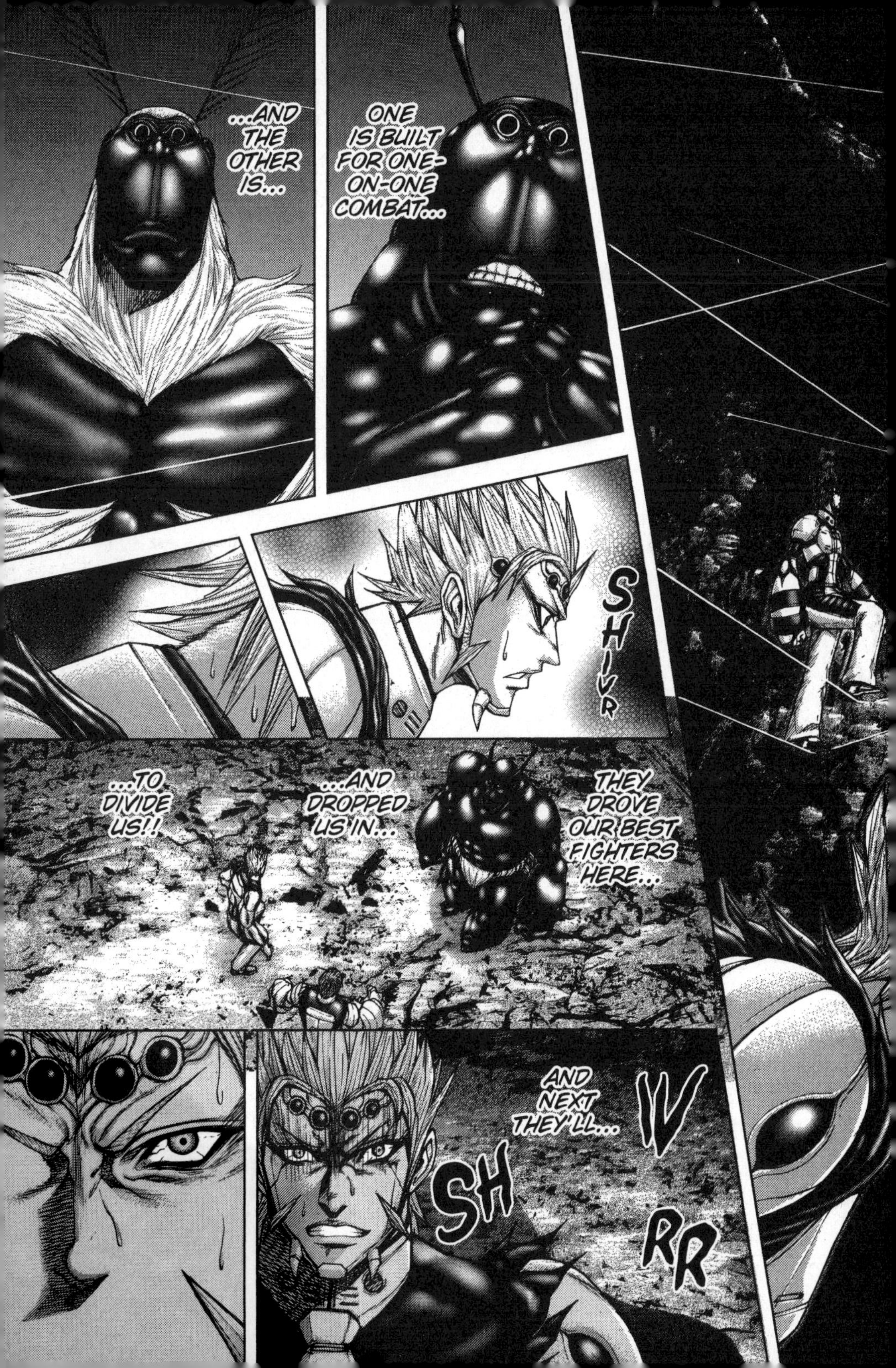
ONE IS BUILT FOR ONE-ON-ONE COMBAT...
...AND THE OTHER IS...
SHIVVR
THEY DROVE OUR BEST FIGHTERS HERE...
...AND DROPPED US IN...
...TO DIVIDE US!!
AND NEXT THEY'LL...
IV
RR
SH

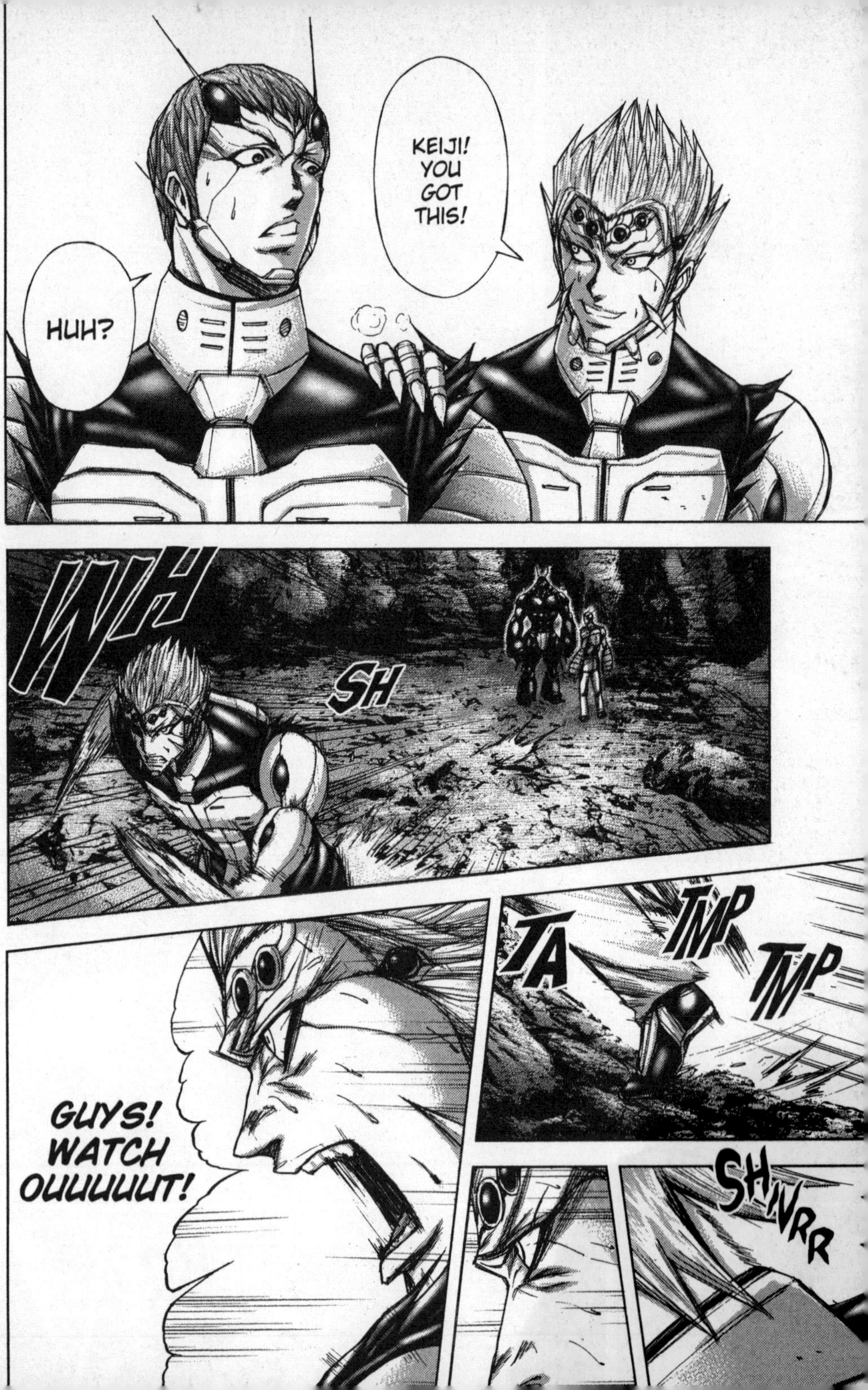
KEIJI! YOU GOT THIS!
HUH?
WH
SH
TA
TMP
TMP
SHNRR
GUYS! WATCH OUUUUUT!

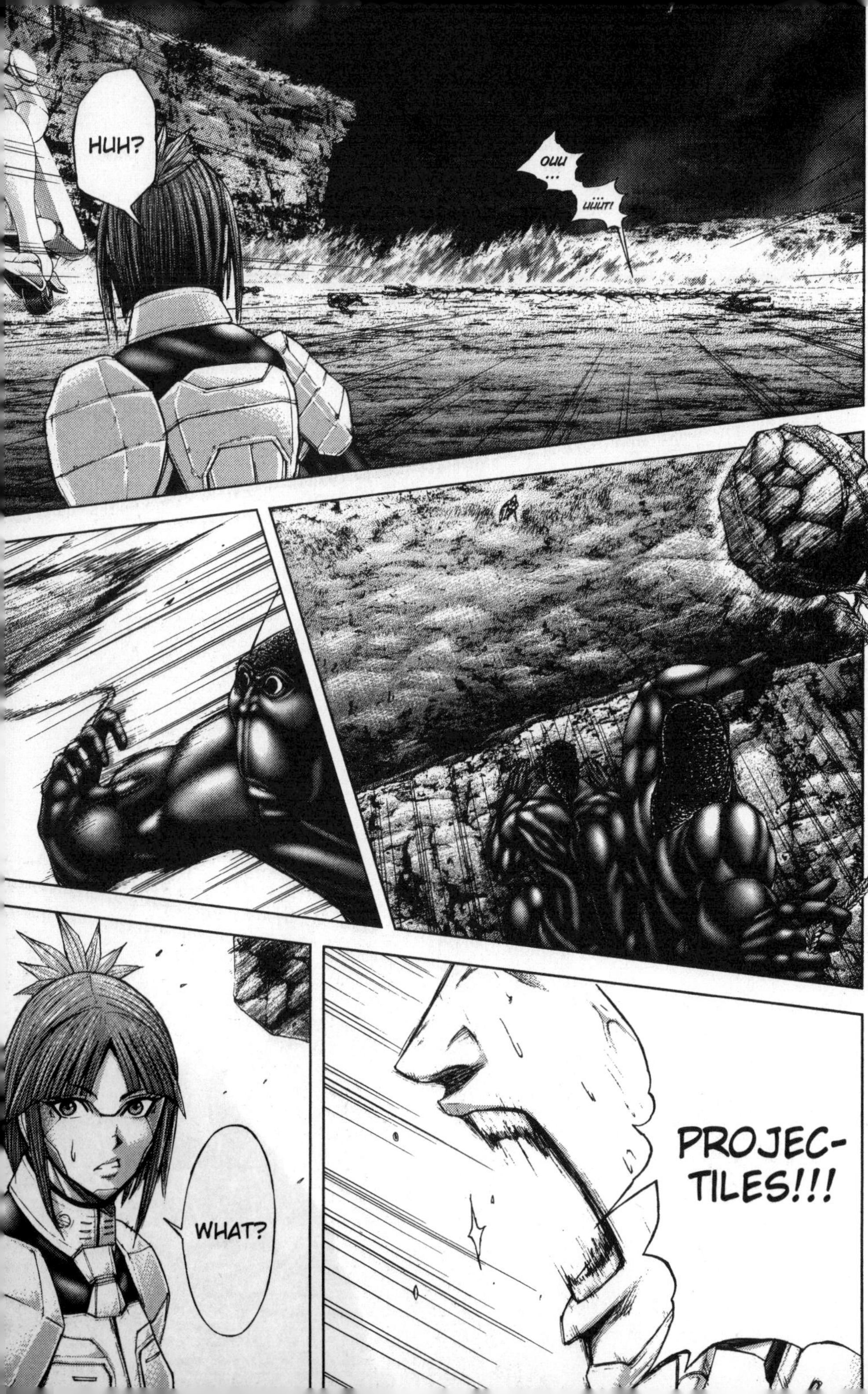
OUU...
...UÜÜT!
HUH?
PROJEC-
TILES!!!
WHAT?

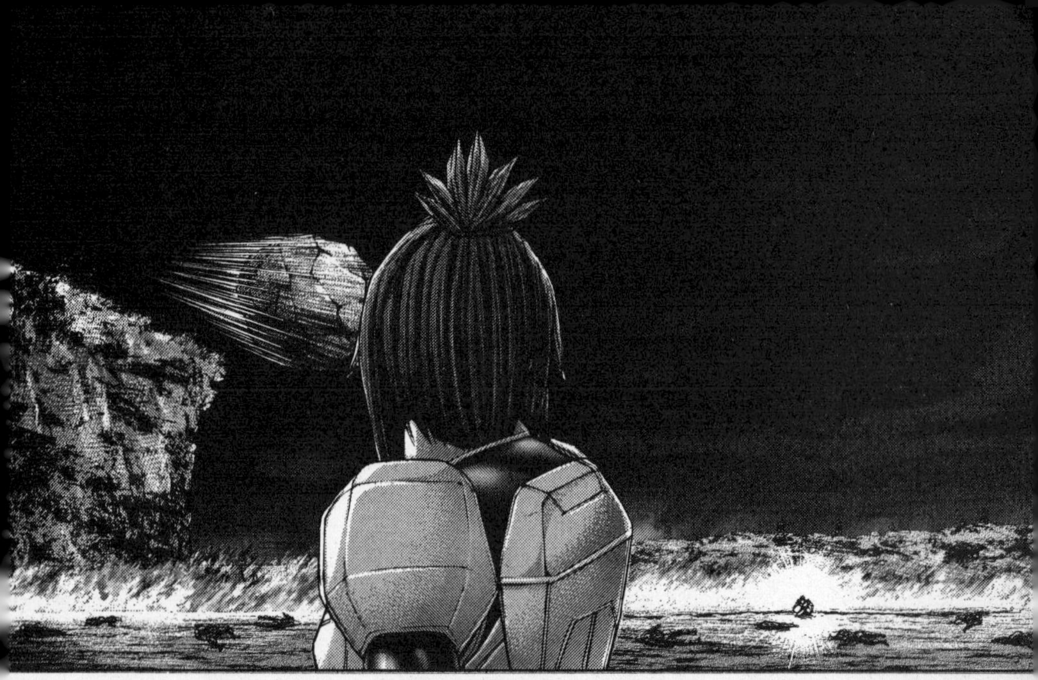

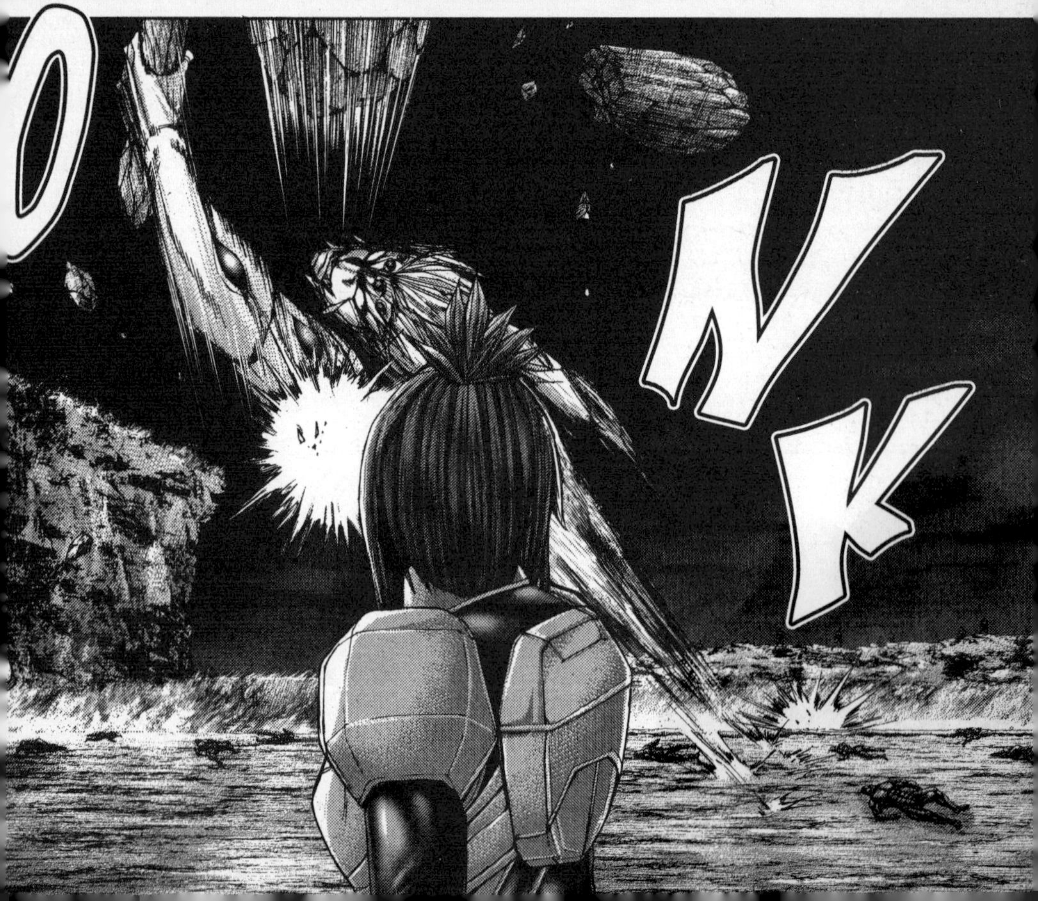
O N K

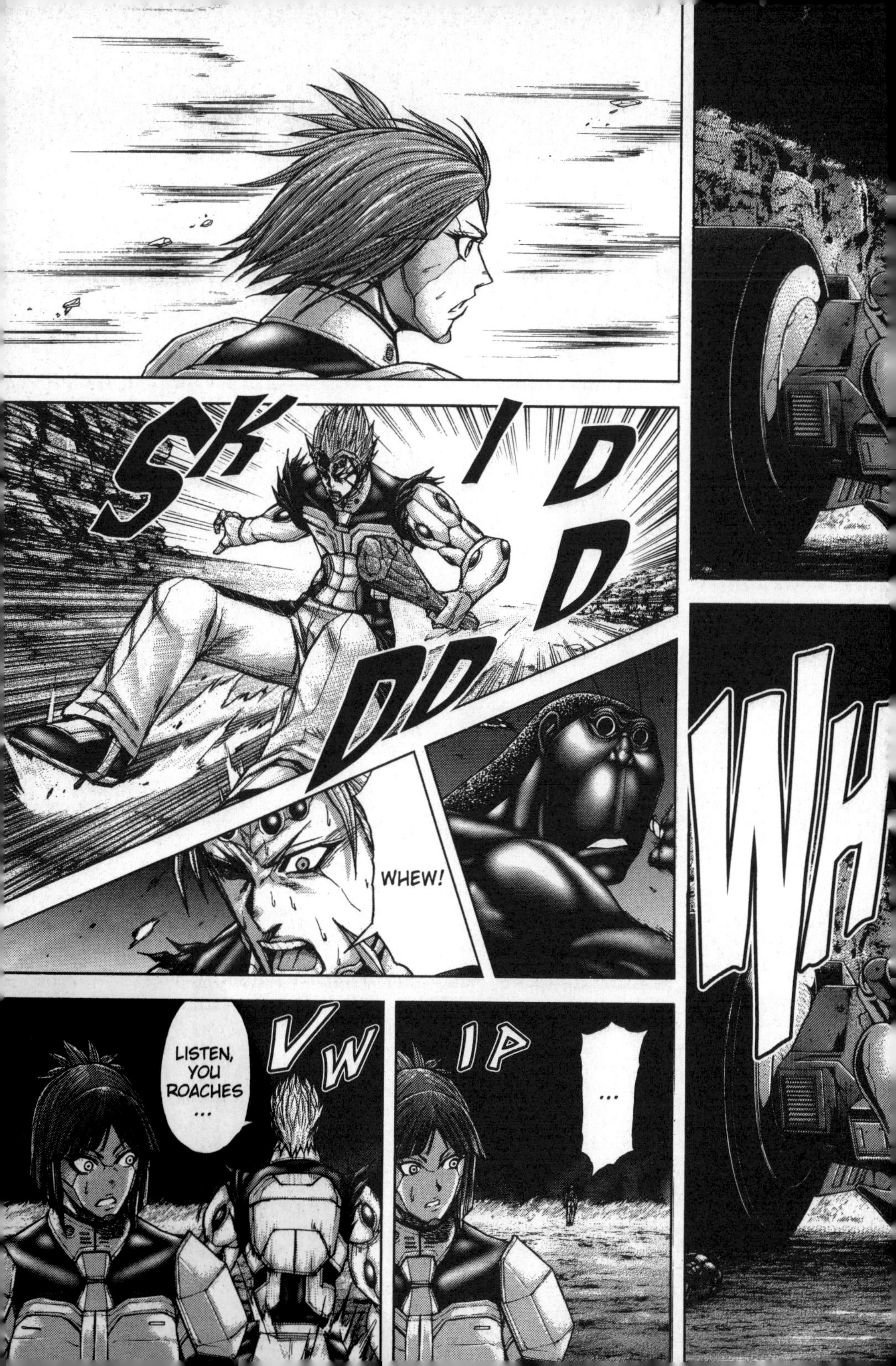
WH
SKIDDDD
WHEW!
VWIP
...
LISTEN, YOU ROACHES ...

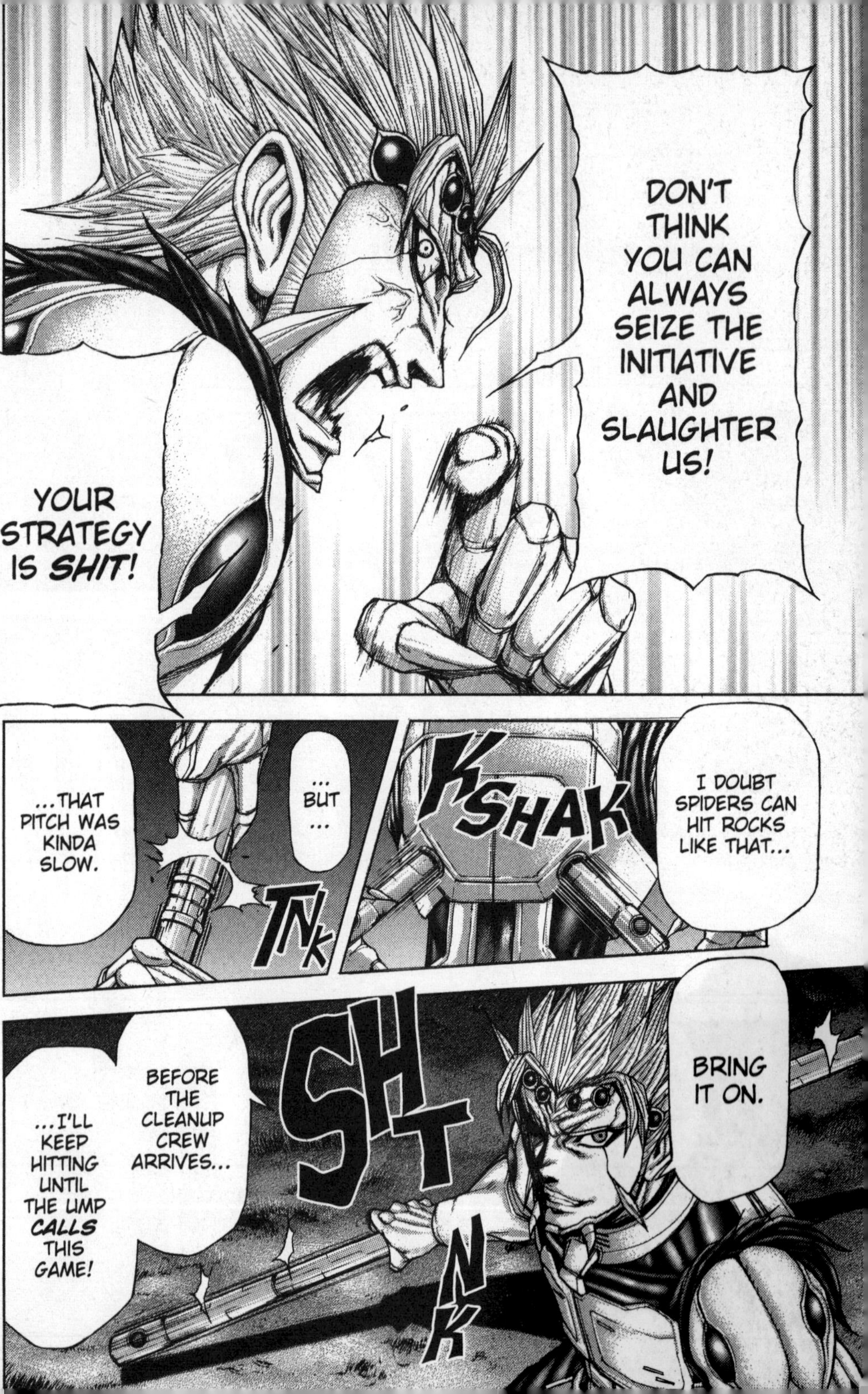
DON'T THINK YOU CAN ALWAYS SEIZE THE INITIATIVE AND SLAUGHTER US!
YOUR STRATEGY IS SHIT!
I DOUBT SPIDERS CAN HIT ROCKS LIKE THAT...
KSHAK
...BUT...
...THAT PITCH WAS KINDA SLOW.
TNK
BRING IT ON.
SHTNK
BEFORE THE CLEANUP CREW ARRIVES...
...I'LL KEEP HITTING UNTIL THE UMP CALLS THIS GAME!

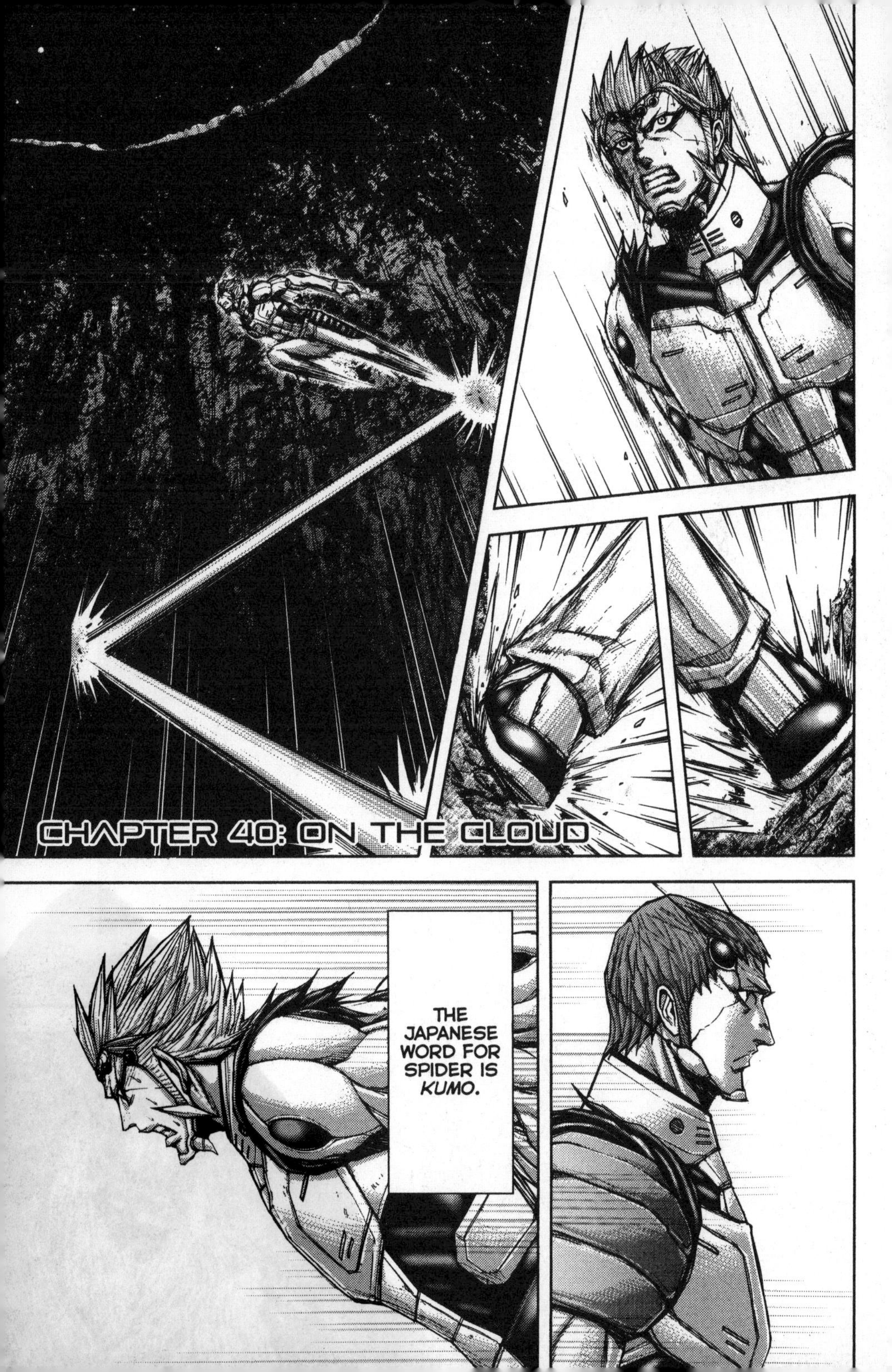
CHAPTER 40: ON THE CLOUD
THE JAPANESE WORD FOR SPIDER IS *KUMO*.

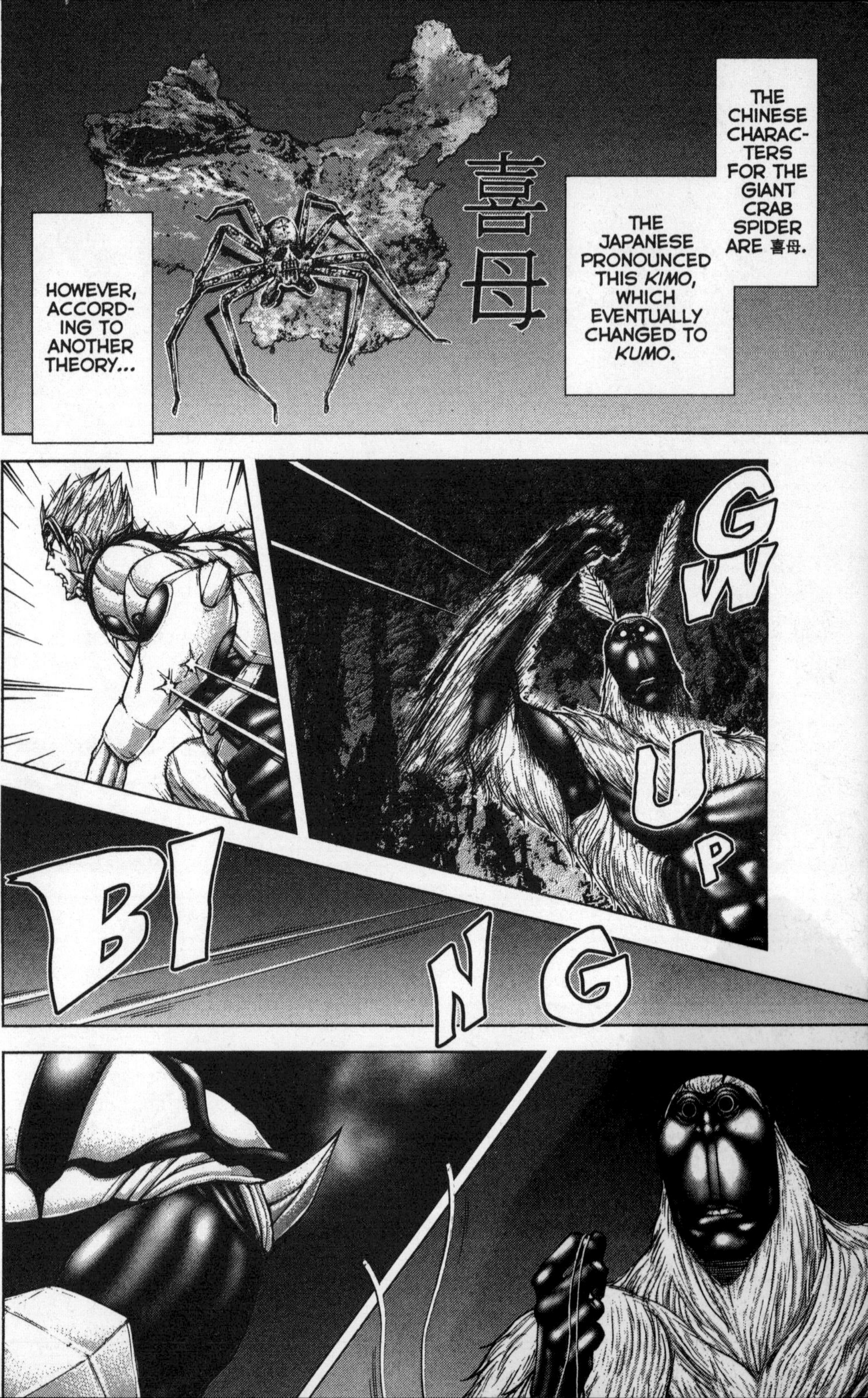
THE CHINESE CHARAC-TERS FOR THE GIANT CRAB SPIDER ARE 喜母.
THE JAPANESE PRONOUNCED THIS *KIMO*, WHICH EVENTUALLY CHANGED TO *KUMO*.
喜母
HOWEVER, ACCORD-ING TO ANOTHER THEORY...
GWUP
BING

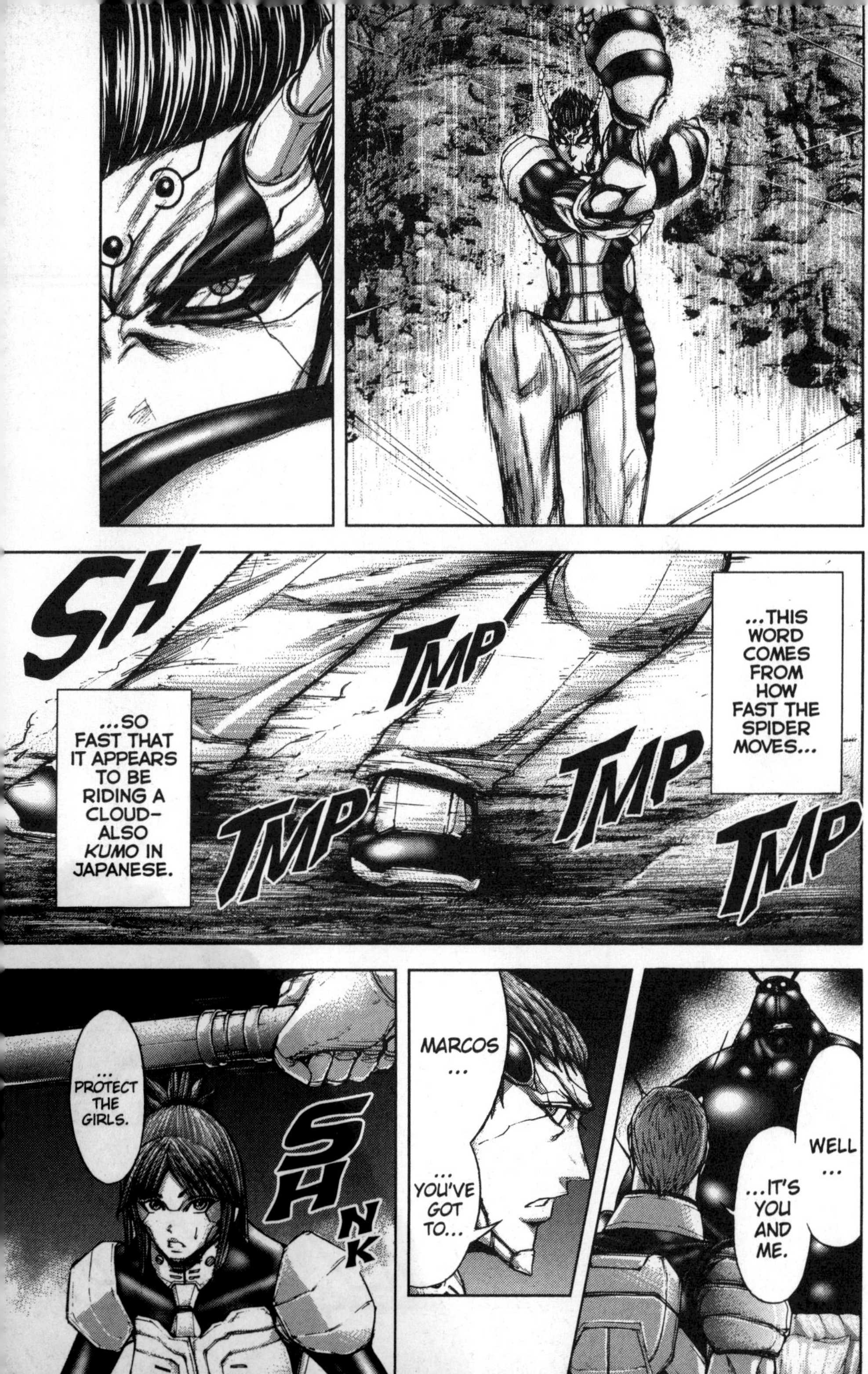
...THIS WORD COMES FROM HOW FAST THE SPIDER MOVES...
SH
TMP
...SO FAST THAT IT APPEARS TO BE RIDING A CLOUD—ALSO *KUMO* IN JAPANESE.
TMP
TMP
TMP
WELL...
...IT'S YOU AND ME.
MARCOS...
...YOU'VE GOT TO...
...PROTECT THE GIRLS.
SHANK

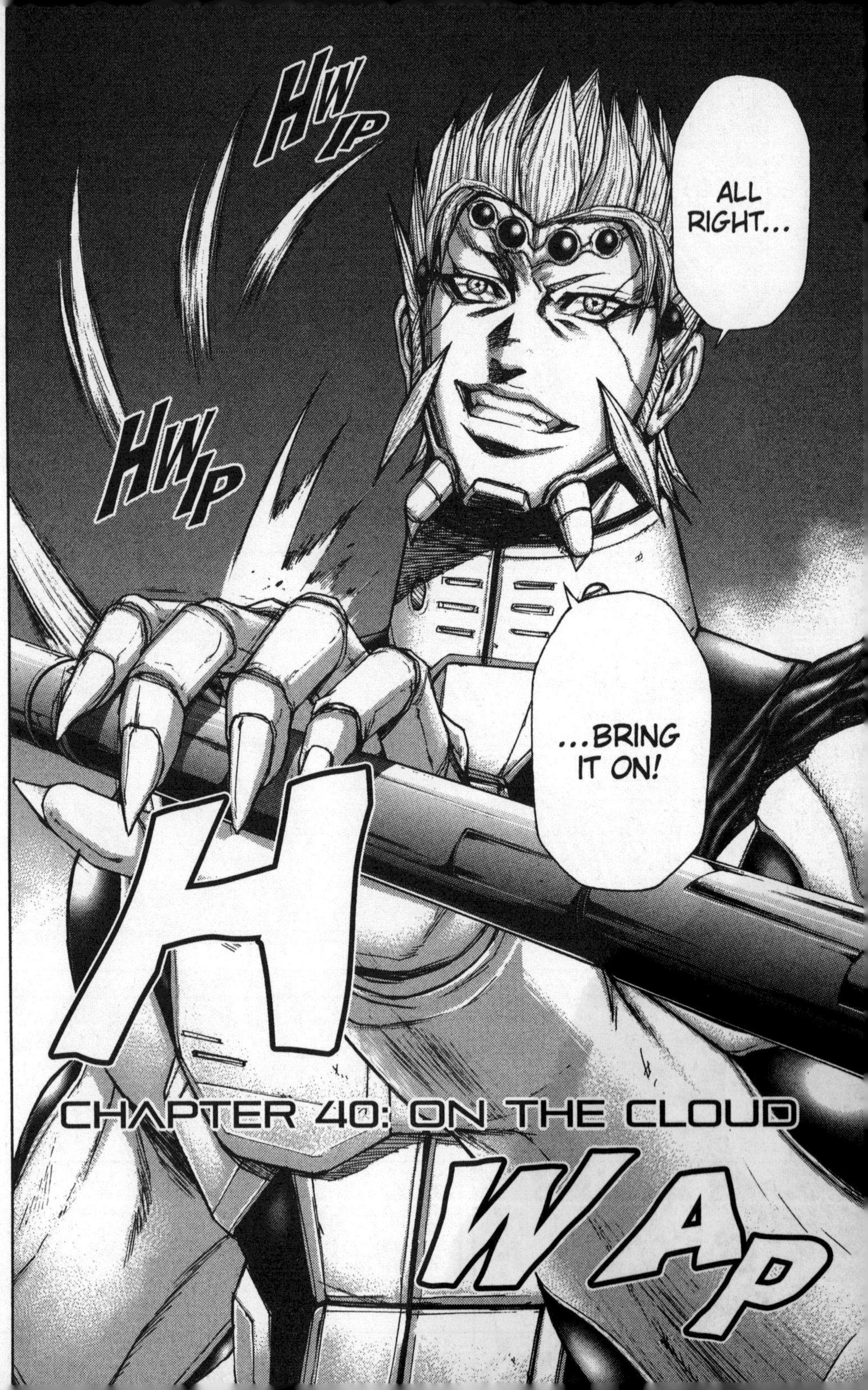
HWIP
ALL RIGHT...
HWIP
...BRING IT ON!
HWAP
CHAPTER 40: ON THE CLOUD

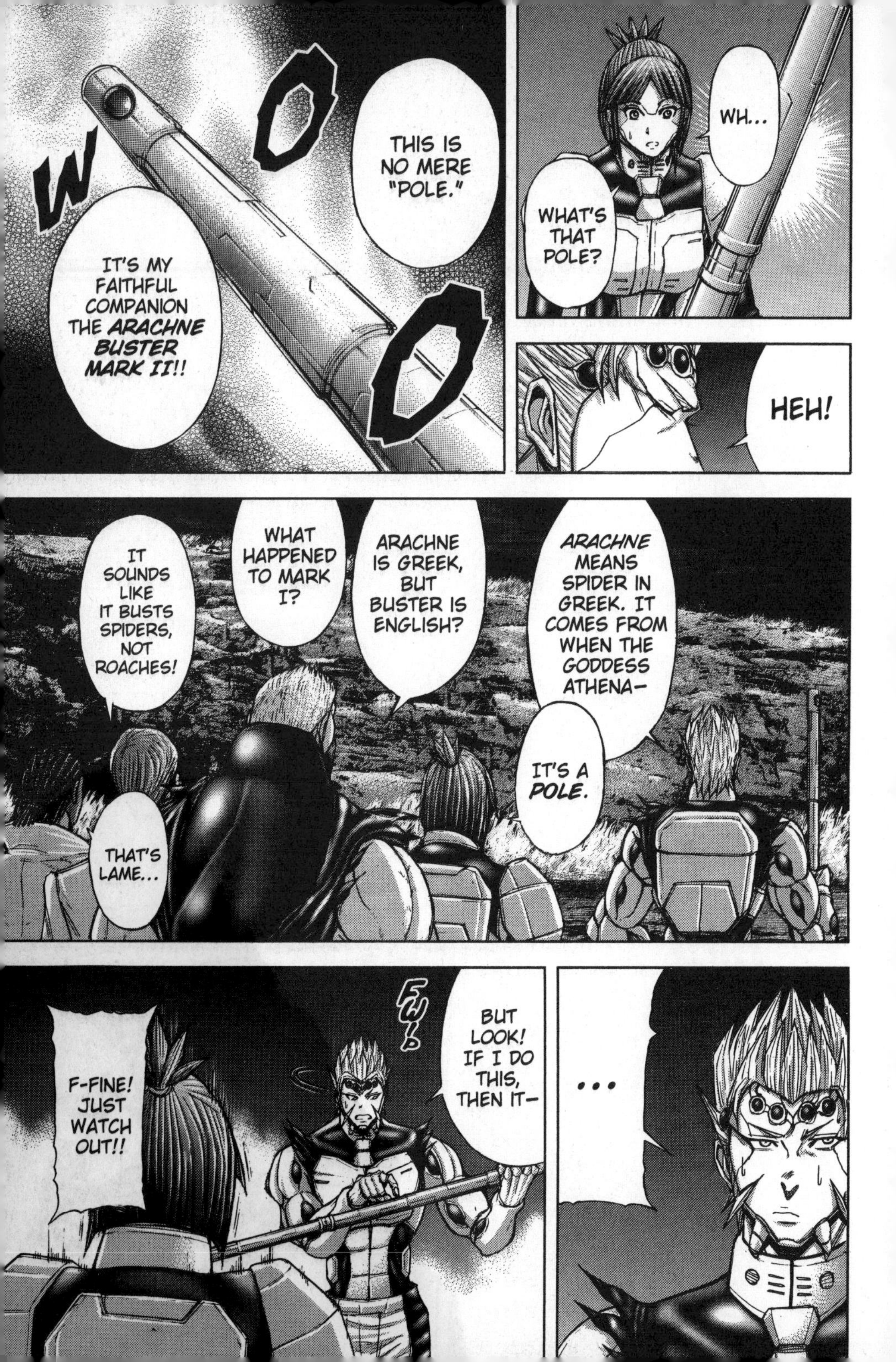
WH...
WHAT'S THAT POLE?
HEH!
THIS IS NO MERE "POLE."
IT'S MY FAITHFUL COMPANION THE *ARACHNE BUSTER MARK II*!!
WOO
ARACHNE MEANS SPIDER IN GREEK. IT COMES FROM WHEN THE GODDESS ATHENA—
IT'S A *POLE*.
ARACHNE IS GREEK, BUT BUSTER IS ENGLISH?
WHAT HAPPENED TO MARK I?
IT SOUNDS LIKE IT BUSTS SPIDERS, NOT ROACHES!
THAT'S LAME...
...
BUT LOOK! IF I DO THIS, THEN IT—
FWIP
F-FINE! JUST WATCH OUT!!

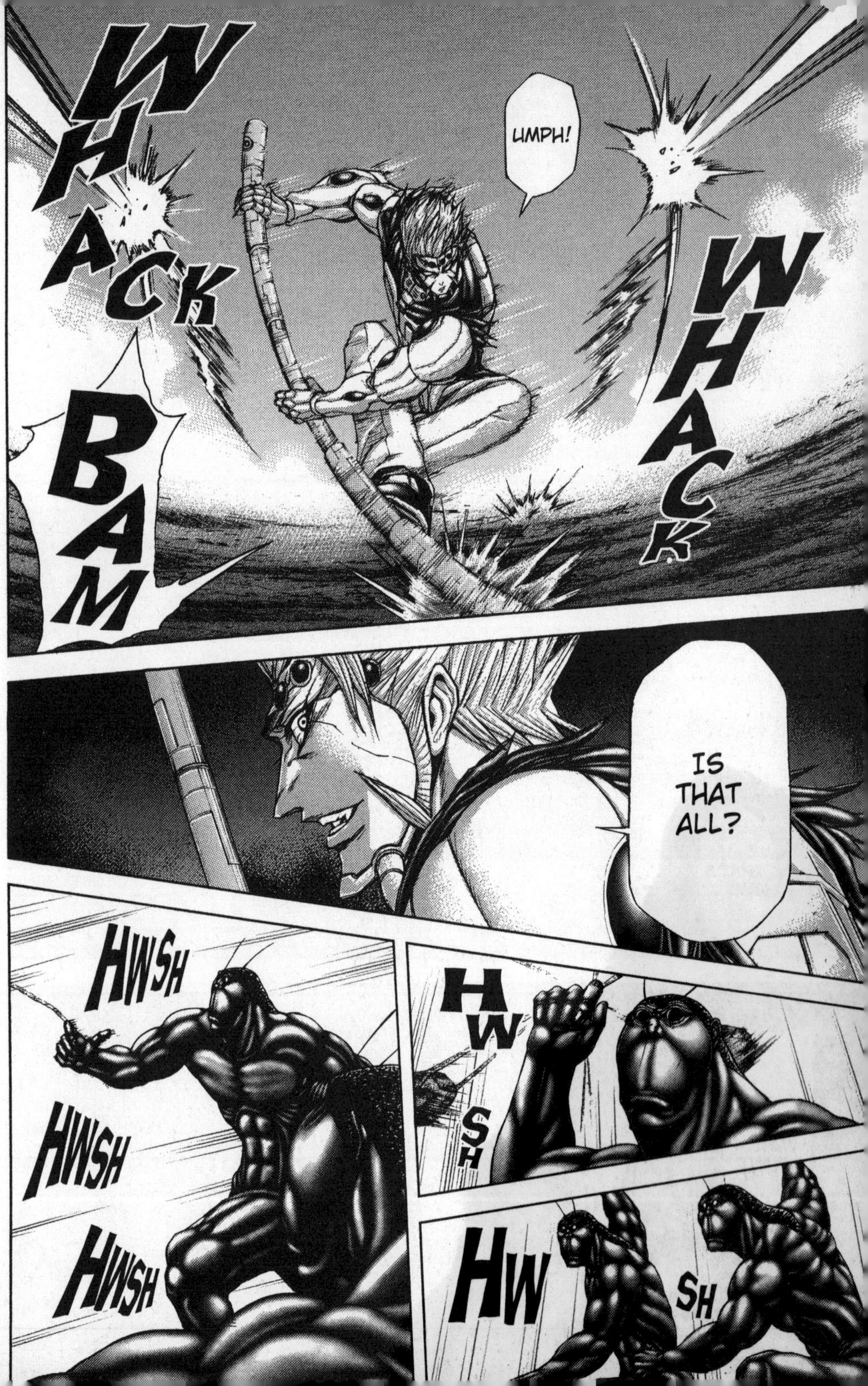
UMPH!
WHACK
WHACK
BAM
IS THAT ALL?
HWSH
HWSH
HWSH
HWSH
HWSH

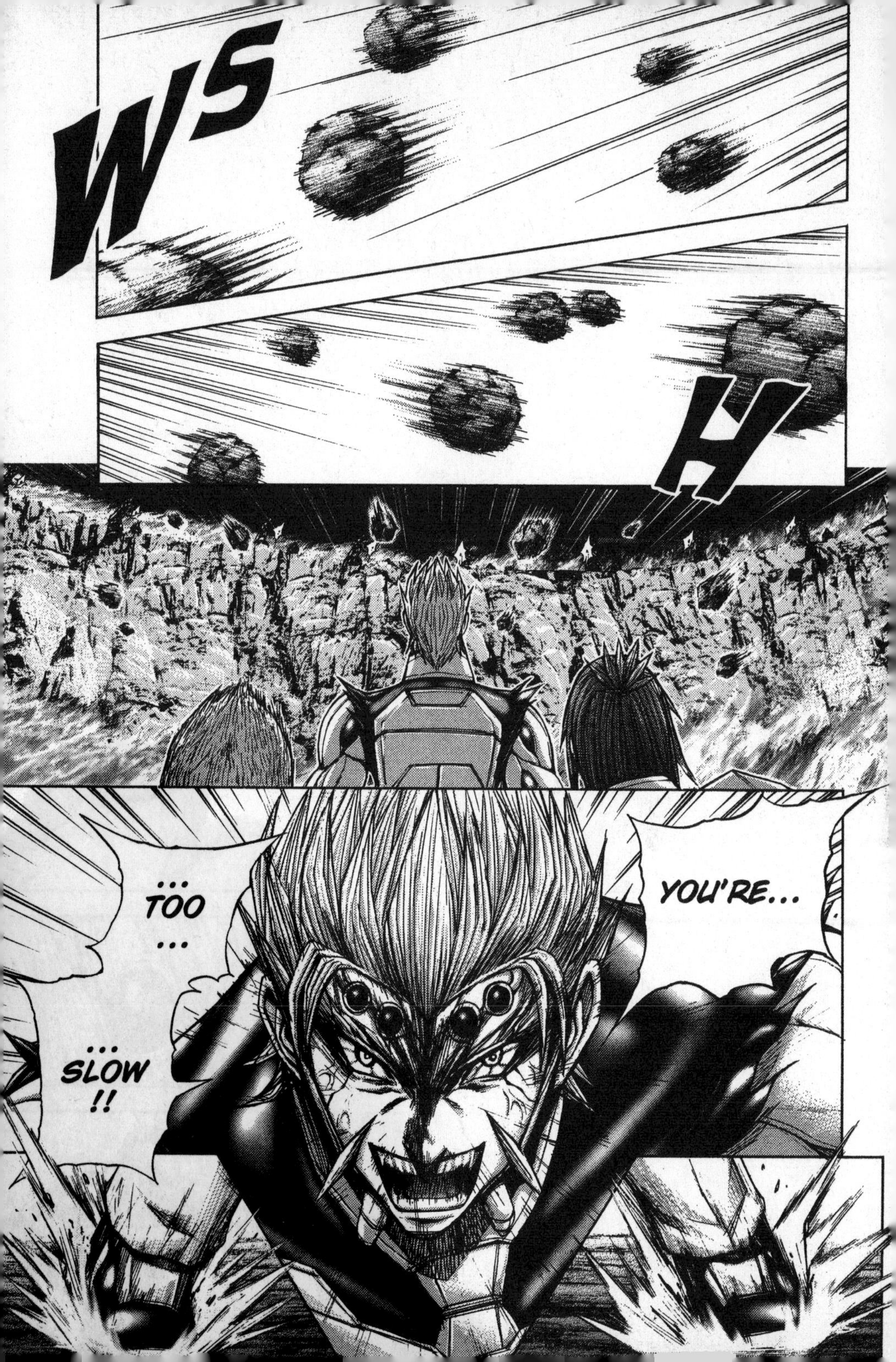
WS
H
YOU'RE...
...TOO...
...SLOW!!

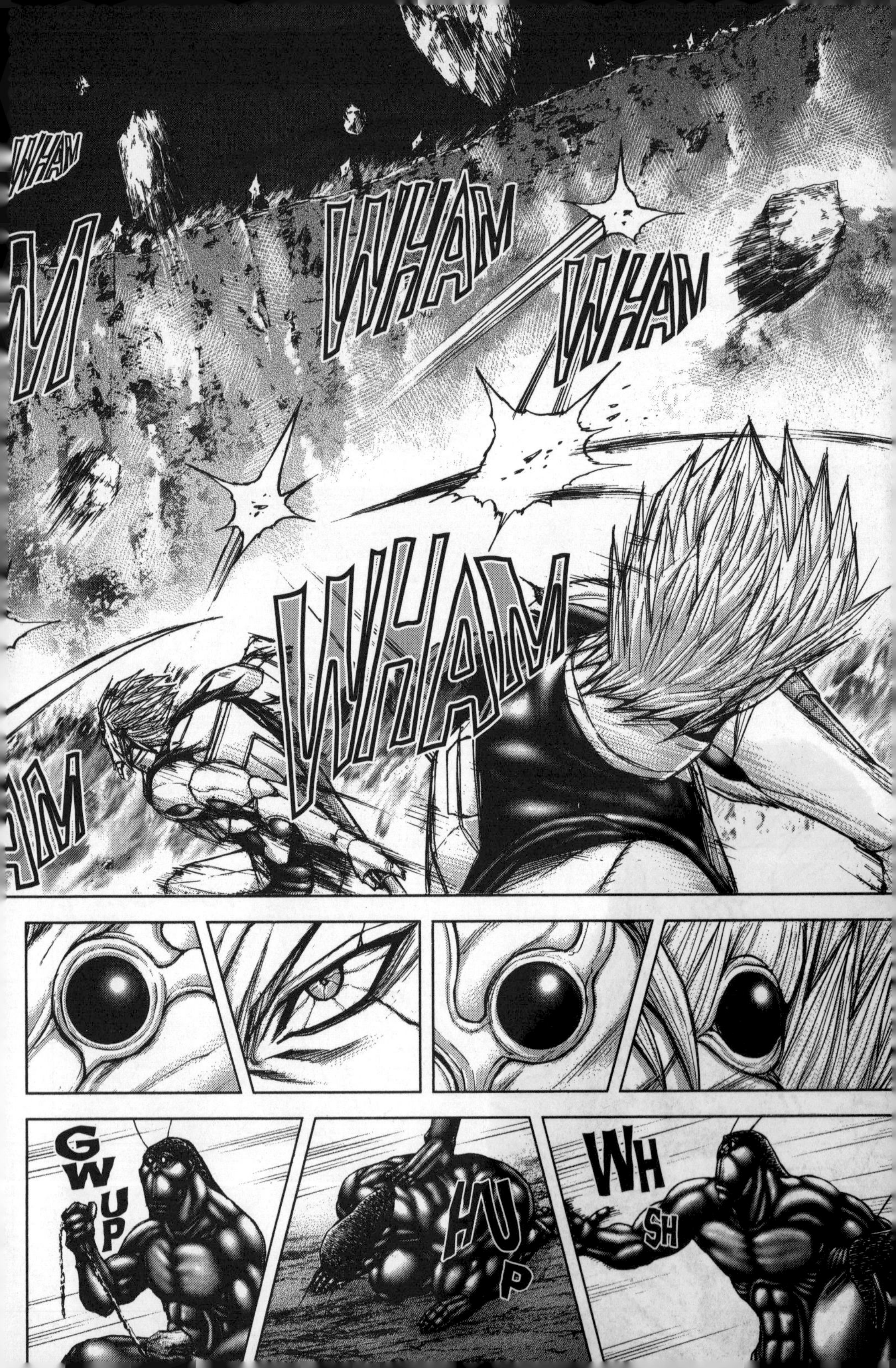

WHAM
WHAM
WHAM
WHAM
WHSH
HUP
GWUP

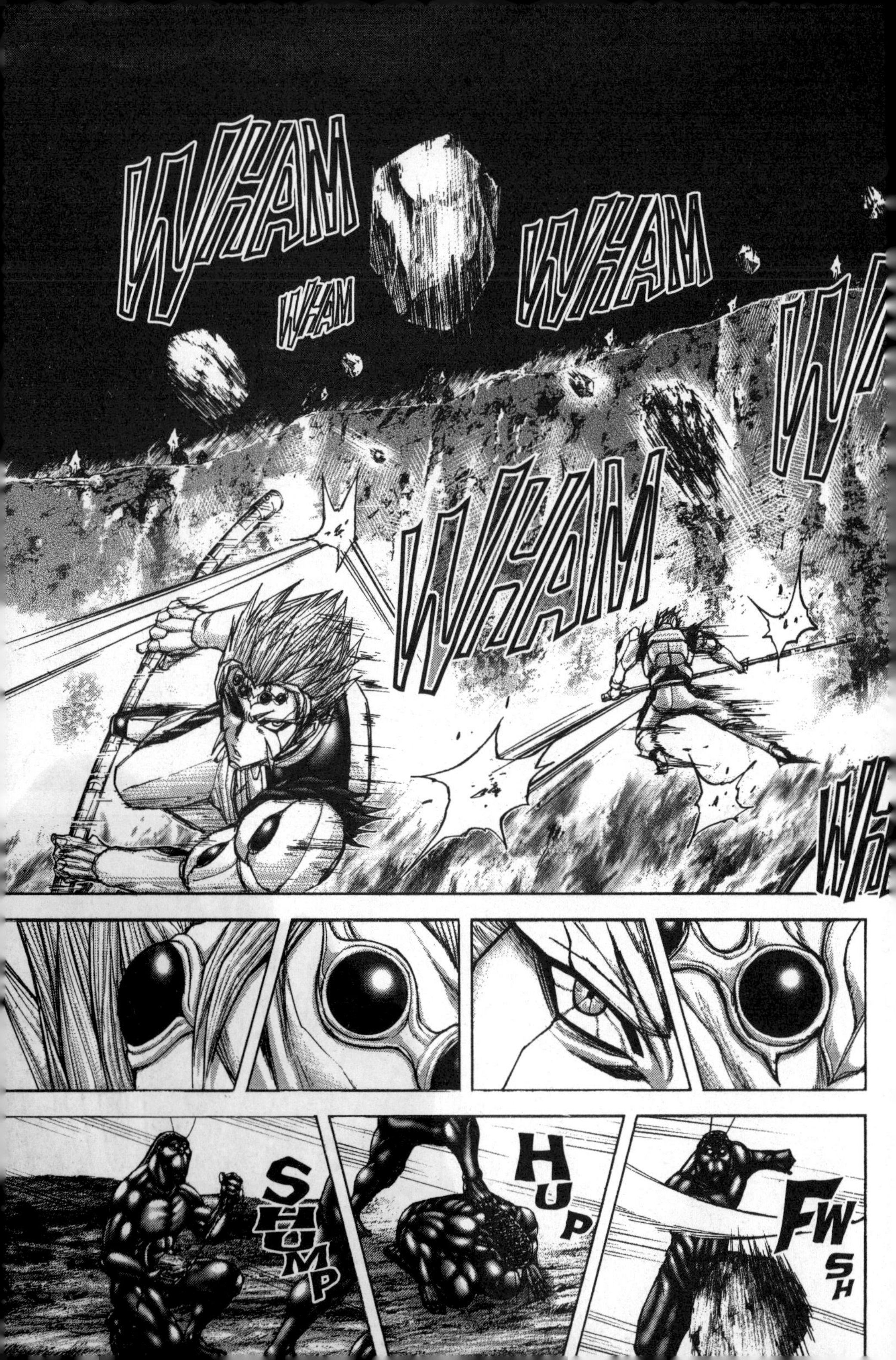
WHAM
WHAM
WHAM
WHAM
FWSH
HUP
SHUMP

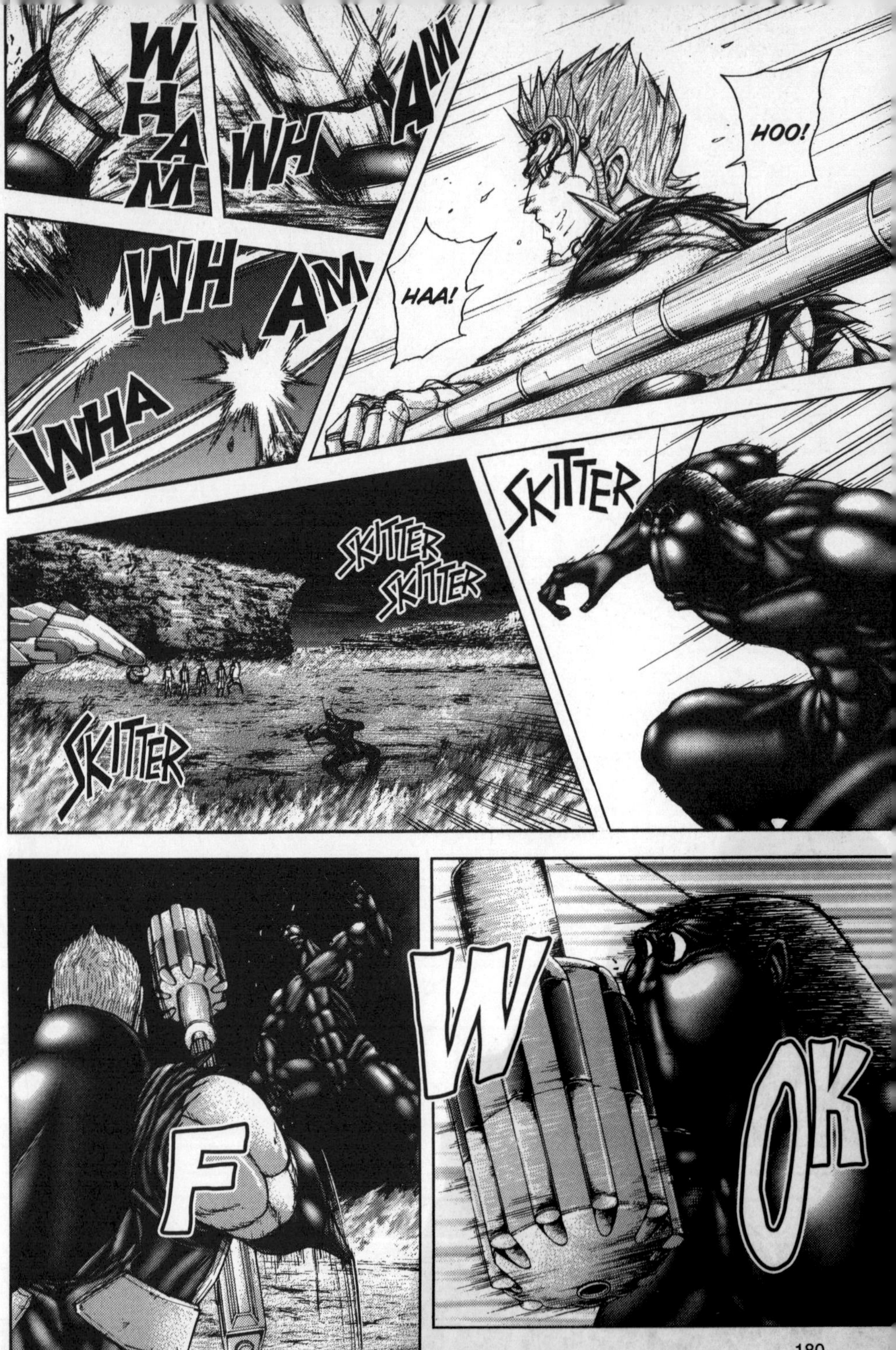
HOO!
HAA!
WH
AM
WHAM
WHA
WH
AM
SKITTER
SKITTER
SKITTER
SKITTER
W
OK
F

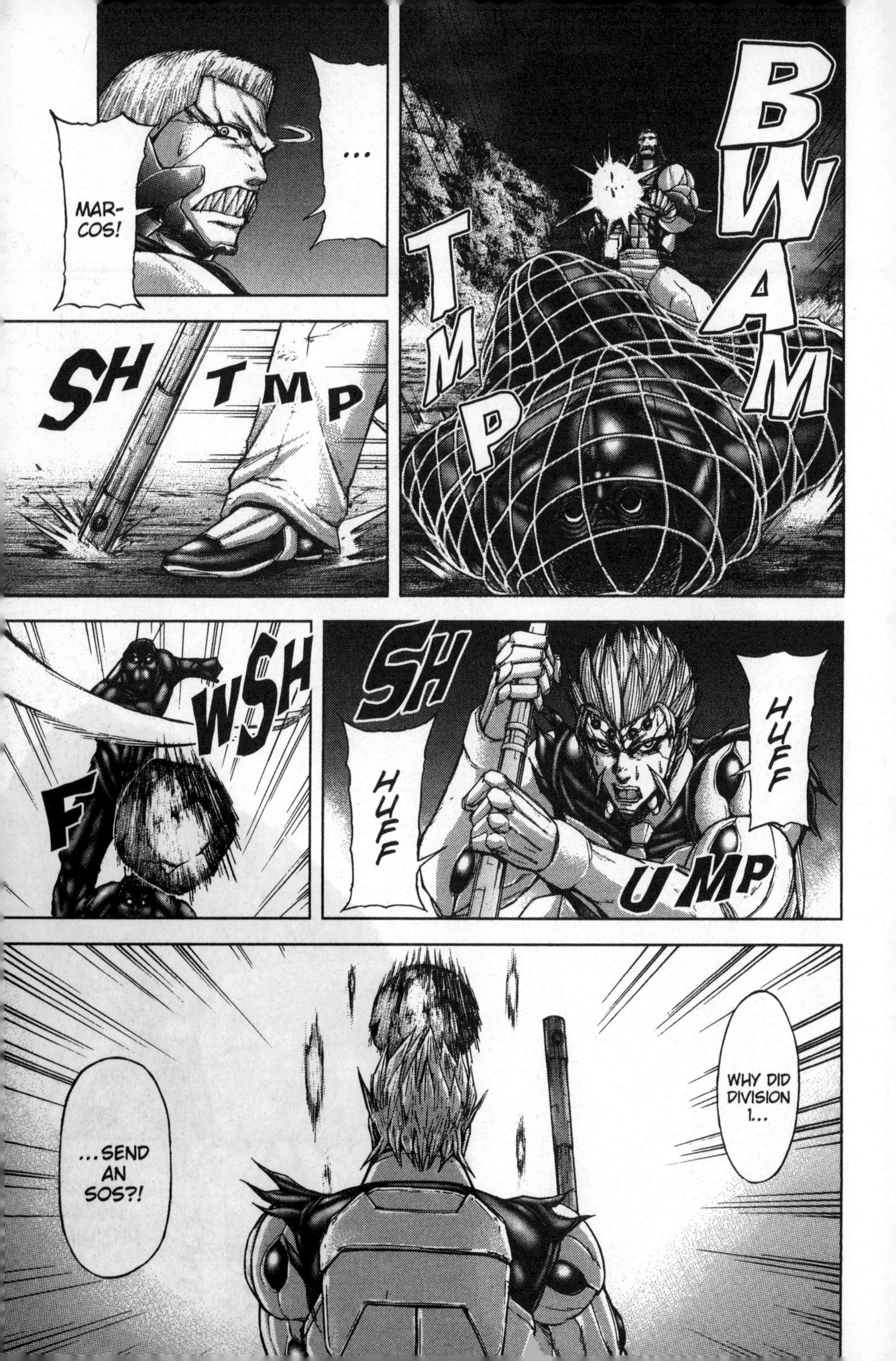
BWAM
TMP
...
MAR-COS!
SH
TMP
HUFF
SH
HUFF
UMP
WSH
F
WHY DID DIVISION 1...
...SEND AN SOS?!

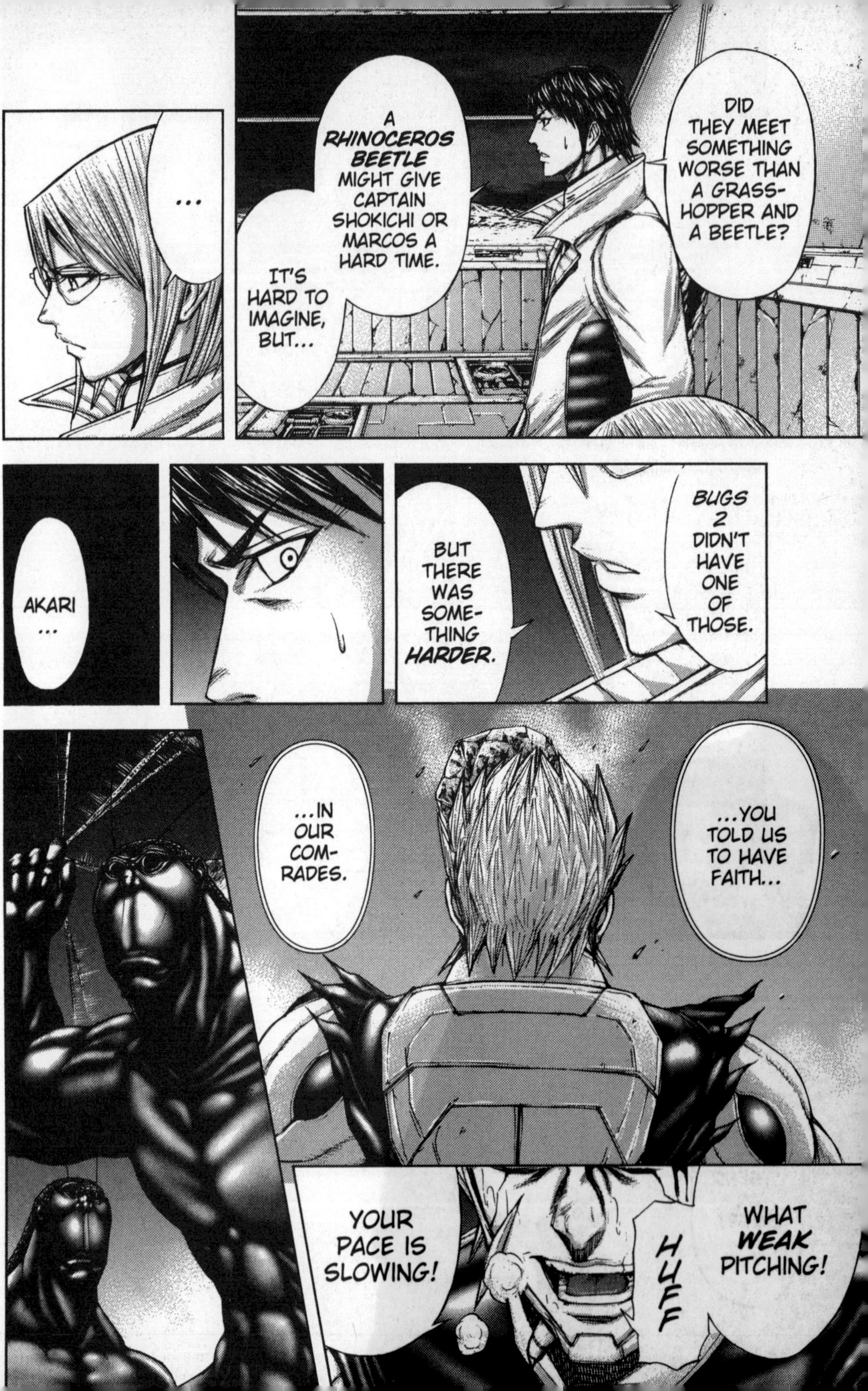
DID THEY MEET SOMETHING WORSE THAN A GRASSHOPPER AND A BEETLE?
A RHINOCEROS BEETLE MIGHT GIVE CAPTAIN SHOKICHI OR MARCOS A HARD TIME.
IT'S HARD TO IMAGINE, BUT...
...
BUGS 2 DIDN'T HAVE ONE OF THOSE.
BUT THERE WAS SOMETHING HARDER.
AKARI...
...YOU TOLD US TO HAVE FAITH...
...IN OUR COMRADES.
WHAT WEAK PITCHING!
HUFF
YOUR PACE IS SLOWING!

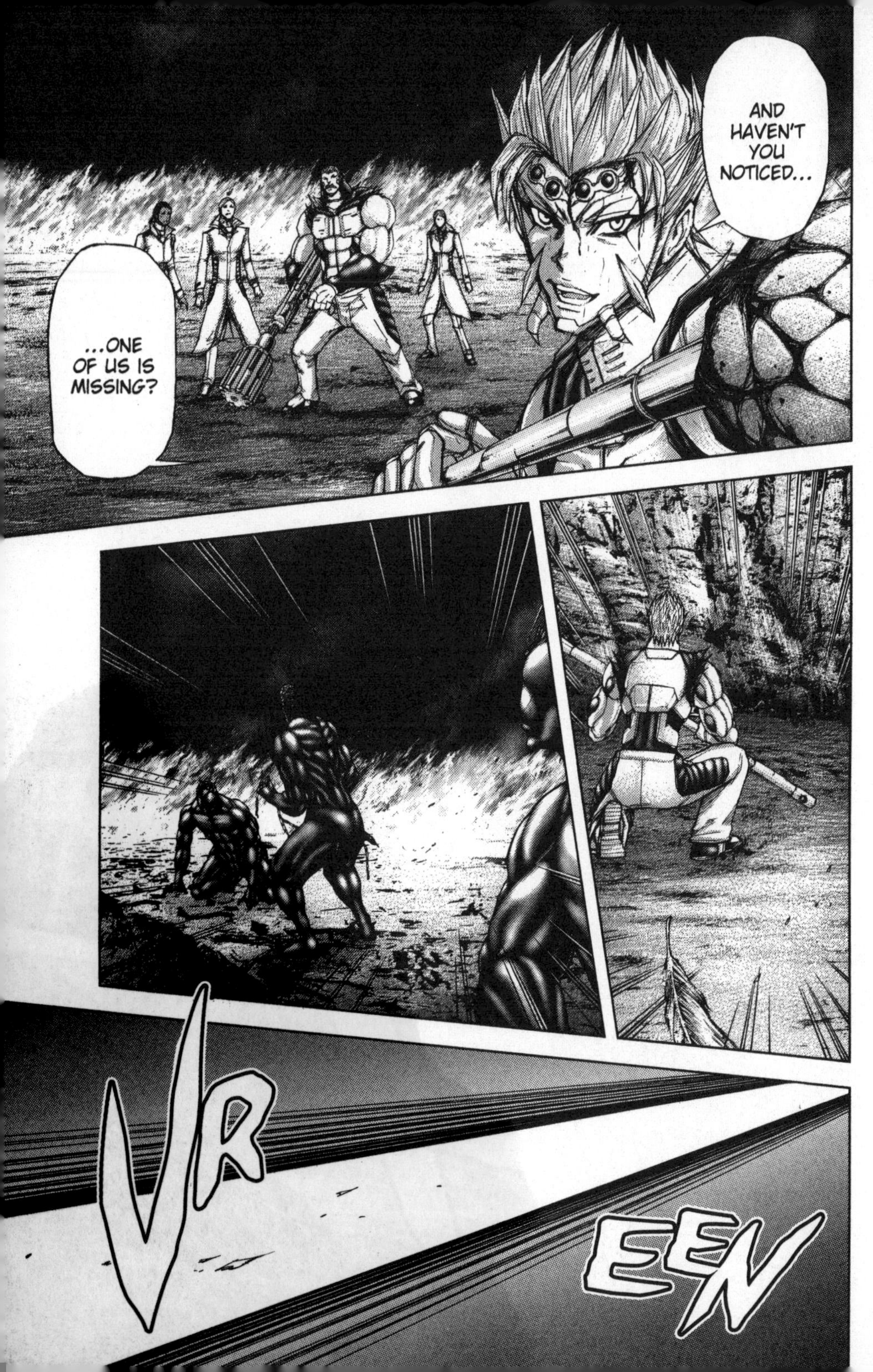
AND HAVEN'T YOU NOTICED...
...ONE OF US IS MISSING?
VR
EEN

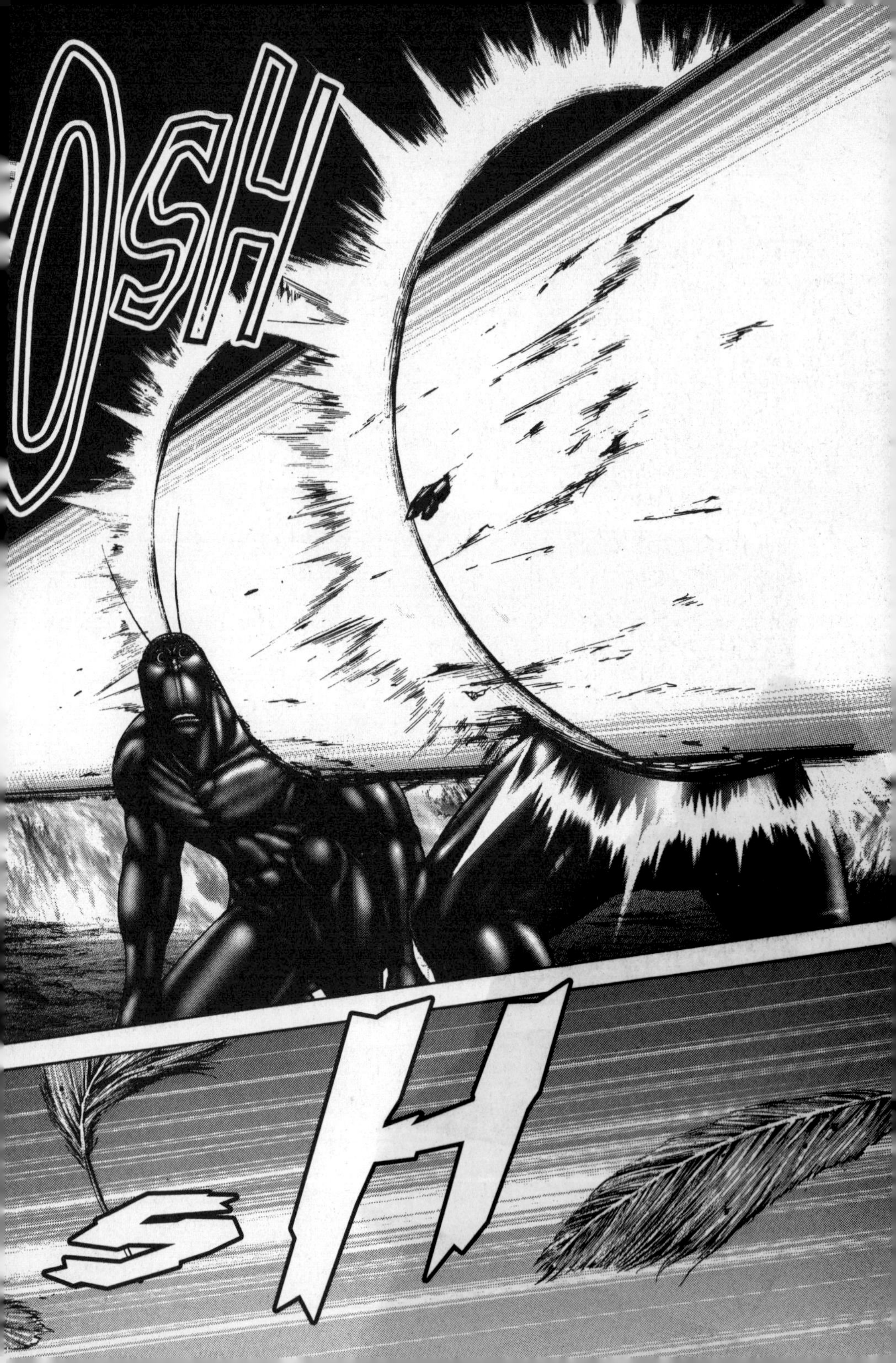
OSH
SH

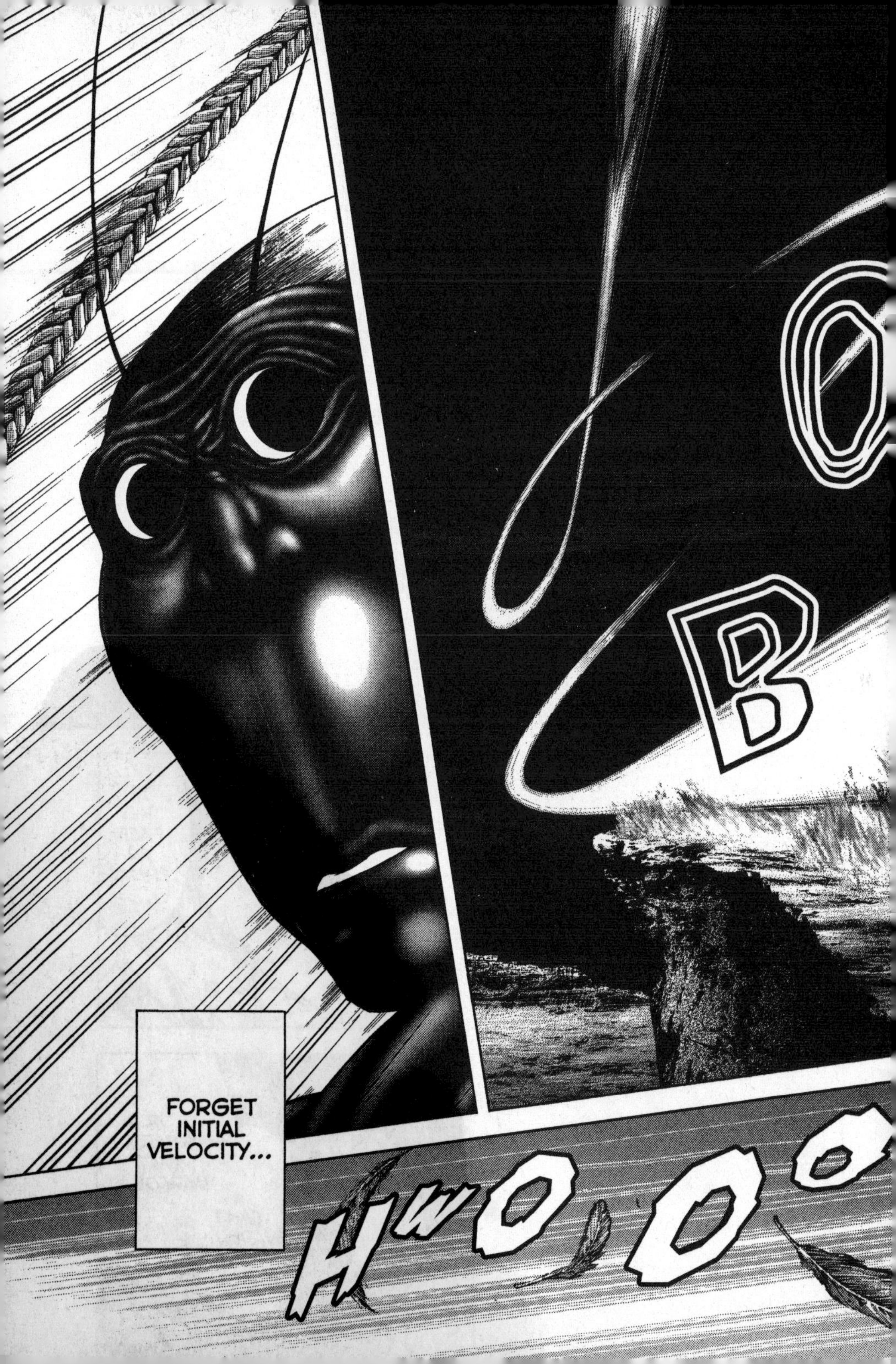
O
B
FORGET INITIAL VELOCITY...
HWOOOO

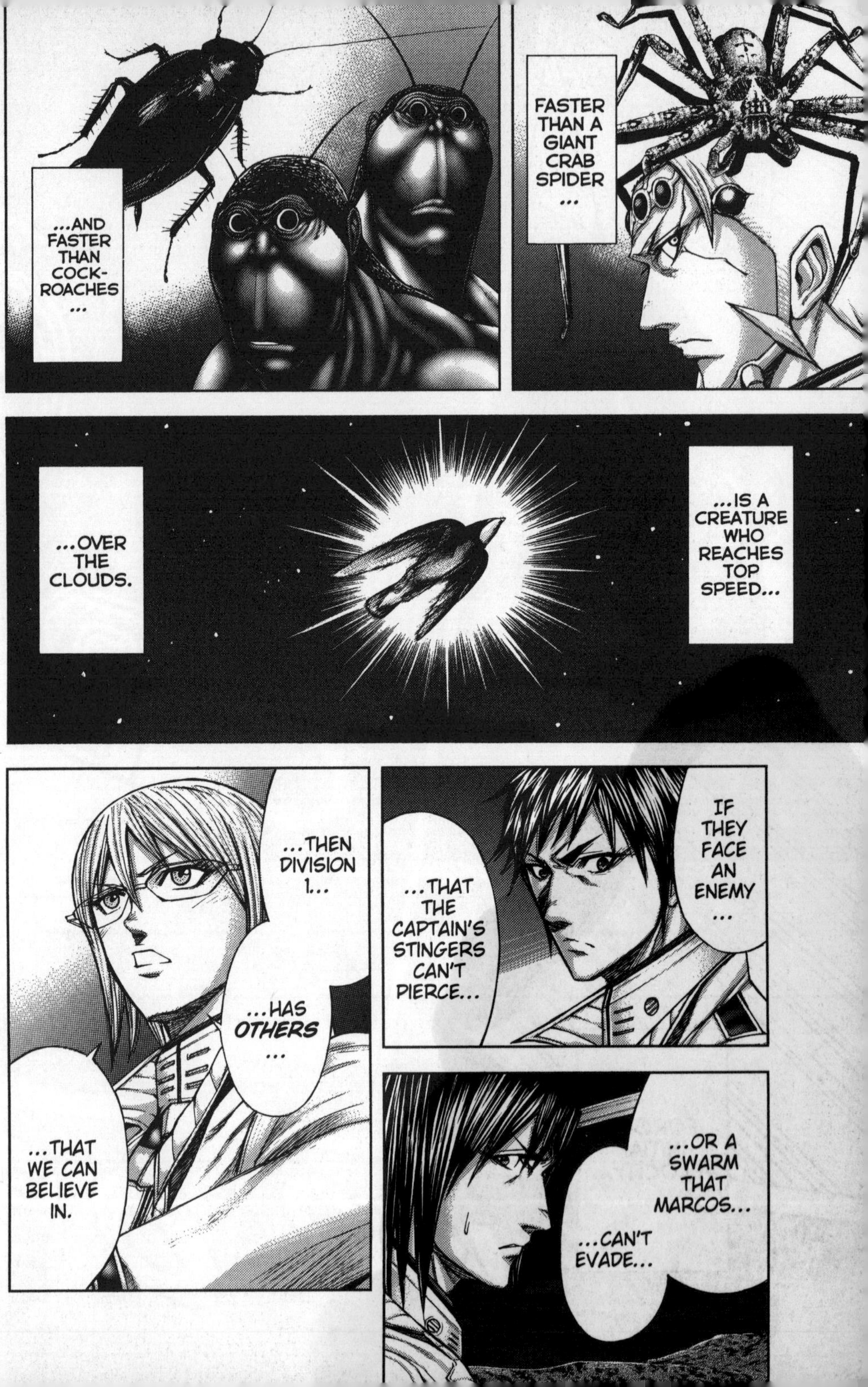

FASTER THAN A GIANT CRAB SPIDER ...
...AND FASTER THAN COCK-ROACHES ...
...IS A CREATURE WHO REACHES TOP SPEED...
...OVER THE CLOUDS.
IF THEY FACE AN ENEMY ...
...THAT THE CAPTAIN'S STINGERS CAN'T PIERCE...
...OR A SWARM THAT MARCOS...
...CAN'T EVADE...
...THEN DIVISION 1...
...HAS *OTHERS* ...
...THAT WE CAN BELIEVE IN.

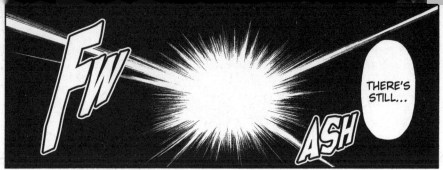

THERE'S STILL...

...KEIJI ONIZUKA!

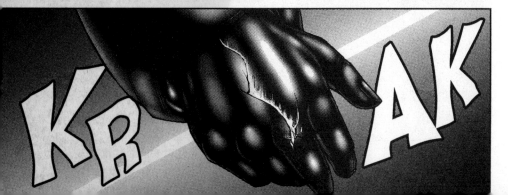

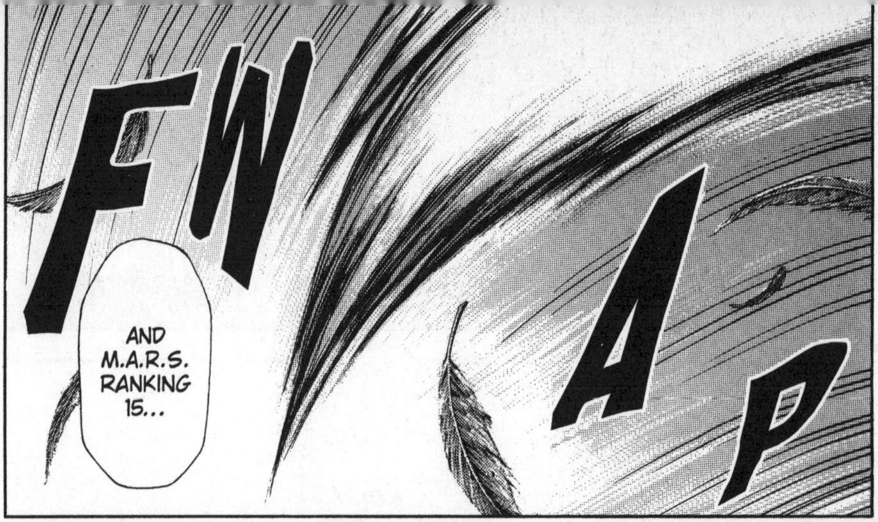
FWAP
AND M.A.R.S. RANKING 15...
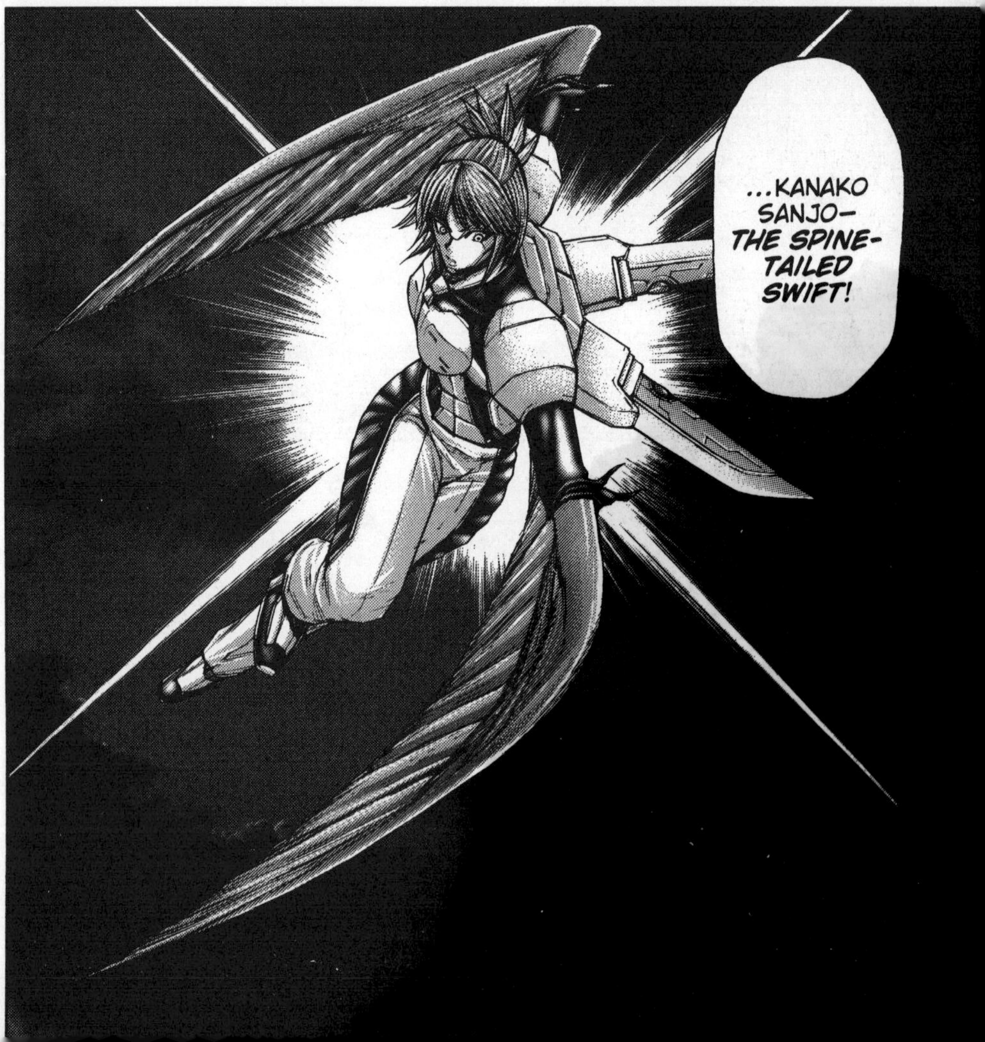
...KANAKO SANJO—THE SPINE-TAILED SWIFT!

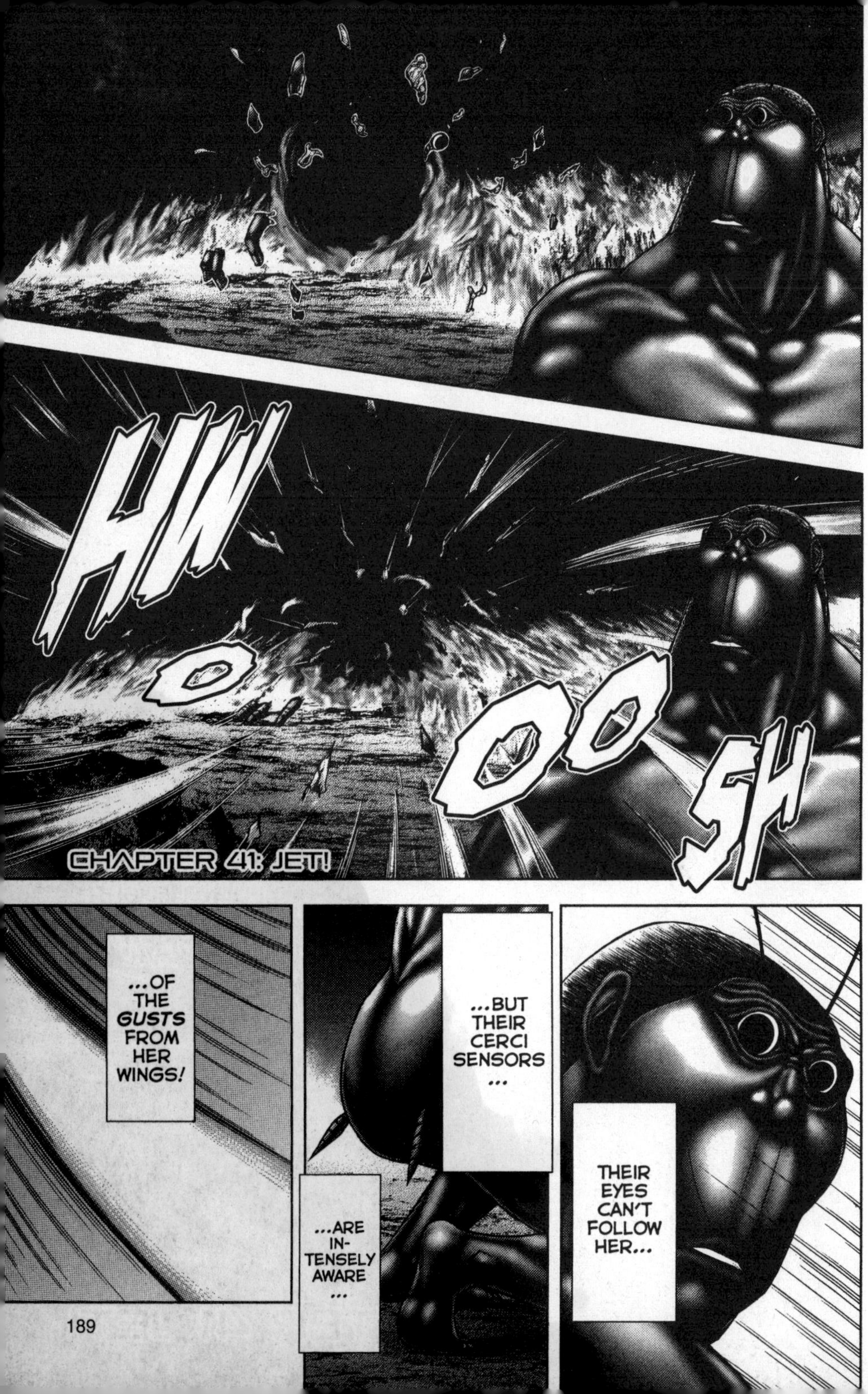
HWOOOSH
CHAPTER 41: JET!
THEIR EYES CAN'T FOLLOW HER...
...BUT THEIR CERCI SENSORS...
...ARE IN-TENSELY AWARE...
...OF THE GUSTS FROM HER WINGS!

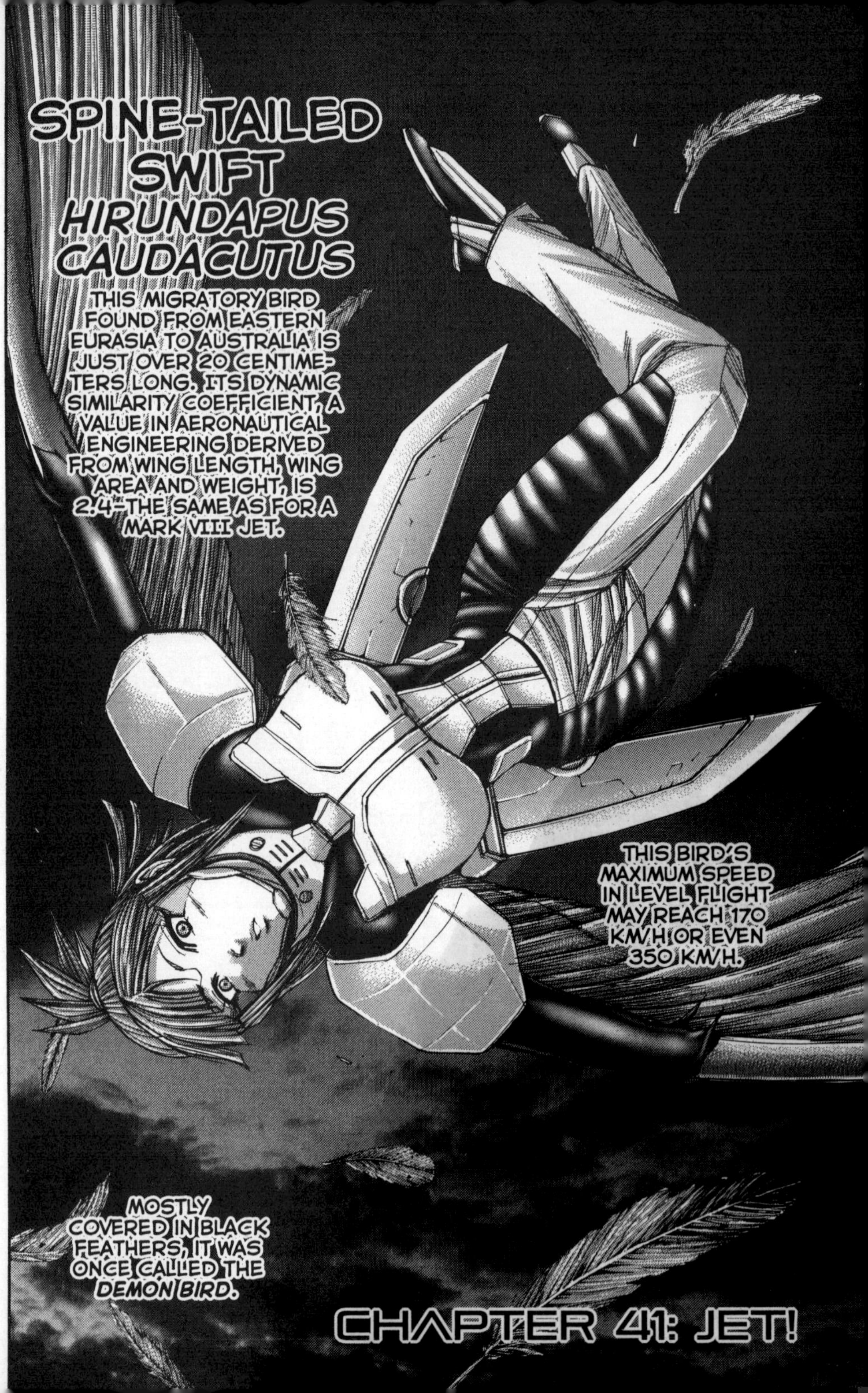
SPINE-TAILED SWIFT
HIRUNDAPUS CAUDACUTUS
THIS MIGRATORY BIRD FOUND FROM EASTERN EURASIA TO AUSTRALIA IS JUST OVER 20 CENTIMETERS LONG. ITS DYNAMIC SIMILARITY COEFFICIENT, A VALUE IN AERONAUTICAL ENGINEERING DERIVED FROM WING LENGTH, WING AREA AND WEIGHT, IS 2.4—THE SAME AS FOR A MARK VIII JET.
THIS BIRD'S MAXIMUM SPEED IN LEVEL FLIGHT MAY REACH 170 KM/H OR EVEN 350 KM/H.
MOSTLY COVERED IN BLACK FEATHERS, IT WAS ONCE CALLED THE DEMON BIRD.
CHAPTER 41: JET!

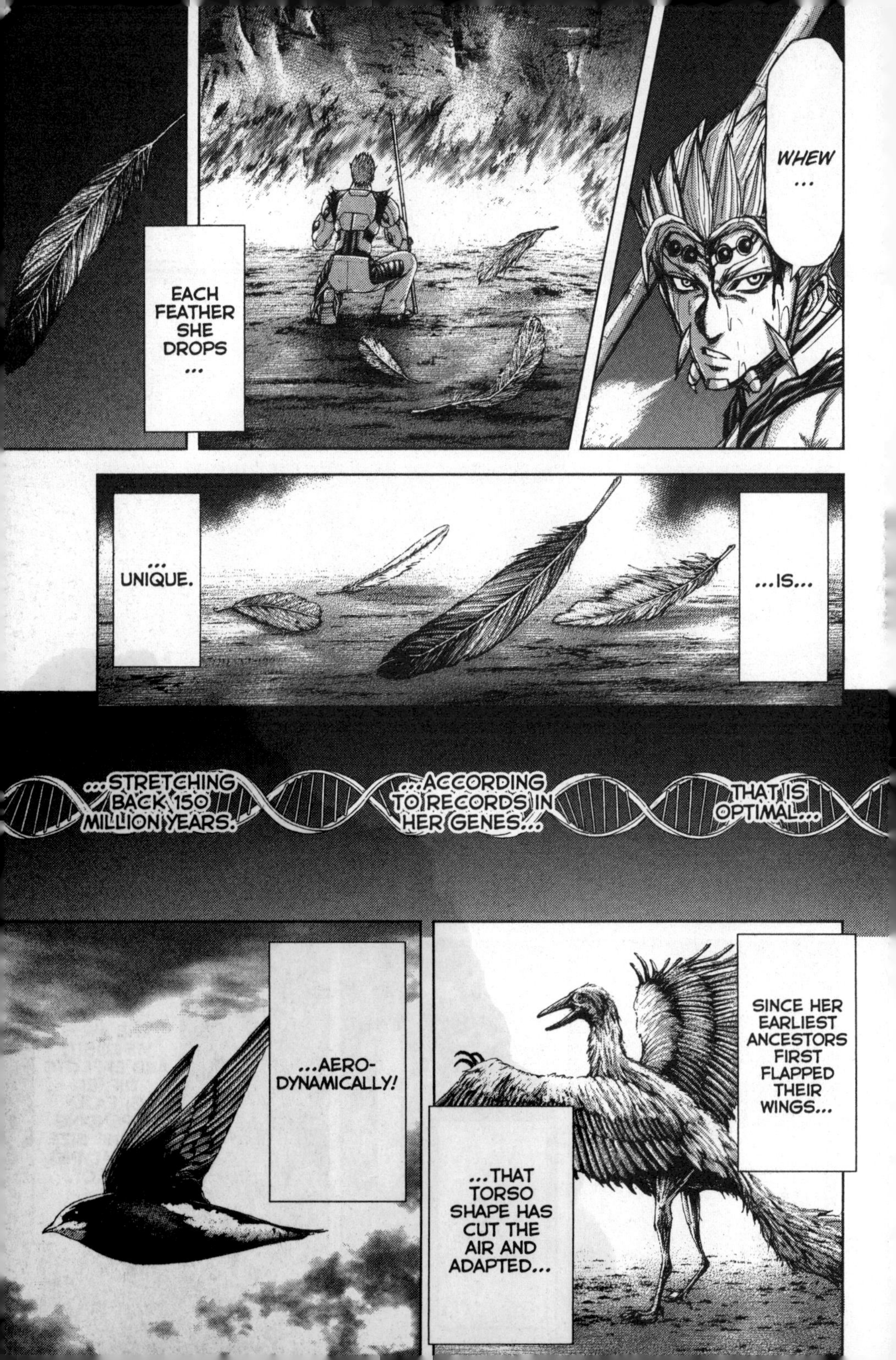

WHEW ...
EACH FEATHER SHE DROPS ...
...IS...
... UNIQUE.
THAT IS OPTIMAL...
...ACCORDING TO RECORDS IN HER GENES...
...STRETCHING BACK 150 MILLION YEARS.
SINCE HER EARLIEST ANCESTORS FIRST FLAPPED THEIR WINGS...
...THAT TORSO SHAPE HAS CUT THE AIR AND ADAPTED...
...AERO-DYNAMICALLY!

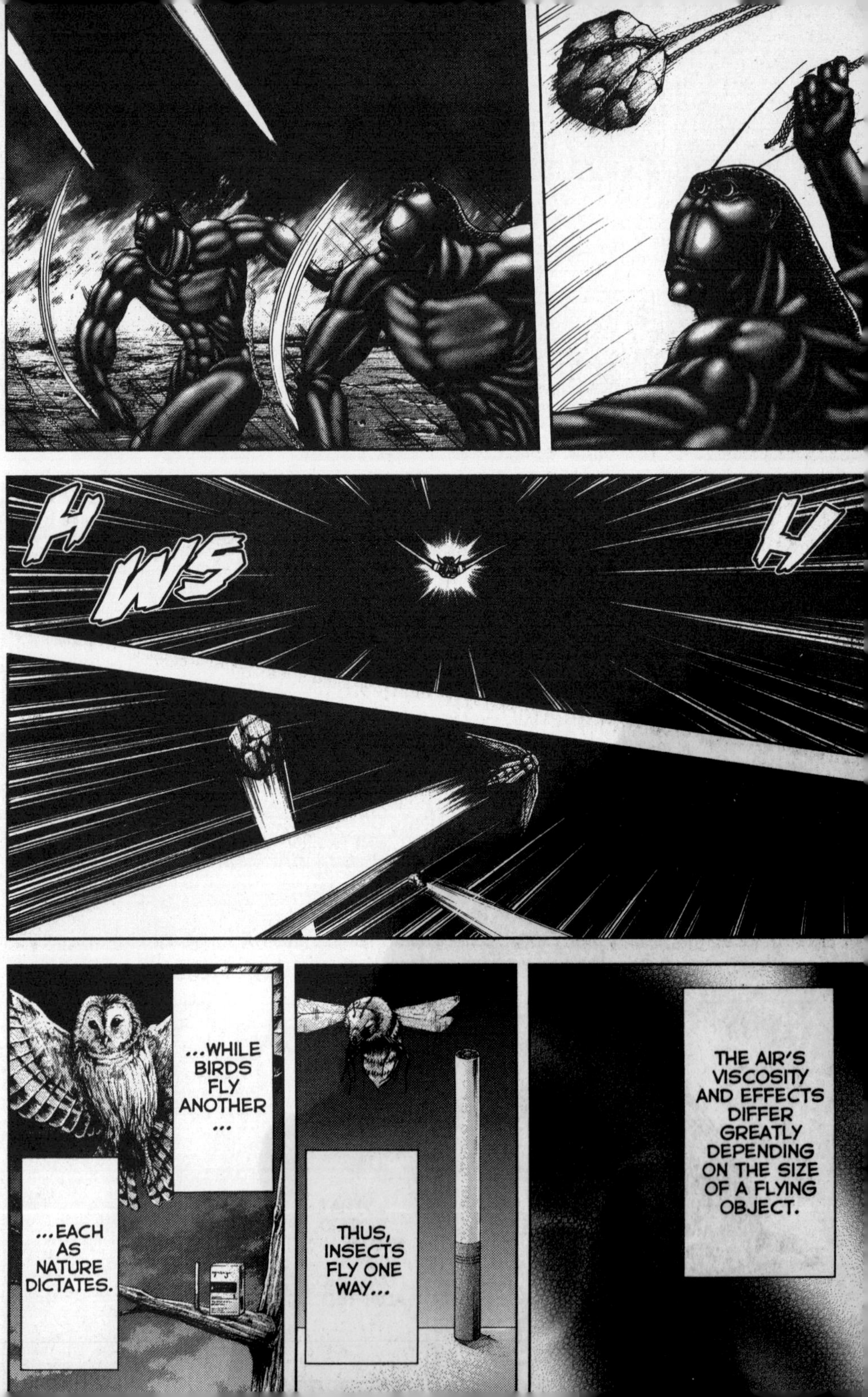
HWSH
THE AIR'S VISCOSITY AND EFFECTS DIFFER GREATLY DEPENDING ON THE SIZE OF A FLYING OBJECT.
THUS, INSECTS FLY ONE WAY...
...WHILE BIRDS FLY ANOTHER...
...EACH AS NATURE DICTATES.

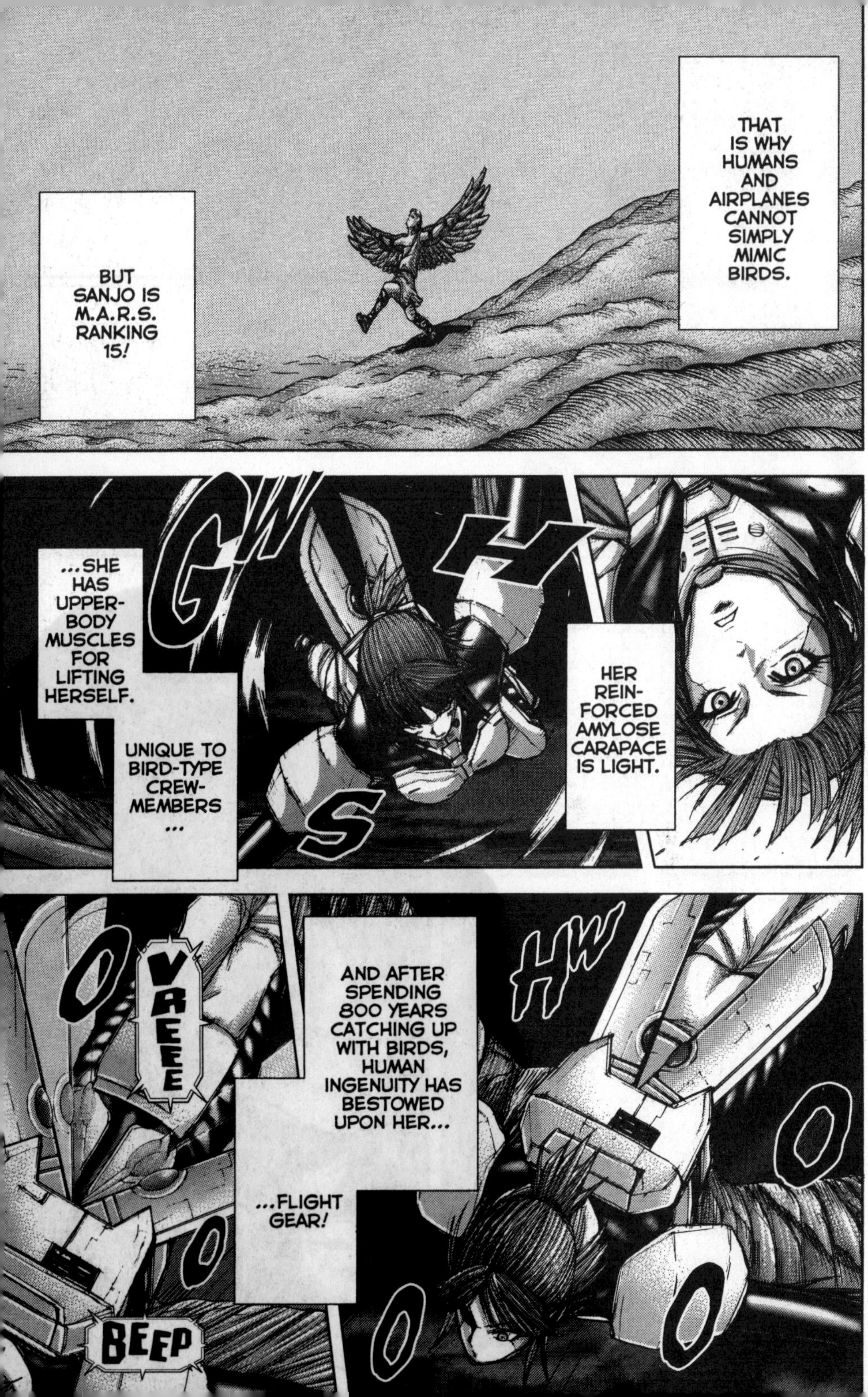
THAT IS WHY HUMANS AND AIRPLANES CANNOT SIMPLY MIMIC BIRDS.
BUT SANJO IS M.A.R.S. RANKING 15!
HER REIN-FORCED AMYLOSE CARAPACE IS LIGHT.
GWHS
UNIQUE TO BIRD-TYPE CREW-MEMBERS ...
...SHE HAS UPPER-BODY MUSCLES FOR LIFTING HERSELF.
HW
AND AFTER SPENDING 800 YEARS CATCHING UP WITH BIRDS, HUMAN INGENUITY HAS BESTOWED UPON HER...
...FLIGHT GEAR!
VREEE
BEEP

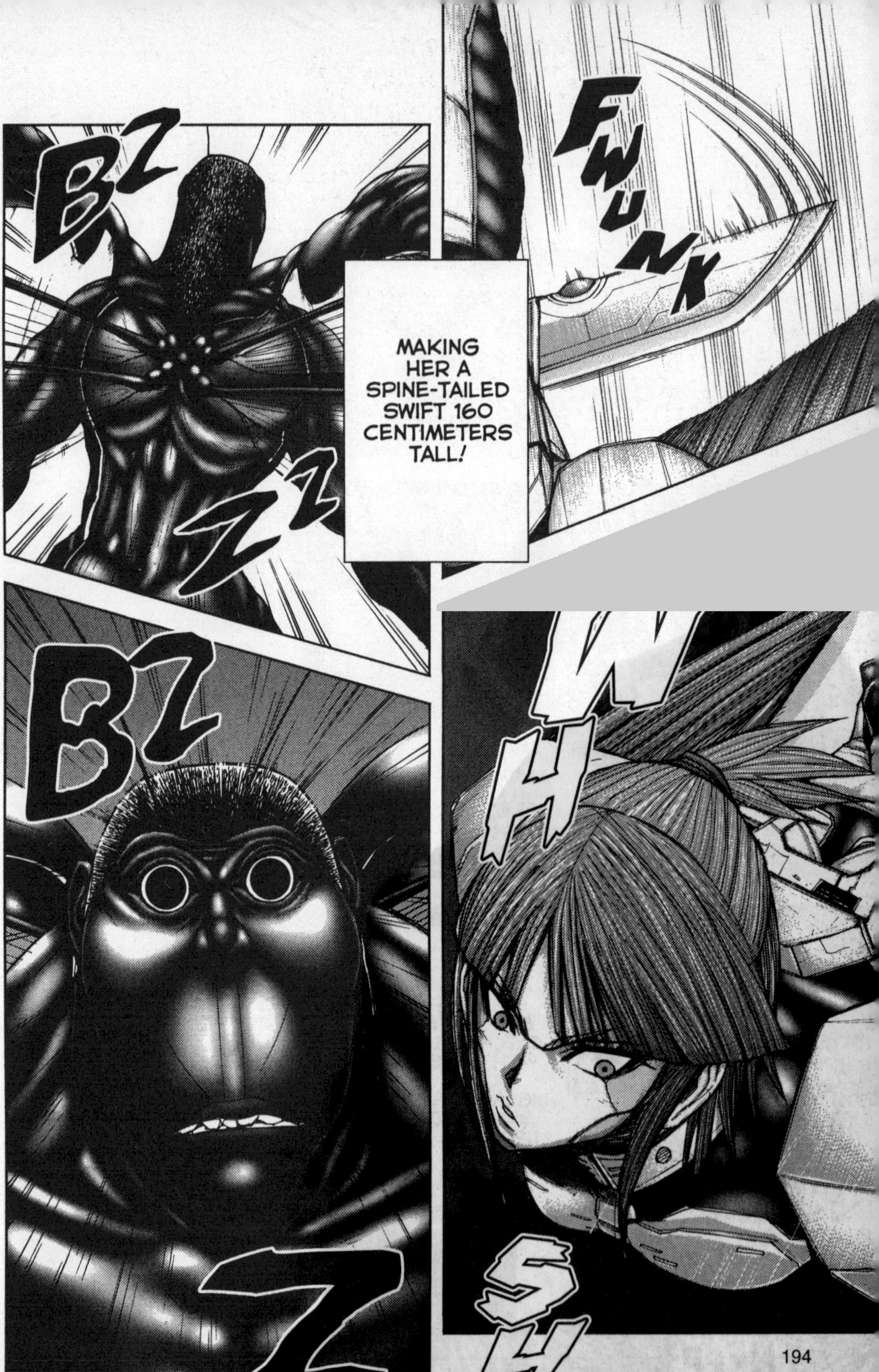
FWUNK
MAKING HER A SPINE-TAILED SWIFT 160 CENTIMETERS TALL!
BZZZZ
WHUSH
BZZ

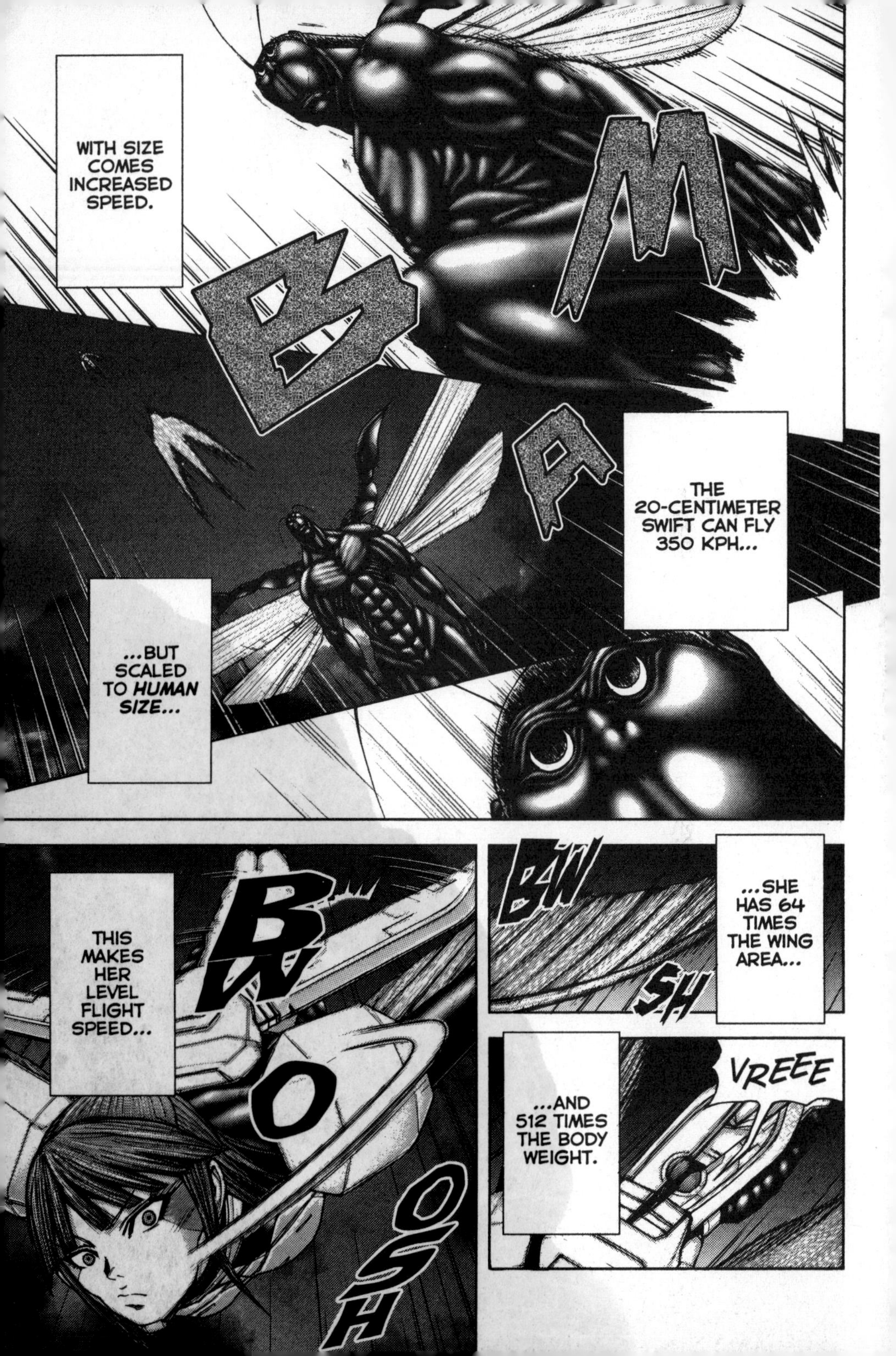

WITH SIZE COMES INCREASED SPEED.
BAM
THE 20-CENTIMETER SWIFT CAN FLY 350 KPH...
...BUT SCALED TO *HUMAN SIZE*...
BWSH
...SHE HAS 64 TIMES THE WING AREA...
VREEE
...AND 512 TIMES THE BODY WEIGHT.
THIS MAKES HER LEVEL FLIGHT SPEED...
BWOOSH

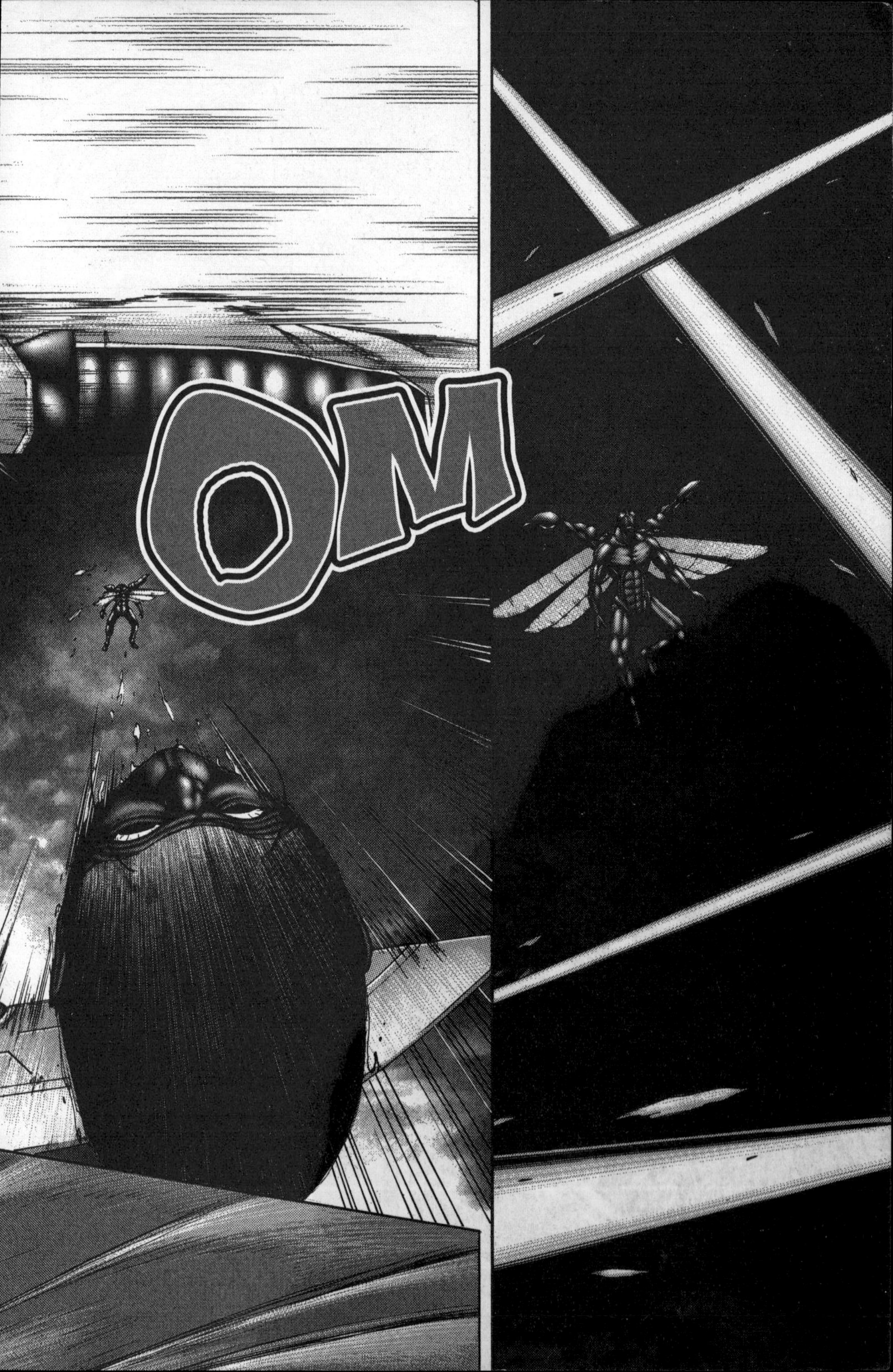
OM

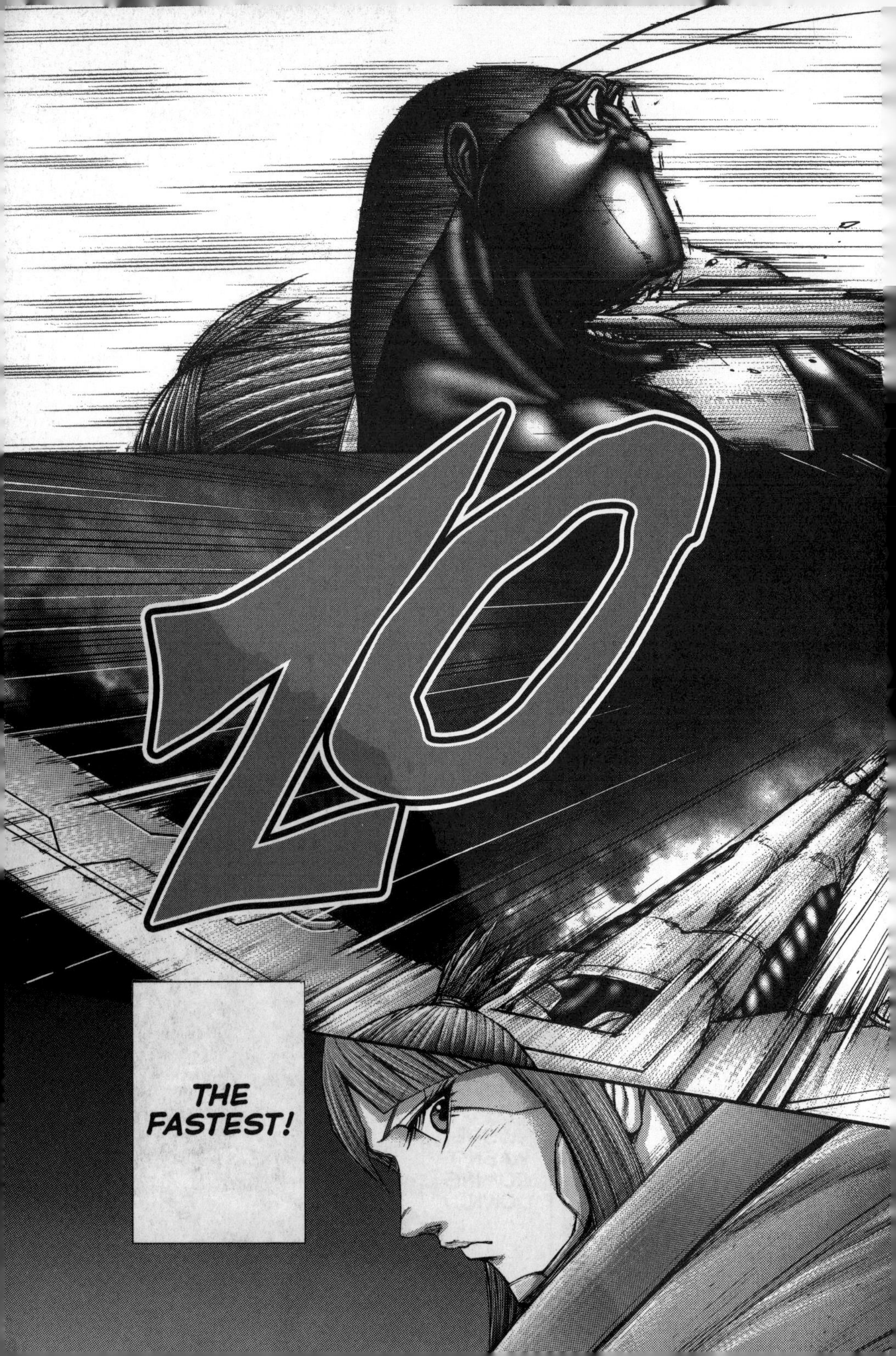
ZO
THE FASTEST!

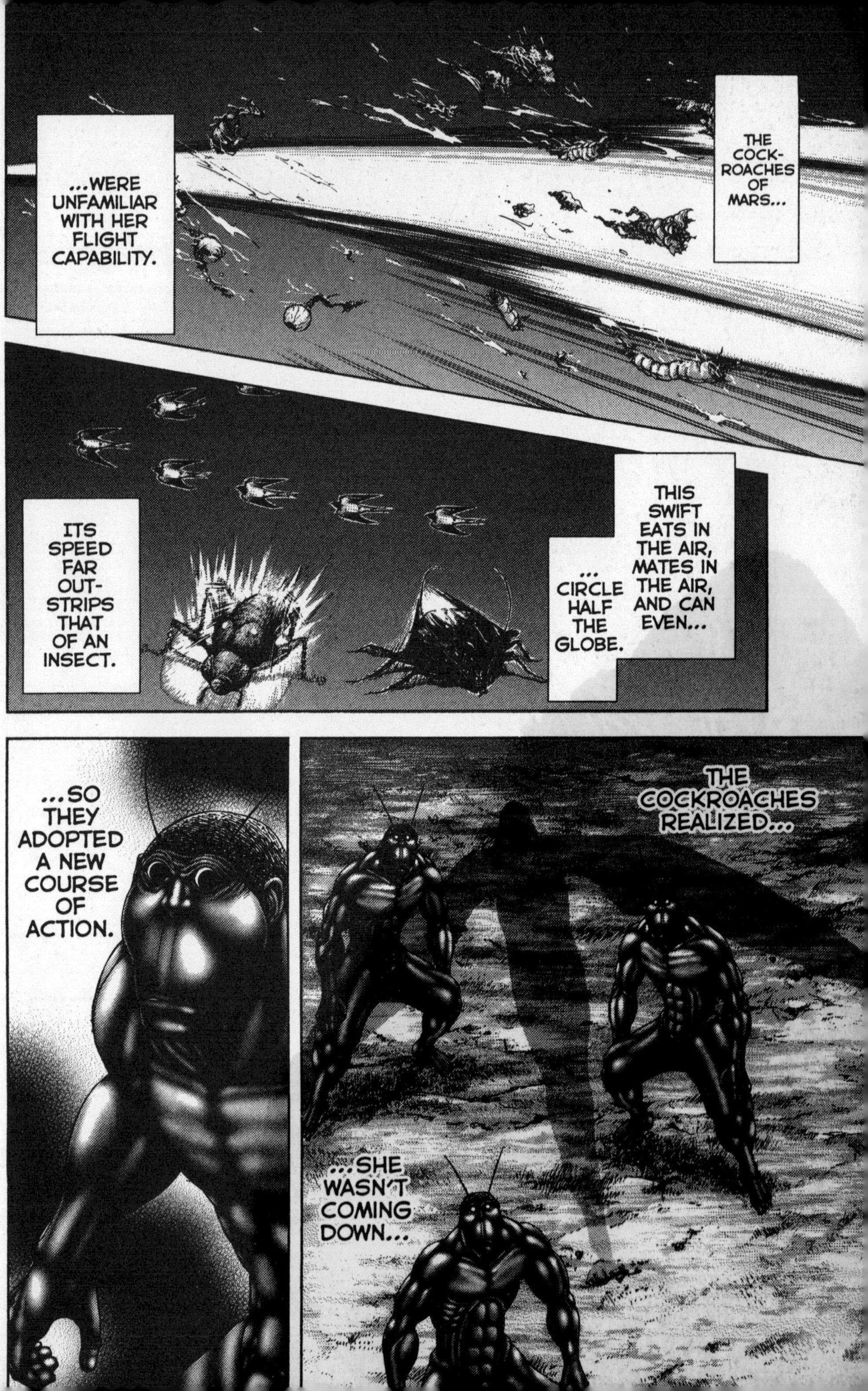
THE COCKROACHES OF MARS...
...WERE UNFAMILIAR WITH HER FLIGHT CAPABILITY.
THIS SWIFT EATS IN THE AIR, MATES IN THE AIR, AND CAN EVEN...
...CIRCLE HALF THE GLOBE.
ITS SPEED FAR OUTSTRIPS THAT OF AN INSECT.
THE COCKROACHES REALIZED...
...SHE WASN'T COMING DOWN...
...SO THEY ADOPTED A NEW COURSE OF ACTION.

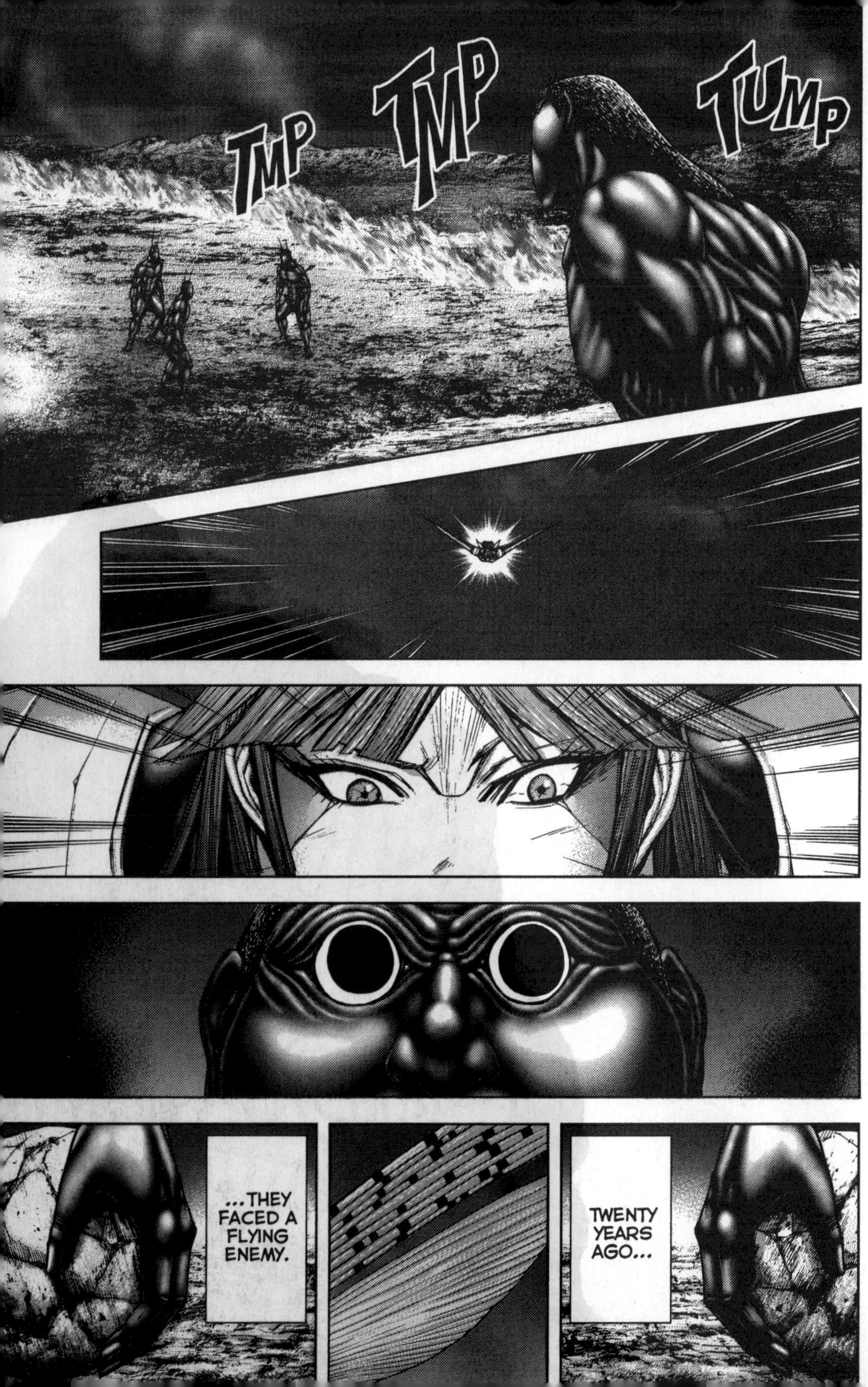
TUMP
TMP
TMP
TWENTY YEARS AGO...
...THEY FACED A FLYING ENEMY.

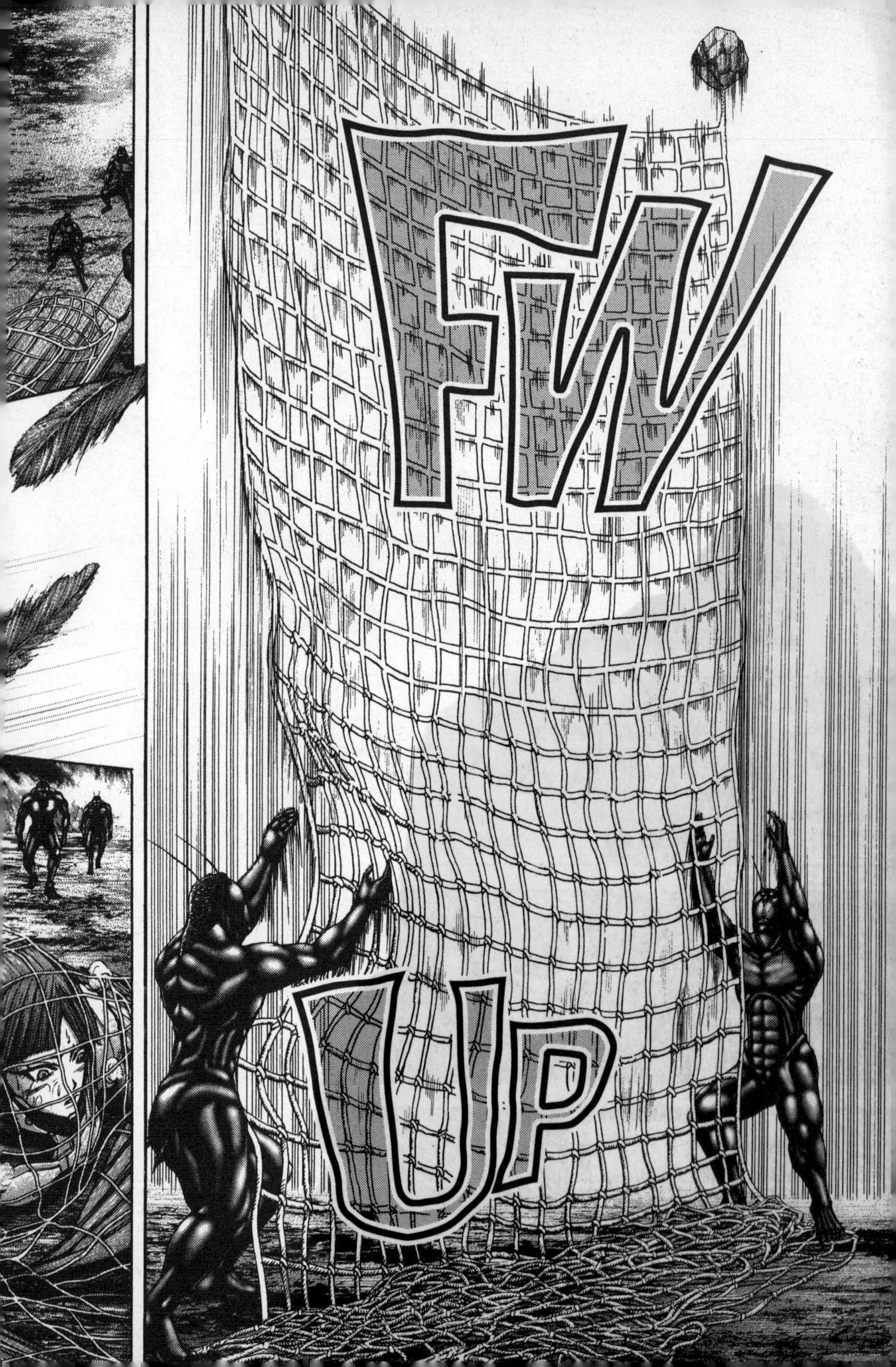
FWUP

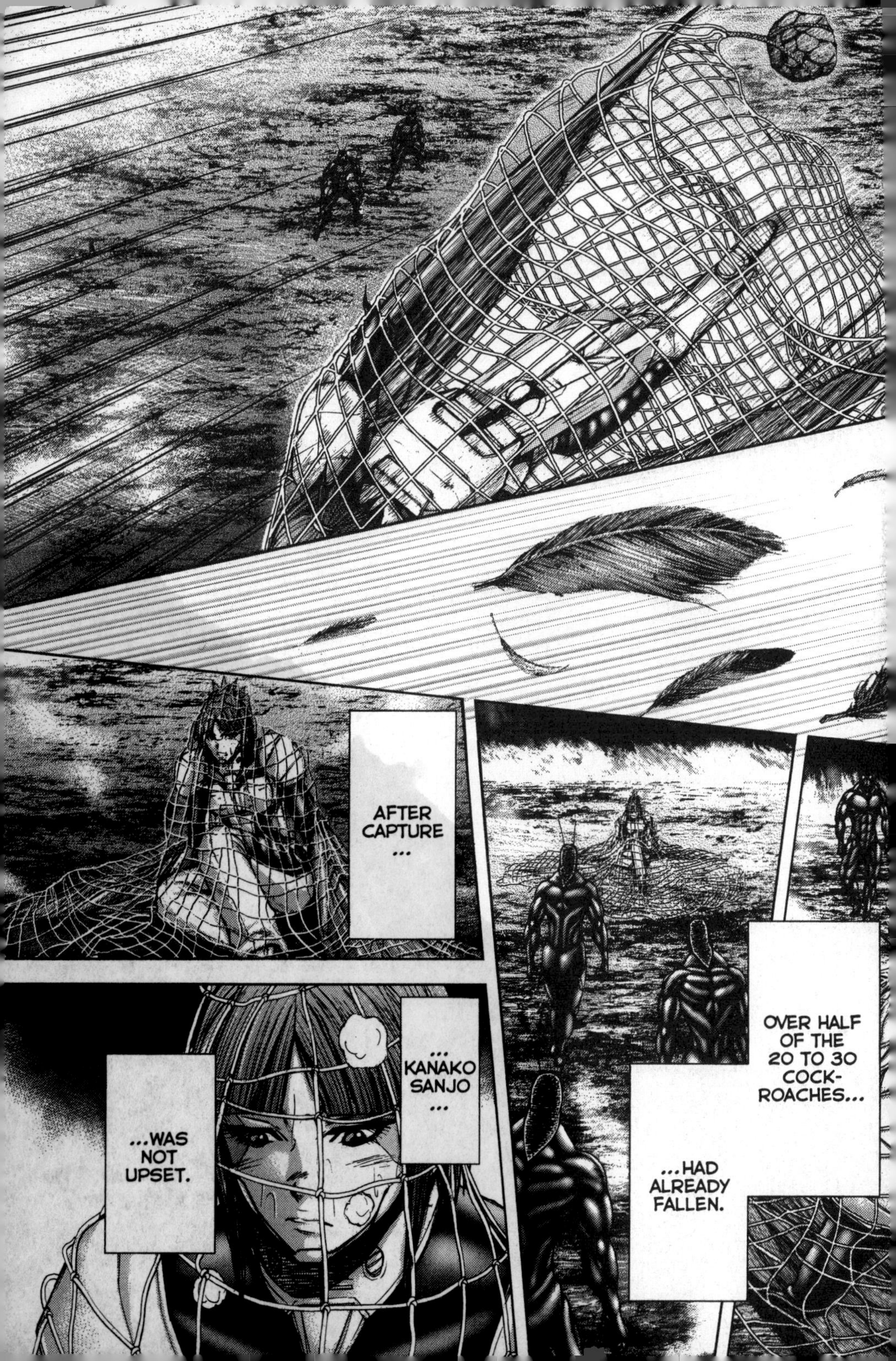

OVER HALF OF THE 20 TO 30 COCK-ROACHES...
...HAD ALREADY FALLEN.
AFTER CAPTURE...
...KANAKO SANJO...
...WAS NOT UPSET.

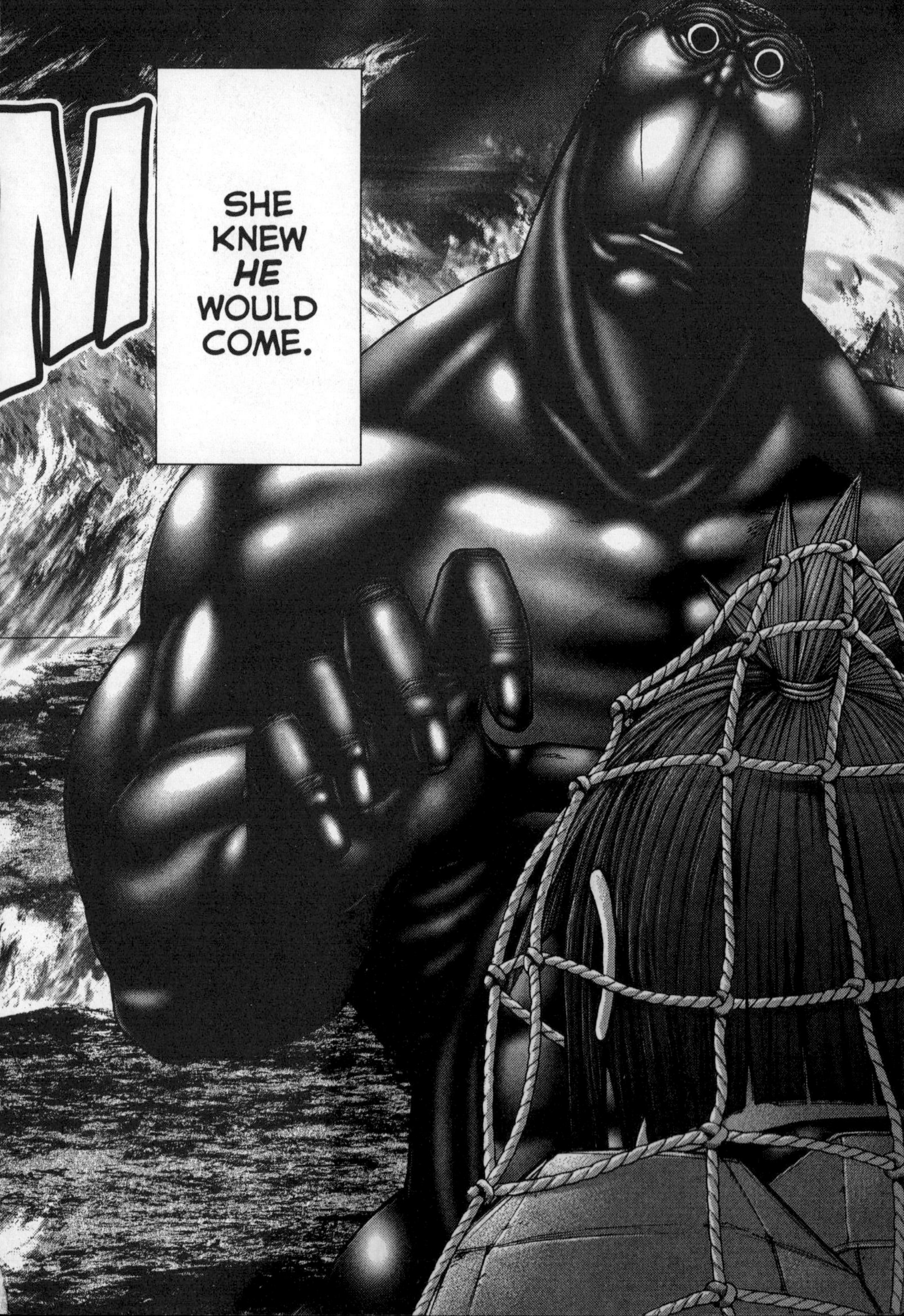
SHE KNEW *HE* WOULD COME.

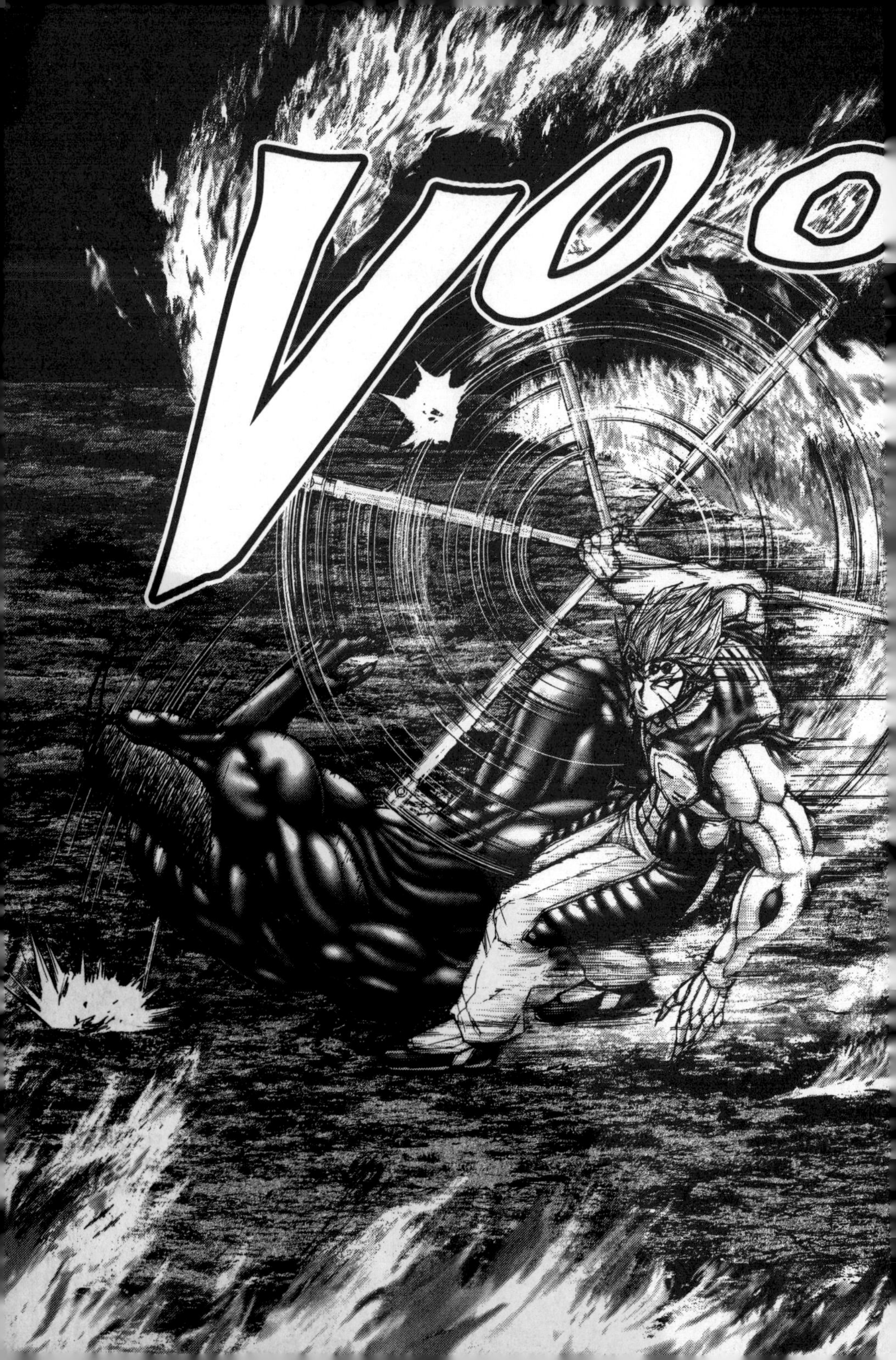
VOO

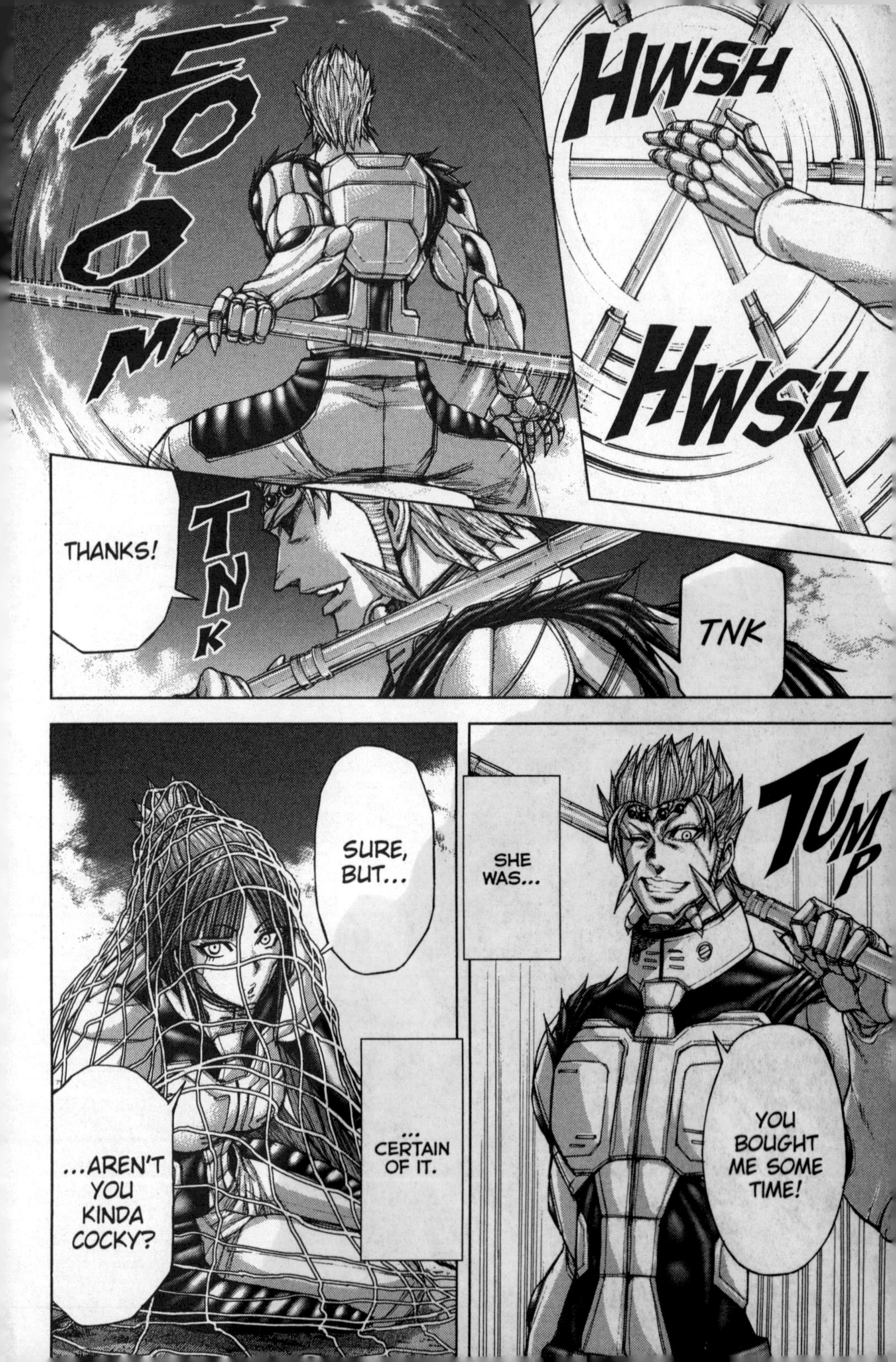
HWSH
HWSH
FOOM
TNK
TNK
THANKS!
TUMP
SHE WAS...
YOU BOUGHT ME SOME TIME!
SURE, BUT...
...CERTAIN OF IT.
...AREN'T YOU KINDA COCKY?

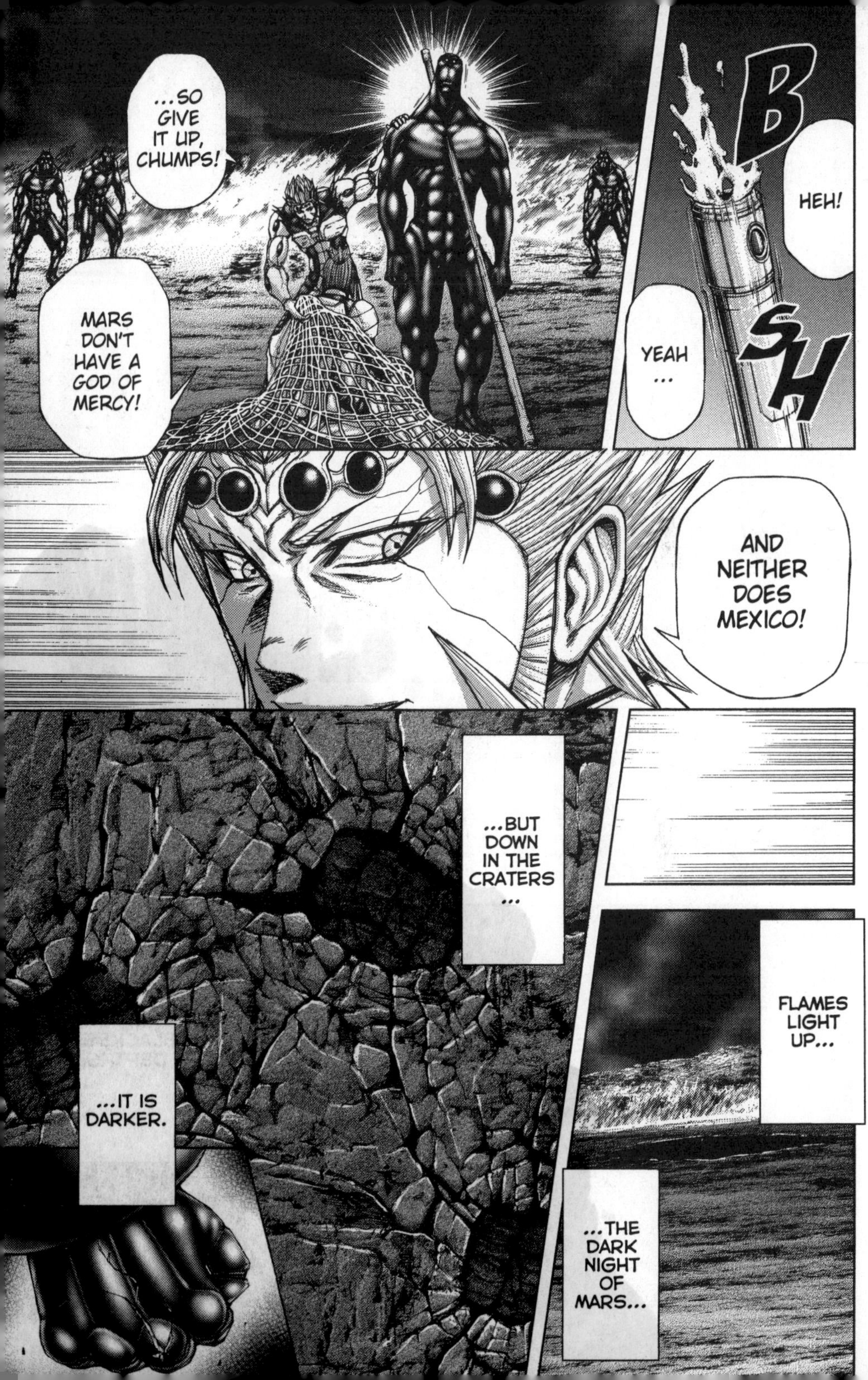
BSH
HEH!
YEAH...
...SO GIVE IT UP, CHUMPS!
MARS DON'T HAVE A GOD OF MERCY!
AND NEITHER DOES MEXICO!
FLAMES LIGHT UP...
...THE DARK NIGHT OF MARS...
...BUT DOWN IN THE CRATERS...
...IT IS DARKER.

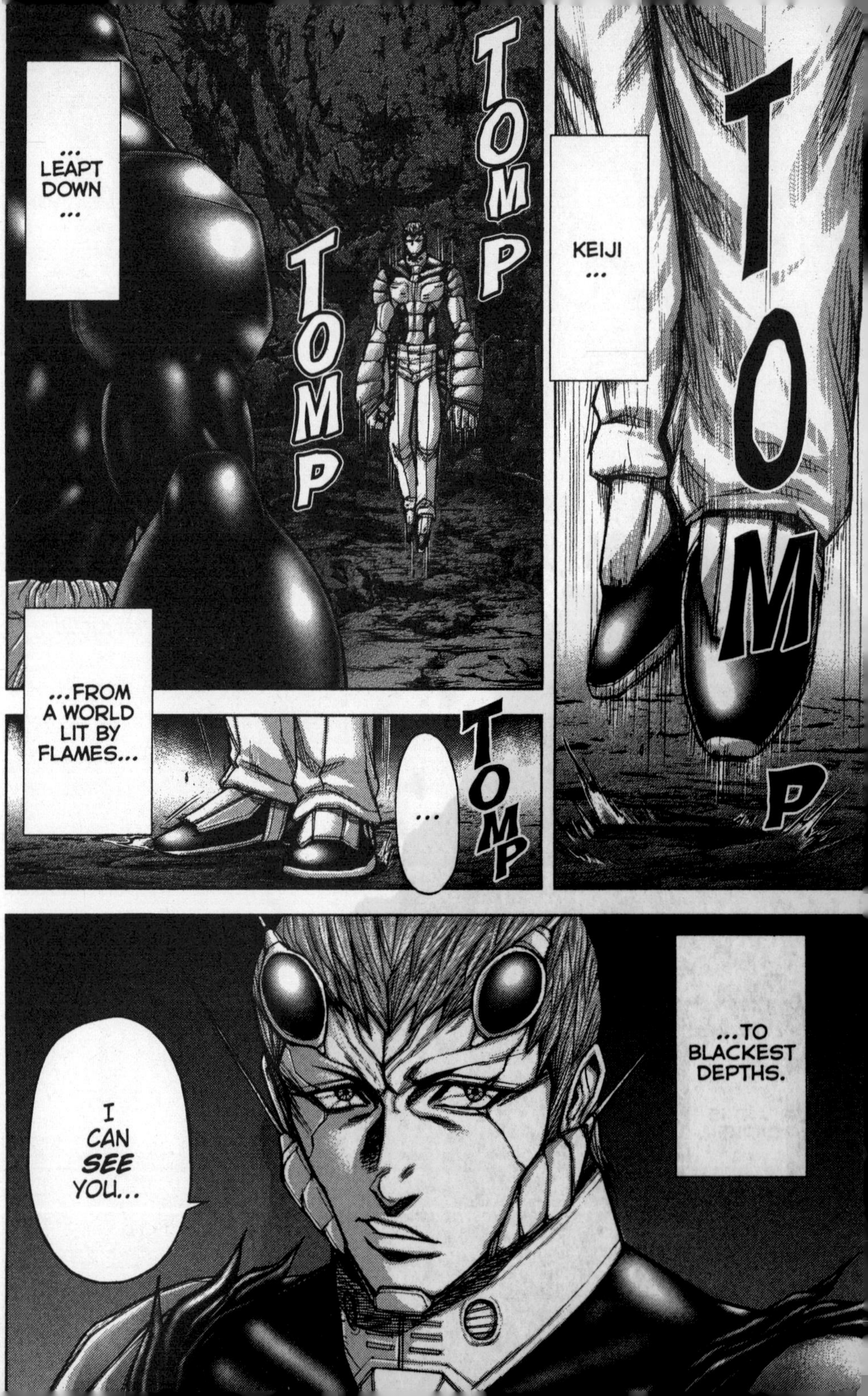
KEIJI ...
TOMP
... LEAPT DOWN ...
TOMP
TOMP
...FROM A WORLD LIT BY FLAMES...
...
TOMP
...TO BLACKEST DEPTHS.
I CAN SEE YOU...

TERRA FORMARS
Volume 5
VIZ Signature Edition

Story by YU SASUGA
Art by KENICHI TACHIBANA

Translation & English Adaptation/John Werry
Touch-up Art & Lettering/Annaliese Christman
Design/Izumi Evers
Editor/Mike Montesa

The stories, characters and incidents mentioned in this publication are
entirely fictional.

Printed in the U.S.A.

Published by VIZ Media, LLC
P.O. Box 77010
San Francisco, CA 94107

10 9 8 7 6 5 4 3 2 1
First printing, March 2015

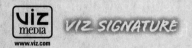

Hey! You're Reading in the Wrong Direction!

This is the **end** of this graphic novel!

To properly enjoy this VIZ graphic novel, please turn it around and begin reading from **right to left.** Unlike English, Japanese is read right to left, so Japanese comics are read in reverse order from the way English comics are typically read.

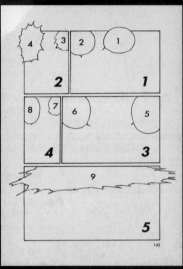

Follow the action this way

This book has been printed in the original Japanese format in order to preserve the orientation of the original artwork.